LAW'S ORDER

LAW'S ORDER

WHAT ECONOMICS HAS TO DO WITH LAW AND WHY IT MATTERS

David D. Friedman

PRINCETON UNIVERSITY PRESS   PRINCETON AND OXFORD

The Library of Congress has cataloged the cloth edition of this book as follows

Friedman, David D.
Law's order : what economics has to do with law and
why it matters / David D. Friedman.
    p.   cm.
Includes bibliographical references and index.
ISBN 0-691-01016-1 (alk. paper)
1. Economics.   2. Law.   I. Title.
HB171.F768 2000
330.1—dc21   99-058555

British Library Cataloging-in-Publication Data is available

This book·has been composed in Sabon

Printed on acid-free paper. ∞

www.press.princeton.edu

Printed in the United States of America

20   19   18   17   16

ISBN-13: 978-0-691-09009-2 (pbk.)

THIS BOOK IS DEDICATED

WITH RESPECT AND AFFECTION TO

Aaron Director and Ronald Coase _____

CONTENTS

LAW'S ORDER

Introduction

What I Am Doing

If there were only one man in the world, he would have a lot of problems, but none of them would be legal ones. Add a second inhabitant, and we have the possibility of conflict. Both of us try to pick the same apple from the same branch. I track the deer I wounded only to find that you have killed it, butchered it, and are in the process of cooking and eating it.

The obvious solution is violence. It is not a very good solution; if we employ it, our little world may shrink back down to one person, or perhaps none. A better solution, one that all known human societies have found, is a system of legal rules explicit or implicit, some reasonably peaceful way of determining, when desires conflict, who gets to do what and what happens if he doesn't.

The legal rules that we are most familiar with are laws created by legislatures and enforced by courts and police. But even in our society much of the law is the creation not of legislatures but of judges, embedded in past precedents that determine how future cases will be decided; much enforcement of law is by private parties such as tort victims and their lawyers rather than by police; and substantial bodies of legal rules take the form, not of laws, but of private norms, privately enforced.

Going farther afield in time and space we encounter a much greater diversity, both in the sources of legal rules and in the ways in which they are enforced. If we are considering all systems of legal rules in all times and places, the ways in which legal rules are created and enforced in America in this century are simply data—one out of many possible solutions to the problem of human conflict, one out of many possible systems of legal rules. This book directs most of its attention to the past century or two of Anglo-American law not because it is more important than other legal systems but because the author, most readers, and most of the scholars whose ideas I will be talking about know more about that legal system than about the legal rules of Homeric Greece, Papua New Guinea, Saga period Iceland, or Shasta County, California. But the ideas I am discussing are as relevant to those systems as to ours—as we will see when we take a brief look at several of them in chapter 17.

There are many ways of looking at a legal system, among them the perspective of a legal historian, a legal philosopher, or a lawyer interested in creating arguments courts will accept or contracts they will enforce. This book is written by an economist. My approach is to try to understand systems of legal rules by asking what consequences they will produce in a world in which rational individuals adjust their actions to the legal rules they face.

While this is not the only possible approach, it is one with very general application. Legal rules exist, at least in large part, in order to change how the people affected by them act. A speed limit exists because someone wants people to drive more slowly. The legal rule that holds that any ambiguity in a contract is to be interpreted against the party who drafted it exists because someone wants people to write contracts more carefully.

The economic approach works in two directions. Starting with an objective, it provides a way of evaluating legal rules, of deciding how well they achieve that objective. Starting with a legal rule, better, a system of legal rules, it provides a way of understanding it—by figuring out what objective it is intended to achieve.

The central assumption of economics is *rationality*—that behavior can best be understood in terms of the purposes it is intended to achieve. The secondary assumption running through this book is that systems of legal rules, or at least large parts of systems of legal rules, make sense—that they can be understood as tools with purposes. The rationality assumption will not be questioned here, although there is an extensive literature elsewhere on the subject, of which the most interesting part, in my judgment, is the recent work in evolutionary psychology. The secondary assumption will be questioned repeatedly. One of the questions running through this book is to what degree the legal rules we observe can be explained as tools—in particular, as tools designed to achieve the particular purpose, economic efficiency, that economic analysis of the law most commonly ascribes to them. In chapter 19 I sum up the evidence and deliver a mixed verdict.

What Is Wrong with It

A system of legal rules is not entirely, perhaps not chiefly, the product of deliberate human design; to a considerable extent it represents the unplanned outcome of a large number of separate decisions, by legislators bargaining over particular provisions in the law or judges trying to find and justify verdicts for particular cases. It is therefore possible that such a system may have no objective for us to find. There is no guarantee that we will be able to make sense of any particular system of legal rules, since there is no guarantee that it makes sense. Human beings are born equipped with a superb pattern-recognition engine—so good that not only can we find patterns that even a well-designed computer would miss, we can sometimes find patterns that aren't there. One of the questions you should be asking yourself, especially as you approach the end of the book, is to what degree economics discovers order in law and to what degree it imposes it.

One objection to the economic approach to understanding the logic of law is that law may have no logic to understand. Another and very different objection is that law has a logic but that it is, or at least ought to be, concerned not with economic efficiency but with justice. We punish criminals not, or at least not entirely, because doing so achieves good consequences but because criminals deserve to be punished. We require tortfeasors to make their victims whole not because doing so gives people an incentive not to be tortfeasors but because it is just that he who did the damage should pay for it. On precisely the same grounds, we insist that if our child has made a mess, he should clean it up.

To this very persuasive line of argument I have two answers. The first is that justice does not give an adequate account of law, both because it is irrelevant to a surprisingly large number of legal issues and because we have no adequate theory of what makes some rules just and some unjust. To a considerable degree, our intuitions of justice are consequence, not cause—we think rules are just because they are the rules we have been brought up with.

My second answer is that in many, although probably not all, cases it turns out that the rules we thought we supported because they were just are in fact efficient. To make that clearer I have chosen to ignore entirely issues of justice going into the analysis. In measuring the degree to which legal rules succeed in giving everyone what he wants, and judging them accordingly, I treat on an exactly equal plane my desire to keep my property and a thief's desire to take it. Despite that, as you will see, quite a lot of what looks like justice—for example, laws against theft and the requirement that people who make messes should clean them up—comes out the other end. That, I think, is interesting.

And for Whom I Am Doing It

This book is aimed at three different sorts of reader. The first is the proverbial intelligent layman—someone who thinks it would be interesting to know about law and economics and what they have to do with each other, himself, and the world in which he lives and so is reading this book for the same sort of reasons that make me read *The Selfish Gene* or *The Red Queen*. The second is the legal professional who would like to know more about the economic approach to his field. The third is the student, most probably in an economics department or a law school, who is reading this book because his professor told him to—and will, I hope, find that that is not the only reason to do so.

One problem in writing for different sorts of readers is that they want different sorts of books. Students, especially law students, and, to some degree, legal professionals expect a scholarly apparatus of footnotes, case cites, extensive bibliographic references, and the like that the intelligent lay reader is likely to find clumsy and unnecessary. I have dealt with that problem by moving the scholarly apparatus to cyberspace. This book is written for the lay reader, with no footnotes and few case cites or references. To go with it, I have produced a web site containing, I hope, everything that the student or legal professional will find missing in the hard copy currently in his hands; think of it as a system of virtual footnotes. The notes are indicated in the text by marginal icons corresponding to different sorts of webbed information:

 Cite to a book or article

 Link to a webbed book or article

 Case

 Math

 Additional comments

To read a virtual footnote, use your browser to go to the web page (www.daviddfriedman.com/laws_order), click on the chapter and then on the page number to bring up an image of the page you are reading. The icons on the image are links; click on one and additional material appears, sometimes including further links to the full text of cases (for some of which you will need a Lexis or Westlaw password), articles, and books. The web page also provides a printable version of the virtual footnotes, in case you plan to read the book at the beach.

of an early book in this field that consisted entirely of hooks to hang footnote references on, with scarcely a sentence that would convey any real information to a reader who did not already know what the book was supposed to be teaching.

My hope is that by paring the book down to what it is really about and taking advantage of modern technology to put everything else somewhere out of the way but within easy reach, I can achieve the benefit of the apparatus without the costs. At the same time I also provide myself a place for continued revision and expansion—without the need for any expensive resetting of type. Readers who want to help with that process will find my e-mail address readily available on the book's Web page.

And, Finally, a Road Map

There are two ways to organize the economic analysis of the law—economic or legal, by economic ideas or by areas of law. In this book I do both. The first part sketches basic economic concepts—rationality, economic efficiency, externalities, value of life, economics of risk allocation, et multae caetera—that can be used to understand a wide range of legal issues. It is followed by a one-chapter intermezzo in which I sketch out how our particular legal system is put together, primarily for the benefit of those readers who are neither lawyers nor law students. The second part then applies the economics to the analysis of the core areas of law— roughly speaking, the courses a law student will take in his first year— and is organized accordingly.

The concluding part applies what we have at that point learned in a variety of different ways: a chapter on legal systems very different from ours (including one located a few hours from where I am sitting), a chapter on the question of why we have two legal systems—tort law and criminal law—to do roughly the same thing in different ways and whether we could dispense with one of them, and a chapter considering the evidence for and against the claim that law, at least judge-made law, is economically efficient. The book ends with a final chapter in which I attempt to sum up what we have learned about systems of legal rules.

1

What Does Economics Have to Do with Law?

YOU LIVE IN A STATE where the most severe criminal punishment is life imprisonment. Someone proposes that since armed robbery is a very serious crime, armed robbers should get a life sentence. A constitutional lawyer asks whether that is consistent with the prohibition on cruel and unusual punishment. A legal philosopher asks whether it is just.

An economist points out that if the punishments for armed robbery and for armed robbery plus murder are the same, the additional punishment for the murder is zero—and asks whether you really want to make it in the interest of robbers to murder their victims.

That is what economics has to do with law. Economics, whose subject, at the most fundamental level, is not money or the economy but the implications of rational choice, is an essential tool for figuring out the effects of legal rules. Knowing what effects rules will have is central both to understanding the rules we have and to deciding what rules we should have.

The fundamental assumption of the economic approach, to law and everything else, is that people are rational. A mugger is a mugger for the same reason I am an economist: Given his tastes, opportunities, and abilities, it is the most attractive profession open to him. What laws are passed, how they are interpreted and enforced, ultimately depend on what behavior is in the rational interest of legislators, judges, and police.

Rationality does not mean that a burglar compiles an elaborate spreadsheet of costs and benefits before deciding whether to rob your house. An armed robber does not work out a precise analysis of how shooting his victim will affect the odds of being caught, whether it will reduce the chances by 10 percent or by 20. But if it is clear that it will reduce the risk of being caught without increasing the punishment, he is quite likely to pull the trigger.

Even in this weaker sense people are not always rational. I, for example, occasionally take a third helping of spaghetti when a careful calculation of my own long-run interests would lead me to abstain. I am well acquainted with my own irrationality and can take steps to deal with it. Having discovered that bowls of potato chips located within arm's reach empty themselves mysteriously, I at least sometimes take the precaution of putting the bowl somewhere else.

But I do not know other people—the vast masses of other people to whom economic analysis of law is intended to apply—well enough to incorporate their irrationalities into my analysis of the effect of legal rules on their behavior. What I do know about them is that they, like me, have purposes they wish to achieve and tend, albeit imperfectly, to correctly choose how to achieve them. That is the predictable element in human behavior, and it is on that element that economics is built.

Whether armed robbers should get ten years or life is not a burning issue for most of us. A question of considerably more importance is the standard of proof. In order for you to be convicted of a crime or to lose a civil case and have to pay damages, just how strong must the evidence against you be?

It is tempting to reply that nobody should be punished unless we are certain he is guilty. But by that standard nobody would ever be punished; the strongest evidence establishes only a probability. Even a confession is not absolute proof: While our legal system no longer permits torture, it does permit plea bargaining, and an innocent defendant may prefer a guilty plea on a minor charge to risking a long prison term on a major one. Scientific evidence is no more conclusive; even if we somehow had a perfect match between the DNA of the suspect and the criminal, there would still be the possibility that someone at the lab made a mistake or that somewhere, perhaps unknown to him, the suspect has an identical twin. If we are to convict anyone at all, we must do it on evidence short of absolute proof.

How far short? Raising the standard of proof reduces the chance of convicting an innocent defendant but increases the chance of acquitting a guilty one. Whether that is on net worth doing depends on the relative costs of the two kinds of mistakes. If, as Blackstone wrote more than two hundred years ago, it is better that ten guilty men go free than that one innocent be convicted, we should keep raising our standard of proof as long as doing so saves one more innocent defendant at the cost of freeing no more than ten guilty ones. We would end up with a high standard.

In fact, law in the United States and similar systems requires a high standard of proof ("beyond a reasonable doubt") in a criminal case but only a low standard ("preponderance of the evidence") in a civil case. Why? The answer cannot simply be that we are more careful with criminal convictions because the penalties are bigger. A damage judgment of a million dollars, after all, is a considerably more severe punishment for most of us than a week in jail.

Economics suggests a simple explanation. The typical result of losing a lawsuit is a cash payment from the defendant to the plaintiff. The result of being convicted of a crime may well be imprisonment or execution. A high error rate in civil cases means that sometimes I lose a case I should have won and pay you some money and sometimes you lose a case you should have won and pay me some money. On average, the punishment itself imposes no net cost; it is simply a transfer. A high error rate in criminal cases means that sometimes I get hanged for a murder I didn't commit and sometimes you get hanged for a murder you didn't commit. In the criminal case, unlike the civil case, one man's loss is not another man's gain. Punishment is mostly net cost rather than transfer, so it makes sense to be a good deal more careful about imposing it.

For an application of economics to a different part of the law, consider the nonwaivable warranty of habitability, a legal doctrine under which some courts hold that apartments must meet court-defined standards with regard to features such as heating, hot water, sometimes even air conditioning, whether or not such terms are provided in the lease—indeed, even if the lease specifically denies that it includes them. The immediate effect is that certain tenants get services that their landlords might not otherwise have provided. Some landlords are worse off as a result; some tenants are better off. It seems as though supporting or opposing the rule should depend mainly on whose side you are on.

In the longer run the effect is quite different. Every lease now automatically includes a quality guarantee. This makes rentals more attractive to tenants and more costly to landlords. The supply curve, the demand curve, and the price, the rent on an apartment, all shift up. The question, from the standpoint of a tenant, is not whether the features mandated by the court are worth anything but whether they are worth what they will cost.

The answer may well be no. If those features were worth more to the tenants than they cost landlords to provide, landlords should already be including them in their leases—and charging for them. If they cost the landlord more than they are worth to the tenant, then requiring them and letting rents adjust accordingly is likely to make both landlord and tenant worse off. It is particularly likely to make poorer tenants worse off, since they are the ones least likely to value the additional features at more than their cost. A cynical observer might conclude that the real function of the doctrine is to squeeze poor people out of jurisdictions that adopt it by making it illegal, in those jurisdictions, to provide housing of the quality they can afford to rent.

If my analysis of the effect of this legal doctrine seems implausible, consider the analogous case of a law requiring that all cars be equipped with sunroofs and CD changers. Some customers—those who would have purchased those features anyway—are unaffected. Others find that they are getting features worth less to them than they cost and paying for them in the increased price of the car.

This is a very brief sketch of a moderately complicated economic problem, and the result is not quite so clear as the sketch suggests. With a little effort one can construct possible situations in which a restriction on the terms of leases benefits some tenants and landlords at the expense of others, or most tenants, or most landlords. With more effort one could construct a situation in which the restriction benefits both landlords and tenants. The important point is not that restrictions on the terms of contracts are a good or a bad thing but that one cannot evaluate their effects by looking only at the terms that are restricted. You also have to look at the effect of the restriction on the other terms of the contract, in my example the rent.

In any particular law case it looks as though what is at stake is how the legal system will deal with this particular set of events, all of which have already happened. From that backward-looking point of view it is often hard to make sense out of existing law. The reason is not that law does not make sense but that we are facing in the wrong direction.

Suppose, for example, that I take advantage of a particularly good opportunity to push my rich uncle off a cliff. By extraordinary bad fortune a birdwatcher happens to have his camera pointed in my direction at just the wrong time, with the result that I am caught, tried, and convicted. During the sentencing phase of the trial my attorney points out that my crime was due to the conjunction of extraordinary temptation (he was very rich, I was very poor) and an improbably good opportunity—and I had only one rich uncle. Besides, once I have been convicted of this crime, potential future victims are unlikely to go rock climbing with me. Hence, he argues, the court should convict me and then let me go. Whatever they do, I will never kill again, and hanging or imprisoning me will not, he points out, bring my uncle back to life.

The conclusion is bizarre, but the argument seems logical. The reply many legal scholars would probably offer is that the law is concerned not only with consequences but also with justice. Letting me go may do no damage, but it is still wrong.

The economist offers a different response. The mistake is not in looking at consequences but in looking at the wrong consequences, backward at a murder that has already happened instead of forward at murders that may happen in the future. By letting me off unpunished, the court is announcing a legal rule that lowers the risk of punishment confronting other nephews faced, in the future, by similar temptations. Executing this murderer will not bring his victim back to life, but the legal rule it establishes may deter future murderers and so save those who would have been their victims. *Legal rules are to be judged by the structure of incentives they establish and the consequences of people altering their behavior in response to those incentives.*

Crime and contract are not the only parts of law in which the economic approach proves useful. Speeding fines are intended, not as an odd sort of tax, but as a way of making it in the interest of drivers to drive more slowly. Tort law determines what happens to people who get in auto accidents and thus affects the incentive to do things that might lead to being in an auto accident, such as not having your brakes checked, driving drunk, driving at all. The rules of civil procedure determine what sorts of information litigants are entitled to demand from each other and thus affect the incentive of firms to keep (or not keep) records, to investigate (or not investigate) problems with their products that might become the subject of litigation, to sue or not to sue. Divorce law determines under what circumstances you can get out of a marriage, which is one of the things relevant to deciding whether to get into it. The subject of economic analysis of law is law. All of it.

The Proper Application of High Explosives to Legal Theory

A physics student who has learned classical mechanics and the theory of electricity and magnetism has the basic equipment to deal with practically any pre-twentieth-century physics problem. Just add facts and mathematics and turn the crank. Throw in relativity and quantum mechanics and you can drop the "pre-twentieth-century" restriction. An economics student who has thoroughly mastered price theory is equipped to deal with very nearly every problem to which economic theory gives a clear answer, with the result that many of the courses offered by an economics department are simply applications of price theory to such particular areas as transportation, agriculture, trade, or law. A law student who has learned to understand tort law has the basic equipment to understand tort law. If he wants to understand criminal law, he must start over again.

Economics changes that. In the next few chapters you will be acquiring a set of intellectual tools. The rest of the book consists of the application of those tools to different areas of law. As you will see, once you understand property, or contract, or tort from the point of view of economics, you have done most of the work toward understanding any of the others. While each raises a few special issues, the fundamental analysis is common to all.

This is one explanation for the controversial nature of economics within the legal academy. On the one hand, it offers the possibility of making sense out of what legal academics do. On the other hand, it asserts that in order for legal academics to fully understand what they are doing, they must first learn economics. In the world of ideas, as in the world of geopolitics, imperialism is often unpopular with its targets.

A second reason economic analysis is controversial is that it sometimes produces conclusions with which many legal academics disagree—for example, that laws "protecting" tenants are quite likely to make tenants worse off. Scholars who apply economic analysis to law are routinely charged with conservatism, not in the literal sense of wanting to keep things unchanged (in that sense the traditional scholars in any field are the conservatives and the challengers the radicals) but in the current political sense.

There is some truth to this claim—more if "conservative" is changed to "libertarian." Part of the reason is the economist's underlying assumption that individuals are rational. While that assumption does not, as we will see, eliminate all reasons for wanting to interfere with market outcomes, it does eliminate many. And while rationality is an optimistic assumption when applied to individuals who are supposed to be acting for their own interest—buying and selling, signing contracts, getting married or divorced—it can be a pessimistic assumption when applied to people who are supposed to be acting in someone else's interests, such as judges or legislators. Their rationality may consist of rationally sacrificing the interests they are supposed to be serving, such as justice and the public good, to their own private interests.

But while economists are more likely to get some answers and less likely to get others than traditional legal scholars, the principal effect of economic analysis is to change not the conclusions but the arguments—for both sides of any controversial issue. It provides a powerful argument for the death penalty as deterrence but also, as we will see in chapter 15, a new argument against the death penalty. Applied to landlord tenant law, the most striking implication is that what legal rules you favor should depend very little on whether you care more for the interests of landlord or tenant. In most cases a bad law will hurt both groups and a good law help both, at least in the long run. In almost every application, economic analysis radically reshapes the arguments out of which legal conclusions come. One implication is that it is a tool or, if you prefer, a weapon, useful to people with a wide range of political agendas.

What the Law Has to Teach Economists

So far I have discussed economic analysis of law from the perspective of an economist, eager to show my legal colleagues why they must study economics if they hope to understand the law. The transaction is not, however, entirely one way. Economists have something to learn as well.

Economics applies its general theory largely to abstract concepts—property, exchange, firms, capital, labor. Quite a lot of what lawyers and law professors do involves dealing with the same concepts in their real-world incarnation.

An economist can talk about someone owning a piece of land and assume that that is the end of it. A lawyer dealing with property is brought face to face with the fact that ownership of land is not a simple concept. How does my ownership of a piece of land apply to someone else who wants to fly over my land, dig a hole next to it that my house might slide into, permit his cattle to wander onto my land and eat my vegetables, erect a structure on his land that shades my swimming pool? And if someone does do something that violates my property rights, just what am I allowed to do about it—ask him to leave, blow him up with a land mine, or sue him for damages?

These issues show up in real cases that real judges and lawyers have to deal with. The more you think about them, the clearer it becomes that what you own is not a piece of land but a bundle of rights related to a piece of land. For example . . .

Someone builds a new hotel in Florida that shades the swimming pool of the next hotel down the beach. The owners of the old hotel sue for damages. Conventional economic analysis holds that they should win. The new hotel imposes a cost on the old; making its builder liable forces him to include that cost—what economists call an external cost or *externality*—in deciding whether or not the new hotel is worth building.

But, as Ronald Coase pointed out in an article that laid an important part of the foundation for the economic analysis of law, that answer is too simple. It may be true that if the builder of the new hotel is not liable he need not consider the cost he imposes by locating his building where it will shade his neighbor's pool. But if he *is* liable, the neighbor at an earlier stage need not consider the cost he imposes by locating his swimming pool where a building on the adjacent lot will shade it—and thus forcing the owner of that lot to either leave it empty or build and pay damages. What we have are not costs imposed by one person on another but costs jointly produced by decisions made by both parties.

Part of Coase's solution to this problem is to restate it in terms not of external costs but of property rights. One of the rights of value to the owners of both hotels is ownership of the stream of sunlight currently falling on the pool. If that right belongs to the owner of the land on which the sunlight now falls—the owner of the old hotel—then the builder of the new hotel can be held legally liable for interfering with it. If it does not, he cannot. The right is of value to the owners of both adjacent pieces of property: One needs it to protect his swimming pool, the other to permit him to build a building that will shade it.

The solution suggested by Coase was not liability but trade. Define the relevant legal rules so that one of the parties has a clear right to the stream of sunlight. If it is worth more to the other—if the gain from building the hotel is more than the cost of moving the swimming pool—the other can buy it. Thus Coase, by looking at real cases in which courts had to decide among competing uses of land, radically revised the economic analysis of externalities—a topic we will return to in chapter 4.

How She Growed: The Three Enterprises of Law and Economics

Economic analysis of law comprises three closely related enterprises: predicting what effect particular legal rules will have, explaining why particular legal rules exist, deciding what legal rules should exist.

The first is the least controversial. While many people believe that the consequences of a law are not the only thing determining whether it is good or not, very few believe that consequences are irrelevant. To the extent that economic analysis helps us perceive consequences of laws and legal decisions, especially consequences that are not obvious, it is useful to anyone trying to make or understand law. If imposing a life sentence for armed robbery results in more murders, that is an argument, although not necessarily a decisive argument, against doing it. If restrictions on the terms of leases make both landlords and tenants worse off, that is an argument, probably a decisive argument, for letting them set the terms themselves.

The second enterprise is using economics to explain the existence of the legal rules that we observe. This is a hard problem. Legal rules are created by legislatures and courts—and we have no very good theory, economic or otherwise, to explain the behavior of either. From a theoretical standpoint, the project is part of the field of economics known as public choice theory, an area still very much on the intellectual frontier. It contains some interesting first steps, such as Niskanen's model of the budget-maximizing bureau and Becker's analysis of the political market on which interest groups bid for legislation, with more concentrated and better organized groups typically using government to benefit at the expense of less concentrated and worse organized groups, but it has not yet provided a fully worked out and generally accepted economic theory of government.

There is, however, one conjecture about law that has played a central role in the development of law and economics. This is the thesis, due to Judge Richard Posner, that the common law, that part of the law that comes not from legislatures but from the precedents created by judges in deciding cases, tends to be economically efficient. I was implicitly relying on that conjecture when I explained the difference between the standard of proof required for criminal conviction and that required for civil conviction; my argument took it for granted that legal rules were somehow shaped in a way that properly traded off the costs of false convictions against those of false acquittals.

Why might one expect legal rules to be like that? One answer offered by Posner is that the two central issues with which we might expect judges to be concerned are efficiency (the effect of legal rules on the size of the pie) and distribution (their effect on who gets how much of it). Common law consists, in large part, of the legal framework for voluntary transactions. The result, as suggested by the earlier example of rental contracts, is that most distributional effects of changes in the law are illusory; when we compel a change in one term of a contract in favor of one party, other terms, such as the price, shift in the opposite direction, wiping out the distributional effect. If using the law to redistribute is difficult, it seems plausible that judges might leave redistribution to legislatures and concern themselves with efficiency instead.

A very different argument offered by others for the same conclusion is that inefficient rules generate litigation, and litigation, eventually, generates changes in the rules. If some rule of the common law prevents people from doing things that are in their mutual interest, those affected will try either to change the law or work around it. Eventually they succeed. We are left with a common law shaped, "as if by an invisible hand," to maximize economic efficiency.

In addition to these theoretical arguments for why we might expect common law to be efficient, there is also the empirical argument, the claim that the common law legal rules we observe are, in most although not all cases, the rules we would get if we were trying to design an economically efficient legal system. Posner's immensely productive career as a legal theorist has largely consisted of piling up evidence for that argument. One of the things we will be doing in future chapters is examining that evidence, comparing the implications of economic theory with the laws we observe. In chapter 19 we will return to the Posner thesis in order to sum up the theoretical and empirical arguments for and against.

The Posner thesis that the common law is efficient leads naturally to the third and most controversial part of law and economics: using economic analysis to decide what the law should be. If we conclude that some particular common law rule—say, the nonwaivable warranty of habitability discussed a few pages back—is economically inefficient, that it makes us on net poorer, one conclusion is that Posner is wrong. Another might be that we should change it.

As a matter of simple logic, the claim that legal rules are efficient is entirely separate from the claim that they ought to be efficient. One might believe that laws should be efficient but are not, or that they are but should not be, that other values should have greater weight than economic efficiency in determining the law. In practice, however, the two claims are easily confused and often combined. Posner makes both, although in each case with substantial qualifications.

I have repeatedly referred to "economic efficiency" without ever explaining precisely what the words mean. In this case as in many others it is dangerous to assume that a word used as a technical term has the same meaning as in other uses. "Strike" means very different things in baseball, bowling, and labor relations. "Efficient" means very different things applied to engines, employees, and economies.

Economic efficiency can most usefully be thought of as the economist's attempt to put some clear meaning into the metaphor "size of the pie." What makes doing so difficult is that the relevant pie is not a single object that we can weigh or measure but a bundle of many different sorts of goods and services, costs and benefits, divided among hundreds of millions of people. It is not obvious how those can be all put in common units and summed to tell us whether some particular change in legal rules (or anything else) increases or decreases the total. Solving that problem will be the subject of the next chapter.

One question that should have occurred to you by now is whether any of this has anything to do with the real world. One way to answer that is to go back to the two examples I started the chapter with, encouraging robbers to kill their victims and making apartments more expensive. The question you should be asking is not whether you are convinced that my analysis of those examples is correct—what I was offering, after all, was only a sketch of an argument. The question is whether you understand more about those issues than you did before you read this chapter. If the answer is yes, then the economic analysis of law has something to do with the real world.

A second way to answer the question is to consider whether you believe that people are, on the whole, rational. If we know that doing something will make someone better off, is that a good—not certain, but good—reason to expect him to do it? If the answer is "yes," are you willing to generalize, to apply it to police, judges, legislators, burglars, muggers, and potential victims? If the answer is still "yes," then you are in agreement with the fundamental assumption on which the theory is built.

2

Efficiency and All That

LEGAL RULES AFFECT lots of people in lots of different ways. In a society
as large and complicated as ours one can be fairly certain that passing or
repealing a law will make some people worse off, including some who
have done nothing for which they deserve to be made worse off, and
make some people better off, including some who have done nothing for
which they deserve to be made better off. How, then, can one decide what
the law ought to be?

One possible answer is that we ought to have whatever laws best serve
our interests—result in people getting more nearly the outcomes they
want. This raises an obvious problem: how to add people up. If a law
benefits some and hurts others, as most do, how can one decide whether
the net effect is loss or gain, cost or benefit? How do you put a pie containing everything that happens to every human being on earth, or even
in the United States, on a scale, so as to get a single measure of its size?

I. A Very Large Pie with All of Us in It

A little over a hundred years ago an economist named Alfred Marshall
proposed a solution to that problem. It is not a very good solution. It is
merely, for many although not all purposes, better than any alternative
that anyone has come up with since. The result is that economists, in both
law schools and economics departments, continue to use Marshall's solution, sometimes concealed behind later and (in my view) less satisfactory
explanations and defenses.

Marshall's argument starts by considering some change—the imposi-
tion or abolition of a tariff, a revision of the tax code, a shift in tort law
from strict liability to negligence. The result of the change is to make some
people better off and some worse off. In principle one could measure the
magnitude of the effects by asking each person affected how much he
would, if necessary, pay to get the benefit (if the change made him better
off) or prevent the loss (if it made him worse off). If total gains were larger
than total losses, making the net effect positive, we would describe the
change as an economic improvement.

Several things are worth noticing about this way of evaluating changes.

One is that we are accepting each person's own judgment of the value to him of things that affect him. In measuring the effect of drug legalization on heroin addicts we ask not whether we think they are better off with legal access to heroin but whether they think they are—how much each addict would pay, if necessary, to have heroin made legal. A second is that we are comparing effects on different people using dollars as our common unit—not dollars actually paid out or received, but dollars as a common measure of value, a way of putting all costs and benefits on the same scale.

II. How to Add People Up

The experiment of asking people such questions is an imaginary one not only because we don't do it but also because, if we did, there is no reason to expect them to tell us the truth. If someone asks you how much you want something, the rational response may be to greatly exaggerate its value to you in the hope that he will then give it to you.

We get the relevant information not by asking questions but by observing behavior, by seeing how much people are willing to give to get things and making deductions from such observations. The reason I believe heroin addicts would be willing to pay quite a lot to have heroin made legal is that I observe heroin addicts paying quite a lot to get illegal heroin. The economist's term for that approach is "revealed preference." Preferences are revealed by choices.

If you are still puzzled, as you probably should be, about how one can make any estimate at all of the net effect of some legal rule on a population of hundreds of millions of people, consider the following, deceptively simple, application of Marshall's approach:

> Mary has an apple. John wants the apple. The apple is worth fifty cents to Mary, meaning that she is indifferent between having the apple and not having the apple but having an additional fifty cents instead. The apple is worth one dollar to John. John buys the apple for seventy-five cents.

Mary no longer has the apple but has seventy-five cents instead—making her, on net, twenty-five cents better off than before, since the apple was only worth fifty cents to her. John no longer has his seventy-five cents but has the apple, making him too twenty-five cents better off than before, since the apple is worth a dollar to him. Both are better off; their net gain is fifty cents. The transfer was an improvement.

It would still be an improvement, and by the same amount, if John, a particularly skilled bargainer, managed to get the apple for fifty cents: he gains fifty cents, she gains nothing, net gain again fifty cents. Ditto if

Mary was the better bargainer and sold her apple for a dollar, its full value to John.

It would still be an improvement, and by the same amount, if John stole the apple—price zero—or if Mary lost it and John found it. Mary is fifty cents worse off, John is a dollar better off, net gain fifty cents. All of these represent the same efficient allocation of the apple: to John, who values it more than Mary. They differ in the associated distribution of income: how much money John and Mary each end up with.

Since we are measuring value in dollars it is easy to confuse "gaining value" with "getting money." But consider our example. The total amount of money never changes; we are simply shifting it from one person to another. The total quantity of goods never changes either, since we are cutting off our analysis after John gets the apple but before he eats it. Yet total value increases by fifty cents. It increases because the same apple is worth more to John than to Mary. Shifting money around does not change total value. One dollar is worth the same number of dollars to everyone: one.

We now expand the analysis by applying Marshall's approach not to a transaction (John buys Mary's apple) but to a legal rule. The rule is freedom of exchange: Anyone who owns an apple is free to sell or not to sell it on any terms mutually acceptable.

In our two-person world the result is efficient. If the apple is worth more to John than to Mary, John will buy it; if the apple is worth more to Mary, she will keep it. Similarly if John starts with the apple. In each case we end up with the outcome that gives the highest total value. That is the efficient outcome, hence freedom of exchange is the efficient rule.

We now add a third party, Anne, an alternative customer for Mary's apple.

First suppose that Anne really likes apples; she is willing to pay up to a dollar fifty for one. Anne outbids John and gets the apple. The apple goes from someone who valued it at fifty cents to someone who values it at a dollar fifty, for a net gain of a dollar, with the distribution of the gain between Mary and Anne depending on how good a bargainer each is. That is a better outcome than having the apple go to John, for a net gain of fifty cents, or stay with Mary, for a net gain of zero. So far, it looks as though freedom of exchange is the efficient rule.

Next suppose that Anne does not like apples so much; she is willing to pay up to seventy-five cents, but no more. This time John outbids Anne and gets the apple. The net gain is fifty cents—superior to the result if the apple went to Anne (now only twenty-five cents) or Mary (again zero).

Thinking through these examples, you should be able to satisfy yourself that freedom of exchange, in our little world of three people and one apple, is the efficient legal rule. Whatever you assume about how much each person values the apple, the rule results in the apple going to whoever values it most, thus maximizing net gain.

This is a simple example in a very small world, but sufficient to illustrate the fundamentals of how Marshall's approach works in practice. The examples depended on particular assumptions about how much the apple was worth to whom, but the argument did not. The form of the argument was not "Anne values the apple more, therefore the rule is efficient" but rather "If Anne values the apple more, she will get it, which is efficient; if John values it more, he will get it, which is efficient."

Arguments about the efficiency of legal rules rarely rest on real-world data about how much different people value things. Typically, we try to take into account all possible, or at least all plausible, valuations and find a legal rule that works for all of them—freedom of exchange in our example. When that is impossible we end up with weaker conclusions, typically of the form "if most people . . . then rule X is more efficient, but if . . ."

Our simple example also illustrates another important point—that money, although convenient for both making transactions and talking about them, is not what economics is about. The same argument could have been worked through, at the cost of an extra page or two of explanation, in a world where money had never been invented. Mary starts with an apple, John a loaf of bread, Anne a pear. All three have knives for making change. No cash needed.

III. Is Efficiency Always a Good Thing?

Marshall's approach to defining economic efficiency has two major virtues:

1. It sometimes makes it possible to answer questions of the form "When and why is strict liability in tort law efficient?" or "What is the efficient amount of punishment for a particular crime?"

2. Although "efficient" is not quite identical to "desirable" or "should," it is close enough so that the answer to the question "What is efficient?" is at least relevant, although not necessarily identical, to the answer to the question "What should we do?"

Put differently, Marshall's version of "more efficient" has at least a family resemblance to what people mean by "better" and is very much more precise and more readily applied. Family resemblance, however, is not the same thing as identity, as my six-year-old son could easily demonstrate by going to a liquor store with my photo ID. Before accepting the usefulness of the concept of economic efficiency, it is worth pointing out its limitations.

1. It assumes that all that matters is consequences. It thus assumes away the possibility of judging legal rules by nonconsequential criteria such as justice.

Consider a sheriff who observes a mob about to lynch three innocent murder suspects and solves the problem by announcing (falsely) that he has proof one of them is guilty and shooting him. Judged consequentially, and assuming there was no better solution available, it seems an unambiguous improvement—by two lives. Yet many of us would have serious moral reservations about the sheriff.

2. It assumes that when evaluating the consequence of a legal rule for a single person, the appropriate values are that person's values as expressed in his actions, that there is no relevant difference between the value of insulin and of heroin.

3. It assumes that, in combining values across people, the appropriate measuring rod is willingness to pay, that a gain that one person is willing to pay ten dollars to get just balances a loss that another is willing to pay ten dollars to avoid. But most of us believe that, measured by some more fundamental standard such as happiness, a dollar is worth more to some people than to others—more to poor than to rich, more to materialist than to ascetic.

If we were claiming that economic efficiency was a perfect criterion for judging legal rules, that whatever legal rule produced a better outcome by Marshall's criterion was always preferable, these would be serious, probably fatal, objections to the claim. They are less serious if our claim is only that it is the best criterion available. To see why, consider the alternatives.

The statement that we should choose just rules, while emotionally satisfying, does not convey much information. Economic value may capture only part of what we want out of a legal system, but at least economic theory tells us how to get it. And consequences are an important part of what we want. The doctrine *fiat justicia, ruat coelum* (let justice be done though the skies fall) is, in my experience, uniformly proclaimed by people who are confident that doing justice will not, in fact, bring down the sky.

As we develop the economic analysis of law we will observe a surprising correspondence between justice and efficiency. In many cases principles we think of as just correspond fairly closely to rules that we discover are efficient. Examples range from "thou shalt not steal" to "the punishment should fit the crime" to the requirement that criminal penalties be imposed only after proof beyond a reasonable doubt. This suggests a radical conjecture—that what we call principles of justice may actually be rules of thumb for producing an efficient outcome, rules we have some-how internalized. Whether that is a sufficient account of justice you will have to decide for yourself.

Defining value by what I act to get may not always give the right an-swer, but it is hard to see how one can do better. If value to me is not defined by my actions, it must be defined, for operational purposes, for controlling what actually ends up happening, by someone else's actions. As long as the statue of justice remains firmly attached to her pedestal instead of stepping down and taking charge, people's actions are the only tools available for moving the world. That leaves us with the problem of finding a "someone else" who both knows my interest better than I do and can be trusted to pursue it.

The final criticism of efficiency, that it ignores the fact that a dollar is worth more to some people than to others, may be the most serious. Marshall's response was that most economic issues involve costs and ben-efits to large and heterogeneous groups of people, so that differences in individual value for money (in the language of economics, differences in the "marginal utility of income") were likely to average out.

At first glance this argument seems inapplicable to law; it is widely believed that some legal rules favor rich people and some poor people, in which case judging rules by their effect on dollar value might give a differ-ent result than judging them by their effect on, say, total happiness. But first glances are often deceptive. One of the things we learn from eco-nomic analysis of law is that it is hard to use general legal rules to redis-tribute wealth, that "pro-rich" or "pro-poor" laws usually are neither.

We saw one example of this in the previous chapter, in the context of the nonwaivable warranty of habitability, a doctrine viewed by many people, including many judges, as a way of benefiting poor tenants at the expense of their landlords. Changing one term of a contract in one case in favor of one tenant may benefit that tenant, but if legal rules consistently change one term in favor of one party, other terms will shift to compen-sate. Viewed from the backward-looking perspective of a single case, re-distribution from one party to the other is obviously an option; viewed from the forward-looking perspective of the effect of a legal rule on how parties affected by it will act, it may not be.

Consider as an extreme example a law "favoring" poor tenants by providing that a landlord may never enforce any term in the lease against them. The result of such a law would be that few people would rent to poor tenants, since there is little point to renting an apartment to someone if you have no way of collecting the rent.

This is not a wholly imaginary argument. It corresponds reasonably well to the eighteenth-century approach to protecting women. Married women were, in most contexts, not permitted to make binding contracts, with the result that they were unable to participate in a wide variety of economic activity. The abandonment of that doctrine in the course of the nineteenth century was an improvement both for women and for men who wanted to do business with women. If, as these examples suggest, most legal issues ultimately involve efficiency rather than the distribution of income, then designing law to maximize efficiency may well be a good, although not perfect, way to maximize happiness.

An alternative argument for efficient law is that, even when legal rules can be used to redistribute, there are better tools available, such as taxation. If so, it may be sensible to use the legal system to maximize the size of the pie and leave to the legislature and the IRS the job of cutting it.

My conclusion is that efficiency, defined in Marshall's sense, provides a useful, although imperfect, approach to judging legal rules and their outcomes. You may find it useful to adopt that conclusion as a working hypothesis in reading this book, while feeling free to drop it at the end.

So far I have been discussing economic efficiency as a normative criterion, a way of deciding what the law should be—what I earlier described as the third and most controversial project of economic analysis of law. In the context of the first two projects, understanding the effect of legal rules and understanding why particular rules exist, the objections I have been discussing are largely irrelevant. The consequences of laws are determined not by what people should value but by what they do value, since that is what determines their actions. And in the machinery that makes law, value measured in dollars is more relevant than value measured in some abstract unit of happiness. A rich man's dollar has the same weight in hiring a lawyer or bribing a legislator as a poor man's dollar, so if outcomes are determined by some sort of net value, dollar value looks like the best candidate.

IV. Alternatives to Marshall, or
Rugs to Sweep the Dust under

Modern economists often try to avoid some of the problems implicit in Marshall's approach by using a different definition of economic improvement, due to Vilfredo Pareto, an Italian economist. Pareto avoided the problem of trading off gains to some against losses to others by defining an improvement as a change that benefits someone and injures nobody.

Unfortunately, this approach eliminates the solution as well as the problem. Consider again our little world. As long as we have two people, freedom of exchange is efficient whether we use Marshall's definition (net gains) or Pareto's (some gain, no loss). At any price between fifty cents and a dollar both Mary and John gain.

But now put Anne back into the picture—with a value for the apple of only seventy-five cents. Anne proposes, on the principle of gender solidarity, a new legal rule: Women can trade only with other women. Going from gender solidarity to freedom of exchange produces a net gain by Marshall's criterion, since it means John instead of Anne getting the apple, and it is worth more to him than to her. But it makes Anne worse off, so it is not a Pareto improvement.

The problem with Pareto's approach becomes still more serious when we add a few hundred million more people. In a complicated society it is very unlikely indeed that a change in legal rules will produce only benefits and no costs. Not even the most enthusiastic supporter of free trade—myself, for example—would deny that the abolition of tariffs makes some people worse off. If we want to make an overall evaluation of the effects of such changes, we are stuck with the problem of balancing gains to some against losses to others, a problem that Marshall solves, even if imperfectly, and Pareto only evades. It is therefore Marshall's approach to defining economic improvements and the efficiency of legal rules that I will be using—and that other economists routinely use, whether or not they say so.

Readers interested in a more detailed discussion of these issues will find it in other books of mine, including one on my web site. Hopefully, what I have provided here is enough to show readers with a background in economics why I consider the Paretian approach that they encountered in their textbooks, along with the more elaborate version due to Hicks and Kaldor that they may have also encountered, evasions of, not solutions to, the problem of evaluating changes that affect many people in a variety of ways.

The Simple Case for Laissez-Faire

The discussion so far suggests a simple solution to the problem of creating efficient legal rules—private property plus freedom of exchange. Everything belongs to someone. Everyone is free to buy or sell on any terms mutually acceptable to buyer and seller.

The generalization to include growing apples as well as trading them is straightforward. Any new good belongs to whoever produced it. So if the cost of producing a good, the summed cost of all the necessary inputs, is less than its value to whoever values it most, it will pay someone to buy the inputs, produce the good, and sell it to the highest bidder. Not only do

all goods end up in their highest valued uses, but all goods are produced
if and only if their value to whoever values them most is greater than their
cost to whoever can produce them most easily.

   If this were a book about price theory, I would now spend the next
seven chapters working through the logic of this argument in a more complicated world, with firms, capital goods, international trade, and a great
variety of other complications; interested readers will find that discussion
in chapters 3–9 of my *Hidden Order*. I will instead assume here that the
basic logic of the argument in favor of freedom of exchange—more generally, of a policy of private property and legal laissez-faire—is clear and go
on to briefly sketch its limitations.

What Is Wrong with the Simple Case for Laissez-Faire

Implicit in the argument so far are a variety of simplifying assumptions.
One of the most important is that all transactions are voluntary. That
assumption was important for two reasons. First, a voluntary exchange
must benefit the parties who make it, otherwise they wouldn't. Second,
while it may make a third party worse off—Anne in the case where John
outbid her for the apple—that loss must be less than the gain to the transacting parties, since otherwise Anne would have offered a higher price
and gotten the apple.

   When I drive my car down the street, both the car and the gasoline
were obtained by voluntary exchange. But the same is not true of the relation between me and pedestrians I might run down or the homeowners
downwind who must breath my exhaust. Nor is there a voluntary relation between me and the thief who steals my hubcaps.

   A second assumption implicit in the argument is that transactions are
costless, that if the apple is worth more to John than to Mary, he will end
up buying it. But suppose Mary believes that the apple is worth a dollar
fifty to John when it is actually worth only a dollar. She holds out for a
price of a dollar twenty-five, he refuses to pay it, and the apple remains
with Mary. The same thing might happen even if nobody misestimates
anyone's value for the apple. Mary holds out for a price of ninety-nine
cents, in the hope of getting most of the gain from the transaction, and
John, with a similar hope, offers only fifty-one cents. And even if the
apple does end up in the right hands, a full analysis ought to include the
costs of getting it there.

   For these and other reasons, the simple argument for a legal regime of
laissez-faire is only the beginning of the analysis. In the next few chapters
we will see some of the ways in which economic theory—and the legal
system—can deal with a more complicated and more realistic picture.

Further Reading

The general argument for the efficiency of market arrangements can be found in a variety of places, including the following:

David Friedman, *Price Theory: An Intermediate Text* (Cincinnati: Southwestern, 1990). Available on the Web page.
David Friedman, *Hidden Order: The Economics of Everyday Life* (New York: HarperCollins, 1996).

3

What's Wrong with the World, Part 1

THE NEXT FEW chapters are concerned with two very simple questions. The first is under what circumstances rational individuals, each correctly acting in his own interest, produce an inefficient outcome. To put it differently, under what circumstances does individual rationality fail to lead to group rationality—to the best possible outcome for the group, with "best" defined in terms of economic efficiency? The second question is what can be done about it—in particular, how can legal rules be designed to minimize such problems.

Start with the simplest case, a situation in which I bear all of the costs and benefits produced by my actions; whatever I do, nobody else is either worse or better off as a result. Being rational, I choose the action that maximizes the net benefit to me. Net benefit to everyone is net benefit to me plus net benefit to everyone else. Since my action maximizes the former and is irrelevant to the latter, it also maximizes the sum.

For a simple example consider my decision of which computer game to play this evening. I own all of the alternative games already, so my decision has no effect on the revenue of the companies that produce them. My office is far enough from the bedrooms so that my decision has no effect on how well my wife or children can sleep. The only effect is on me, and, being rational, I choose the game that I currently find most entertaining.

We can expand the range of examples by considering cases in which my action affects other people but the effects cancel. Suppose I decide to put my house up for sale. One result is that my neighbor ends up selling his house for five thousand dollars less than he otherwise would have because he had to cut his price in order to keep his customer from buying my house instead. My neighbor is worse off by five thousand dollars as a result of my action, but the person who bought his house at the lower price is five thousand dollars better off, so the net effect on other people is zero. Such effects are called "pecuniary" or "transfer" externalities—effects on other people that result in a net transfer between them but not a net cost to them. Since I impose no net cost on others, when I take the action that maximizes net benefit to me I am also maximizing net benefit to everyone.

Situations in which individual rationality leads to group rationality are surprisingly common in market settings. In a competitive market the price at which something sells equals both the cost of producing it (more precisely, the cost of producing one more unit of the good—*marginal cost*) and the value to the purchaser of consuming it (more precisely, the value of consuming one more unit of the good—*marginal value*). When you buy an apple or an hour of labor on a competitive market, what you pay just compensates the person who sells it; when you sell an apple or an hour of labor, what you receive just measures the value to the purchaser of what you sold him. Prices end up transmitting all of the costs and benefits associated with your actions back to you. Thus, when you make the decision that maximizes your benefit, you are also making the decision that maximizes net benefit. It is this fact that is at the heart of the proof that a perfectly competitive market produces an efficient outcome. For the details see a good price theory text.

Although such situations are common, they are by no means universal. When my steel mill produces a ton of steel, I pay my workers for the cost of their labor, I pay the mining firm for the cost of its ore, but I do not pay the people downwind for the sulfur dioxide I am putting into their air. In deciding how much steel to produce and how to produce it, I make the decision that maximizes net gain to me, that maximizes net gain summed over me, my suppliers and customers, and everyone upwind, but not the decision that maximizes net gain to everyone.

Since the cost to me of producing steel is less than the true cost, I end up selling the steel at below its real cost; since the amount people buy depends in part on price, other people end up buying too much steel. Total value summed over everyone concerned, including my downwind neighbors, would be larger if we produced and consumed a little less steel and substituted some other material instead.

The existence of such external costs results in my producing too much steel. It also results in my producing too little pollution control. There may be ways to reduce the amount of pollution my mill produces: a different production process, cleaner coal, taller smokestacks, filters. If I can eliminate two dollars worth of pollution damage at a cost of one dollar of pollution control, it is worth doing from the standpoint of efficiency—cost one dollar, benefit two. But the cost is paid by me, and the benefit goes to the people downwind, so it is not in my interest to do it.

The problem is not simply that pollution is bad. All costs are bad; that is why they are costs. We are willing to bear some costs because we get benefits in exchange; we are willing to work, even when we would rather play, because work produces useful goods. The problem with external costs such as pollution is that they get left out of the calculation of what things are or are not worth doing, with the result that we end up with not only efficient pollution, pollution whose prevention would cost more than it is worth, but inefficient pollution as well.

One solution is direct regulation: some government agency such as the EPA makes rules requiring steel mills to filter their smoke, or build high smokestacks, or in various other ways reduce their pollution. While this is an obvious solution, it has some serious problems.

The first is that the EPA may not be interested in maximizing efficiency. Steel producers, coal producers, and the makers of filters and scrubbers are also voters and potential campaign contributors. It is not obvious that the summed effect of their political activities will make it in the interest of the politicians who ultimately control the EPA to use their power to produce an efficient outcome. If (to take a real-world example) senators from states producing high-sulfur coal have sufficient political clout, the regulations will be rigged to encourage the use of scrubbers even when switching to low-sulfur coal would be a more efficient way of controlling pollution.

The second problem is that, even if the EPA wants to maximize efficiency, it does not know how to do it. Figuring out what pollution control measures are or are not worth taking and how much steel ought to be produced after properly allowing for the external costs of producing it are hard problems. Answering them requires detailed information about the costs and benefits of different measures for different steel mills, most of which is in the hands of the firms, not the regulators. If the EPA simply asks a firm whether it knows any cost-effective way of controlling its pollution, the obvious answer is "no," since if the EPA believes that there is no cost-effective form of control, the firm will get to pollute without having to pay any control costs at all. The answer may even be true. There is, after all, very little reason to learn things when the knowledge will only make you worse off.

Because of such problems economists interested in the problem of controlling negative externalities, of which pollution is one example, usually favor a less direct form of regulation. Instead of telling the firm what it must do, the regulator simply charges the firm for its pollution. If making a ton of steel produces twenty pounds of sulfur dioxide, which does four dollars worth of damage, the firm is billed for its sulfur dioxide output at twenty cents a pound.

This approach, labeled "effluent fees" in the context of pollution (more generally, "Pigouvian taxes," after A. C. Pigou, the economist who thought up the idea), has several advantages over direct regulation. To begin with, the regulator does not have to know anything about the costs of pollution control; he can safely leave that to the firm. If the firm can reduce its emissions at a cost of less than twenty cents per pound, it is in its interest to do so. If the firm protests that there is no way it can produce steel without pollution, the EPA politely accepts its word and sends it a bill for the pollution it produces.

A second advantage is that this approach generates not only the right amount of pollution control but the right amount of steel as well. When the firm produces steel, its costs now include both the cost of controlling pollution and the cost of any pollution it fails to control. So the price steel is sold at now represents the true cost of producing it. When steel is cheaper than concrete, buildings will be built of steel; when concrete is cheaper, they will be built of concrete.

Effluent fees do not solve all of the problems of controlling pollution, unfortunately. For one thing, they do not solve the problem of making it in the political interest of the regulators to do the right thing. They might deliberately set the fee too low in exchange for political contributions or future jobs for the regulatory officials, or deliberately set the fee too high to punish firms for making contributions to the wrong candidate.

Even if the regulators are trying to produce the efficient outcome, it may not be easy to measure the damage actually done by each additional pound of sulfur dioxide, or CO_2, or whatever. But at least the informational problems are less than with direct regulation, since the regulators no longer need to know how pollution can be controlled or at what cost. And the political problems, although they still exist, should be reduced, since it is harder to provide special favors to your friends when decisions are made pollutant by pollutant instead of firm by firm.

So far I have been describing Pigouvian taxes in the context of a regulatory agency such as the EPA. But the same analysis can be used to explain large parts of tort law. Instead of having the EPA impose effluent taxes, we permit the people downwind to sue the steel mill for the damage its pollution is doing to their houses, laundry, and lungs. The steel mill has the choice of eliminating the pollution, paying damages, or reducing the pollution and paying damages on what is left.

The analysis can be applied to parking fines and speeding tickets as well. When I drive fast I am imposing a cost, in additional accident risk, on other drivers. The law forces me to take account of that cost in my actions by fining me when I am caught exceeding the speed limit.

There are, of course, differences among these examples. An effluent fee goes to the state. Tort damages go to the victim and his attorney. Fines go to the state. There are other important differences as well, many of which will be discussed in later chapters.

But the fundamental logic of all three cases is similar. Someone takes an action that imposes costs on others. It is in his interest to take the action as long it produces a net benefit for him, even if including the effects on the rest of us converts that to a loss. We solve the problem with legal rules that force the actor to bear the external cost himself, to internalize the externality. His net cost now equals net cost to everyone, so he takes the action if and only if it produces a net benefit. Individual rationality has been harnessed to produce group rationality. It is an elegant solution although far from a perfect one, as you will see in subsequent chapters.

Rent Seeking: How Not to Give Things Away

I mentioned earlier a special sort of externality called a pecuniary externality, one that imposes no net cost, since the effects on other people cancel out. Unlike other externalities, a pecuniary externality does not lead to inefficiency, since the actor's private net costs are equal to total net costs, just as they would be if there were no externality at all. My example was the externality I imposed on my neighbor by putting my house on the market when he is trying to sell his.

The implication of the argument is that my neighbor ought not to be able to collect damages from me for the reduction in the price of his house. Competition should not be, and is not, a tort. That particular legal principle appears in the common law at least as early as 1410, when the owner of one school sued a competitor for taking students away from him—and lost.

A clever—and mischievous—reader might suggest extending the argument from competition to theft. When a pickpocket steals fifty dollars from me, he is fifty dollars better off and I am fifty dollars worse off. The net effect is only a transfer, so there is no reason for an economist, concerned only with efficiency, to object. Does it follow that, just as competition ought not to be a tort, theft ought not to be a crime?

It does not. A pecuniary externality occurs when an action by A results in a transfer from B to C. The logic of the situation is rather different when an action by A results in a transfer from B to A.

Picking pockets is not a costless activity; it involves time, training, and a variety of risks. Suppose the total cost to me of picking your pocket works out, on average, to twenty dollars. I gain fifty dollars at a cost of twenty, so it is worth it for me to pick your pocket; I am thirty dollars better off. But the net effect is to transfer fifty dollars from you to me at a cost of twenty, making us on net twenty dollars worse off.

To carry the argument a little further, consider what happens if there are lots of other people about as talented as I am at this particular activity. Since twenty dollars worth of effort yields fifty dollars worth of income, picking pockets is an attractive opportunity for them too. The number of pickpockets increases rapidly.

As the number increases, the profitability of that line of work declines. Someone who carelessly flashes a big roll of bills is instantly targeted by six pickpockets, leaving numbers two through six out of luck. As the risk of having your pocket picked rises, so does the incentive to take precautions. People start carrying money in their shoes, which are harder to pick than their pockets.

The process stops only when it is no longer profitable for any more people to become pickpockets. We end up with lots of pickpockets, most of whom have abandoned productive jobs in order to make a little more money picking pockets. Most of the money the victims lose goes to re-imburse the criminals for their time and effort, making the net loss roughly equal to the amount stolen—a little less, since some especially talented pickpockets make more in that profession than they could in any other.

So far we have omitted the cost to the victims of their precautions—sore feet from walking on small change and sore eyes from trying to keep a close watch on everyone around them. If we include that, the net cost of theft increases; it may well be more, not less, than the total amount stolen.

The general term for this phenomenon is "rent seeking." It occurs when there is an opportunity for people to spend resources transferring wealth from others to themselves. As long as the gain is more than the cost, it is worth making the transfer—from the standpoint of the recipient. As more people compete to be recipients, the gain falls. In equilibrium the marginal recipient (the least talented pickpocket) just breaks even. The inframarginal recipients (especially talented pickpockets) make some gain, although less than what the victims lose (even talented pick-pockets have some costs). The victims lose both the amount transferred and the cost to them of their defensive efforts.

Rent seeking occurs in a wide variety of contexts, many relevant to the subjects of this book. The term was coined to describe competition for government favors—in the original example import permits that permit-ted the holders to buy foreign currency at an artificially cheap price. Firms competed to get those valuable favors by public relations efforts, lobby-ing, campaign contributions, bribes. As long as a million-dollar favor can be obtained for substantially less than a million, some other firm is willing to bid a little higher, so winning firms end up, on average, paying about what the favors are worth. Anne Krueger, who originated the term "rent seeking," estimated that the governments of India and Turkey, two poor countries that at the time had systems of exchange controls and import permits, were burning up between 5 and 10 percent of their GNP in such unproductive competition.

For a somewhat less clear example, consider litigation. Each side is spending money on lawyers, expert witnesses, and the like in order to increase its chance of winning the case. The plaintiff is spending money to increase the chance of a transfer from the defendant to him, the defendant to decrease it. The transfer itself is neither a net gain nor a net loss; the expenditures on litigation are a net loss.

This is a less clear example of rent seeking because it is at least possible that the expenditures are producing something valuable: an increased probability of a correct verdict, resulting in better incentives elsewhere in the system. Controlling pollution by allowing suits against polluting factories by people living downwind works only if factories that pollute are more likely to lose suits than factories that don't, or, in other words, if the court has at least some tendency to reach the correct verdict. Expenditures by both sides on producing evidence and argument may make that more likely.

Getting It Wrong: Fraud on the Market Suits

The CEO of a company gives an optimistic speech. Six months later the newest product turns out to be a flop, and the company's stock falls. An enterprising lawyer files a class action suit on behalf of everyone who bought stock in the company between the speech and the stock drop. His argument is that the speech, by omitting relevant facts that might have led to a more pessimistic conclusion, fraudulently induced people to buy the stock for more than it was worth and that the company should therefore make up their losses. Such "fraud on the market" suits occasionally succeed. Since the potential damages are enormous, even a small chance of success is enough to make it in the interest of some defendants to settle out of court, making such litigation a profitable enterprise for entrepreneurial attorneys.

There are a number of problems with the theory underlying such suits. CEOs are no more omniscient than anyone else, making it a considerable stretch to treat an optimistic statement that turns out to be wrong as actionable fraud. Customers are free to decide for themselves whose predictions to believe. An investor who takes optimistic speeches and press releases for gospel might be wiser to keep his money under his mattress instead.

One problem particularly relevant to this chapter has to do with the calculation of damages. Even if we concede that the speech was deliberately fraudulent, liability ought to depend on net damage done. Suppose I bought a share from you for a hundred dollars and it later fell to fifty. If the speech (and my purchase) had not been made, the stock would still have gone down; the only difference is that you, rather than I, would have been holding it. I am fifty dollars worse off as a result of my believing the CEO, but you are fifty dollars better off.

Insofar as the CEO's optimism merely resulted in different people holding the stock when it fell, the externality is purely pecuniary and should give rise to no liability at all. We get a net externality only if I bought the stock from the CEO, making the effect of his speech a transfer from him to me and converting the situation from pecuniary externality to rent seeking.

Courts, in accepting the plaintiffs' theory of how damages should be calculated, have produced an economically inefficient verdict. One result is to penalize executives for making predictions that might turn out to be wrong, thus reducing the total amount of information available to investors. Another is to divert real resources from producing useful goods and services to producing litigation.

Defenders of that theory might—and sometimes do—argue that even if the damage payment is unrelated to the actual damage done, it provides injured stockholders an incentive to sue and thus deters fraudulent statements by corporate executives. The problem is that the higher the potential damage award, the higher the incentive to sue even on a weak case—and suits with large sums at stake produce high litigation costs. One might, on similar grounds, argue that since we want to deter illegal parking, anyone who finds an illegally parked vehicle should be allowed to claim it for his own. What we want, here as in many other cases, is not an incentive but the right incentive, a point we will return to in later chapters.

Question: I have just described a case not only of pecuniary externalities but of rent seeking as well—and not by the CEO. Explain.

Further Reading

The term "rent seeking" was originated by Anne Krueger in "The Political Economy of the Rent-Seeking Society," *American Economic Review* 64 (June 1974): 291–303. The idea, however, was presented earlier and more generally by Gordon Tullock in "The Welfare Consequences of Tariffs, Monopoly and Theft," *Western Economic Journal* 5 (June 1967): 224–32.

4

What's Wrong with the World, Part 2

Where two carriages come in collision, if there is
no negligence in either it is as much the act of the
one driver as of the other that they meet.
  (*Bramwell, B., in* Fletcher v. Rylands,
  3 H. & C. 774 [Ex. 1865])

THE ARGUMENT of the previous chapter can be stated quite simply:

A takes an action that imposes a cost upon B. In order to make A take the action
if and only if it produces net benefits, we must somehow transfer the external
cost back to him. The polluting company is charged for its pollution, the careless motorist is sued for the damage done when he runs into someone else's car.
The externality is internalized, the actor takes account of all relevant costs in
deciding what action to take, and the result is an efficient pattern of decisions.

That view of externalities, originally due to Pigou, was almost universally accepted by economists until one evening in 1960, when a British
economist named Ronald Coase came to the University of Chicago to
deliver a paper. He spent the evening at the house of Aaron Director,
the founding editor of the *Journal of Law and Economics*. Counting
Coase, fourteen economists were present, three of them future Nobel
Prize winners.

When the evening started, thirteen of them supported the conventional
view of externalities described above. When the evening ended, none of
them did. Coase had persuaded them that Pigou's analysis was wrong,
not in one way but in three. The existence of externalities does not necessarily lead to an inefficient result. Pigouvian taxes do not in general lead
to the efficient result. Third, and most important, the problem is not really externalities at all. It is transaction costs.

I like to present Coase's argument in three steps: Nothing Works,
Everything Works, It All Depends (on transaction costs).

Nothing Works

An external cost is not simply a cost produced by one person and borne
by another. In almost all cases, the existence and size of external costs

depend on decisions by both parties. I would not be coughing if your steel mill were not pouring out sulfur dioxide. But your steel mill would do no damage to me if I did not happen to live downwind from it. It is the joint decision, yours to pollute and mine to live where you are polluting, that produces the cost. If you are not liable to me for the damage done by your pollution, your decision to pollute imposes a cost on me. If you are liable, my decision to live downwind imposes a cost, in liability or pollution control, on you.

Suppose pollution from a steel mill does $200,000 a year worth of damage and could be eliminated at a cost of $100,000 a year (from here on all costs are per year). Further assume that the cost of shifting all of the land downwind to a new use unaffected by the pollution, timber instead of summer resorts, is only $50,000. If we impose an emission fee of $200,000 a year, the steel mill stops polluting, and the damage is eliminated at a cost of $100,000. If we impose no emission fee, the mill keeps polluting, the owners of the land stop advertising for summer visitors and plant trees instead, and the problem is again solved, this time at a cost of $50,000. The result without Pigouvian taxes is efficient—the problem is eliminated at the lowest possible cost—and the result with Pigouvian taxes is inefficient.

Even draconian limits on emissions in southern California would be less expensive than evacuating that end of the state; indeed, it is unlikely that moving the victims is often an efficient solution to the problems of air pollution. But consider the same logic applied to the externalities produced by testing high explosives. A thousand-pound bomb produces substantial external effects if it lands fifty feet from your campsite. Keeping campers out of bomb ranges seems a more sensible solution than letting them in and permitting them to sue for the resulting damage.

For a less exotic example consider airport noise. One solution is to reduce the noise. Another is to soundproof the houses. A third is to use the land near airports for wheat fields or noisy factories instead of housing. There is no particular reason to think that one of those solutions is always best. Nor is it entirely clear whether the victim is the landowner who finds it difficult to sleep in his new house with jets going by overhead or the airline forced by a court or a regulatory agency to adopt expensive sound control measures in order to protect the sleep of people who chose to build their new houses in what used to be wheat fields, directly under the airport's flight path.

Finally, consider an example in which the sympathies of most of us would be with the "polluter." The owner of one of two adjoining tracts of land has a factory that he has been running for twenty years with no complaints from his neighbors. The purchaser of the other tract builds a recording studio on the side of his property immediately adjacent to the factory. The factory, while not especially noisy, is too noisy for something located two feet from the wall of a recording studio. The owner of the studio demands that the factory shut down or else pay damages equal to the full value of the studio. There are indeed external costs associated with operating a factory next to a recording studio. But the efficient solution is building the studio at the other end of the lot, not building the studio next to the factory and then closing down the factory.

So Coase's first point is that since external costs are jointly produced by polluter and victim, a legal rule that assigns blame to one of the parties gives the right result only if that party happens to be the one who can avoid the problem at the lower cost. In general, nothing works. Whichever party the blame is assigned to, by government regulators or by the courts, the result will be inefficient if the other party could prevent the problem at a lower cost or if the optimal solution requires precautions by both parties.

One advantage of effluent fees over direct regulation is that the regulator does not have to know the cost of pollution control in order to produce the efficient outcome; he just sets the tax equal to damage done and lets the polluter decide how much pollution to buy at that price. But one implication of Coase's argument is that the regulator can guarantee the efficient outcome only if he knows enough about the cost of control to decide which party should be considered responsible for preventing the jointly produced problem and so required to bear the cost if it is not prevented.

Everything Works

The second step in Coase's argument is to observe that, as long as the parties can readily make and enforce contracts in their mutual interest, neither direct regulation nor a Pigouvian tax is necessary in order to get the efficient outcome. All you need is a clear definition of who has a right to do what, and the market will take care of the problem.

Our earlier case of the steel mill and the resorts showed one way of getting to the efficient result without legal restrictions on pollution. The lowest-cost avoiders were the owners of the land downwind; since they could not prevent the pollution they shifted from operating resorts to growing timber, which happened to be the efficient outcome.

What if, instead, the legal rule had been that the people downwind had a right not to have their air polluted? The final result would have been the same. The mill could eliminate the pollution at a cost of $100,000 a year. But it is cheaper to pay the landowners some amount, say $75,000 a year, for permission to pollute. The landowners will be better off, since what they are getting is more than the cost to them of changing the use of the land. The steel mill will be better off, since what it is paying is less than the cost of eliminating the pollution. So it pays both parties to make such an agreement.

Next suppose we change our assumptions, lowering the cost of pollution control to $20,000. If the mill has the right to pollute, the landowners will pay more than the $20,000 cost of pollution control in exchange for a guarantee of clean air. If it does not have the right to pollute, the most the steel mill will be willing to offer the landowners for permission to pollute is $20,000, and the landowners will turn down that offer. Either way, the mill ends up controlling its pollution, which is now the efficient solution.

The generalization of this example is straightforward: *If transaction costs are zero, if, in other words, any agreement that is in the mutual benefit of the parties concerned gets made, then any initial definition of property rights leads to an efficient outcome.* This result is sometimes referred to as the *Coase Theorem.*

We have just restated the simple argument for laissez-faire in a more sophisticated form. What people own are not things but rights with regard to things. Ownership of a steel mill is a bundle of rights: the right to control who comes onto the property, the right to decide how the machinery is used, . . . It may or may not also include the right to produce pollution. If that right is more valuable to the owner of the bundle of rights we call "ownership of the steel mill" than to anyone else, he will keep it if he owns it and buy it if he does not. If it is more valuable to property owners downwind, they will keep it if they own it and buy it if they do not. All rights move to those to whom they are of greatest value, giving us an efficient outcome.

It All Depends (On Transaction Costs)

Why, if Coase is correct, do we still have pollution in Los Angeles? One possible answer is that the pollution is efficient, that the damage it does is less than the cost of preventing it. A more plausible answer is that much of the pollution is inefficient, but that the transactions necessary to eliminate it are blocked by prohibitively high transaction costs.

Let us return again to the steel mill. Suppose it has the right to pollute but that doing so is inefficient; pollution control is cheaper than either putting up with the pollution or changing the use of the land downwind. Further suppose that there are a hundred landowners downwind.

With only one landowner there would be no problem; he would offer to pay the mill for the cost of the pollution control equipment plus a little extra to sweeten the deal. But a hundred landowners face what economists call a *public good problem.* If ninety of them put up the money and ten do not, the ten get a free ride—no pollution and no cost for pollution control. Each landowner has an incentive to refuse to pay, figuring that his payment is unlikely to make the difference between success and failure in the attempt to raise enough money to persuade the steel mill to eliminate its pollution. If the attempt is going to fail even with him, it makes no difference whether or not he contributes. If it is going to succeed even without him, then refusing to contribute gives him a free ride. Only if his contribution makes the difference does he gain by agreeing to contribute.

There are ways in which such problems may sometimes be solved, but none that can always be expected to work. The problem becomes harder the larger the number of people involved. With many millions of people living in southern California, it is hard to imagine any plausible way in which they could voluntarily raise the money to pay all polluters to reduce their pollution.

This is one example of the problem of transaction costs. Another occurs if we reverse our assumptions, making pollution (and timber) the efficient outcome but giving landowners the legal right to be pollution free. If there were one landowner, the steel mill could buy from him the right to pollute. With a hundred, the mill must buy permission from all of them. Each has an incentive to be a holdout, to refuse his permission in the hope of getting paid off with a large part of the money the mill will save from not having to control its pollution. If too many landowners try that approach, the negotiations break down and the parties never get to the efficient outcome.

Seen from this perspective, the problem is not externalities but transaction costs. With externalities but no transaction costs there would be no problem, since the parties would always bargain to the efficient solution. When we observe externality problems (or other forms of market failure) in the real world, we should ask not merely where the problem comes from but what the transaction costs are that prevent it from being bargained out of existence.

Coase Plus Pigou Is Too Much of a Good Thing

There is one more use for our polluting factory before we move on to more pastoral topics. This time we have only one factory and one landowner, so bargaining between them is simple. Pollution does $60,000 worth of damage, pollution control costs $80,000, switching the land use from resorts to timber costs $100,000. The efficient outcome is pollution, since the damage done is less than the cost of avoiding it.

The EPA, having been persuaded of the virtues of Pigouvian taxes, informs the factory that if it pollutes, it must pay for the damage it does—a $60,000 fine. What happens?

Controlling the pollution costs more than the fine, so one might expect the factory to pay the fine and continue to pollute, which is the efficient solution. That is the obvious answer, but it is wrong.

We have forgotten the landowner. The fine goes to the EPA, not to him, so if the factory pays and pollutes, he suffers $60,000 of uncompensated damage. He can eliminate that damage by offering to pay part of the cost of pollution control, say $30,000. Now, when the factory controls its pollution, it saves a $60,000 fine and receives a $30,000 side payment from the landowner, for a total of $90,000, which is more than the $80,000 cost of pollution control. The result is pollution control that costs more than it is worth.

We are adding together Pigou's incentive (a fine for polluting) and Coase's incentive (a side payment from the victim for not polluting), giving the factory twice the proper incentive to control its pollution. If the cost of control is less than twice the benefit, the factory buys it even if it shouldn't.

One solution is to replace administrative law with tort law, converting the fine paid to the EPA into a damage payment to the landowner. Now he is compensated for the damage, so he has no incentive to pay the factory to stop polluting.

Coase, Meade, and Bees

Ever since Coase published "The Problem of Social Cost," economists unconvinced by his analysis have argued that the Coase Theorem is merely a theoretical curiosity, of little or no practical importance in a world where transaction costs are rarely zero. One famous counterexample concerns bees.

Writing before Coase, James Meade (who later received a Nobel Prize for his work on the economics of international trade) offered externalities associated with honeybees as an example of the sort of problem for which the market offered no practical solution. Bees graze on the flowers of various crops, so a farmer who grows crops that produce nectar benefits the beekeepers in the area. The farmer receives none of the benefit himself, so has an inefficiently low incentive to grow such crops.

Since bees cannot be convinced to respect property rights or keep contracts, there would seem to be no practical way to apply Coase's approach to the problem. We must either subsidize farmers who grow nectar-rich crops (a negative Pigouvian tax) or accept inefficiency in the joint production of crops and honey.

It turns out that it isn't true. As supporters of Coase have demonstrated, contracts between beekeepers and farmers have been common practice in the industry at least since early in this century. When the crops were producing nectar and did not need pollination, beekeepers paid farmers for permission to put their hives in the farmers' fields. When the crops were producing little nectar but needed pollination (which increases yields), farmers paid beekeepers. Bees may not respect property rights, but they are, like people, lazy and prefer to forage as close to the hive as possible.

That a Coasian approach solves that particular externality problem does not imply that it will solve all such problems. But the observation that an economist as distinguished as Meade assumed an externality problem was insoluble save by government intervention in a context where Coase's market solution was actually standard practice suggests that the range of problems to which the Coasian solution is relevant may be much greater than many would at first guess. And whether or not externality problems can be bargained away, Coase's analysis points out fundamental mistakes in the traditional way of thinking about externalities: the failure to recognize the symmetry between "polluter" and "victim" and the failure to allow for private approaches to solving such problems.

A different way of putting the point is to observe that the Pigouvian analysis of the problem is correct, but only under special circumstances, situations in which transaction costs are high, so that transactions between the parties can safely be ignored, and in which the agent deciding which party is to be held liable already knows who the lowest-cost avoider of the problem is. Air pollution in an urban area is an obvious example. Coase provides the more general analysis, covering both that case and all others.

Considered from the standpoint of a court there are at least two different ways in which these insights might be applied. Courts could follow a policy of deciding, in each case, whether plaintiff or defendant was the lowest-cost avoider, awarding damages for pollution only if it concluded that the polluter could solve the problem more cheaply than the victim. Alternatively, courts could try to establish general rules for assigning liability, rules that usually assigned liability to the right party.

One example of such a general rule is the tort defense of "coming to the nuisance." Under this doctrine if you build your housing development next to my pig farm, I may be able to avoid liability by arguing that, because I was there first, you were the one responsible for the problem. An economic justification for the doctrine is that it is less expensive to change the location of a development, or a pig farm, before it is built than after, making the second mover usually the lower-cost avoider of the problem. We will return to this example, along with some complications, in later chapters.

General rules have several advantages over case-by-case decisions. They are usually more predictable, making it possible for parties to take decisions without having to guess who some future court will think was the lowest-cost avoider of future problems. They reduce litigation costs, since using expensive legal resources to convince a court that the other party can solve the problem more cheaply than you can is more likely to work than using similar resources to convince a court that your housing development was built ten years earlier than it really was. The disadvantage of a general rule is that it can be expected to give the wrong answer in some specific cases, which means that a general rule will do a worse job of guaranteeing efficient outcomes than would a perfectly wise court deciding each case on its individual merits.

General rules that yield easily predictable results are sometimes referred to as *bright line rules*; rules that require a case-by-case decision by courts are sometimes referred to as *standards*. Consider, as one example, the requirement in the U.S. Constitution that a candidate for president must be at least thirty-five years old. Presumably the purpose is to ensure that candidates be sufficiently mature for the job. It is a bright line rule, but not a very good one, since chronological age is only a very rough measure of maturity; all of us can think of examples of people over thirty-five who are less mature than many people under thirty-five. Some of us may even be able to think of ones who have been elected president.

But consider the alternative—a standard specifying that a candidate for president must be as mature as the average thirty-five-year-old. That is a very fuzzy rule indeed—one that reduces, in practice, to the requirement that any candidate must be acceptable to a majority of the justices on the Supreme Court.

A still more important example of a bright line rule is the general principle that all human beings, with some narrow exceptions for children and lunatics, have the same legal rights—very different from the legal rights of animals. The features of human beings that give rise to legal rights are not all-or-none matters; most humans are more rational and better able to communicate than most animals, but again many of us can think of exceptions. A perfect legal system with perfectly wise judges would presumably enforce legal rights that varied from person to person (and animal to animal), tracking the variation in the features that gave rise to those rights. The result might well be that a sufficiently retarded human being would have fewer rights than a very smart chimpanzee.

Our legal system does not work that way and probably shouldn't. The human/not human distinction is not a perfect measure of intelligence, linguistic ability, and the like, but it is a very good one—and it generates a bright line rule that avoids most of the problems of some humans trying to persuade courts that they have different rights than others.

Coase, Property, and the Economic Analysis of Law

Coase's work radically altered the economic analysis of externalities. It also suggested a new and interesting approach to the problem of defining property rights, especially property rights in land.

A court settling disputes involving property, or a legislature writing a law code to be applied to such disputes, must decide which of the rights associated with land are included in the bundle we call "ownership." Does the owner have the right to prohibit airplanes from crossing his land a mile up? How about a hundred feet? How about people extracting oil from a mile under the land? What rights does he have against neighbors whose use of their land interferes with his use of his? If he builds his recording studio next to his neighbor's factory, who is at fault? If he has a right to silence in his recording studio, does that mean that he can forbid the factory from operating or only that he can sue to be reimbursed for his losses? It is simple to say that we should have private property in land, but ownership of land is not a simple thing.

The Coasian answer is that the law should define property in a way that minimizes costs associated with the sorts of incompatible uses we have been discussing: airports and residential housing, steel mills and re- sorts. The first step is to try to define rights in such a way that, if right A is of most value to someone who also holds right B, they come in the same bundle. The right to decide what happens two feet above a piece of land is of most value to the person who also holds the right to use the land itself, so it is sensible to include both of them in the bundle of rights we call "ownership of land." But the right to decide who flies a mile above a piece of land is of no special value to the owner of the land, hence there is no good reason to include it in that bundle.

If, when general legal rules were being established, we always knew what rights belonged together, the argument of the previous paragraph would be sufficient to tell us how property rights ought to be defined. But that is rarely the case. Many rights are of substantial value to two or more parties; the right to decide whether loud noises are made over a particular piece of property, for example, is of value both to the owner of the prop- erty and to his next-door neighbors. There is no general legal rule that will always assign it to the right one.

In this case the argument underlying the Coase Theorem comes into play. If we assign the right initially to the wrong person, the right person, the one to whom it is of most value, can still buy it from him. So one of the considerations in the initial definition of property rights is doing it in such a way as to minimize the transaction costs associated with fixing, via private contracts, any mistakes in the original assignment.

An example may make this clearer. Suppose damages from pollution are easy to measure and the number of people downwind is large. In that case the efficient rule is probably to give downwind landowners a right to collect damages from the polluter but not a right to forbid him from polluting. Giving the right to the landowners avoids the public good problem that we would face if the landowners (in the case where pollution is inefficient) had to raise the money to pay the steel mill not to pollute. Giving them a right to damages rather than giving each landowner the right to an injunction forbidding the steel mill from polluting avoids the holdout problem that the mill would face (in the case where pollution is efficient) in buying permission from all of the landowners.

A more complete explanation of how Coase's argument can be applied to figuring out what the law ought to be appears in the next chapter; a full explanation would require a book—one that has not yet been written. I hope I have said enough to make the basic idea clear. Coase started with a simple insight, based in part on having read cases in the common law of nuisance, the branch of law that deals with problems such as noisy factories next door to recording studios. He ended by demonstrating that what everyone else in the profession thought was the correct analysis of the problem of externalities was wrong and, in the process, opening up a whole new approach to the use of economics to analyze law.

Coase's argument first saw print in "The Problem of Social Cost," the most cited article in the economic analysis of law and one of the most cited articles in economics. In addition to showing what was wrong with the conventional analysis of externalities, the article made a number of related points.

Economists (and others) tend to jump from the observation that the market sometimes produces an inefficient outcome to the conclusion that, when it does, the government ought to intervene to fix the problem. Part of what Coase showed was that there may be no legal rule, no form of regulation, that will generate a fully efficient solution, the solution that would be imposed by an all powerful and all knowing dictator whose only objective was economic efficiency. He thus anticipated public choice economists such as James Buchanan (another Nobel winner) in arguing that the choice was not between an inefficient solution generated by the market and an efficient solution imposed by the government but rather among a variety of inefficient alternatives, private and governmental. In Coase's words, "All solutions have costs and there is no reason to suppose that government regulation is called for simply because the problem is not well handled by the market or the firm." He further argued that the distinction between market solutions and government solutions was itself in part artificial, since any market solution depended on a particular set of legal rules established by the legislature and the courts.

A second interesting feature of Coase's work was mentioned in chapter 1. Coase got to his conclusions in part by thinking about economic theory and in part by studying law. He based his argument on real cases in the common law of nuisance—a Florida case where one landowner's building shaded an adjacent hotel's swimming pool, a British case where a physician built a new consulting room at the edge of his property adjacent to a neighboring candy factory and then demanded that the candy factory shut down machinery whose vibrations were making it hard to use his consulting room, and many others. He concluded that common law judges had recognized and attempted to deal with the problem of joint causation of externalities, a problem that the economic analysis of externalities had entirely missed.

Further Reading

Ronald Coase, "The Problem of Social Cost," *Journal of Law and Economics* 3 (1960): 1–44.

Defining and Enforcing Rights: Property, Liability, and Spaghetti

COASE'S WORK provides one possible approach to the problem of constructing efficient legal rules. To make that approach clearer I spend most of this chapter using Coase's ideas to analyze how legal rights ought to be defined in the context of a particular real-world problem, one that Pigou used to explain the problem of externalities and that Coase in turn used to show why Pigou was wrong.

Having seen how, in principle, we would find the efficient legal rules for that particular situation, we then generalize the argument to the question of how to decide whether rights ought to be protected by property rules ("steal a car, go to jail"), liability rules ("dent my car, pay to fix it"), or fines.

Flaming Rails: An Extended Exercise

Railroad trains in the nineteenth century threw sparks; the sparks sometimes started fires in adjacent fields. Railroad companies could reduce the problem either by running fewer trains or by installing a spark arrester, an apparatus on the train's smokestack designed to keep sparks from getting out. Farmers could reduce the problem by leaving land near the railroad track bare or planting some crop unlikely to catch fire.

For purposes of my example I am going to simplify the situation a little. Farmers have only two alternatives: wheat, which burns, and clover, which does not. I assume that growing clover is less profitable than growing wheat, since otherwise everyone grows clover and the problem disappears. The railroad also has only two alternatives: to install or not install a spark arrester. All costs in the example can be thought of as annual costs: the lost revenue per year from growing clover instead of wheat, the lost revenue per year from occasional fires in wheat fields, the annual cost of spark arresters on railroad engines. Finally, I assume that the area we are considering contains one railroad company and a hundred farmers and that all farmers are equally at risk from sparks.

We consider four different legal rules:

1. *Property right by the railroad.* The railroad is free to throw sparks if it wants to.

2. *Property right by the farmers.* The railroad may only throw sparks if it has permission to do so from all the farmers; any one farmer can go to court and enjoin the railroad from throwing sparks.

3. *Liability right by the farmers.* The railroad is free to throw sparks but must compensate the farmers for any damage that results.

4. *Liability right by the railroad.* Any farmer may enjoin the railroad from throwing sparks but must then compensate the railroad for the cost of having to put on a spark arrester.

This way of stating the rules partly obscures the symmetry of the alternatives. In particular, alternative 4 (the legal term for which is "incomplete privilege") seems less natural than the other three. The symmetry is clearer if we think of each rule as answering two questions:

Who decides whether the railroad throws sparks?
Who bears the costs implied by that decision?

There are two possible answers to each question: Railroad or farmers. Combining the possible answers gives us our four rules:

1. Railroad decides, farmers bear
2. Farmers decide, railroad bears
3. Railroad decides, railroad bears
4. Farmers decide, farmers bear

In addition to four rules we also have four possible outcomes:

A. *Sparks + Wheat = Fires:* Railroad throws sparks, farmers grow wheat, the result is occasional fires.

B. *Sparks + Clover = No Fires:* Railroad throws sparks, farmers grow clover, no fires because there is nothing to burn.

C. *Spark Arrester + Wheat = No Fires:* Railroad installs the spark arrester, farmers grow wheat, there are no fires because there are no sparks to start them.

D. *Spark Arrester + Clover = No Fires:* Railroad installs the spark arrester, farmers grow clover, no fires.

Each legal rule can lead to any of several different outcomes, either directly or via a transaction between railroad and farmer, as shown in figure 5.1. Each outcome has a cost, as shown in table 5.1. The objective of the game is to pick the right starting point, the efficient legal rule. As will become clear, which one that is depends on where you want to go—more precisely, on how likely each outcome is to be the efficient one.

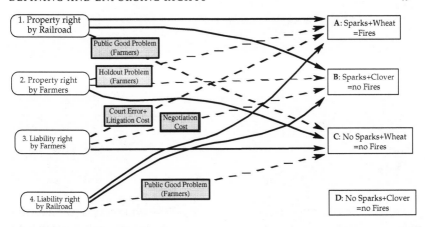

Figure 5.1. Spaghetti diagram.

TABLE 5.1
Cost of Outcomes

Cost of	Cost of	a	b	c	d
Outcome A	Fires	**$400**	$800	$800	**$600**
Outcome B	Clover	800	**400**	400	800
Outcome C	Spark Arrester	1000	1000	**200**	1000

Note: The lowest-cost solution in each column is boldfaced.

We begin with rule 1: The railroad has a right to throw sparks and is liable to nobody for the consequences. What happens?

First suppose that the damage done by fires in wheat fields is $400, switching to clover costs $800 ($8 per farmer), and a spark arrester costs $1,000 (column a of the table). The cost of the fires is less than the cost of either way of preventing them, so the efficient outcome is A: Sparks + Wheat. That outcome occurs with no transactions necessary between the parties and costs $400. The railroad throws sparks; the farmers reject the possibility of switching to clover because it would cost them more than the savings from preventing fires. The farmers could try to pay the railroad to put on a spark arrester, but the most they would offer would be $400, and the cost of the spark arrester is $1,000, so there would be no point to making the offer. We have the efficient outcome, and we have gotten there with no transactions among the parties and no transaction costs, as indicated by the solid arrow linking rule 1 to outcome A.

Next suppose we reverse the costs of clover and fires; switching to clover now costs $400, and fires do $800 worth of damage (column b). The railroad throws sparks. The farmers consider their options and switch to clover, since the savings from eliminating fires make it worth doing. This time outcome B, Sparks + Clover, is the efficient one, and we have again gotten there with no transactions between the parties and no transaction cost, shown by another solid arrow.

Finally, suppose the cost of a spark arrester drops to $200 (column c). The railroad is still legally free to throw sparks if it wants to. But now it is in the interest of the farmers to buy the railroad a spark arrester, since doing so will cost them less than switching to clover, which is their next best alternative.

It is in their interest, but it may not happen. The reason is the public good problem mentioned earlier. As long as enough money is contributed to pay for the spark arrester, farmers who choose not to contribute get a free ride. With a hundred farmers one farmer's contribution is unlikely to make the difference between success and failure. Many farmers may refuse to pay, figuring that if everyone else refuses, their contribution will not be enough to make a difference, and if enough other farmers pay, they can get a free ride: receive the benefit of a spark-free world without paying for it.

There are a variety of ways in which the farmers might try to overcome such a problem. For example, they might draw up a contract by which each agrees to contribute only if all of the others do. A potential holdout will realize that if he refuses, the project will fall through, while if he agrees but someone else refuses, his agreement will not cost him anything, so it is in his interest to agree.

This solution depends on our assumption that all farmers are equally at risk from sparks. If that is not the case, then what each farmer's fair share is becomes a complicated and debatable issue. If even one farmer thinks he is being charged more than the spark arrester is worth to him, the whole deal falls through. And a sufficiently strong-minded farmer may simply announce that he is not going to contribute; if the others want to raise the money, they had better draw up a new contract with his name omitted. As this example suggests, the situation provides a lot of opportunity for bargaining, bluffing, threats, and counterthreats. The result may well be no spark arrester. That is why rule 1 is linked to outcome C by a dashed line, blocked by a box representing the public good problem faced by the farmers.

What about outcome D—Spark Arrester + Clover? As long as both the spark arrester and the switch to clover are costly, that can never be the efficient outcome, since both precautions are costly and either one is sufficient. That is why there are no arrows linking any of the four rules to outcome D. That would change if the invention of diesel locomotives eliminated sparks at no cost while the import of lots of foreign wheat made clover the more profitable crop, but under those assumptions the problem we are analyzing vanishes.

Turn now to rule 2. This time it is the farmers who have the absolute property right; the railroad is permitted to throw sparks only if it has permission from every farmer. What happens?

If the efficient outcome is C—No Sparks + Wheat—it happens immediately with no need for any transactions. The railroad could offer to buy the farmers' permission, but that would cost more than a spark arrester, so it is not in the railroad's interest to make the offer. Rule 2 is linked to outcome C by a solid line.

Suppose, however, that the efficient outcome is A or B—sparks, with or without a switch to clover. To get there the railroad must buy permission to throw sparks from the farmers. Such a transaction, at any price lower than the cost of a spark arrester and higher than the cost of either fires (A) or clover (B), is in the interest of both railroad and farmers.

It is in their interest but, again, may not happen, this time because of a *holdout problem*. Suppose the railroad offers each farmer $6 for permission to throw sparks; the cost to the farmers (fires or clover, whichever is cheaper) is only $4. It occurs to one of the farmers that if the deal goes through, the railroad reduces its cost from $1,000 (for a spark arrester) to $600 (paid to farmers), for a net savings of $400. It also occurs to him that if he refuses to agree to the deal, the $400 savings will vanish. Being a reasonable man, he offers to split the gain; he will agree, but only if the railroad pays him an extra $200.

If only one farmer adopts this strategy, the deal still goes through, and the efficient outcome is reached, although there may be some grumbling when the other farmers discover the terms. But if more than two farmers decide to charge $200 for their assent, the railroad refuses to pay, and the deal collapses. And it is quite likely that multiple farmers will do so. Their risk is the loss of the $2 profit they make by agreeing to accept $6 for something that costs them $4. Their potential gain from strategic bargaining is $200. Here again there are ways that the farmers might try to resolve the situation, but none that is guaranteed to work. So rule 2 is linked to outcomes A and B by dotted arrows blocked by the holdout problem.

So far we have been dealing with property rules: One side or the other gets to decide whether or not sparks are thrown. Next we consider liability rules: One party gets to decide but owes compensation to the other for the resulting costs.

Rule 3 is a liability rule in which the railroad controls the decision of whether to throw sparks, but the farmers have a right to be compensated for any resulting damage. What happens?

Suppose first that the costs are those shown by column a on the table, making A the efficient outcome. The railroad can either throw sparks and pay the farmers $400 for the resulting fires or else pay $1,000 for a spark arrester; it chooses the former option.

The result is a little more complicated than it was under rule 1; this time when the railroad's sparks start fires, the farmers sue for damages. We have gotten to the efficient outcome, but with an additional cost: the litigation cost of the resulting tort suits.

Implicit in that conclusion is an important assumption: that the court can accurately measure damages. Suppose that is not the case. The fires actually do $400 worth of damage, but the court, impressed by pictures of smoldering fields, overestimates the damages and awards $1,200 in compensation to the farmers. If the overestimate is predictable, it is in the interest of the railroad to put on the spark arrester instead even though that is an inefficient outcome.

The solution to this problem requires another transaction. The railroad goes to the farmers and offers to buy their liability right, to pay each of them $8 in exchange for his agreement not to sue. Just as with rule 2, the parties may be able to bargain to an efficient outcome, but to do so they must overcome a holdout problem. Fortunately it is an easier one than before. A single farmer can no longer force the railroad to put on a spark arrester, since the railroad has the option of throwing sparks and paying him $12 in damages instead. So the most the holdout can hope for is a $12 payment for his assent.

So far we have been assuming that switching to clover costs more than the damage done by the fires, making A the efficient outcome. Suppose we now reverse the assumption: Clover costs $400, and fires do $800 worth of damage. B is now the efficient outcome. How do we get it?

The answer depends on how much the court knows when it awards damages. If the court simply measures the damage from fires, the obvious tactic for the farmers is to grow wheat, suffer fires, and send the bill to the railroad. The cost to them is zero. If instead they switch to clover, they pay the $400 cost of the switch and receive no reimbursement—since there are no longer any fires, hence no visible damage to sue for. So they end up at outcome A, even though B is efficient.

We can solve this problem by having the railroad pay the farmers to switch to clover. Here again there is a potential holdout problem, but it is reduced by the fact that the railroad can pay some farmers to switch to clover, eliminating fires in their fields and the resulting liability, and pay damages to the ones who refuse to switch.

There is an easier route to the efficient outcome if the court is smart enough. Under conventional principles of common law, the victim of a

tort is obliged to take action after the fact to minimize the damage. A
sufficiently well-informed court, applying the same principle to precautions against a continuing problem, could refuse to award the farmers the
full $800 cost of their burning wheat on the grounds that half the cost is
their fault; they should have switched to clover. If the farmers do switch
to clover, the sufficiently smart court will recognize that they are suffering
a real cost from the sparks even though there are no visible fires and
award them $400 in damages. Under those rules farmers are better off
switching to clover ($400 cost, fully reimbursed by what the court makes
the railroad pay them in damage payments) than staying with wheat
($800 cost, only $400 of it reimbursed). We go directly to B, with no
further transactions necessary. Do not stop at Go. Do collect $400.

A Brief Digression on a Too Often Neglected Topic

As we will see in more detail in chapter 14, the competence of courts is a
crucial factor in determining efficient legal rules. If courts were fully informed about everything, if they knew, in detail, what every party ought
to do, we would not need a liability system. The court could simply announce what everyone ought to do and hang anyone who didn't do it.
That is the centralized solution to the problem of coordinating human
activity. We have massive historical evidence that it does not work, save
for very small societies, and lots of economic theory to tell us why.

At the other extreme, if courts knew nothing at all and produced their
verdicts by rolling dice, legal liability, law in general, would make little
sense as a solution to the coordination problem. To make sense out of our
legal system we require a picture of the courts somewhere between total
ignorance and omniscience. Exactly where is one of the critical assumptions of our theory, and one rarely made explicit.

In the particular example we have been working with, a property rule,
1 or 2, only requires a court smart enough to tell whether or not the
railroad has been throwing sparks and starting fires. Rule 3 gets us directly to outcome A (sparks, wheat, and fires) when that is efficient, provided the court is smart enough to measure the cost actually imposed by
fires that actually happen. It gets us directly to outcome B (sparks and
clover) only if the court is smart enough to measure not merely the actual
cost of the fires, but the cost of precautions taken to avoid that cost (farmers who switch to clover) and the potential cost of precautions not taken
that would have avoided that cost (farmers who don't switch to clover),
and include that information in its calculation of damages. Whichever
outcome we are headed for, if the court is not smart enough to get us there

directly, the Coasian solution cuts in: The parties bargain to the efficient rule, provided the transaction costs associated with such bargaining are not too high.

Back to Our Regularly Scheduled Tangle

Before I so rudely interrupted myself, we were applying rule 3 to situations where the efficient solution was for the railroad to continue to throw sparks. We now shift to the opposite case. The efficient outcome is C: the railroad should buy a spark arrester, leaving the farmers free to plant wheat without worrying about fires. As long as the court can accurately measure damages, there is no problem. The railroad calculates the cost in damage payments of continuing to throw sparks and puts in an order for a spark arrester.

Rule 4 is rule 3 run backwards. The farmers get to decide whether or not a spark arrester goes on but are liable for the cost of their decision; if they insist on a spark arrester, they must pay for it. Getting to outcomes with sparks is now easy: Each farmer correctly calculates that putting up with fires or growing clover, whichever is cheaper, costs less than buying the railroad a spark arrester. Rule 4 is linked to outcomes A and B by solid arrows.

Getting to C is harder because of the same sort of public good problem that we encountered earlier. If any one farmer enjoins the railroad from throwing sparks, he will have to pay the full cost of the spark arrester, giving the other farmers a free ride. In order to get to C, the farmers must somehow agree to share the cost of the spark arrester, just as under rule 1.

Under rule 1 the price paid by the farmers to the railroad to get it to stop throwing sparks was determined by bargaining among the parties; under rule 4 it is determined by the court. If one or more farmers is willing to pay for the spark arrester, the railroad no longer has the option of refusing the deal in hopes of being offered a higher price. Which transaction works better depends on the costs of bargaining and litigation and the relative accuracy of the two procedures for reaching the correct price.

We have now completed our spaghetti diagram. What do we do with it?

What we do with it is choose a legal rule. In order to do so, we need additional information: estimates of how likely it is that each of the alternative outcomes will be the efficient one and of how serious the various transactional problems are.

Suppose we knew that, in all of the cases the legal rule would apply to, outcome A was the efficient one. We choose legal rule 1. It takes us directly to A with no transactions and no need for the court to measure damages. A real-world example is the externality that I impose every time I exhale, increasing the amount of carbon dioxide in the world and thus contributing my little bit to global warming. The cost may be real, but we are quite confident that continuing to breathe and putting up with the consequences is the least costly solution to the problem, so we give each individual a right to breathe, free of tort liability for costs that his breathing may produce.

Suppose, on the other hand, we were sure it was outcome C that would always be efficient. Now the same argument implies that we want rule 2. An example is my absolute property right not to be deliberately shot at by my neighbors. While losing the opportunity to practice their marksmanship and take out their frustrations may cost them something, we are pretty sure that it costs them less than being shot costs me.

Things get more complicated if we do not know which outcome will be optimal. Now we have to estimate the probabilities, how likely it is that A, B, or C will be the right answer. Given the probabilities, we can look at each rule and see how easily we can get from it to each of the places we might want to go. Whichever rule performs best on average, minimizes the summed cost of transactions that happen and inefficiency due to transactions that don't happen, is the one we want.

The calculation requires estimates not only of probabilities but also of transaction costs. If we know that courts can measure damages accurately and cheaply, taking into account all possible precautions, then rules 3 and 4 look very attractive; either takes us directly to A, B, or C without requiring any transaction between farmers and railroad. If we believe that courts are cheap and accurate but can measure only direct damages, then how attractive rule 3 looks depends on how likely we think it is that the efficient outcome is B, since that is the only one that requires bargaining to get to.

Similarly, if we believe that it is easy for the farmers to solve their public good problem, perhaps because there are not very many of them and they are all friends and neighbors, rule 1 looks attractive. It takes us directly to outcomes A and B and indirectly but inexpensively to C. It is especially attractive, relative to the alternatives, if we believe courts are costly to use and incompetent at estimating damages.

The basic logic of what we are doing should now be clear. Given beliefs about the world we face (probability of each outcome being efficient) and our technology for dealing with it (costs of transactions, accuracy of court judgments), we can deduce the average cost resulting from each legal rule and pick the least costly. We have, in principle, an intellectual apparatus for designing law.

"In principle" conceals a multitude of problems, since most of what we need in order to pick the right rule is information we don't have. The point of the exercise is, by seeing how we would do the exact calculation if we had all the necessary information, to understand how to attempt the much more approximate calculation, which is the best we can do with our very imperfect data. While we may not be able to prove for certain what rule is best for determining the liability of railroads for fires started by their sparks, we can show what factors make one rule or another more attractive.

Before restating the argument in this form, however, it is worth considering one more possible rule—controlling sparks by Pigouvian taxes. We therefore add to the argument (but not to the diagram, which is quite complicated enough already)

>5. *Fine for sparks.* Railroad pays a fine equal to the damage done by its sparks.

At first glance, this rule seems to solve all problems. If the damage done is less than the cost of the spark arrester (outcome A or B is efficient), the railroad pays the fine and throws the sparks. The farmers, who are now receiving no compensation, grow wheat or clover according to which minimizes their cost. If the damage done is more than the cost of the spark arrester, the railroad buys the spark arrester, and we are safely at outcome C. No transactions between farmers and railroad are required.

There are some problems, however. Suppose the regulatory agency assessing the fine, like the only moderately smart court of an earlier example, can measure and charge only for direct damages. Further suppose that switching to clover costs less than putting up with fires but more than a spark arrester. The efficient outcome is C; the costs are shown in column c of the table.

The railroad continues to throw sparks and pay fines. When questioned by irate stockholders about why it is paying fines when it would be cheaper to put on a spark arrester, its president tells them to be patient. The farmers, observing that the railroad continues to throw sparks, switch to clover. The fires cease. So do the fines.

Railroad and farmers are engaged in a game of mutual bluff. The farmers could try to force the railroad to put on a spark arrester by refusing to switch to clover, just as the railroad can try to force the farmers to switch to clover by refusing to put on a spark arrester. But it is a game where the railroad is in much the stronger position—because there is one railroad and a hundred farmers. Each individual farmer has an incentive to switch to clover in order to avoid the cost of fires, while hoping that enough others will grow wheat to maintain the railroad's incentive to put on the spark arrester. The farmers, in trying to keep each other in the business of burning wheat until the railroad backs down, face a public good problem.

A second problem was mentioned in the previous chapter: Coase plus Pigou is too much of a good thing. Suppose the spark arrester costs $1,000, switching to clover costs $800, fires cost $600 (column d). The efficient solution is to keep throwing sparks. Under this solution, each year the railroad pays a $600 fine, and the farmers suffer $600 worth of damage. If the railroad installs a spark arrester, both fine and damage disappear, for a combined gain of $1,200 at a cost of $1,000. The farmers offer to pay the railroad $500 toward the cost of a spark arrester, the railroad agrees, and we have gotten to the inefficient outcome C.

We are now finished with the details of this particular example. The next step is to see what it has taught us, not about railroads and farmers but about the advantages and disadvantages of different sorts of legal rules.

Property or Liability Rules

If someone breaks a window or a contract, he gets sued for damages roughly equal to the cost he has imposed on the victim. If instead he steals a car and is caught and convicted, he ends up in jail. The right to performance of a contract, or the right not to have your property accidentally damaged, is a liability right, protected by civil (contract and tort) law. The right to possession of your car is a property right, protected by criminal law.

A liability right to something means that if it is taken, the taker owes you compensation. A property right means that if it is taken, the taker is punished in a fashion intended to make it in his interest not to have taken it. Very roughly, we may think of the liability rule as "damages equal to damage done" and the property rule as "damages high enough always to deter." Real-world property rules, of course, do not always deter, an issue that will be discussed in chapter 15. But it will simplify the present discussion if we ignore that complication for the moment.

Imagine a world with only liability rules. If someone wants your car, he doesn't have to come to you and offer you a price. He simply takes the car and lets you sue him for its value. What is wrong with that approach? Why would it not lead to an efficient outcome?

In a world where courts could accurately measure value and enforce liability judgments at negligible cost, it would. The damage payment equals the cost to you of having your car stolen, so it pays to steal a car only if it is worth more to the thief than to the owner, in which case stealing it is an efficient transaction. And, unlike the (uncompensated) theft discussed in chapter 3, such a legal rule would lead to no rent seeking. I would have no incentive to spend time and money guarding my car against thieves, since if it were stolen I would be fully compensated—and besides, theft would be rare in a world where the thief had to fully compensate the victim. The cost to thieves of stealing cars would be negligible, since owners would take no precautions. All you have to do is walk up to a car, open the (unlocked) door, and start it with the key that the owner has left in the ignition.

In the real world courts cannot measure the value of my car to me very accurately, not nearly as accurately as I can. Furthermore, the cost of finding out who stole the car, proving that he did it, and establishing an estimate of its value, is substantial. Protecting my right to my car with a liability rule would be an expensive approach and one that could frequently lead to inefficient transfers.

That would not be a sufficient reason to reject that approach if we had no better alternative, but we do. The better approach is a property rule: You can take my car only with my permission. If you take it without my permission, very bad things will happen to you.

The reason that is a better approach was sketched out by Anne, Mary, and John back in chapter 2. If my car is worth more to you than to me, you will be willing to make me an offer that I will be willing to accept. You don't have to steal it; you buy it instead. Value is demonstrated not by a court's best guess but by what offers you are willing to make and I am willing to accept. The transaction cost of selling you the car is a great deal less than the transaction cost of your stealing the car and my then suing you and collecting.

If property rules work so well, why do we ever use liability rules? The answer is that there are some cases in which the transaction cost of selling is higher than of suing. Every time I pull out of my driveway I impose a tiny risk of injury on every driver and pedestrian for miles around. The transaction cost of getting permission from all of them before I turn on the ignition is prohibitively high. So instead of enforcing their right not to be run into or over by a property rule, we enforce it by a liability rule: If I injure someone under circumstances in which the court finds me at fault, I must compensate him.

These examples suggest a very simple conclusion. *Property rules are attractive when the cost of allocating rights by market transactions is low. Liability rules are attractive when the cost of allocating rights by litigation is low.* We use property rules in contexts, such as allocating cars, where allocation through the market works well, allocation by courts works badly. Reverse the situation, and we use liability rules. In a world where both costs were zero, either approach would lead to an efficient outcome. In a world where both sets of costs are high, we may have to look for other alternatives.

Consider the distinction between trespass by people and trespass by cattle. If I deliberately trespass on your land, I am liable without regard for how much damage I did or how reasonable my action was. If my cattle stray onto your land, I am liable only for the damage they actually do. Thus your right not to have people walk on your land without your permission is enforced by a property rule; your right not to have cattle stray onto your land is enforced by a liability rule.

The obvious explanation is that if crossing your land is worth more to me than it costs you, I can buy permission—permanently, in the form of an easement, if that is what I require. But if I want to keep cattle on my land, I cannot readily buy the permission of every landowner onto whose property they might stray.

For a second example, consider the difference between the legal treatment of an accident and the legal treatment of a continuing nuisance. If my haystack spontaneously ignites and the fire spreads to your nearby buildings, you sue me for damages. If the smell from your tannery makes my apartment building unfit for human habitation, I go to court and ask to have the tannery enjoined as a nuisance. In the former case I am asking the court to apply rule 3, to give me a liability right not to have my buildings burned down. In the latter I am asking it to apply rule 2, to give me a property right not to have my building fumigated without my consent.

Part of the explanation for the difference may relate to the ability of the court to determine who is the least-cost avoider. With a continuing nuisance the cost to either party of eliminating or tolerating the nuisance is to some degree observable. So the court has a reasonable chance of figuring out who is the least-cost avoider and assigning the property right accordingly, thus getting directly to the efficient outcome either on a case-by-case basis or by general rules such as the doctrine of coming to the nuisance. But accidents are uncertain, making their expected cost uncertain, making it hard, perhaps impossible, for the court to know who is the least-cost avoider. By using a liability rule it puts the burden of deciding whether to take precautions, by keeping flames from my hay or locating the stacks farther from my neighbor's building, on me. All the court has to do is to estimate damages when and if the accident happens.

A second reason for the difference may be that reallocating rights by a private transaction is often more practical in the case of the continuing nuisance. If my tannery is polluting your factory, both of us know it. So if the wrong person is assigned the right by a court deciding whether or not to grant an injunction, the other person can buy it from him, at least as long as only one or two people are affected. This doesn't work as well for accidents. If the legal system gives you an absolute right not to have your buildings burnt down by accident, enforced after the fact with statutory damages or criminal punishments, I may not know which of my neighbors I need to buy what rights from in order to avoid being found liable if an accident occurs.

Liability Rules versus Fines

One way of treating pollution and similar externalities is as torts; if your neighbor's noisy candy factory makes it impossible to use your consulting room, you sue him for damages. Under modern environmental law they are more commonly treated as violations of federal regulations and punished with fines. If our objective is efficiency, how do we choose between the two approaches?

One answer is that the two approaches have different effects on the incentives of the victim to take precautions. If, when a railroad throws sparks, farmers whose wheat burns are compensated for the loss, they have no incentive to switch to clover even if that would be a cheaper solution than either fires or a spark arrester. If the railroad is fined but the money does not go to the farmers, they have an incentive to minimize the damage by switching to clover. That is one respect in which fines are a better approach. How important the advantage is depends in part on how easy it is for the railroad to negotiate with the farmers. If transaction costs are low, a liability rule leads to the efficient solution too, because the railroad will pay the farmers to switch to clover.

Low transaction costs not only make a liability rule work better, they also make a fine work worse, for a reason already discussed. If transaction costs are low and the fine does not go to the farmers, the railroad has a double incentive to put on the spark arrester; not only can it eliminate its fine, it can also get the farmers to help pay the cost. So it may be in the railroad's interest to install a spark arrester even if doing so costs more than the damage done by the sparks.

So far I have ignored a second basis for choosing between these two rules: the incentive each provides to report and prosecute the offense. In order for someone to be punished, his violation must be reported and prosecuted. A liability rule gives the victim an incentive to do so, since he is the one collecting the damage payment. A fine does not.

One way of thinking of tort liability is as a Pigouvian tax, designed to force tortfeasors to internalize their externality. Another is as a way of compensating victims, a sort of court-ordered insurance policy. A third is as a bounty system, in which private law enforcers, also known as tort victims, bring malefactors to justice and are rewarded with the fines paid by the guilty parties. Only the first approach has been dealt with here; the others will make their appearance in later chapters.

A Postscript

One possible response to the problems I have been discussing in this chapter is that I have not considered enough legal rules. One might, for example, argue that the solution to both the public good and holdout problems faced by the farmers is a legal rule that allows a majority of farmers to set the terms on which all farmers will deal with the railroad. If the majority decides that each farmer will chip in $4 to buy a spark arrester, every farmer must do so; if the majority agrees to permit sparks or to grow clover in exchange for a payment from the railroad, every farmer is bound by that agreement. Versions of that rule are used not only in democratic governments and many private organizations but in some legal contexts as well, such as the rules for unitizing oil fields.

That particular set of institutions solves the problems I have discussed here at the cost of producing a different set of problems. Consider, for example, the costs shown in column b of the table, with a slight modification of our assumptions: Forty of the farmers are already growing clover; the other sixty have soil suited only for wheat and suffer the whole $800 cost of the fires.

The legal rule is 1; the railroad is free to throw sparks. One of the farmers who is at risk of fire proposes that each farmer contribute ten dollars toward the cost of buying the railroad a spark arrester. For the farmers who are at risk, it is an attractive proposal, since each is losing more than ten dollars to fires. The proposal passes by sixty to forty. The result is outcome C, even though A would be more efficient. The railroad ends up with a spark arrester that costs more than the fires it prevents.

As this example suggests, it is not enough to come up with a legal rule that works better under one set of assumptions; it may work worse under another. I could have added this additional rule and several others to the figure, along with additional columns on the table to describe a greater range of possible cost distributions. Doing so would make the analysis, which already occupies most of a chapter, still more complicated but would not change the essential point—a demonstration not of what the efficient rule is but of how one goes about finding it.

One point that may have occurred to you is that choosing the right legal rules requires a good deal of specific information about the problems they are going to be applied to—information that a court may not have. That is one argument for the principle of freedom of contract, which allows the parties to a contract to set their own rules for the little two-person society that the contract creates; they, after all, are the experts on the problems that particular society is likely to encounter. More broadly, it suggests that there may be much to be said for a legal system sufficiently decentralized so that legal rules are created by people reasonably close to the problems those rules will apply to.

6

Of Burning Houses and Exploding Coke Bottles

WHEN SOMETHING goes wrong, legal rules help determine who pays for it. When, on a hot summer day, a Coke bottle does a plausible imitation of a hand grenade, product liability law determines whether you or Coca-Cola pays the cost of removing fragments of glass from your skin. When a company that ordered goods from you finds that it no longer needs them and refuses to take delivery, contract law determines whether you or they bears the resulting costs. Legal rules allocate risk.

Insurance companies also allocate risk—to themselves, at a price. The economic analysis of that activity was worked out well before the economic analysis of law. The economics of insurance—why people buy it, what costs are associated with it, and how they can best be minimized— provides a useful shortcut to understanding a wide variety of legal issues. Hence this chapter.

The Economics of Insurance

There is one chance in a hundred that my house will burn down this year, costing me $100,000. I go to an insurance company to buy insurance on the house. The company agrees with my estimate of the odds and concludes that, on average, it will end up paying out $1,000 on the policy. In addition to paying out on claims, the insurance company also has to pay salaries, rent on its office, and the like, so it offers to insure my house for one year at a price of $1,100.

On average I am paying out a hundred dollars more than I am getting back, so why should I buy the insurance? The answer is that a dollar is not a dollar is not a dollar. If my house burns down, I am going to be much poorer than if it doesn't, hence dollars will be worth much more to me. I am trading cheap dollars in a future in which my house doesn't burn down, dollars not worth very much to me because I will have lots of them, for valuable dollars in a future in which the house does burn down and I will need them badly. The difference in value is enough so that I am willing to trade eleven cheap dollars for ten valuable ones, leaving the insurance company enough over to pay its rent.

This explains why I am willing to buy insurance. Why is the insurance company willing to sell it? If the stockholders of the insurance company have the same pattern of tastes as I do, less value for additional dollars the more of them they have, why are they willing to accept my risk?

The answer is that transferring risk does not eliminate it, but pooling risk does. With a large number of policies most of the uncertainty averages out. The insurance company that insures a hundred thousand houses can predict with considerable confidence that it will have to pay out on about a thousand fires a year.

We have encountered dollars of varying value before. In chapter 2, when I was explaining economic efficiency, I pointed out that one of the things wrong with it as a measure of how well off people are is that it compares gains and losses to different people on the assumption that a dollar is worth the same amount to everyone—and the assumption isn't true. My example there was the difference between the value of a dollar to a rich person and its value to a poor person. My example now is the difference in its value to the same person under different circumstances.

The example this time is actually a better one, for two reasons. To begin with, the poor person and the rich person may differ in many ways other than wealth. Perhaps the rich person is rich because he values material goods very highly, continues to do so even when he has a lot of them, and therefore works very hard to get more money to buy things with, while the poor person is poor because he has the opposite attitude. If so, the rich person, even rich, may value a dollar more than the poor. In the context of insurance we are comparing the same person in different circumstances. All that has changed is how much money he has.

A second reason this example is a better one is that we do not have to limit ourselves to theory; we have evidence. People buy insurance even though most of them probably know that, on average, they can expect to collect less in claims than they pay out in premiums. That suggests that purchasers of insurance are measuring its value in something other than dollars and, by that measure, expect a dollar to be worth more to them if their house burns down than if it doesn't. Diminishing marginal utility is a fact about most people's preferences, revealed by their choices.

Risk Aversion Is Not about Risk: A Necessary Digression

Economists refer to this pattern of tastes as *risk aversion*. By insuring your house against fire you convert an uncertain future, a 99 percent chance you will have your current wealth and a 1 percent chance you will have your current wealth minus $100,000, into a certain future in which you have a 100 percent chance of your current wealth minus $1,100. You are paying $100 to make the conversion, since your expected wealth falls by $100 when you buy the insurance. Your willingness to pay to reduce risk shows that you are risk averse.

This terminology is widely used and almost as widely misunderstood. To begin with, it makes it sound as though risk preference is a statement about your taste for the excitement of risk, when it is actually a statement about how the value of money to you varies with the amount of it you have. There is nothing logically inconsistent about someone who both buys fire insurance and jumps out of airplanes for fun. The cautious sky-diver has both declining marginal utility of income and a taste for thrills.

A further problem is that what we call risk aversion is really aversion to monetary risks. The fact that one more dollar is worth less to you the more you have does not mean that the same pattern holds for things other than dollars.

Shortly after getting married you discover that you are suffering from a rare and very serious medical problem. If you do nothing about it, you can expect to die in about fifteen years. The alternative is a medical procedure that gives you a 50 percent chance of living for another thirty years—and a 50 percent chance of never waking up from the operation.

Measured in life expectancy, it is a fair gamble—on average you will live for another fifteen years either way. Whether you take the gamble depends on how the value of additional years depends on how many you have.

Suppose you very much want to have children—but only if you are going to live long enough to bring them up. Your choice is between a certainty of fifteen years without children and a 50 percent chance of thirty years with them. You grit your teeth, take several deep breaths, and arrange for the operation.

I have just described someone who is a risk preferrer measured in years of life, as demonstrated by his preference for an uncertain outcome over a certain outcome when the expected value is the same for both. He might simultaneously be a risk averter when it was a matter of insuring his house. "Risk averse" is not a statement about tastes for risk but about tastes for outcomes.

Back to Insurance

Risk aversion explains why we sometimes buy insurance, even at a price that covers not only our future claims but the insurance company's rent and salaries as well. To explain why we often don't buy insurance, it is worth introducing two other concepts: *moral hazard* and *adverse selection*.

You own a factory worth a million dollars. You estimate that each year it has a 4 percent chance of burning down. By spending ten thousand dollars a year on buying and maintaining a sprinkler system and having occasional inspections for fire hazards, you can cut the risk in half. Should you do it?

On average you are saving twenty thousand dollars a year in expected fire damage at a cost of ten thousand a year in precautions. If you are risk neutral, neither risk preferring nor risk averse, that is a good deal. If you are risk averse, it is an even better deal. Your precautions are the equivalent of an insurance policy that costs only half what it pays out.

Suppose, however, that you have already insured the factory for its full value. Now if it burns down you lose nothing. Your precautions are still worth more than they cost—but not to you, since it is the insurance company that benefits by the reduced risk. So you don't bother putting in a sprinkler system.

In the insurance literature this problem is referred to as "moral hazard"—the failure of the insured to take cost-justified precautions once he has shifted the risk the precautions protect against to the insurance company. It implies that insured buildings are, on average, more likely to burn down than uninsured buildings. Rational insurance companies take that fact into account in setting their rates. Ignoring your insurer's operating expenses and assuming, for simplicity, that it sells policies at their expected value, your policy will cost you forty thousand dollars a year. That is the expected loss from fire if you do not take precautions, and, if you are fully insured, you will not take precautions.

The cost of moral hazard is not merely a transfer from insured to insurance company but a net loss—in our example a loss of ten thousand dollars a year. That is the difference between what the precautions you are no longer taking now that you are insured are worth and what they cost.

Moral hazard is one example of a problem we discussed earlier: inefficiency due to externalities. By buying insurance you transfer the benefit of precautions against fire and the cost of risky behavior, such as smoking near piles of waste paper, from you to the insurance company. Precautions now have a large positive externality, so you take inefficiently few; risks have a large negative externality, so you take inefficiently many.

Does it follow that an efficient legal system should ban insurance? No. The inefficiency due to moral hazard is a real cost of insurance, but the gain due to pooling risks is a real gain. Insurance is a voluntary transaction between the insurer and the insured and so will take place only if both parties believe that the gain at least balances the loss.

The problem of moral hazard does not imply that insurance should not exist, but it does imply that insurance companies should and will try to design their policies in ways that reduce the problem. One way of doing so is to specify precautions the insured must take, such as installing an adequate sprinkler system. Another is for the insurance company itself to pay for some precautions, such as inspections.

A less direct approach is coinsurance. The insurance company insures the factory for only part of its value. The lower the fraction insured, the more precautions it is in the interest of the owner to take. If the factory is insured for half its value, precautions whose payoff is at least twice their cost, such as those described earlier, are worth taking. Thus coinsurance eliminates the most inefficient consequences of moral hazard: the failure to take precautions that have a payoff much larger than their cost. At the other extreme, if an insurer is so careless as to insure a factory for 150 percent of its value, the probability of fire may become very large indeed.

Moral Hazard: Bug or Feature?

> That's not a bug. That's an undocumented
> feature.
> (*Old software joke*)

Consider our factory again, with one change. This time the factory belongs to a large corporation with thousands of such facilities, and I am the employee in charge of managing this one. My employer, like many corporations, judges its employees by results, which in my case means output (the higher the better) and operating costs (the lower the better).

It occurs to me that by doing without fire precautions I can save my employer ten thousand dollars a year, substantially improving my chances for promotion. With only one chance in twenty-five that the factory will burn down each year, the odds that it will happen while I am still in charge are pretty low. And if it does, the million dollar loss comes out of my employer's pocket, not mine; the most they can do to me is to fire me. It looks as though skimping on precautions, while a poor decision from the standpoint of my employer's long-run interest, may be a good one from the standpoint of my long-run interest.

My head office, in charge of thousands of facilities, does not know enough about each one to judge which precautions are or are not worth taking; that is why they have to judge me by results. They don't know it, and they know they don't know it. They can run through the calculation of my interests as well as I can and come to the same conclusion—that there is a conflict between what they want me to do and what it is in my interest to do. Their problem is what to do about it.

One solution is to hire another employee to look over my shoulder and second-guess all my decisions, but that would be expensive, and they would then have the problem of making it in his interest to do the right things. An alternative solution is to transfer both the costs and the risks to someone in the business of keeping factories from burning down.

My employer goes to a company that specializes in fire insurance. In exchange for a fee of somewhat over thirty thousand dollars a year, they agree to insure the factory against fires, pay for sprinkler systems, and arrange for regular inspections. I get a message from the head office telling me that precautions against fire are no longer my business. I am to do what the insurance company tells me and send them the bill.

This is a situation wherein moral hazard is a feature, not a bug. In my earlier discussion I took it for granted that the owner of the factory was in the best position to prevent the fire. He was, to use a term from our earlier discussion of externalities, the lowest-cost avoider. Often that is the case; sometimes, as in the example of the large corporation, it is not. If I am the lowest-cost avoider, the incentive effect of transferring the loss from me to the insurance company is a disadvantage of insurance, since it is no longer in my interest to take all precautions that are worth taking. But it is an advantage of insurance if it is the insurance company that is the lowest-cost avoider.

"Moral hazard" may be a misleading way of thinking about the issue, since it implicitly assumes that the person buying the insurance is the only one whose incentives matter. The risk of fires or other insurable accidents is affected by the decisions of more than one actor. Putting all the cost on one party gives him the right incentive but other parties the wrong one. If the insurance company is in a better position than the insured to prevent the loss, transferring it to them via insurance raises efficiency more by increasing the incentives of the insurance company than it lowers it by reducing the incentive of the owner. The right rule is to put the incentive wherever it will do the most good.

Seen from this standpoint, coinsurance, insuring the property for only a fraction of the loss, looks like a sensible, although imperfect, solution to the problem. Each party has some incentive, although neither has the efficient incentive, since precautions whose payoff is only a little larger than their cost will not get taken. That leads to some inefficiency. But it may not be a lot of inefficiency since precautions that cost almost as much as they are worth produce only a modest gain. The precautions that you want to make sure are taken are the ones that produce a large reduction in risk for a small cost. Those are the ones that coinsurance makes it in the interest of either party to take.

Recognizing that moral hazard is sometimes a feature rather than a bug helps explain why large corporations sometimes insure their factories. My imaginary employer, after all, has no need to hire an insurance company to pool its risks; it is big enough to pool them itself. Like an insurance company that insures a thousand houses, a company with a thousand factories can rely on the law of large numbers to produce a predictable outcome. Nonetheless such companies sometimes buy insurance. One possible explanation is that they do so in order to give the insurance company an incentive to keep their factories from burning down.

A different version of the same argument explains another puzzle: why people sometimes buy insurance against small losses, even though a small loss is unlikely to change your wealth by enough to significantly change the value to you of another dollar.

Consider a customer who buys a new washing machine from Sears and decides to pay for an extended service contract. From the standpoint of risk aversion, buying the contract makes little sense. But from the standpoint of finding a competent person to fix the machine if something goes wrong, and getting the job done well and at a reasonable cost, it may be a sensible decision. Sears knows a great deal more than I do about how to repair its washing machines and about the competence and honesty of the people who do it. By purchasing a service contract, I turn over the job of finding someone to fix the machine to them and give them an incentive to see that the job is done well, since if it is not they will be hearing from me again. Here again, although in a somewhat different way, we are shifting the incentive from the owner of the property at risk to somewhere else where it will be more useful.

We will return to this issue in chapter 14, where we discuss product liability. A legal rule that makes Coca-Cola responsible if a Coke bottle blows up is, in effect, mandatory insurance; Coca-Cola is insuring its customer against that particular risk. One disadvantage is that doing so reduces your incentive to be careful not to shake warm bottles of Coke. One advantage is that it increases Coca-Cola's incentive to improve the quality control on their bottles.

Adverse Selection: What He Knows That You Don't

You are in the life insurance business. One morning a man comes running into your office and tells you that he wants to buy a large policy—right now. At what price should you sell it to him? Actuarial tables showing risk of death for men of his age and health may not be very relevant, since his behavior suggests that he knows something you don't that is relevant to his chance of living out the day.

The same argument applies, with somewhat less force, to everyone who comes into your office. The fact that someone wants to buy insurance is evidence that you should not sell it to him—more precisely, that he is a worse risk than the actuarial tables imply. Most people, after all, have some private information about their own risks, whether those risks involve jumping out of airplanes, paying too much attention to arguing with radio talk show hosts while driving in heavy traffic, or being shot at by jealous husbands. That private information affects how likely their family is to collect on their life insurance, hence how much they are willing to pay for it. People who buy insurance represent, not a random sample of possible customers, but a sample weighted toward those most likely to collect. A prudent insurance company takes that into account in setting prices.

If the insurance company knew the risk for each customer, there would be no problem; high-risk and low-risk customers would have their policies priced accordingly and would buy or not buy according to whether or not the protection was worth the price. But the insurance company cannot charge different prices to high- and low-risk customers if it does not know which is which, so it ends up charging both the same price. That makes insurance a better deal for customers whose private information implies that they are particularly likely to collect than for those whose private information goes in the opposite direction. The result is that members of the first group are more likely to buy insurance than are members of the second.

The insurance company prices its policies to allow for that fact, which makes insurance an even worse deal for the low-risk customers, since they are being charged a price that assumes they are probably high-risk customers. As low-risk customers respond by dropping out, buying insurance becomes even stronger evidence that you are a bad risk; the price rises accordingly. The result is that some of the good risks fail to buy insurance even though, at an actuarially fair price, it would be worth buying. That is the problem known in the insurance literature as adverse selection—an inefficient outcome due to asymmetric information.

To see the same pattern in another context, consider the market for used cars. Sellers know more about their cars than buyers do, and the worse the car, the more willing the owner is to sell. This time it is the seller who has private information—with the result that his willingness to sell is at least weak evidence that the car is a lemon. Buyers reduce what they are willing to offer to take account of that evidence, making sale even less attractive to owners of cars in good condition. One can model extreme cases where only the worst car sells or more realistic cases in which many cars go unsold, even though they are worth more to a potential buyer than to their current owner.

Solving One Problem and Creating Another

Sellers with cars in good condition could solve the problem by providing guarantees—any repairs in the first year to be paid by the seller. Their willingness to offer such guarantees would demonstrate that they believe their own claims about the car's condition. Unfortunately, while a guarantee eliminates inefficiency due to adverse selection, it creates inefficiency due to moral hazard. The buyer, knowing that someone else will pay for repairs, has an inefficiently low incentive to take good care of the car.

Such conflicts appear with disturbing frequency when trying to design efficient legal rules: Fixing one problem often creates another. The fully efficient rule, one that gives everyone the correct incentives on every margin, may turn out to be an impossible ideal. If so, we are left, as Coase suggested, with the problem of choosing the least bad among a set of imperfect alternatives.

A friend of mine who was looking for a used car devised an ingenious way of inducing sellers to reveal their private information. Having located a car he liked, he asked the seller if he was willing, for an additional payment, to provide a one-year guarantee. The seller declined. My friend continued looking. Eventually he found a car he liked whose seller was prepared to sell him a guarantee as well as a car. He bought the car—without the guarantee.

This method works only if the seller does not know about it; otherwise he can offer to guarantee a lemon, knowing that the buyer will buy the lemon but not the guarantee. Perhaps it would be prudent for me to continue to omit my friend's name from this story, on the chance that he might some day try to buy a car from one of my readers.

The Risks of Regulated Biotech or How to Hurt People by Helping Them

It is now becoming possible to identify genetic tendencies toward diseases and test for them. This leads to some interesting problems.

Some people have bad hearts, some do not. As long as nobody knows which is which, it is possible to insure against the risk of a heart attack. Suppose a cheap and reliable genetic test is discovered by which we can tell who is in which group. Consider some possible legal rules:

1. The test is banned; nobody is allowed to use it.

2. Individuals are permitted to get tested. Insurance companies are permitted to make testing a condition of insurance and take account of the result in setting rates.

3. Individuals are permitted to get tested; the results are confidential. Insurance companies are forbidden to make testing a condition of insurance and take account of the result.

4. Individuals are permitted to get tested, but the fact of the test (not the outcome) is recorded. Insurance companies are not permitted to require testing

as a condition of insurance but are permitted to know whether or not a potential customer has been tested and to take account of that fact in setting the rate they charge him.

What are the consequences of each rule? Is it possible that, under some or all rules, the invention of the test makes us worse off?

To see why the answer is "yes," compare rules 1 and 2. Under rule 1, which corresponds to the situation before the test is invented, neither the insurance company nor the customer knows the condition of the customer's heart, so the risk of having a bad heart is insurable. Under rule 2 if you try to buy insurance and refuse to be tested, the company will take that as evidence that you know you have a bad heart and set the price accordingly. You can still get tested, show the results to the insurance company, and insure against whatever uncertainty is left after knowing the condition of your heart, but the risk of having a bad heart is now uninsurable.

The result of rule 3 is worse still; we are back in the market for lemons. Anyone who tries to buy insurance against a heart attack signals by doing so that he has a bad heart; the insurance company no longer has the option of testing applicants and pricing insurance accordingly. People with good hearts cannot get insurance unless they are willing to pay far more than the actuarial value of their risk, which few are. Only people with bad hearts are insurable—against the residual uncertainty of just when their hearts will fail.

Rule 4, if it is an option, provides the best outcome. People who want to insure against the risk of a bad heart can buy insurance before being tested; since they can prove to the insurer that they have not been tested, the price will correspond to what it costs to provide insurance to a random customer. After they have bought insurance they can then decide whether the advantage of better information about what health precautions they should take and how long they can expect to live outweighs the risk of learning something they may not want to know.

Unfortunately rule 4 may not be an option in a world of many countries and high mobility. Even if the United States insists that all tests be recorded and successfully suppresses any black market in secret tests, American citizens can still get their genes tested somewhere with less restrictive rules. The same problems apply to rule 1. So it is possible that the invention of the test, by moving us from the world of rule 1 to the world of rule 2 or 3, may make the risk of being born with a bad heart uninsurable—just as the risk of being born poor is now. If that effect is large enough to outweigh the benefits that individuals get from knowing more about their own health risks, the invention of the test will have made us, on net, worse off.

I was introduced to this problem by a commencement speech proposing rule 3 as a way of protecting people from misuse of genetic information by their insurance companies. I concluded that the speaker had never heard of adverse selection.

For Further Thought

I rent land with buildings on it. Six months into my one-year lease some of the buildings burn down. Do I still owe full rent for the remainder of the year? The common law answer was that, unless there was a contrary provision in the lease, I did. The risk associated with a fire was placed on the tenant, not the landlord, at least for the duration of the lease.

I sell a piece of land, accepting as payment a sack of gold coins. A year or two later, after discovering that the coins are actually lead plated with gold, I attempt to cancel the sale, only to learn that the buyer has resold the land and skipped town. I try to reclaim the land from its current owner, arguing that since it was procured by fraud the buyer never really owned it and so could not sell it. I lose. In the view of most courts I am entitled to void the purchaser's deed but not the deed of an innocent third party.

Suppose that instead of defrauding me with fake coins, the villain adopts a more direct approach: He forges a deed to my land and then sells the land to an innocent purchaser. This time, when I try to reclaim the land, I win the case.

All three of these cases make sense in terms of one simple rule for allocating risk: Put the incentive where it does the most good. Can you see why?

7

Coin Flips and Car Crashes: *Ex Post* versus *Ex Ante*

SOMEONE OFFERS you a bet on the flip of a coin: Heads he pays you two dollars, tails you pay him one. You agree. He flips the coin. It comes up tails, and you pay him a dollar.

Whether you should have made the bet depends on whether you judge it *ex ante* or *ex post*. *Ex ante*, judged by the information available to you at the time, it was a good bet, since on average you could expect to come out fifty cents ahead. *Ex post*, judged by the information available to you after the coin was flipped and you had lost, it was a bad bet, since it cost you a dollar.

When dealing with decisions under uncertainty it is important to distinguish between these two ways of evaluating them. *Ex ante*, almost all gambles in Las Vegas are losing ones; the casino, like an insurance company, sets its rates so that the money that comes in when it wins covers not only the money it pays out when it loses but also its operating expenses. Nonetheless, some gamblers win their bets *ex post*.

The same distinction is useful in analyzing how the legal system can be used to prevent undesirable outcomes such as automobile accidents. One approach punishes people for doing things that increase the probability of accidents *ex ante*: speeding, drunk driving, failing to get their brakes inspected. The other punishes the undesirable outcome observed *ex post*, via tort liability for the damage done to the car you collide with or criminal penalties for drunk drivers who run over people.

Why Punish Attempts?

For a less obvious example of the *ex post/ex ante* distinction, consider the puzzle of why we punish attempted murder. I shoot at you, and the bullet goes into a tree instead. Judged *ex post*, based on the damage done, there should be no punishment: Both you and the tree are fine.

The explanation is that punishment for attempted murder is, like a speeding ticket, an *ex ante* punishment, a way of preventing undesirable outcomes by punishing behavior that increases their probability. Driving fast makes it more likely that you will run into someone. Shooting at people makes it more likely that you will hit them. The odd thing about punishment for attempted murder is that the *ex ante* behavior is discovered only after we know that it did not actually produce the undesirable outcome—this time. A different way of putting it is that our legal system imposes an *ex ante* punishment for trying to kill people plus an additional *ex post* punishment for succeeding.

Choosing the Right Rule(s)

These examples of *ex post* and *ex ante* punishments suggest an interesting question for the economic analysis of law: Why does the legal system sometimes uses one approach, sometimes the other, and sometimes both? What are the advantages and disadvantages of each?

The *ex post* approach has one important advantage over the *ex ante*: By making it in the driver's interest to avoid accidents, it exploits his private knowledge of how to do so. Consider, for a simple real-world example, my own behavior. The most dangerous thing I do when driving is not speeding, nor driving drunk, nor driving an unsafe car. The most dangerous thing I do is to pay attention to my conversations with other people, real conversations with real people sitting next to me or arguments inside my head with radio talk show hosts or imaginary opponents, when I ought to be paying attention to my driving.

That is the most dangerous thing I do as a driver, but I have never gotten a ticket for it. *Ex ante* punishments can be imposed only on behavior that a traffic cop can observe; so far, at least, that does not include what is going on inside my head. *Ex post* punishments can be imposed for outcomes that can be observed due to behavior that cannot—when what is going on inside my head results in my running a red light and colliding with another automobile. *Ex ante* punishment makes it in my interest to take those precautions that the legal system, here represented by the legislature and the traffic cop, knows I should take and can tell if I am taking. *Ex post* punishment makes it in my interest to take any precautions that I know I should take and can tell if I am taking.

Ex post punishment takes account of two sorts of private information that *ex ante* ignores: information about what I am doing (paying attention to my thoughts instead of the road) that cannot be observed by others, and information about what I should be doing. The speed limit is the same for everyone, from the race car driver to the teenager with a brand-new license, because the traffic cop has no easy way of distinguishing competent drivers from incompetent ones. I, on the other hand, know when I am sleepy and inattentive, or upset, or distracted, and thus a worse driver than usual; *ex post* punishments make it in my interest to drive slower at those times than at others. And I can (and do) exploit my knowledge of my own inattentiveness by letting my wife drive when we are both in the car.

We have seen this argument before in a different context. The advantage of *ex post* over *ex ante* punishment is very much like the advantage of an effluent fee over direct regulation. Direct regulation controls inputs to pollution—scrubbers, coal quality, smokestack height—just as speed limits control one input to having accidents. Effluent fees punish the unwanted output, pollution, and leave it to the polluter to decide how best to reduce it, just as liability for accidents punishes the output, accidents, and leaves it to the driver to decide how best to avoid them. Both effluent fees and *ex post* punishment thus reduce the amount of information the legal system requires to do its job. But both still require some information. The EPA must estimate the damage done by additional pollution in order to set the fee, and someone must estimate the damage done by an accident in order to decide just how high the *ex post* punishment should be.

Seen from a somewhat different perspective, however, the speeding ticket looks more like an effluent fee. Drivers who believe that getting somewhere fast is very important are free to speed and pay for it, at least as long as they are not caught too often. Thus even *ex ante* punishment takes advantage of some private information, not about what the driver is doing or how it affects the chance of an accident but about how costly it is to him to take precautions that the law wants him to take, such as driving slowly.

The example of using private information to decide how fast I should drive suggests a possible disadvantage, as well as a possible advantage, of *ex post* punishment. *Ex ante* punishment provides incentives based on the beliefs of the people making the laws; *ex post* provides incentives based on the beliefs of the people the law applies to. If I believe that I can drive just fine after a shot of whiskey and two beers, the knowledge that if I have an accident terrible things will happen to me provides no special reason to avoid driving when drunk. The knowledge that if I am stopped and fail the Breathalyzer exam I will go to jail does.

It is said that if you poll people on their driving ability, you discover that the vast majority are above average drivers. The teenager with a brand-new license may not actually be a race car driver, but that does not keep him from believing that he could win the Indianapolis 500 if he only had a chance to enter it. If people consistently misestimate their abilities, and if the legislators setting *ex ante* rules are better informed, then the *ex ante* rules have the advantage of substituting the legislators' opinion of what behavior lead to accidents for the drivers' opinion.

This argument depends on more than mere ignorance. If the legislators know facts about driving—that roads are especially slippery when it has just started to rain, for example—that drivers do not know, the legislators can (and do) pass that information on to the drivers in safety ads or in the booklet that everyone reads before taking his driver's test. That does not work perfectly, since the driver may not see the ad or pay attention to the booklet. But the same problem of getting information to the drivers exists if the legislators try to use *ex ante* punishment to make the drivers embody the legislators' expertise in their driving decisions. A law requiring all drivers to slow down when it has just started raining works only if the driver knows the law exists. It is only when drivers not only don't know things but think they do, and are therefore unwilling to believe what the legislators tell them, that *ex ante* punishment has an advantage—assuming, of course, that the drivers are wrong and the legislators are right.

So the advantage of *ex post* punishment is that it utilizes the driver's information about what he is doing, which is almost always better than the legal system's information about what he is doing, and the driver's information about what he ought to be doing to avoid accidents, which is often but not always better than the legal system's information. What are the advantages of *ex ante* punishment?

The obvious answer is that the *ex ante* approach prevents accidents before they happen, while *ex post* only punishes afterwards. Like many obvious answers, it is wrong.

Being found liable for an accident does not prevent that accident—but then, getting a speeding ticket does not prevent that act of speeding. The point of giving speeding tickets is that the knowledge that you might get one gives you an incentive not to drive fast. The point of punishing people for being in accidents is that the knowledge that if you are in accident you will get punished gives you an incentive not to have accidents. Both speeding tickets and tort liability are approaches to preventing accidents before they happen.

To see the real advantage of *ex ante* punishments, consider two alternative patterns of punishment, each of which collects the same number of dollars. Under the pure *ex ante* rule you end up paying two hundred dollars in speeding tickets every year, and, if you injure someone else's person or property in an accident, there is no penalty. Under the pure *ex post* rule there are no speed limits, and each year you have one chance in a thousand of being in an accident and having to pay a two hundred thousand dollar fine. Unfortunately, you don't have two hundred thousand dollars in your bank account. So the result of an accident is that you forfeit everything you own, including your house, and must spend the next five years working sixty hours a week to pay back the rest of the fine.

Most of us would prefer the former pattern of punishment because most of us are risk averse. All else being equal, we prefer a high probability of a low cost to a low probability of a high cost. *Ex post* punishment is imposed only when an accident occurs, which is rarely, so in order to provide a significant incentive to avoid accidents *ex post* punishments must be large. If we are risk averse, *ex ante* punishment can provide the same incentive at a lower cost.

So far I have assumed that you can and must pay the *ex post* fine, even though doing so may be very difficult. But suppose the *ex post* fine necessary to give you an adequate incentive to avoid accidents is ten million dollars, and there is no way you can expect ever to pay that much. How can we give you an incentive equivalent to the ten million dollar fine you cannot pay?

The obvious answer is to switch from fines to other sorts of punishments, such as execution or imprisonment; even if you don't have the money to pay a fine, you can still pay with your life or liberty. But while such punishments may provide adequate deterrence, they do so at a high cost. If you pay a fine, whether for speeding or being in an accident, someone collects it; your loss is someone else's gain. If the fine is a speeding ticket, the money goes to the state; if it is a liability payment, it goes to the victim. But if your punishment is execution, you lose a life and nobody gains one. If your punishment is imprisonment, you lose your liberty, and the rest of us have to pay for the jail. Hence both execution and imprisonment are costly punishments compared to fines. Here the relevant cost is not simply cost to the person being punished—imposing a cost on him is the point of the punishment, after all—but net cost on everyone affected, including the person punished, the people who collect fines, and the taxpayers who pay for prisons. It is net cost to everyone that is relevant to economic efficiency.

It follows that while the advantage of *ex post* punishment is that it takes advantage of the private information of the people whose behavior it is intended to control, the advantage of *ex ante* punishment is that it can be done efficiently, using relatively small fines imposed with relatively high probability. Doing so avoids both the cost of risk aversion from very high fines imposed with low probability and the high net cost of such inefficient punishments as execution and imprisonment.

Does the Law Get It Right?

We now have some idea of the advantages, from the standpoint of economic efficiency, of each approach. By combining that with Posner's conjecture that the common law tends to be economically efficient, we should be able to predict and explain when *ex post* punishment will be used, when *ex ante*, and when both.

Risk aversion is important for large losses but not for small ones, since the value to you of a dollar does not change much when your income changes by only a few dollars. That is one of the reasons you buy insurance against your house burning down but not against spilling ink on your best pair of pants. The difficulty of collecting fines, and thus the need to substitute less efficient punishments, arises only when the fines are large relative to the offender's assets. It follows that where the damage done by accidents is small enough so that the appropriate *ex post* fine is one that everyone can easily pay, there is no reason to use *ex ante* punishments.

This seems to fit what we actually observe. Traffic accidents do lots of damage, and the legal system attempts to prevent them by both *ex ante* and *ex post* punishments. Many other activities that do small amounts of damage, a broken window due to overly enthusiastic baseball playing in a neighbor's yard, for example, are controlled by a pure *ex post* approach via tort law.

Criminal law typically relies on costly punishments, at least in part because convicted criminals cannot pay adequate fines. Tort law typically relies on damage payments. I argued earlier that punishment of attempts was a form of *ex ante* punishment. If so, the argument I have just offered implies that attempted crimes should be punished and attempted torts should not. That corresponds reasonably well to actual law. If I try to photocopy your copyrighted book but carelessly put the pages into the copier upside down, I owe you no damages for the resulting blank copy. If I set off to trespass on your property but lose my way and end up somewhere else, you have no tort claim against me.

A second prediction is that we should never observe systems of pure *ex ante* punishment, such as a legal system that punishes speeding but fully insures drivers against all costs of accidents. Low levels of *ex post* punishment, such as a fine equal to a month's salary, are almost always superior to *ex ante* punishment, since they can be paid in money, impose little cost through risk aversion, and provide an incentive for actors to use their private information to avoid accidents. So an efficient system that uses *ex ante* punishments will supplement them with at least some level of *ex post* punishment. I cannot think of a real-world counterexample to this prediction; perhaps you can.

For a hypothetical exception, consider pollution regulation, not in the real world but in books such as this one. Polluters are required to obey a variety of regulations specifying the precautions they must take to keep down their pollution. Having met those regulations they then pay no cost for whatever pollution occurs.

If this pattern existed in the real world, it would be inefficient—although, since pollution regulations are set by legislators and regulators, not by courts, it would not contradict Posner's conjecture that common (i.e., judge-made) law is efficient. But it does not. Even if a polluter obeys the regulations, he is still at risk of being sued by the downwind victims. Obedience to the regulations provides him a defense, but not an absolute defense.

A Market for Legal Rules

So far I have been discussing legal rules made by legislators and judges. One problem with all such systems is that even if we know what rule is efficient, it is not obvious that it is in the interest of legislators or (*pace* Posner) judges to set efficient rules. That observation suggests that it might be worth looking for other ways of generating efficient legal rules—in particular, an efficient mix of *ex ante* and *ex post*.

One such mechanism was described in the previous chapter: insurance. The inefficiency of *ex post* rules comes in part from risk aversion. The inefficiency of *ex ante* rules comes from the fact that unobservable decisions by me, such as how much attention to pay to my driving, impose costs on others, costs I ignore when making such decisions. The last time we encountered that problem we called it moral hazard.

Insurance provides a market mechanism for trading off costs of risk aversion against costs of moral hazard in order to find the least costly combination; could that mechanism be applied here? Imagine that the optimal pure *ex post* system imposes a fine of two hundred thousand dollars for an accident, and that that is a fine that drivers can (barely) pay, making the problem one of risk aversion rather than the need to shift to less efficient punishments. We abolish all speed limits and similar regulations, set a two hundred thousand dollar fine, and permit drivers to insure against having to pay it.

The more insurance I have, the lower my incentive to avoid accidents, just as, in the previous chapter, the more insurance I had on my factory the lower my incentive to avoid fires. Insurance companies will take account of that in setting rates. They will also consider ways of reducing the risk. One obvious approach to reducing the risk of fire is requiring sprinklers. One obvious approach to reducing the risk of accidents is requiring speed limits.

There are practical problems in the second case, since while insurance companies sometimes employ inspectors they do not normally have their own traffic cops. We could solve that problem by making the traffic cops subcontractors to insurance companies. Instead of enforcing laws, they enforce contracts. A customer who has agreed not to drive over sixty miles an hour as a condition of his insurance has a giant bar code on his bumper announcing the fact. Traffic cops are provided, along with their radars, with equipment for automatically reading bumper bar codes. When they spot a car driving faster than it should, on goes the siren and flashing lights.

Under such a system the insurance company has an incentive to calculate the optimal tradeoff between *ex post* and *ex ante*, the optimal amount of the former, and the optimal pattern of the latter. The higher the fraction of the loss it insures, the lower the costs due to risk aversion but the greater the costs due to moral hazard. It can control those costs via *ex ante* punishments, contractually set. The degree to which that is worth doing depends on how well or badly *ex ante* punishments work relative to *ex post* ones, given the advantage of using the latter to exploit the driver's private information. The full analysis of such a system would carry us well beyond the limits of this book, but the general logic should be clear.

In some contexts, such as buildings burning down, private insurance is routinely used to trade off costs of risk aversion against costs of moral hazard. In the context of traffic regulation, of course, it is a fantasy, at least at present—as fantastic as the idea of auctioning off part of the electromagnetic spectrum was when Ronald Coase first suggested it in 1959.

The Rational Voodoo Killer: Should We Punish Impossible Attempts?

In explaining why we punish attempted murder, I argued that it was a form of *ex ante* punishment. Shooting at people sometimes kills them, so we punish you for it even if you happen to miss. But what if I am attempting murder by a method that never works, such as sticking pins in a voodoo doll? Should that be criminal? Should we punish impossible attempts?

The argument against is obvious: Sticking pins in voodoo dolls does no harm, so why punish it? Why pay the cost of catching people and locking them up in order to deter behavior that we have no reason to deter?

To see what is wrong with this argument, imagine that I am considering committing a murder in one of two ways—poison or voodoo. The poison I am considering is invariably lethal, whereas sticking pins in a voodoo doll will have no effect at all on the prospective victim's life expectancy. If I were aware of these facts, I would either choose poison or not attempt the murder at all. The problem arises because I am not aware of them. I know that one of the methods works and one does not but not which is which. The legal rule we are considering is *Attempts by impossible means are not punishable.* Since I do not know which method is impossible (if I did, I would not bother using it), this does not translate, for me, into *attempts by voodoo are not punishable.*

Since I am unsure which method works I must allow in my calculations for the possibility that I will choose the wrong one. If impossible attempts are not punished, then the wrong choice means that I will not succeed in my crime but will also not be punished, even if caught. If impossible attempts are punished, I risk using an impossible method and being punished for doing so. That risk is one of the costs to take into account in deciding whether or not to try to kill someone.

So a policy of punishing impossible attempts tends to deter real murders, murders with poison, by people who do not know whether what they think is poison will actually work. The cost of that deterrence is that some people caught making attempts that actually are impossible must be punished for doing so.

Even if punishing impossible attempts provides some deterrence, would it not make more sense to get that deterrence by punishing possible attempts (and successful murders) instead, thus concentrating our efforts on those most likely to do damage? The answer is that it would if we could costlessly impose adequate punishments. We are back again to the *ex post/ex ante* argument.

Punishing the outcome does a better job of putting the punishment where it does the most good—some attempted voodoo killers, after all, may be people who know perfectly well that voodoo does not work and are merely posturing for less well-informed friends. But punishing attempts, even impossible ones, lets us increase the probability of the punishment and thus achieve the same deterrence with less costly punishments.

A different way of making the same argument is to assume that there is some maximum punishment we are willing to impose—life imprisonment but not execution, or execution but not by torture. Supplementing that maximum punishment for murder with a lesser punishment for unsuccessful attempts allows us to increase the *ex ante* cost of the attempt to the aspiring murderer. We can increase it still more by including punishment for impossible attempts.

One thing you may find a little bizarre about this discussion is the assumption that the behavior of voodoo killers will be affected by the incentives provided by legal rules. How likely is it that anyone sufficiently irrational to believe in voodoo will be well enough informed about the law to know whether or not impossible attempts are punished, or sufficiently prudent to care?

One reply is that while rationality may not always be an accurate way of predicting behavior, it is the best tool we have—and ignorance in one part of life does not guarantee ignorance or irrationality in others. All of us, after all, get quite a lot of our beliefs about what does or does not work from the people around us, and a rational person may accept irrational beliefs if everyone he knows accepts them.

Another reply is to point out that impossible attempts are not limited to voodoo. Voodoo is unlikely to kill anyone, but so is shooting a tree. Trying to pick an empty pocket is perfectly rational behavior but unlikely to succeed. There is a sense in which all failed attempts are impossible, judged by what we know after they fail.

Seen from this perspective the question of whether to punish impossible attempts is simply the question of whether to punish attempts. In either form the essential argument is the same: Since someone does not know whether his attempt is impossible before he makes it, the knowledge that it will still be punished even if it turns out to be impossible, whether in the obvious sense of voodoo or the subtler sense of picking an empty pocket, is an incentive not to make the attempt.

Further Reading

Readers interested in a more extensive analysis of these issues will find it in my "Impossibility, Subjective Probability, and Punishment for Attempts," *Journal of Legal Studies* 20 (January 1991).

8

Games, Bargains, Bluffs, and Other Really Hard Stuff

There Are Two kinds of people in the world:
Johnny von Neumann and the rest of us.
  (*Attributed to Eugene Wigner,*
  a Nobel Prize–winning physicist)

ECONOMICS ASSUMES that individuals rationally pursue their own objectives. There are two quite different contexts in which they may do so, one of which turns out to be much easier to analyze than the other. The easy context is the one where, in deciding what to do, I can safely treat the rest of the world as things rather than people. The hard context is the one where I have to take full account of the fact that other people out there are seeking their objectives, and that they know that I am seeking my objectives and take account of it in their actions, and they know that I know . . . and I know that they know that I know . . . and . . .

A simple example of the easy kind of problem is figuring out the shortest route home from my office. The relevant factors—roads, bridges, paths, gates—can be trusted to behave in a predictable fashion, unaffected by what I do. My problem is to figure out, given what they are, what I should do.

It is still the easy kind of problem if I am looking for the shortest distance in time rather than in space and must include in my analysis the other automobiles on the road. As it happens, those automobiles have people driving them, and for some purposes that fact is important. But I don't have to take much account of the rational behavior of those people, given that I know its consequence—lots of cars at 4:30 P.M., many fewer at 2 P.M.—by direct observation. I can do my analysis as if the cars were robots running on a familiar program.

For a simple example of the harder kind of problem, assume I am in a car headed for an intersection with no stop light or stop sign, and someone else is in a car on the cross-street, about the same distance from the intersection. If he is going to slow down and let me cross first, I should speed up, thus decreasing the chance of a collision; if he is going to try to make it through the intersection first, I should slow down. He faces the same problem, with roles reversed. We may end up both going fast and running into each other, or both going slower and slower until we come to a stop at the intersection, each politely waiting for the other.

To make the problem more interesting and the behavior more strategic, assume that both I and the other driver are male teenagers. Each of us puts what others might regard as an unreasonably low value on his own life and an unreasonably high value on proving that he is courageous, resolute, and unwilling to be pushed around. We are playing a variant of the ancient game of "Chicken," a game popular with adolescent males and great statesmen. Whoever backs down, slows enough so that the other can get through the intersection, loses.

If I am sure he is not going to slow down, it is in my interest to do so, since even an adolescent male would rather lose one game of Chicken than wreck his car and possibly lose his life. If he knows I am going to slow down, it is in his interest to speed up. Precisely the same analysis applies to him: If he expects me to go fast, he should slow down, and if he is going to slow down, I should speed up.

This is strategic behavior, behavior in which each person's actions are conditioned on what he expects the other person's actions to be. The branch of mathematics that deals with such problems, invented by John von Neumann almost sixty years ago, is called game theory. His objective was a mathematical theory that would describe what choices a rational player would make and what the outcome would be, given the rules of any particular game. His purpose was to better understand not merely games in the conventional sense but economics, diplomacy, political science—every form of human interaction that involves strategic behavior.

It turned out that solving the general problem was extraordinarily difficult, so difficult that we are still working on it. Von Neumann produced a solution for the special case of two-person fixed-sum games, games such as chess, where anything that benefits one party hurts the other. But for games such as Chicken, in which some outcomes (a collision) hurt both parties, or games like democratic voting, in which one group of players can combine to benefit themselves at the expense of other players, he was less successful. He came up with a solution of a sort, but not a very useful one, since a single game might have anything from zero to an infinite number of solutions, and a single solution might incorporate up to an infinite number of outcomes. Later game theorists have carried the analysis a little further, but it is still unclear exactly what it means to solve such games and difficult or impossible to use the theory to provide unambiguous predictions of the outcome of most real-world strategic situations.

Economics, in particular price theory, deals with this problem through prudent cowardice. Wherever possible, problems are set up, the world is modeled, in ways that make strategic behavior unimportant. The model of perfect competition, for example, assumes an infinite number of buyers and sellers, producers and consumers. From the standpoint of any one of them his actions have no significant effect on the others, so what they do is unaffected by what he does, so strategic problems vanish.

This approach does not work very well for the economic analysis of law; however tightly we may close our eyes to strategic behavior, we find ourselves stumbling over it every few steps. Consider our experience so far. In chapter 2 John was buying an apple that was worth a dollar to him from Mary, to whom it was worth fifty cents. What price must he pay for it? The answer was that it might sell at any price between fifty cents and a dollar, depending on how good a bargainer each was. A serious analysis of the bargaining—which, at that point, I deliberately omitted— would have led us to something very much like the game of Chicken, although with lower stakes. Mary insists she won't sell for less than ninety cents, John insists he won't pay more than sixty, and if neither gives in, the apple remains with Mary, and the potential gain from the trade disappears.

We encountered strategic behavior again in chapters 4 and 5, this time concealed under the name of transaction costs. When one farmer refuses to permit the railroad to throw sparks in the hope of selling his consent for a large fraction of what the railroad will save by not putting on a spark arrester, he is engaging in strategic behavior, generating what I called a holdout problem. So is the free rider who, under a different legal rule, prevents farmers from raising enough money to pay the railroad to put on the spark arrester. So is the railroad when it keeps throwing sparks and paying fines even though a spark arrester would be cheaper, in order to pressure the farmers to switch to clover.

One reason strategic behavior is so important in the economic analysis of law is that it deals with a lot of two-party interactions: litigation, bargaining over permission to breach a contract, and the like. When I want to buy corn I have my choice of thousands of sellers, but when I want to buy permission to be released from a contract the only possible seller is the person I signed the contract with. A second reason is that our underlying theory is largely built on the ideas of Coase, transaction costs are central to Coase's analysis, and transaction costs often involve strategic behavior.

Faced with this situation, there are two alternative approaches. One is to bite the bullet and introduce game theory wholesale into our work. That is an approach that some people doing economic analysis of law have taken. I am not one of them. In my experience if a game is simple enough so that game theory provides a reasonably unambiguous answer, there are probably other ways of getting there.

In most real-world applications of game theory the answer is ambiguous until you assume away large parts of the problem in the details of how you set it up. You can get mathematical rigor only at the cost of making real-world problems insoluble. I expect that will remain true until there are substantial breakthroughs in game theory. When I am picking problems to work on, ones that stumped John von Neumann go at the bottom of the stack.

The alternative approach, and the one I prefer, is to accept the fact that arguments involving strategic behavior are going to be well short of rigorous and try to do the best one can despite that. A first step in this approach is to think through the logic of games we are likely to encounter in order to learn as much as we can about possible outcomes and how they depend on the details of the game. Formal game theory is helpful in doing so, although I will not be employing much of it here.

In the next part of the chapter I work through the logic of two games: bilateral monopoly and prisoner's dilemma. Those two, along with closely related variants, describe a large part of the strategic behavior you will encounter, in this book and in life.

Bilateral Monopoly

Mary has the world's only apple, worth fifty cents to her. John is the world's only customer for the apple, worth a dollar to him. Mary has a monopoly on selling apples, John has a monopoly (technically, a *monopsony*, a buying monopoly) on buying apples. Economists describe such a situation as *bilateral monopoly*. What happens?

Mary announces that her price is ninety cents, and if John will not pay it, she will eat the apple herself. If John believes her, he pays. Ninety cents for an apple he values at a dollar is not much of a deal—but better than no apple. If, however, John announces that his maximum price is sixty cents and Mary believes him, the same logic holds. Mary accepts his price, and he gets most of the benefit from the trade.

This is not a fixed-sum game. If John buys the apple from Mary, the sum of their gains is fifty cents, with the division determined by the price. If they fail to reach an agreement, the summed gain is zero. Each is using the threat of the zero outcome to try to force a fifty cent outcome as favorable to himself as possible. How successful each is depends in part on how convincingly he can commit himself, how well he can persuade the other that if he doesn't get his way the deal will fall through.

Every parent is familiar with a different example of the same game. A small child wants to get her way and will throw a tantrum if she doesn't. The tantrum itself does her no good, since if she throws it you will refuse to do what she wants and send her to bed without dessert. But since the tantrum imposes substantial costs on you as well as on her, especially if it happens in the middle of your dinner party, it may be a sufficiently effective threat to get her at least part of what she wants.

Prospective parents resolve never to give in to such threats and think they will succeed. They are wrong. You may have thought out the logic of bilateral monopoly better than your child, but she has hundreds of millions of years of evolution on her side, during which offspring who succeeded in making parents do what they want, and thus getting a larger share of parental resources devoted to them, were more likely to survive to pass on their genes to the next generation of offspring. Her commitment strategy is hardwired into her; if you call her bluff, you will frequently find that it is not a bluff. If you win more than half the games and only rarely end up with a bargaining breakdown and a tantrum, consider yourself lucky.

Herman Kahn, a writer who specialized in thinking and writing about unfashionable topics such as thermonuclear war, came up with yet another variant of the game: the Doomsday Machine. The idea was for the United States to bury lots of very dirty thermonuclear weapons under the Rocky Mountains, enough so that if they went off, their fallout would kill everyone on earth. The bombs would be attached to a fancy Geiger counter rigged to set them off if it sensed the fallout from a Russian nuclear attack. Once the Russians know we have a Doomsday Machine we are safe from attack and can safely scrap the rest of our nuclear arsenal.

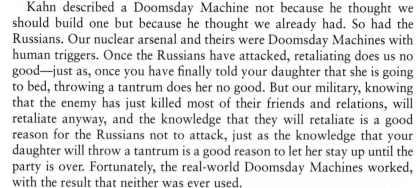

The idea provided the central plot device for the movie *Doctor Strangelove*. The Russians build a Doomsday Machine but imprudently postpone the announcement—they are waiting for the premier's birthday—until just after an American Air Force officer has launched a unilateral nuclear attack on his own initiative. The mad scientist villain was presumably intended as a parody of Kahn.

Kahn described a Doomsday Machine not because he thought we should build one but because he thought we already had. So had the Russians. Our nuclear arsenal and theirs were Doomsday Machines with human triggers. Once the Russians have attacked, retaliating does us no good—just as, once you have finally told your daughter that she is going to bed, throwing a tantrum does her no good. But our military, knowing that the enemy has just killed most of their friends and relations, will retaliate anyway, and the knowledge that they will retaliate is a good reason for the Russians not to attack, just as the knowledge that your daughter will throw a tantrum is a good reason to let her stay up until the party is over. Fortunately, the real-world Doomsday Machines worked, with the result that neither was ever used.

For a final example, consider someone who is big, strong, and likes to get his own way. He adopts a policy of beating up anyone who does things he doesn't like, such as paying attention to a girl he is dating or expressing insufficient deference to his views on baseball. He commits himself to that policy by persuading himself that only sissies let themselves get pushed around—and that not doing what he wants counts as pushing him around. Beating someone up is costly; he might get hurt, and he might end up in jail. But as long as everyone knows he is committed to that strategy, other people don't cross him, and he doesn't have to beat them up.

Think of the bully as a Doomsday Machine on an individual level. His strategy works as long as only one person is playing it. One day he sits down at a bar and starts discussing baseball with a stranger—also big, strong, and committed to the same strategy. The stranger fails to show adequate deference to his opinions. When it is over, one of the two is lying dead on the floor, and the other is standing there with a broken beer bottle in his hand and a dazed expression on his face, wondering what happens next. The Doomsday Machine just went off.

With only one bully the strategy is profitable: Other people do what you want, and you never have to carry through on your commitment. With lots of bullies it is unprofitable: You frequently get into fights and soon end up either dead or in jail. As long as the number of bullies is low enough so that the gain of usually getting what you want is larger than the cost of occasionally having to pay for it, the strategy is profitable and the number of people adopting it increases. Equilibrium is reached when gain and loss just balance, making each of the alternative strategies, bully or pushover, equally attractive. The analysis becomes more complicated if we add additional strategies, but the logic of the situation remains the same.

This particular example of bilateral monopoly is relevant to one of the central disputes over criminal law in general and the death penalty in particular: Do penalties deter? One reason to think they might not is that the sort of crime I have just described, a barroom brawl ending in a killing—more generally, a crime of passion—seems to be an irrational act, one the perpetrator regrets as soon as it happens. How then can it be deterred by punishment?

The economist's answer is that the brawl was not chosen rationally, but the strategy that led to it was. The higher the penalty for such acts, the less profitable the bully strategy. The result will be fewer bullies, fewer barroom brawls, and fewer "irrational" killings. How much deterrence that implies is an empirical question, but thinking through the logic of bilateral monopoly shows us why crimes of passion are not necessarily undeterrable.

The Prisoner's Dilemma

Two men are arrested for a burglary. The District Attorney puts them in separate cells. He goes first to Joe. He tells him that if he confesses and Mike does not, the DA will drop the burglary charge and let Joe off with a slap on the wrist—three months for trespass. If Mike also confesses, the DA cannot drop the charge but will ask the judge for leniency; Mike and Joe will get two years each.

If Joe refuses to confess, the DA will not feel so friendly. If Mike confesses, Joe will be convicted, and the DA will ask for the maximum possible sentence. If neither confesses, the DA cannot convict them of the robbery, but he will press for a six-month sentence for trespass, resisting arrest, and vagrancy.

After explaining all of this to Joe, the DA goes to Mike's cell and gives the same speech, with names reversed. Table 8.1 shows the matrix of outcomes facing Joe and Mike.

TABLE 8.1
Prisoner's Dilemma

		Mike	
		Confess	Say Nothing
Joe	Confess	2 years, 2 years	3 months, 5 years
	Say Nothing	5 years, 3 months	6 months, 6 months

Joe reasons as follows:

> If Mike confesses and I don't, I get five years; if I confess too, I get two years. If Mike is going to confess, I had better confess too.
>
> If neither of us confesses, I go to jail for six months. If Mike stays silent and I confess, I only get three months. So if Mike is going to stay silent, I am better off confessing. In fact, whatever Mike does I am better off confessing.

Joe calls for the guard and asks to speak to the DA. It takes a while; Mike has made the same calculation, reached the same conclusion, and is in the middle of dictating his confession.

Both Joe and Mike have acted rationally, and both are, as a result, worse off. By confessing they each get two years; if they had kept their mouths shut, they each would have gotten six months. That seems an odd consequence for rational behavior.

The explanation is that Joe is choosing only his strategy, not Mike's. If Joe could choose between the lower right-hand cell of the matrix and the upper left-hand cell, he would choose the former; so would Mike. But those are not the choices they are offered. Mike is choosing a column, and the left-hand column dominates the right-hand column; it is better whichever row Joe chooses. Joe is choosing a row, and the top row dominates the bottom.

Mike and Joe expect to continue their criminal career and may find themselves in the same situation again. If Mike double-crosses Joe this time, Joe can pay him back next. Intuitively, it seems that prisoner's dilemma many times repeated, with the same players each time, should produce a more attractive outcome for the players than a single play.

Perhaps—but there is an elegant if counterintuitive argument against it. Suppose Joe and Mike both know that they are going to play the game exactly twenty times. Each therefore knows that on the twentieth play future retaliation will no longer be an option. So the final play is an ordinary game of prisoner's dilemma, with the ordinary result: Both prisoners confess. Since they are both going to confess on the twentieth round, neither has a threat available to punish betrayal on the nineteenth round, so that too is an ordinary game and leads to mutual confession. Since they are going to confess on the nineteenth . . . The whole string of games comes unraveled, and we are back with the old result. Joe and Mike confess every time.

Many people find that result deeply counterintuitive, in part because they live in a world where people have rationally chosen to avoid that particular game whenever possible. People engaged in repeat relationships requiring trust take care not to determine the last play in advance, or find ways of committing themselves to retaliate, if necessary, even on the last play. Criminals go to considerable effort to raise the cost to their co-workers of squealing and lower the cost of going to jail for refusing to squeal. None of that refutes the logic of prisoner's dilemma; it simply means that real prisoners, and other people, are sometimes playing other games. When the net payoffs to squealing have the structure shown in table 8.1, the logic of the game is compelling. Prisoners confess.

For a real prisoner's dilemma involving a controversial feature of our legal system, consider plea bargaining:

> The prosecutor calls up the defense lawyer and offers a deal. If the client will plead guilty to second-degree murder, the District Attorney will drop the charge of first-degree murder. The accused will lose his chance of acquittal, but he will also lose the risk of going to the chair.

Such bargains are widely criticized as a way of letting criminals off lightly. Their actual effect may well be the opposite—to make punishment more, not less, severe. How can this be? A rational criminal will accept a plea bargain only if doing so makes him better off—produces, on average, a less severe punishment than going to trial. Does it not follow that the existence of plea bargaining must make punishment less severe?

To see why that is not true, consider the situation of a hypothetical District Attorney and the defendants he prosecutes. There are a hundred cases per year; the DA has a budget of a hundred thousand dollars. With only a thousand dollars to spend investigating and prosecuting each case, half the defendants will be acquitted. But if he can get ninety defendants to cop pleas, the DA can concentrate his resources on the ten who refuse, spend ten thousand dollars on each case, and get a conviction rate of 90 percent.

A defendant faces a 90 percent chance of conviction if he goes to trial and makes his decision accordingly. He will reject any proposed deal that is worse for him than a 90 percent chance of conviction but may well accept one that is less attractive than a 50 percent chance of conviction, leaving him worse off than he would be in a world without plea bargaining. All defendants would be better off if none of them accepted the DA's offer, but each is better off accepting. They are caught in a many-player version of the prisoner's dilemma, alias the public good problem.

Prisoner's dilemma provides a simple demonstration of a problem that runs through the economic analysis of law: Individual rationality does not always lead to group rationality. Consider air pollution, not by a few factories but by lots of automobiles. We would all be better off if each of us installed a catalytic converter. But if I install a converter in my car, I pay all of the cost and receive only a small fraction of the benefit, so it is not worth doing. In much the same fashion everybody may be better off if nobody steals, since we are all potential victims, but my decision to steal from you has very little effect on the probability that someone else will steal from me, so it may be in my interest to do it.

Constructing efficient legal rules is largely an attempt to get out of prisoner's dilemmas: criminal penalties to change the incentives of potential thieves, pollution laws to change the incentives of potential polluters. We may not be able to succeed completely, but we can at least try, whenever possible, to choose rules under which individual rationality leads to group rationality instead of rules that produce the opposite result.

I started this chapter with a very simple example of strategic behavior: two motorists approaching the same intersection at right angles. As it happens, there is a legal rule to solve that problem, one that originated to solve the analogous problem of two ships on converging courses. The rule is "Starboard right of way." The ship, or the car, on the right has the right of way, meaning that the other is legally obliged to slow down and let him go through the intersection first.

Conclusions

So far our discussion of games has yielded only two clear conclusions. One involves a version of bilateral monopoly in which each player precommits to his demands, pairs of players are selected at random, and the outcome depends on what strategies that particular pair has precommitted to. That is the game of bullies and barroom brawls, the game sociobiologists have christened "hawk/dove." Our conclusion was that increasing the cost of bargaining breakdown, making a fight between two bullies or two hawks more costly, decreases the fraction of players who commit to the bully strategy. That is why we expect punishment for crimes of passion to deter. Our other clear conclusion was that rational players of a game with the payoff structure of prisoner's dilemma will betray each other.

Even these results become less clear when we try to apply them to real-world situations. Real-world games do not come with payoff matrices printed on the box. Prisoner's dilemma leads to mutual betrayal, but that is a reason for people to modify the game, using commitment, reputation, altruism, and a variety of other devices to make it in each party's interest to cooperate instead of betraying. So applying the theoretical analysis to the real world is still a hard problem.

We can draw some other and less rigorous conclusions from our discussion, however. It seems clear that in bilateral monopoly commitment is an important tactic, so we can expect players to look for ways of committing themselves to stick to their demands. A small child says, "I won't pay more than sixty cents for your apple, cross my heart and hope to die." The CEO of a firm engaged in takeover negotiations gives a speech arguing that if he offers more than ten dollars a share for the target, he will be overpaying, and his stockholders should fire him.

Individuals spend real resources on bargaining: time, lawyers' fees, costs of commitment, and risk of bargaining breakdown. The amount they will be willing to spend should depend on the amount at stake—the same problem we encountered in our earlier discussion of rent seeking. So legal rules that lead to bilateral monopoly games with high stakes should be avoided where possible.

Consider, for a simple example, the question of what legal rules should apply to a breach of contract. Suppose I have agreed to sell you ten thousand customized cams, with delivery on March 30, for a price of a hundred thousand dollars. Late in February my factory burns down. I can still, by extraordinary efforts and expensive subcontracting, fulfill the contract, but the cost of doing so has risen from ninety thousand dollars to a million dollars.

One possible legal rule is specific performance: I signed the contract, I must deliver the cams. Doing so is inefficient; the cams are worth only $110,000 to you. The obvious solution is for us to bargain; I pay you to permit me to cancel the contract.

Agreement provides you a net gain so long as I pay you more than the $10,000 you expected to make by buying the cams. It provides me a net gain so long as I pay you less than the $900,000 I will lose if I have to sell you the cams. That leaves us with a very large bargaining range to fight over, which is likely to lead to large bargaining costs, including some risk of a very expensive breakdown: We cannot agree on a price, you make me deliver the cams, and between us we are $890,000 poorer than if you had let me out of the contract. That suggests one reason why courts are reluctant to enforce specific performance of contracts, usually preferring to permit breach and award damages, calculated by the court or agreed on in advance by the parties.

For another example, suppose a court finds that my polluting oil refinery is imposing costs on my downwind neighbor. One possibility is to permit the neighbor to enjoin me, to forbid me from operating the refinery unless I can do it without releasing noxious vapors. An alternative is to refuse an injunction but permit the neighbor to sue for damages.

If the damage to the neighbor from my pollution is comparable to the cost to me of preventing it, the court is likely to grant an injunction, leaving me with the alternatives of buying permission to pollute from my neighbor or ending my pollution. If the cost of stopping pollution is much greater than the damage the pollution does, the court may refuse to grant an injunction, leaving my neighbor free to sue for damages.

If the court granted an injunction in such a situation, the result would be a bilateral monopoly bargaining game with a very large bargaining range. I would be willing, if necessary, to pay anything up to the (very large) cost to me of controlling my pollution; you would be willing to accept, if necessary, anything more than the (small) damage the pollution does to you. Where between those points we ended up would depend on how well each of us bargained, and each of us would have an incentive to spend substantial resources trying to push the final agreement toward his preferred end of the range.

Further Reading

Readers interested in a somewhat more extensive treatment of game theory will find it in chapter 11 of my books *Price Theory* and *Hidden Order*. Readers interested in a much more extensive treatment will find it in *Game Theory and the Law* by Douglas G. Baird, Robert H. Gertner, and Randal C. Picker (Cambridge, Mass.: Harvard University Press, 1994). Readers who would like to watch a first-rate mind working its way through a really hard problem will find at least the early chapters of *The Theory of Games and Economic Activity* by John Von Neumann and Oskar Morgenstern (Princeton: Princeton University Press, 1980) worth reading.

9

As Much as Your Life Is Worth

Your money or your life.
Take my life; I'm saving my money for my old age.

IN CHAPTER 3 I described one approach to producing efficient outcomes: If someone imposes costs on others, charge him an amount equal to the damage done in order to force him to take those costs into account in his decisions. This chapter will deal with a problem raised by that approach, one that may have occurred to you during the discussion of auto accidents in chapter 7. Some accidents destroy cars; we know, at least roughly, how to measure the cost of a car. But other auto accidents destroy people. How does one price a life?

Economists measure costs and value by revealed preference, by people's actual behavior. If someone offered to buy your heart for a million dollars, even ten million, it is unlikely that you would agree. By that standard it looks as though most people put an infinite value on their life.

But consider the decision of how often to get a medical checkup or have your brakes checked. Such activities buy you life in the form of a slightly lower chance of an undetected heart blockage or a lethal skid. If life is of infinite value to you, you ought to divert time and money from activities that do not prolong your life to activities that do as long as the latter have any payoff at all, however small.

For the same reason, somebody who puts infinite value on his life ought to avoid all dangerous activities: hang gliding, skiing, or driving a car for any purpose not directly related to survival. He should not smoke, drink only on doctor's orders, and never touch ice cream or spare ribs. Exercise should be half an hour on a treadmill, avoiding the risk of unlikely but potentially lethal accidents on a tennis court or a jogging track. The result would be a long life. If you call it living.

The Problem Isn't Multiplying by Infinity but Dividing by Zero

That is not how the people I know act. It is not the way I act. I doubt it is the way you act.

Consider again your reaction to an offer of a million dollars for your life. Why do you refuse, and keep refusing even when the buyer offers to raise his price? The obvious answer is not because your life is of infinite value but because money is of no use to a corpse.

Suppose we switch to a probabilistic version of the same deal: Someone offers you a gamble based on the roll of a hundred-sided die. On any roll from 1 to 99 he pays you a hundred thousand dollars. If it comes up 100, he shoots you. You might still decline the offer, but not as fast. If he raises the offer to a million dollars and a thousand-sided die, you may change your mind.

The decrease in the probability of death from 100 percent to 1 percent or .1 percent explains why the price you charge falls, but not why it falls from infinity to a million dollars, perhaps much less. What explains that is the increase in the chance of being able to collect the money from zero to a near certainty. Zero times a hundred million dollars is still zero. Ninety-nine hundredths times a hundred thousand dollars is a substantial sum.

This way of looking at the problem also explains why people sometimes do accept a near certainty of death—charging into machine-gun fire in the First World War, piloting a kamikaze bomber in the Second, or giving someone dear to you the last seat in the lifeboat. Those are all cases where you can die and still collect. One can even imagine someone accepting a million dollars in cash for his life if there were some person or cause sufficiently important to him that could make good use of the money. What makes no sense is accepting a million dollars for your life with the intention of spending the money on yourself.

Back to Law

The economic question of how to value a life is also a legal question. If someone accidentally destroys your car under circumstances in which he is legally liable, he owes you the price of a new car. What should he owe you—or your heirs—if he also destroys you?

The traditional common law answer, oddly enough, was "nothing." This may have been a consequence of the unwillingness of tort law to treat civil claims as transferable property, which meant that your claim for being killed died with you. Alternatively, it may have been a result of viewing tort damages as compensation to the victim rather than disincentive to the tortfeasor. It is hard to compensate someone for being dead. Legal reforms in the mid–nineteenth century made it possible for your wife and children to sue for the cost to them of your dying, roughly speaking for your future income minus the amount of it that you would have spent on yourself. But nobody could claim for the cost to you of losing your life.

Suppose, however, that we are constructing our own legal system along the general lines suggested by Pigou's analysis of externalities—ignoring, for the moment, the problems with that analysis raised by Coase. We want to impose a cost on those whose actions destroy or injure people for the same reason we want to impose a cost on those whose actions destroy or injure property, in order that the actor will take proper account of those consequences in deciding what to do. How, in principle, should we set the price?

Start with an actor who already bears all of the costs: yourself, deciding whether to take risks, spend money on medical care or in other ways trade off your own life against other values. Even quite risky activities rarely result in immediate death, so you expect the payment for the little bit of life you are sacrificing to be in a form that you can almost certainly collect. Under those circumstances your behavior demonstrates that your value for your life is high but not infinite.

How might we measure that value? One way is by looking at the wage premium for risky professions. Trucking companies have to pay more to get people to drive trucks full of dynamite than trucks full of sand. By estimating the risk of death in risky jobs and measuring their wage premium relative to safer jobs that are otherwise similar, we get at least a rough estimate of the value of life to the people accepting those risky jobs: the amount they have to be paid to take them. Such calculations have been done; the result is a value of life, for ordinary Americans, ranging from about one to ten million dollars.

This is an imperfect measure for at least two reasons. First, the people who accept such jobs are the ones most willing to do so; all else being equal they will be the ones with the lowest value for their lives. Second, driving a dynamite truck may be less pleasant work than driving a truck loaded with sand; the driver is under more pressure, which some will see as an extra cost. Of course, there may also be people who regard the tension as a benefit—the sort of people who get their fun jumping out of airplanes or climbing cliffs. The protagonist of Neil Stephenson's *Snow Crash,* set in the twenty-first century, delivers pizza for the Mafia. He takes the job precisely because the Mafia has converted pizza delivery into a high-risk, high-pressure profession.

Problems such as these imply that estimates of value for life based on the risk premium for risky professions might be off in either direction. But they still provide at least a first approximation, and one that can be improved by more detailed studies.

If we accept this approach to calculating the value of life, we seem to have a simple solution to the optimal incentive problem. If someone causes another person's death under circumstances that make him liable for the loss—just what that means will be taken up in chapter 14—he owes his victim's estate damages corresponding to the value of the victim's life to himself, as reflected in his behavior. If we somehow know that the victim would have required an extra thousand dollars a year to agree to drive a dynamite truck instead of a sand truck, and if we also know that driving a dynamite truck increases the probability of dying each year by a tenth of a percentage point, the tortfeasor owes a million dollars to the victim's estate, since a million dollars times a probability of one in a thousand is equal to a thousand dollars.

To see the implications of this legal rule, imagine that you are considering dynamiting some tree stumps, which is a lot less work than digging them up. The only catch is that there is one chance in ten thousand of a lethal accident. If it happens, since the victim values his life at a million dollars, you will owe his heirs a million dollars in damages. In deciding whether to go ahead, you must add to the cost of the dynamite an additional expected cost of a hundred dollars, one chance in ten thousand of a million-dollar liability. That is precisely the price the victim would have required to accept a one in ten thousand chance of death. It is also what a fully informed insurance company would charge you (plus something extra for overhead) to insure your stump-removal project against liability. You use dynamite if it produces net benefits, if the cost savings to you outweigh the risk to third parties. That is the efficient outcome. Through the magic of the tort system, you have been induced to make the same choice the victim would have made.

Optimal Deterrence, Optimal Insurance, and Never the Twain Shall Meet

This provides the correct incentive to people not to take chances with other people's lives, but there is still a problem. Suppose the victim has no dependents and no worthy causes he cares about. The only thing he can buy with the million dollars (specified in his will, which happens to provide for the unlikely contingency that he will be tortiously blown up) is a spectacular tomb. We have provided the right deterrence to the tortfeasor, but we have done it at the cost of transferring money from people who can use it to someone who cannot.

The example is an extreme one, but it points to a general problem. Tort liability serves at least two different functions. One is to deter actions that injure others. Another is to compensate the victims, to insure them. There is no reason to expect the optimal damage payment for purposes of deterrence to be equal to the optimal damage payment for purposes of insurance.

Consider again our hypothetical victim. Given the choice, he would buy no life insurance, since money is more useful to him alive than dead. The fact that his optimal insurance is zero does not mean that someone who kills him has done him no damage.

This way of putting the question also suggests the solution. A potential victim with no need for life insurance wants to transfer his damage payment from the future in which he gets blown up to the future in which he is alive to enjoy the money. Our society has a very large industry in the business of transferring money from one future to another: the insurance industry. When you buy fire insurance you are giving up money in a future in which your house does not burn down in order to collect money in a future in which it does, transferring wealth from one future to another.

The potential victim whose damage award will overcompensate him solves the problem not by buying insurance but by selling it. In exchange for a fixed payment now he transfers to an insurance company the right to collect damages if he is ever tortiously killed. If he faces one chance in a thousand of being tortiously killed and getting a million dollars in damages, and if, for simplicity, we ignore the insurance company's operating costs and assume it buys and sells insurance at its actuarial value, the company will pay him a thousand dollars. They have bought life insurance on him, but insurance that only pays off if his death is the result of someone else's tort. To put the same thing in different words, they have bought an *inchoate tort claim*, a claim for a tort that has not yet happened.

This set of institutions not only provides potential tortfeasors with the right deterrence, assuming that we can estimate the value of life reasonably accurately, it also gives the payment to the victim when it is most valuable to him. If he wants to have money if he dies, if, in other words, he wants life insurance, he gets the damage payment then. If he doesn't want it then, he transfers the money back to when it is most useful to him.

A Perfect Information Fantasy and How to Get It

Imagine how we would handle risky activity in a world where all risks were known. Every time you imposed a risk on someone else you would owe him the amount of money he would have required to voluntarily accept that risk. Not only would that give people whose actions might injure others the right incentives, it would also achieve, *ex ante*, the nominal objective of tort liability—compensating victims at the expense of tortfeasors—an objective that cannot be achieved *ex post*, since we have no way of adequately compensating someone for the loss of his life.

Now consider the system described in the previous section, with one addition: Potential tortfeasors buy insurance against their liability. The cost to me of risks I impose on others shows up in my insurance premium, representing the insurance company's estimate of the risk that they will have to pay out on the insurance. The cost to you of risks others impose on you is balanced by the money you can get by selling the right to collect damages if you are killed. It is just the result described in the previous paragraph, except that we are now in a world where risks can be estimated but not known with certainty, with the insurance companies providing a market mechanism to estimate the relevant risks.

Why do these institutions not exist; why is there is no market on which you can sell your future claims for the tortious loss of your life? There are two answers. The first is that, as I mentioned earlier, traditional common law did not award you or your estate damages for the loss of your life, on the principle that your claim dies with you. This has changed in recent decades, as states have passed survival statutes allowing your heirs to collect damages for your death. While these laws permit your heirs to claim for your pain and suffering, they do not usually permit a claim based on the value to you of your life; as a result they badly understate the real loss. The second and related reason is that the common law does not treat tort claims as transferable property. While you can, in principle, sell life insurance on yourself, subject to the restrictions of your state's regulatory regime, you cannot sell your claim to future damage payments.

This is an issue we will return to again in chapters 18 and 19. In the former I will argue that making tort claims, including claims for torts that have not yet occurred, marketable would help solve some of the problems of using tort law to replace criminal law. In the latter I will argue that the failure of the common law either to permit claims based on the value of the victim's life to himself (what have recently come to be called "hedonic damages") or to treat tort claims as property is evidence against Posner's thesis of the efficiency of the common law.

Damages for Injury

We have been considering the problem of compensating people for being killed, but similar arguments apply to lesser injuries as well. When someone is tortiously blinded or crippled, he is made worse off in at least three different ways. The injury imposes pecuniary costs: medical bills, lost wages, and the like. It imposes nonpecuniary costs: Life is less fun from a wheelchair. Finally, the injury reduces the value to the victim of additional money, at least once the medical bills and the wheelchair are paid for, since many of the ways in which he could have used money in the past are no longer available to him.

How might we measure his loss in order to calculate the damages that someone responsible for it would owe? One way is to simply measure pecuniary loss: lost wages, medical expenses, and the like. To a considerable degree, this is the traditional common law approach; its obvious advantage is that these are the easiest costs to measure. Its obvious disadvantage is that it may badly underestimate total costs. Very few of us would be willing to give up our eyesight, or our legs, in exchange for full medical expenses plus lost wages.

An approach more consistent with the language of tort law would be to require the tortfeasor to fully compensate the victim, to "make him whole." That would mean paying him enough so that a potential victim, knowing he would be compensated, would not care whether or not the accident happened. One practical problem with doing that is that injuries not only make people worse off, they also make money less useful to them. Even if it were possible, by enormous payments, to just barely recompense the victim, it is not obvious that the creation of blind billionaires living in profligate luxury, and so just barely compensating with pleasures that large amounts of money can buy for lost pleasures that it cannot buy, is a good idea.

Another way of putting this is to observe that full compensation represents more insurance than a potential victim would want to buy. To see this, imagine that the victim first receives full compensation for his pecuniary losses, so that he can afford to consume exactly the same things as if he had not been injured. Since some of those things (color television if he has been blinded) are no longer useful to him, he will transfer some of his expenditure to things that before the accident were not worth their cost. He is worse off, since he is buying a thousand dollars of gourmet dinners worth a thousand units of happiness instead of a thousand dollar color television that would be worth two thousand—if he could see it. With fewer ways of spending the same amount of money he is getting less happiness per dollar.

If we now award him enough more money to return him to his old level of happiness, he will be using that money to buy things even less valuable to him, with the result that the last dollar will provide even less happiness. This is a less extreme version of the reason you would not sell your life for a million dollars. It implies that the price for which you would sell your eyesight is high, perhaps infinite.

I have already offered the solution to this problem in the more extreme case: Award damages based on what potential victims would have accepted in exchange for the risk. Since that may well overcompensate from the insurance standpoint, permit potential victims to transfer part of their future awards to their uninjured state by selling part of their damage claim in advance.

The same solution applies here. It implies damage payments higher than mere compensation for pecuniary loss, since after suffering an injury and being compensated for pecuniary loss the victim is still worse off than if the injury did not occur. It implies damage payments lower than those that would fully compensate since, by allowing the victim to shift some of the money to his uninjured state, we increase the value to him of the compensation. The consequence, as in the earlier case, is full compensation *ex ante*. *Ex post*, potential victims who do not get injured are better off as a result of the risk imposed on them; they have the money from selling part of the damage claim for an accident that did not happen. Actual victims are worse off as a result of the risk.

I believe I have now solved the puzzle with which I started this chapter: How can we adequately compensate people for loss of life or limb? The answer is that, *ex post*, we often cannot and usually should not. But our inability to compensate *ex post* does not mean that life is infinitely valuable, nor does it imply that we should avoid any activity that imposes any risk of death on other people, any more than it is a reason to avoid any act that imposes any risk of death on oneself.

In both cases the relevant question is whether the cost of the risk is worth paying for the associated benefit. We make that calculation implicitly for ourselves every time we drive, or eat ice cream, or decide to have a baby. We could force people to make the same calculation for risks they impose on others by imposing *ex post* liability sufficient to reimburse potential victims *ex ante*.

The American Legal System in Brief

MODERN ECONOMIC analysis of law originated in the United States a few decades ago; the first issue of the *Journal of Law and Economics*, the first law and economics journal, was published in Chicago in 1958. One result is that although the theory is relevant to all systems of legal rules in all times and places, most applications, including most of this book, are to modern Anglo-American law.

Chapter 17 will change that, applying ideas developed in the preceding chapters to the legal institutions of medieval Iceland and eighteenth-century England and the private norms of a rural county in twentieth-century California. Until then we will mostly be looking at the legal institutions that most of us live under. The purpose of this chapter is to provide a sketch of those institutions before we go on to examine the system of legal rules they implement.

Where Does Law Come from?

> There is some difference of opinion on the subject
> in American jurisprudence brought about by
> differing views as to the correctness or
> applicability of the decision of the English courts
> in *Rylands v. Fletcher*, L. R. 3 H. L. 330.
> (*Annie Lee Turner et al. v. Big Lake
> Oil Company et al.*)

The year is 1936. The Supreme Court of Texas must determine what compensation, if any, Big Lake Oil Company owes Annie Lee Turner and her neighbors for damage done to their property by the escape of polluted water from Big Lake's storage pools. A key issue is whether Big Lake is liable only if it failed to take reasonable precautions (was *negligent*) or whether it is automatically liable for any damage done (is *strictly liable*).

To answer that question the Texas judges looked first not to the statute law of Texas but to a case decided in another country in another century: *Rylands v. Fletcher*, decided by a committee of the British House of Lords in 1868. That case too dealt with liability for spilled water; it held that the appropriate rule was strict liability. The Texas court, for reasons that we will return to in chapter 19, reached the opposite conclusion, holding that Big Lake was not liable unless it had been negligent. To justify that conclusion it spent a considerable part of the written opinion explaining its disagreement with the British House of Lords.

The obvious question is why it bothered. England had never ruled Texas, and its authority over the American colonies ended almost a century before *Rylands v. Fletcher* was decided. The British legislature had no authority over the law of Texas.

Law is not entirely the work of legislatures. The House of Lords, in addition to functioning as part of the British legislature, also appoints a committee of "law lords," judges who function as Britain's high court. It was that committee that decided *Rylands v. Fletcher.* In doing so it was both a court deciding the outcome of a particular case—requiring Fletcher to pay damages to Rylands, a matter of interest only to them and their attorneys—and an expert body interpreting the common law of England. In that second role the conclusion it reached was relevant to, although not determinative of, the deliberations of a Texas court deciding a similar case based on the same underlying system of law. An English judge has authority over an American case in precisely the same sense in which an English scholar has authority over a dispute in his field carried on by American scholars: He is an expert whose opinion is relevant to deciding a disputed question of fact.

In the Anglo-American legal system judges as well as legislators make law. One way in which they do so is by interpreting legislation and constitutions, resolving ambiguities, filling in gaps. Under the doctrine of *stare decisis*, decisions by one court are usually, although not inevitably, binding on another, so a decision in one case creates precedents that affect decisions in later cases.

But judges do more than merely interpret statutes or constitutions. They also create law, gradually, through a long series of decisions, out of thin air. The Court's opinion in *Turner v. Big Lake Oil* did cite one Texas statute but only to argue that, "interpreted . . . in the light of the Constitution and of the common law and Mexican civil law," it was irrelevant to the case. The decision was based not on statute but on past cases, in Texas and elsewhere, demonstrating that American courts had generally refused to apply strict liability in the fashion implied by *Rylands v. Fletcher.*

One of the startling discoveries that students make in the first year of law school is how much of law is created, modified, and in some cases later repealed, entirely by judges:

> Defendant strongly urges that if said immunity is to be abolished, it should be done by the legislature, not by this court. With this contention we must disagree. The doctrine of school district immunity was created by this court alone.

Having found that doctrine to be unsound and unjust under present conditions, we consider that we have not only the power, but the duty, to abolish
that immunity. (Mr. Justice Klingbiel in *Molitor v. Kaneland Community Unit
District No. 302*, 18 Ill. 2d 11, 22–26)

The Structure of the Court System

You are arrested, tried, and convicted of playing your accordion without
a license, in violation of a state statute as interpreted and expanded by a
series of court decisions. Being a litigious sort, you decide to appeal.

In the original case you faced both a judge and jury, the former with
the job of determining the relevant law, the latter of determining the facts
relevant to whether you violated it. The appeals court, if it accepts your
appeal, will consist of a judge or group of judges. Its job is to review the
work of the judge in the first trial. Since it is concerned with law, not facts,
neither side will be able to introduce additional evidence about what
happened, although both may, if they wish, introduce additional legal
arguments.

If the appeals court finds that the judge's decisions on matters of law
were correct, your conviction will stand. You may, if you can afford it,
attempt a further appeal all the way up to the state supreme court, if it is
willing to hear the case.

Suppose the appeals court rules that the judge below made an error of
law. The result is not that you go free; the fact that the judge made a
mistake does not imply that you are innocent. Typically, the higher court
sends the case back down to the lower to be retried, with the necessary
amendment in the judge's ruling. This time you get to introduce evidence
on the quality of your performance, ruled out as irrelevant the first time
around. Only if the matter of law on which the lower court erred was so
important that once it is corrected there is no case left does your victory
above translate into an automatic victory below.

The higher the court that makes a ruling, the more authority that precedent will have in future cases. If it was the supreme court of your state
that decided to admit your evidence, generations of accordion players yet
unborn may benefit by being able to introduce similar evidence in their
trials.

One result of this system of appeals is that most of the decisions that
law students and lawyers study are by appeals courts, especially ones near
the top level of the system, since those decisions set precedents that can be
used in arguing later cases. A further result is that law school education
consists in large part of reading the middle of stories without ever learning either what really happened at the beginning—the appeals court takes
the original findings of fact, however implausible, as gospel—or what

finally happened when the case was sent back down and resolved. Some day an enterprising writer will fix that problem with a book written for curious law students telling them just what was going on between the plaintiff in *Bird v. Holbrook*, "a youth of the age of nineteen years," and the "female servant" on behalf of whom he pursued a fugitive peacock into Holbrook's walled tulip garden, where he fell victim to a spring gun, and what became of them thereafter. We may finally learn how much of the implausible chain of causation alleged by the plaintiff in *Palsgraf v. Long Island R. Co.* actually happened, and whether Mrs. Palsgraf retained her stammer after she lost her case. He can call it *The Rest of the Story.*

So far I have limited my example to the courts of a single state. Expanding the picture raises the problem of deciding what court has jurisdiction and what law applies in a particular case. Consider a suit for breach of contract brought by a corporation headquartered in one state against a corporation headquartered in another for events that occurred in a third, or a product liability suit by the owner of a car that was built in Michigan, sold in Illinois, and crashed in New York.

The rule for deciding jurisdiction is simple in principle, if not always in practice. Suppose I am a citizen of California and you of New York. Since I am suing you, I make the initial decision of what court to sue in. If I sue you in a state court in New York, your home state, the case will be decided by the New York court system. If I try to sue you in California, my home state, and if the California court decides that the case has sufficient connection to California to make my doing so appropriate (and the amount in controversy is more than $75,000), you then have the option of removing the case to federal court. The federal court, deciding a state law case under its diversity jurisdiction, then resolves the case according to California law. Alternatively, I could start by suing you in a federal court in New York.

Diversity cases are one way in which disputes get into the federal system. Another is by being appealed all the way up to the state's supreme court and from there to the U.S. Supreme Court on the grounds that they involve federal issues, such as claims that state law is inconsistent with federal law or the federal Constitution. A third is when the initial dispute involves federal rather than state law—for example, a criminal prosecution for violation of a federal narcotics law or a civil case involving charges that an employer violated federal antidiscrimination law. A fourth possibility is for the defendant in a state court to go to a federal court and initiate a suit asking to have the relevant state law declared invalid on federal grounds.

The pattern of the court system at the federal level is similar to that at the state level. A case comes into the system either as a case of first impression, to be tried by a federal court, or on appeal to the Supreme Court from a verdict already given by a state supreme court. A federal case may be appealed up the hierarchy of courts, first to a federal circuit court and from there to the Supreme Court. A circuit court must decide all cases appealed to it. The Supreme Court does not; it refuses far more cases than it accepts. Decisions at any level provide precedents for that level and those below.

Within the federal system there are multiple circuits, geographical areas, each with its own system of appeals courts. A case decided by a district court in the seventh circuit will be decided by the law of the seventh circuit, meaning that decisions by courts in that circuit, especially the circuit's highest level courts, will be given more weight as precedent than decisions by federal judges in other circuits. One reason the Supreme Court accepts cases is to resolve a conflict between the law of different circuits; opinions by the Supreme Court are, at least in theory, binding on everyone. A similar situation exists within the state court system, with disagreements ultimately decided by the state's supreme court.

It may have occurred to you by now to wonder how we can have a consistent legal system, rule by laws rather than by men, if law is judge-made, so that for a wide range of issues the law is whatever the judge says it is. One answer is provided by the system of appeals. If a judge is frequently reversed on appeal, that fact will be known both to his colleagues, who will conclude that he is incompetent, and to the attorneys who appear before him. Other judges will decline to follow his precedents; attorneys will routinely appeal his decisions. Thus a judge who rules according to his own preferences rather than his interpretation of the legal rules set by precedent may suffer serious reputational penalties and find that his decisions have limited effect on the final outcome of cases.

The obvious exception is the federal Supreme Court, which cannot be reversed, save by its future self. In my experience, at least, reading the explanations provided by the justices for their decisions can be a depressing experience, in part because they are written by men who know that, however bad their arguments, what they say goes:

> A federal judge can be lazy, lack judicial temperament, mistreat his staff, berate without reason the lawyers who appear before him, be reprimanded for ethical lapses, verge on or even slide into senility, be continually reversed for elementary legal mistakes, hold under advisement for years cases that could be decided perfectly well in days or weeks, leak confidential information to the press, pursue a nakedly political agenda, and misbehave in other ways that might get even a tenured civil servant or university professor fired; he will retain his office. (Richard Posner, Chief Judge of the Seventh Circuit, *Overcoming Law*, p. 111)

The Structure of Law

Seen from a suitable vantage point, say the first semester of law school, Anglo-American law is a confused and tangled mess of laws and precedents, torts and crimes, procedure and substance. One purpose of this book is to untangle it at a deep level, to develop a pattern of ideas in terms of which it is possible to make sense out of most of law. In this section I attempt a more modest task—to sort the mess into suitable piles, so that, in the next few chapters, we can try to make sense of one pile at a time.

The first big division is between criminal law and civil law. Under criminal law the plaintiff is the government; a typical case might be labeled "State v. Friedman." In civil law the plaintiff is normally a private party, although governments can and do dress up as private parties from time to time in order to prosecute cases under civil rather than criminal law.

One consequence of this difference is that fines under criminal law go to the government while damage payments under civil law go to the victim, the private party who is suing. Another is that only the government can drop a criminal prosecution. Legally speaking, the victim is not a party to the case, merely a witness. A civil case, on the other hand, can be settled out of court by an agreement between private plaintiff and private defendant.

Other differences between civil and criminal law will be discussed at greater length in later chapters, especially chapter 18, which deals with the question of whether we need both systems and if so why. Among the more notable are that criminal law makes use of punishments such as imprisonment and execution, while civil law relies mostly on money damages, and that criminal law requires a higher standard of proof for conviction, proof "beyond a reasonable doubt," rather than the civil requirement of "by the preponderance of the evidence."

Within civil law there are further divisions, not always sharply drawn, into categories such as property, tort, and contract. Property law deals with the ownership of things, especially but not exclusively land and buildings (referred to in the law as "real property," from which it follows that the computer on which I am writing this book is unreal, hence the book does not exist, hence I am free to go home and play computer games instead of finishing this chapter). Included in the law of property is the law of intellectual property: patent, copyright, trademark, trade secret, and related areas.

Tort law deals with torts, literally wrongs, actions by one person that wrongfully injure another person or his property. If you carelessly run me down with your automobile, I will sue you for damages, a tort action. If you publish a hostile review of this book, I may sue you for defamation (and lose, even though everything you said is wrong, since it is well established that the rules limiting attacks on authors do not apply to attacks on their books), another tort action. Very loosely, one may think of tort law as the civil counterpart of criminal law, a set of legal rules designed to impose costs on people who do things that injure other people. But tort law, unlike criminal law, has built into it the principle of compensation; the tortfeasor is supposed to pay sufficient damages to his victim to "make him whole"—as well off as if the wrongful act had not occurred.

A third area of civil law is the law of contracts, the legal rules that determine when a contract has been formed, what obligations it imposes on the parties, and what recourse one party has against another for violating the agreement.

In trying to make some rough sense out of these categories, a useful starting point is the question of who has a right against whom, what determines what it is, and why. Contract law is the clearest case. I have a right against you (and you against me) because we have signed a contract. The particular rules of this contract were drawn up by us, within the constraints permitted by more general rules of contract law created by courts and legislatures.

The most striking difference between contract law and property law is that while a contract right is good only against the other party to the contract, a property right is good against the world; I can legally prevent you from trespassing on my land, or violating my copyright, without first getting your agreement. The same is true of tort law; my right not to be assaulted or defamed by you does not require your consent either. But while property law defines a bundle of rights associated with objects— somewhat metaphorical objects in the case of intellectual property—that belong to one person and can be transferred to another, tort law's central concern is with a bundle of rights associated with a person.

Contract law and property law resemble each other, however, in a different way: In both cases what rights you have in part depend on past agreements. But while contract rights are created out of thin air by the contracting parties, the owner of property starts with a preexisting bundle of rights defined by property law: the right to prevent people from trespassing on his land by the use of fences but not by the use of land mines, to prevent trespassers from passing a foot above his land but not airplanes from passing a mile above. Those rights can be transferred to someone else, and to some limited extent they may be unbundled first, as when a landowner sells an easement permitting a neighbor to cross his land, and then sells the land, subject to the easement, to someone else. But property transactions do not create new rights. To do that requires contract.

The traditional categories of property, tort, and contract are convenient ways of thinking about the law, but it does not follow that an actual legal dispute can always be neatly classified as one of them. An important issue in property law is just what rights ownership of property implies—and it shows up, among other places, in tort suits by one landowner against another under the common law of nuisance. Breach of contract is, under some, but not all, circumstances, a tort, and it is tortious for A to persuade B to breach his contract with C. A lease is both a contract between landlord and tenant and the transfer of a property interest, the right to control the land for a certain number of years.

Putting things in the right piles is a useful first step in housekeeping—too often, in my case, also the last step. In the case of legal rules, these particular piles are of considerable practical significance for those involved in litigation. Tort, contract, and property each has its own set of legal rules, differing in a variety of details. Whether a particular breach of contract is or is not tortious determines, among other things, what is or is not included in the damages that the successful plaintiff is entitled to collect.

Beyond these large categories, there are additional areas of law that either do not fit neatly into any of them, such as antitrust law and regulatory law, or provide a background for all of them, such as rules of procedure and jurisdiction.

One final distinction among sorts of laws is implicit in the first section of this chapter, the distinction among laws according to where they come from. On this basis there are three major classes of law in the United States: statutory law, judge-made or common law, and constitutional law.

Here again the distinction is far from tidy. Statutes such as the copyright act exist to implement parts of the Constitution, so disputes involve the question of what the act says and of what the Constitution implies that the act must, or may not, do. And neither statutes nor constitutions interpret themselves, so statute law and constitutional law, at the point at which they actually decide cases, are heavily overlaid with the decisions of the judges that have interpreted them in the past.

One result is to make "common law" a somewhat ambiguous term. Broadly speaking, it describes judge-made law in contrast to legislative or constitutional law. But where that line should be drawn is far from clear. This question is of particular interest to us because the economic analysis of law, as it has actually developed, has been heavily influenced by Judge Posner's conjecture that common law, but not statutory law, tends to be economically efficient. In order to test that conjecture one must first figure out what law is or is not common.

Our perspective on law in this book is functional: We view a system of legal rules as a tool with a purpose. But legal rules are also historical facts, produced by a long history of legal development. Even if it turns out that a large part of the structure can be explained on functional grounds, we must also expect to find embedded in it rules that can be explained, if at all, only by historical accident.

10

Mine, Thine, and Ours: The Economics of Property Law

PROPERTY SEEMS SUCH a simple idea: Things belong to people, and the owner of each thing gets to control how it is used. Like many simple things it becomes more and more complicated the longer you think about it.

In chapter 5 we looked at some of the complications and saw how, in principle, one might determine an efficient set of property rights. In this chapter we extend the argument in two directions: What an owner owns, and why some things, property, are owned and some, commons, are unowned.

Bundling Rights: What an Owner Owns

The idea of a thing belonging to a person is fairly clear when the thing is an automobile or a pair of pants. It is less clear when the thing is a piece of land. What rights does my ownership give me? Almost certainly I can farm the land, or build on it, or keep off trespassers. But can I prevent airplanes from flying over it, miners from tunneling under it, neighbors from making loud noises near it? If it is my land, does that mean I can forbid radio stations from broadcasting without my permission, on the theory that if I can pick up the signal, the radio waves must be trespassing on my property?

What I own is not a thing called land but a bundle of rights. Some rights almost always go in the bundle associated with a particular piece of land, such as the right to walk on it and forbid others from doing so. Other rights associated with the land, such as the right to forbid trespassers at various distances above or below it and the right to have the surface stay put instead of sliding into someone else's coal mine, may or may not be found in the same bundle.

Chapters 4 and 5 sketched out the economic approach to designing efficient legal rules. It starts with two questions: To whom is a particular right most valuable, and, if we do not know that for certain, what initial definition of rights makes it easiest to move the rights to the person to whom they turn out to be most valuable?

When constructing bundles of rights the first question becomes "Which rights belong together?" If I own the right to farm the land, the right to walk on the land is worth more to me than to anyone else, so the two belong in the same bundle. Since it is hard to grow crops if other people are free to tramp through your fields, the right to exclude trespassers probably belongs in the bundle as well. But that depends in part on how the land is going to be used. If it is timber instead of corn, the argument is not so clear. In some legal systems ownership of land implies only a very limited right to exclude trespassers.

The right to forbid radio waves from passing over my property, on the other hand, is of very little use to me. If every property owner had that right, setting up a radio station would require unanimous consent from every owner within range of the broadcast, making a transfer of the right from the owners to the person to whom it is of most value a prohibitively difficult transaction. It makes more sense to have legal rules in which the right to broadcast on a particular frequency is entirely separate from the ownership of the land over which the broadcast passes. Similar arguments suggest that the right to forbid airliners from trespassing a mile above my fields would be of little value to me, and moving it to those to whom it was of most value would be hard. That right, too, is left out of the bundle.

A more difficult problem arises when a single right is associated with two different, typically adjacent, pieces of land. The right to control sound waves crossing into my property, to forbid you from playing loud music or setting off firecrackers close to my property line at three in the morning, for example, is valuable to me. But the right to control sound waves crossing out of your property, to make noises that I can hear from my side of the property line, is valuable to you.

The same problem arises when two properties are adjacent vertically rather than horizontally. In Pennsylvania, a state constructed largely out of coal, rights to land are made up of three separable estates: the surface estate, the mineral estate, and the support estate. If I own the surface estate and the support estate and you own the mineral estate, you are free to mine the coal under my land but must leave enough of it to support the surface. If my house falls into your mine, you have violated my rights. If, on the other hand, you own both the mineral estate and the support estate, I may own the surface, but I have no legal right to have it supported by anything. The support estate is valuable both to the owner of the surface, who wants something under his house to hold it up, and to the miner, who wants to be able to get out all of the coal. So it makes sense for the law to permit transactions between the owner of the surface and the owner of the mining rights to move the support right to whoever values it most.

The same problem sometimes arises between neighbors who are adjacent horizontally. If I dig too deep a pit on my side of the property line, your land may start to slide into it. Under English common law, a landowner has a right to lateral support, meaning that his neighbor has a duty to continue to provide the support that the adjacent land would receive under natural conditions.

Such conflicts are the subject of the common law of nuisance, the area of law that inspired Coase's work. The analysis of railroads and farmers in chapter 5 was a sketch of how, at least in principle, questions about who owns which rights in the bundle and how they can be enforced would be decided in an efficient legal system. We will return to the subject again in chapter 14.

In chapter 5, after discussing property and liability rules as alternative approaches to enforcing property rights, I briefly mentioned another alternative, controlling property by majority vote. That turns out to be a common, and arguably efficient, rule for controlling the use of fugitive mineral resources: oil and gas.

Consider a group of landowners sitting on top of a large pool of oil. If I drill a well on my property and start pumping, all the oil will eventually belong to me, since as oil flows out from under my land it is replaced by oil flowing in from under yours. (Geologists, including the one I am married to, will, I hope, forgive my oversimplification of the geological facts.) My well imposes an externality on you in the form of lost oil; your well, if you drill it, will impose a similar externality on me. It is in each person's interest to drill too many wells and pump them too fast, making all of us worse off. We are in a prisoner's dilemma with multiple prisoners.

One solution is unitization. In some states a sufficiently large majority of the landowners over such a pool—frequently two-thirds are required—can vote to unitize the pool. Doing so converts the oil from the private property of whoever owns the land immediately above it to the joint property of all the landowners. The landowners as a group then agree on how the oil is to be extracted and share the resulting income. Conflicts of interest among the landowners are reduced by legal rules requiring equal treatment; a majority group cannot simply vote to pump all the oil and give the income to its members. Similar rules forbid a majority group of stockholders in a corporation from transferring the firm's assets to themselves at the expense of the minority stockholders.

In all of these cases the relevant legal rules can be thought of as a way of defining and bundling rights so as to achieve the most efficient possible outcome. Whether that approach explains the rules we have or provides reasons why we should have different rules is less clear. Coase's conclusion was that, in the case of the common law of nuisance, the evidence suggested that judges were at least trying to produce something close to efficient rules.

Property versus Commons

For a noneconomist the first and most obvious question about private property is why we have such a silly institution. Why not forget selfish notions of thine and mine and let everyone use everything whenever he needs it?

There are two reasons why that does not work. The first is that you and I cannot simultaneously drive the same car to different places, nor can I drive my car very far if your previous use has left it with an empty gas tank and a flat tire. We need some way of deciding who gets to use what when, preferably a way that results in the person to whom something is most valuable getting it. Private property and exchange solve that problem, for reasons sketched in chapter 2. If the use of my property is more valuable to you than to me, you will be willing to offer a price that I will be willing to accept.

The second reason is that most of the things we treat as private property are things that somebody must make, and making things is costly. If making things results in owning them, that gives you a reason to make them. Not only does it provide an incentive, it provides the right incentive: You will make something if and only if its value to whoever values it most, either you or the person you plan to sell it to, is at least as great as the cost of making it. That is the efficient rule.

The puzzle for the noneconomist is why anything is private property. The puzzle for the economist is why anything is not. Having found such an elegant solution to the problem of producing and allocating things, why not apply it universally?

If you think the answer is that we should, consider extending intellectual property law to cover the English language. Words become private property, each belonging to its first user or his heir or assign. Before speaking a sentence you must first license rights to each word.

There would be some advantages to propertizing language. The owner of a word could prevent the sort of overuse by which words are rendered almost meaningless: "nice," for example, or "awful." Perhaps more important, it would provide an incentive for creative neologism. The English language is sadly lacking in gender-neutral pronouns, leaving us with the choice of "he-she-or-it" or misusing "they" to produce such ungrammatical barbarisms as "this policy covers the customer even if they drop dead of a heart attack tomorrow." If the first person to invent and popularize a euphonious and intuitive set of gender-neutral pronouns were able to collect license fees thereafter from everyone who used them, perhaps the problem would be solved.

There are advantages to propertizing the language, but also very large disadvantages. The transaction costs associated with writing or speaking, in a world of private words, would be very high. I suspect that they would more than outweigh any advantage due to more rapid linguistic innovation. It would be a very quiet world.

The argument is not limited to intellectual property. Consider property rights among primitive peoples. Some have private property in land, some do not. Why?

It is tempting to answer that the ones who do not have private property in land are too primitive to have thought of the idea. But that cannot be an adequate answer, because some groups have private property in land for only part of the year. They know of the concept and practice it—part time.

A more plausible answer starts with the observation that, since primitive people probably know more about their conditions than we do, their legal rules may well be efficient ones for their circumstances. Consider land used part of the year for agriculture and part of the year for hunting large animals across. Private property is very useful for agriculture, since there is little point in planting and weeding if other people are free to do the harvesting and eating. Private property in land being hunted over, on the other hand, means stopping at every border to ask permission to cross, while your quarry vanishes into the distance. The sensible rule is for the animal you are hunting to be private property, belonging to the hunter who first spotted it, while the land you are hunting it over is common property. If hunters depend on the rest of the community to bring them word of game, that rule may be efficiently modified to include a claim by others to a share of the kill.

For a less exotic example of land owned in common, consider the various sorts of joint tenancy, common tenancy, tenancy by the entirety, and life interest with reversion that law students encounter in studying prop- erty law. All raise the usual problem of common ownership, the risk that each party, in deciding how to use the land, will ignore the interests of the other. Legal doctrines such as the law of waste, which forbids a life tenant from altering property in ways injurious to the interest of the person to whom the property will revert, have evolved as attempts by the common law to deal with that problem.

A more recent example of common property is information on the Internet. While some providers choose to charge for information, many others, myself among them, deliberately give it away to all comers. And the standard procedure for getting e-mail from computer A to computer G through intermediate computers B–F involves no charge by the owners of the intermediate machines to the owners of the machines whose mail they are forwarding.

Charging for information online, although possible, is costly, with the result that porn sites do it and most of the rest of us don't bother. Instead we rely on indirect ways of getting paid for the information we give away—advertising for commercial sites, the pleasure of spreading our ideas and showing off pictures of ourselves and our children for non-commercial sites. That works because the cost of distributing information, measured per user, is small enough to be covered by such indirect methods. Charging for forwarding the packets of information into which e–mail dissolves itself when it leaves the host computer would require enormous numbers of tiny charges, currently an unreasonably expensive procedure (although that may be changing). Instead the ground rule for host computers is "I'll forward your packets if you'll forward mine."

There are many examples of firms that routinely give things away. An all-you-can-eat restaurant charges for entry, but once inside additional food is free. Most Internet service providers follow the same policy—a fixed monthly fee for unlimited service. Whether or not we can explain the failure of primitive people to maintain property rights in land by simple ignorance, we cannot explain AOL's pricing policy that way. A more plausible explanation is that such firms are balancing the inefficiency due to overuse, an additional serving of food that is worth ten cents to you and costs the restaurant twenty cents to produce, against the cost savings from not having to restrict and monitor use.

These examples suggest one reason why private property is sometimes not worth having: the cost of the transactions necessary to move it from one person to another. That is the obvious explanation of why we do not want English words to be private property. A second is the cost and difficulty of defining and recognizing boundaries—which brings me to the story of the floating island.

The Floating Island

Stack Island in the Mississippi belonged to someone. Over a period of many years the river's current eroded the upstream end of Stack Island and deposited sediment at the downstream end, with the result that Stack Island gradually drifted downstream.

Some distance below Stack Island the west bank of the river belonged to someone else, along with all islands in the section of river east of his property. After a very long time one of them was Stack Island. Who owned it?

The resulting law case was settled on grounds of adverse possession: The court, by holding that the owner of the coastal strip had waited too long to assert his rights, avoided having to rule on whether he had any rights to assert. What I like about the case is that it illuminates one of the unstated assumptions of ordinary property law—that boundaries stay where they are put, permitting us to define what we own in an unambiguous way. The property rights that came into conflict in that case were defined in a perfectly clear and sensible fashion as long as islands stayed put. In a world where Stack Island was the norm instead of the exception, where the physical boundaries defining property claims shifted around in an unanticipated and ambiguous fashion, defining those boundaries and arbitrating the resulting disputes might be a significant cost of maintaining a system of private property.

Consider the following description of land law in the Sudan:

> You cannot understand a Nile land case without understanding how the river behaves. As it rises and falls in its annual cycle, fertile land in the riverbed is arable for seven or eight months, then disappears again beneath the water. One year a particular tract may fail to reappear, and the owner loses his land. Five years later land appears again in that same place. Does the old owner still have rights to it? If he is dead, who does have rights to it? Perhaps an island has vanished under the flood. It reappears a quarter of mile downstream in slightly different form. Does the owner of the lost island own the new one? . . . The banks of the Nile also occasionally tend to swing back and forth, and, according to the custom that prevails in most places, as the riverbanks move, so does riverbank land. Everyone's property swings with the river. Even people whose land is some distance from the water are affected when the channel takes a turn in their direction. Properties near and far move like connected pieces of armor, in concert with the unpredictable water. (John McPhee, *A Roomful of Hovings*, pp. 162–63, in part quoting Carroll W. Brewster)

That is a topic we will return to in the next chapter. In the law of real property fuzzy boundaries are the exception. In patent law, which tries to draw boundaries around ideas, they are the norm.

Why We Owe Civilization to the Dogs

The date is 10,000 or 11,000 B.C. You are a member of a primitive tribe that farms its land in common. Farming land in common is a pain; you spend almost as much time watching each other and arguing about who is or is not doing his share as you do scratching the ground with pointed sticks and pulling weeds.

You are primitive but not stupid—stupid people don't live long in your environment—and it has occurred to several of you that the problem would disappear if you converted the common land to private property. Each person would farm his own land; if your neighbor chose not to work very hard, it would be he and his children, not you and yours, that would go hungry.

There is a problem with this solution, one you observed when a neighboring tribe tried it a few years back. Private property does not enforce itself. Someone has to make sure that the lazy neighbor doesn't solve his food shortage at your expense. Instead of spending your days making sure your fellow tribesmen are working hard harvesting the common fields, you will have to spend your nights making sure they are not working hard harvesting your fields. All things considered, you conclude that communal farming is the least bad solution.

Agricultural land continues to be treated as a commons for another thousand years, until somebody makes a radical technological innovation: the domestication of the dog. Dogs, being territorial animals, can be taught to identify their owner's property as their territory and respond appropriately to trespassers. Now you can convert to private property in agricultural land and sleep soundly. Think of it as the bionic burglar alarm.

I do not remember who first proposed this explanation for the rise of private property in land, and I do not know enough anthropology and prehistory to judge how plausible it is. But, *Si non e vero, e ben trovato*— if it isn't true, it ought to be. Just as the story of the floating island conveniently symbolizes the problem of defining boundaries, so the tale of the bionic burglar alarm, of how we owe the crucial step in human civilization to the dog, symbolizes the problem of enforcing those boundaries and the fact that if enforcing them is too costly it may not be worth doing. That subject too will be revisited in the next chapter, where we see how changes in the technology of copying have taken us from a world where publishers successfully enforced rights that, legally speaking, they did not have to a world where they are unable to enforce rights that, legally speaking, they do have.

The Most Expensive Mistake the U.S. Government Ever Made?

So far we have discussed problems associated with defining property and enforcing property rights. Additional problems arise with the initial creation of property rights, the process that determines who owns what.

Like many things we will discuss, the incentive to acquire property rights is sometimes a bug and sometimes a feature. In the case of things whose value is created by human efforts, it is a feature; the fact that you get ownership of a car by building one provides people an incentive to build cars.

In the case of land, on the other hand, most of which is not created by human effort, the incentives associated with the creation of property rights may have less attractive consequences. Consider the economic implications of homesteading, the mechanism by which large parts of the United States became private property. Under the Homestead Act of 1862 a settler obtained ownership of a quarter section of land, 160 acres, by farming it for a fixed number of years and meeting a variety of other requirements such as successfully growing fruit trees on it.

The year is 1862; the piece of land we are considering is beyond the margin of settlement, too far from railroads, feed stores, and other people to be cultivated at a profit. As time passes and settlement expands, that situation changes. The efficient rule would be to start farming the land the first year that doing so becomes profitable, say 1890.

But if you set out to homestead the land in 1890, you will get an unpleasant surprise; someone else is already there. Homesteading land that it is already profitable to farm is an attractive proposition, since you not only make money in the process, you also end up with valuable real estate. When valuable rights are being given away for free, there is no shortage of takers. If you want to get the land you will have to come early. By farming it at a loss for a few years you can acquire the right to farm it thereafter at a profit.

How early will you have to come? To make things simple, assume the value of the land in 1890 is going to be twenty thousand dollars, representing the present value of the profit that can be made by farming it from then on. Further assume that the loss from farming it earlier than that is a thousand dollars a year. If you try to homestead it in 1880, you again find the land already taken. Someone who homesteads in 1880 pays ten thousand dollars in losses for twenty thousand dollars in real estate—not as good as getting it for free, but still an attractive deal. Working through the logic of the argument, we conclude that the land will be claimed about 1870, just early enough so that the losses in the early years balance the later gains. It follows that the effect of the Homestead Act was to wipe out, in costs of premature farming, a large part of the land value of the United States.

If you think this argument looks familiar, you are right. The logic of homesteading is the same as the logic of theft, discussed back in chapter 3; both are examples of rent seeking. The thief spends resources in time and effort in order that he rather than you will end up possessing your television set. The homesteader spends resources in order that he, rather than the next possible claimant, will end up possessing a particular piece of land. In each case actors are competing with each other to get something valuable that already exists and, in the process, spending resources roughly equal to the value of what they are getting.

In this case as in the other one, a full analysis would be somewhat more complicated. Some people are better at settling land than others, just as some are better at stealing than others. In equilibrium the marginal homesteader or the marginal thief just breaks even. The particularly skilled homesteader or thief makes a profit. It follows that homesteading did not dissipate all of the value of the land, just a large part of it.

Or Maybe Not—In Defense of Homesteading

Terry Andersen and P. J. Hill, the economists whose argument I have just summarized, concluded that what the government should have done was to auction off the land. That way the settlers' rent-seeking expenditure would have gone to pay the federal government's bills instead of being wasted growing crops not worth the cost of growing and trying to keep fruit trees alive in places nature intended for prairie. What they did not explain was why the government, which owned the land and, then as now, always had uses for money, didn't do it that way.

The answer is that they tried. From shortly after the Revolution there were repeated attempts by both state and federal governments to raise money by auctioning off land from the public domain. But there was a problem.

The federal government has announced that a particular territory is about to be opened to the public, with land auctions held locally to allow buyers to inspect the land they are bidding on. You, as the representative of a real estate syndicate in Boston, head out to the Wild West, somewhere in what will be eastern Ohio, to buy some land.

To your surprise you discover that, although the land has not yet been opened for settlement, it is already settled. Most of the people at the auction, held ninety miles from nowhere, are squatters, illegal settlers bidding for the land they are already farming, rough, tough frontiersmen with knives in their boots and flintlock rifles leaned up against the wall. They make it very clear to you that whatever may happen back east, out here bidding against a settler for "his land" just isn't done—and leave it to you to figure out for yourself what may happen to you if you do it. Each settler ends up buying a quarter section of land, the best land he could find when he arrived and settled a few years earlier, at the minimum auction price, because nobody else is bidding for "his" land. All that is left for you is the land that nobody else wants.

Sometimes the process was even simpler. When the land was about to be opened for settlement, the people already living there would petition Congress, arguing that as brave frontiersmen they were entitled to special treatment. The government could raise revenue auctioning off other land to other people, but they were entitled to buy the land they had settled at the minimum legal price. Quite often it worked. Settlers, even squatters, are also voters.

As these examples, somewhat stylized from the real history, suggest, land sales in law often turned into homesteading in practice, which may be why the federal government eventually gave up and wrote homesteading into the law.

As a final note in defense of homesteading, there is the possibility that the squatters were right and the economists were wrong. The squatters, after all, really were brave frontiersmen. One of the things they did by settling was help maintain the U.S. claim to the land against both native inhabitants and rival governments to north and south. One way of de-

fending homesteading is to argue that giving homesteaders a claim to land they settle, like giving auto companies a claim to the cars they produce, actually produced a useful incentive—not to create the land but to go out and defend it. From the standpoint of the government that gave out the land, homesteading was a productive activity. From a broader standpoint, one that includes in the calculation of economic efficiency the interests of Canadians, Mexicans, and American Indians, it was still rent seeking, but on a larger scale.

Whether or not that is a plausible defense for what happened, the logic of inefficient homesteading, the Hill and Andersen story of how the government burned up the value of the public lands, provides one more reason why making things into property may not always be a good idea. We will return to that subject in the next chapter, where we consider intellectual property law as a way of propertizing previously unowned intellectual property and see under what circumstances the result is inefficient rent seeking.

On the Other Hand: The Benefits of Property

So far we have been looking at costs of treating things as property, problems of defining, enforcing, and transacting over property rights. Whether it is worth paying those costs depends on how large the benefits are that flow from the incentives for efficient production and allocation created by private property.

Suppose you believe that, even without copyright, plenty of novels would be written. Great writers, you might argue, are motivated not by money but by the desire for fame or love for their art. As evidence, you point out that much of the world's great literature, including the work of Homer, Dante, and Shakespeare, predates copyright law.

If this argument is right, then the incentive to produce property in order to own it is not very important in the case of literature, which weakens the argument for copyright law. The second advantage of property rights is better allocation of existing goods, and since my reading a novel does not keep you from reading the same novel, allocation is not a problem in the case of literature. We cannot simultaneously drive the same car to our different homes, but we can simultaneously read (different copies of) the same novel. And what copyright law propertizes is the novel, the sequence of words, not the physical book. The book would be private property even without copyright law.

To put the argument in slightly more technical language, the benefit from an additional incentive to produce depends on supply elasticity, on how sensitive the amount produced is to the price the producer gets for producing it. If supply is very inelastic, then incentives don't matter very much, and you get almost as many novels without copyright law as with it. If supply is very elastic, on the other hand, abolishing copyright law would result in a drastic reduction in the supply of new literature.

A similar argument applies on the demand side. Consider an all-you-can-eat restaurant. If it serves salad, the fact that additional servings are free will result in only a small inefficiency. Additional servings cost the restaurant twenty cents apiece but cost me nothing; underpricing them by twenty cents causes only a modest increase in how much I eat. And my extra consumption, although inefficient, is not very inefficient; in the worst case I am consuming a serving of salad that is worth about a penny to me and costs the restaurant twenty cents, for a net efficiency loss of nineteen cents.

Contrast to that an all-you-can-eat sushi bar—in my experience a much rarer institution. Making sushi is a skilled job, and the individual pieces are, as a result, quite expensive. Dropping the price I pay for additional servings from three dollars to zero would result in my leaving inefficiently full. And the last sushi I ate before finally surrendering to the geometric limits of my stomach would represent an efficiency loss of about $2.99.

So in deciding whether it is worth making something property, you must consider two different questions. How large, for this particular sort of something, are the costs associated with treating it as property rather than commons, how easy is it to define boundaries, enforce rights, transact? How large, for this particular sort of something, are the benefits of treating it as property? How sensitive are producers and consumers to the perverse incentive effects of a zero price?

Real Property and Unreal Property

All property consists of bundles of rights with regard to things. But property in land, known in law as *real property*, has a special characteristic—to a considerable extent owners are free to rebundle it. I can sell my neighbor an easement, such as permission to cross my property. Once I have done so the easement is not merely a contract between him and me but, like other property, a right good against the world. If I sell the property to someone else, the easement binds him too—even though he never agreed to it and may not have known it existed. This feature of property law makes it easier for owners of adjacent pieces of property to coordinate their activity. Having purchased an easement to cross your land, I can build a new house without worrying that a future owner might withdraw his permission, leaving me stranded.

Suppose, on the other hand, that I sell you a car. As a member of a particularly extreme sect of Orthodox Judaism, I believe that not only should I not work on the Sabbath, my car should not work on the Sabbath either. So one of the conditions of the sale, to which you agree, is that, from the time the sun sets Friday to the time the sun sets Saturday, the car may not be driven.

That condition is a contract, enforceable against you. But if you sell the car to someone else, it is not enforceable against her. I might have provided in the original contract that you would sell only to a purchaser who accepted the agreement, but that term would bind you, not the new buyer. I can sue you for breach of contract, but I cannot stop her from taking a Saturday drive.

There is a simple and obvious reason for this difference between real property and everything else. Ownership of land is controlled by an elaborate recording system, involving title deeds, land registries, and the like. Restrictions such as easements that run with the land are part of that system, so a diligent buyer will in fact know about the easement. A diligent buyer of a car will know if the car is encumbered by loans, because that encumbrance is included in our system for registering title, but that is all he will know. And a diligent buyer of most other goods will not know even that much.

To put the same argument in the language of an earlier part of this chapter, Stack Island is the exception not the rule. Most property in land is easy to draw lines around. Not only is it easy to draw lines marking the physical boundaries of a piece of land, it is also, thanks to the registration system, fairly easy to draw boundaries around the bundle of rights that the owner has with regard to that piece of land—boundaries that other people can, if they wish, observe. Thus it is practical to allow a considerable degree of rebundling. The argument in favor of doing so is implied by several of the arrows on chapter 5's spaghetti diagram. Permission to throw sparks is an easement.

Property in other things is still good against the world, but it comes in a one-size-fits-all version. You either own something or you don't. The purchaser of stolen property does not, as a general rule, have good title, although there are exceptions. But the purchaser of property whose use is encumbered by contract, for example a contract not to drive the property on Saturday, does have good title. Property title is good against the world; contractual obligations are good against the person who signed the contract.

If our willingness to permit rebundling of real property is due to a recording system that makes it possible for third-party purchasers to find out what they are getting, one implication is that the ability to rebundle should be limited by the ability of third parties to find out about it. Roughly speaking, it is. As a general rule, an easement is binding on later purchasers only if its existence can be deduced, or at least suspected, from inspecting the land, or if a prudent search of the relevant records would reveal it.

Rule versus Regulation: The Touch and Concern Doctrine

> A servitude . . . is invalid if the restraint is
> unreasonable. Reasonableness is determined by
> weighing the utility of the restraint against the
> injurious consequences of enforcing the restraint.
> (*Restatement (third) of Property, Servitudes,*
> *§3.4, 1991*)

Property rights can be rebundled, making it possible to create rights associated with land that are good against future owners. Such rights include not only easements, such as the right to cross land, but also licenses, such as the right to use land—to hunt on it or mine under it. They also include covenants running with the land, such as an agreement that plots in a residential development will be used only for residential, not commercial, purposes—the private equivalent of zoning regulations. An elaborate body of law determines under what circumstances such agreements are enforceable against whom.

One interesting feature of that body of laws is that, although the details vary over time and from jurisdiction to jurisdiction, it is generally easier to pass a benefit to future buyers than a burden. Suppose I have made a legally binding covenant with my neighbor, agreeing not to build a factory on my land near his residence. It is more likely that my selling my property will extinguish that covenant, leaving him with no recourse against the new owner, than that his selling his property will extinguish the covenant, leaving the new owner with no recourse against me.

There is an economic reason for that pattern. The right to rebundle makes sense because of the ability of buyers to know what they are buying. If you are selling land with a benefit attached—a right not to have your neighbor do things that would reduce the value of the land—you have every reason to tell the purchaser about it. If, on the other hand, I am selling land with a burden attached—an obligation not to use land in ways in which a new owner might want to use it—I have an incentive not to tell the purchaser. Hence the legal requirements that define, roughly speaking, how obvious the existence of the covenant must be in order for it to be binding on a new owner are stricter for passing burdens than for passing benefits.

A second issue that arises when we are rebundling rights to land is just what can be included in the bundle. If there is no restriction at all, then all rights become rebundleable. All I have to do is to merge my ownership of my car with my ownership of a piece of land, making all of the rights associated with both of them sticks in a common bundle of rights. Since that bundle is a set of rights associated with real property, it can be rebundled. So I pull out the right to drive the car six days a week and sell it to you, retaining the right to drive—or not drive—the car on Saturday.

The common law prevented such juggling by requiring that any covenant that ran with the land must involve a burden or benefit that touched or concerned the land. Your Saturday driving of the car I sold you does not touch or concern my land, so that right cannot run with my land.

What if I sold you a piece of my land, along with a covenant by which I agreed to supply, and you to buy at a fixed price, water from my well? Access to water may be relevant to the value of your land, so your right to get it concerns the land you bought. But once you have chosen to drill your own well, does my right to be paid for the water you no longer want to buy still run with your land?

Modern courts have to some degree abandoned this doctrine in favor of the rule quoted at the beginning of this section: Covenants are enforceable if they are reasonable. Roughly speaking, that means that they are enforceable if the court believes that they are economically efficient and unenforceable otherwise.

In chapter 4 I pointed out two different ways in which a court might deal with externalities. It might decide in each case which party was the lowest-cost avoider of the problem and assign rights accordingly on a case-by-case basis, or it might establish general rules designed to get problems resolved as efficiently as possible. The same issue arises here. The old approach was to use a general rule, the "touch and concern" doctrine, to help determine whether a covenant was merely a contract between two parties or was part of the ownership of land, and thus to determine what rights could be rebundled. The new approach moves closer to judicial determination, in each case, of whether rebundling is or is not desirable.

One reason for the change may have been that the rule the common law had come up with did not serve the function of a rule very well—it was sufficiently vague so that parties were faced with considerable uncertainty as to whether courts would or would not enforce particular covenants. Whether the new approach will do better remains to be seen.

Further Reading

Terry Anderson and P. J. Hill, "Privatizing the Commons: An Improvement?" *Southern Economic Journal* 50, no. 2 (October 1983): 438–50.

The source for my discussion of property rights among primitive people is Martin Bailey, "The Approximate Optimality of Aboriginal Property Rights," *Journal of Law and Economics* 35 (1992): 183.

11

Clouds and Barbed Wire: The Economics of Intellectual Property

> The Congress shall have power . . .
> To promote the progress of science and useful arts
> by securing for limited times to authors and
> inventors the exclusive right to their respective
> writings and discoveries.
>   (*U.S. Constitution, Article I, Section 8*)

THE CLAUSE in the Constitution that covers intellectual property mentions two categories of protectable creations: writings and discoveries. It says nothing about differences in how the two sorts of creations are to be protected. Yet U.S. law, following earlier English law, provides two entirely different systems of protection: copyright law for writings, patent law for inventions. In this chapter we will try to make sense of the differences in the two bodies of law and the allocation of the various sorts of intellectual creation to the different categories, using ideas worked out in chapter 10. The first step is a brief sketch of copyright law, patent law, and how they differ.

Copyright: The Law

> [W]here both . . . central characters have
> miraculous strength and speed; conceal their
> strength, along with their skin-tight acrobatic
> costumes, beneath their ordinary clothing; are
> termed champions of the oppressed; crush guns;
> stop bullets; and leap over or from buildings.
>   (*Detective Comics, Inc. v. Bruns Publications*)

Copyright was originally available only for writings but has since been expanded to cover computer programs, pictures, music, and much else. What it controls is the right to make copies (and derivative works, such as translations). This raises the question of exactly what feature of the work it is that you are not permitted to copy. The standard answer is that copyright law protects expression but not idea. If I copy a chapter from your novel, I have violated your copyright. If I instead copy the plot, the idea of your novel, while providing my own characters, incidents, and background, your copyright has not been violated. Patent law, in contrast, protects idea, not expression. What you patent is not a particular machine but a set of ideas that are embodied in that machine and could be embodied in other machines.

The distinction between idea and expression blurs on close study. Is a superhero who can see through walls, is impervious to bullets, and jumps over tall buildings at a single bound an *idea*, expressed in a particular Superman comic, or an *expression* of the idea of a superhuman being?

That particular question has been settled by the courts; Superman won an infringement suit against an imitator who had borrowed too many of his characteristics. The issue remains unsettled in the newer and more important context of software copyrights. Is the Lotus 123 menu tree, the particular pattern of commands used by what was for some years the dominant spreadsheet, an idea, expressed in the form of a particular program, or an expression of the idea of using key commands to make a spreadsheet do things?

That became an important legal issue some years back when several software companies produced clones of Lotus 123. Their programs, written from scratch without copying any Lotus code, were designed to work like Lotus, using the same commands in the same pattern so as to make it easy for customers to switch over without retraining. The result of extended litigation was ambiguous, with some courts taking one side, some the other; the one decision that reached the Supreme Court was permitted to stand on a 4-4 tie vote. While it is clear that copying someone else's computer code or the precise appearance of the screens it produces is a violation of copyright, it is unclear at what point beyond such literal copying protectable expression turns into unprotectable idea.

One restriction of copyright is that it applies only to expression, not idea. A second is that it applies only to copies, not independent creations, even if they happen to be identical to the copyrighted material. If I independently write a chapter that reads exactly like your chapter and can prove it, my chapter is not covered by your copyright.

The probability that two authors will independently write the same chapter is not very high. But consider the analogous case in computer law. In order to clone the IBM PC, to make computers that would run the same software in the same way, it was necessary to produce functional equivalents for the ROM chips built into the original. Those chips contained firmware, bits of computer code that the computer used for various basic functions. Computer code is covered by copyright. The companies designing the chip sets that would make cloning possible had to find some way of reproducing the function of the chips without copying them.

The solution was to set up two teams of engineers. Team A examined the IBM chips, read the computer instructions built into them, and figured out, in agonizing detail, exactly what they did. The result was a set of functional specifications: If you put this number in this memory location, this is what happens. When the specifications were complete, describing what the engineers believed to be all of the functions of the chip, they were handed to team B.

Members of team B, the "clean room" team, were never permitted to look at either the original chips or the code they contained. Their function was to reverse engineer the chip. They had to write code that would do exactly what the IBM code did, based on the specifications produced by team A, without seeing or copying the original.

If you set out to duplicate the detailed functionality of a lot of short bits of computer code, including the exact memory locations that numbers have to be put into or read out of, the code you produce is likely to look very much like the code in the original. It might even be identical. But for the purpose of the copyright law that doesn't matter. Copyright law protects only against copying.

For me to write the same chapter you wrote is quite unlikely; if we wanted to wait until it happened by pure chance, we would need a good supply of candles, since the sun is unlikely to last that long. And if it did happen by accident, perhaps with something much shorter than a chapter, it would be very hard to prove. For the clean room team to end up re-creating from the specifications large chunks of the original code is very much more likely, which is why their employers took great care to make sure they could prove in court that what they came up with was independently created, not copied. They were copying the function of the code, but function is idea, not expression, hence not protected by copyright.

Independent invention is one loophole in copyright. Another is the doctrine of *scènes à faire*, which holds that if there is only one way of expressing an idea, or only a very small number of ways, copying that expression is not a violation of copyright. Without that a copyright on the expression would implicitly include ownership of the idea.

Another loophole is the doctrine of fair use, which sometimes permits copying of otherwise protected materials. The criteria are the nature of the use (nonprofit and educational are good, commercial bad), the nature of the work, the amount copied (less is better), and the effect on the revenue of the copyright holder.

How do you get a copyright? The short answer is that you get a copyright by creating a protectable work. While the United States maintains a copyright registry, and registration of your work gives you some additional protection against infringers, it is not necessary to register in order to be covered by copyright. It is not even necessary to attach a copyright notice.

How long does copyright last? In the United States the term of protection has varied somewhat over the years but has always been long. Currently it is life of the author plus fifty years.

In summary, copyright is easily obtained, long-lasting, clearly applies to literal copying of writings and a variety of other things, and may sometimes apply to less than literal copying.

Patent: The Law

Popular usage to the contrary, there is no such thing as a patented machine. Patents are not on objects but on ideas. To apply for a patent you specify your claims, explaining precisely what ideas you claim to have invented, and describe the best way known to you of practicing your invention. If you have invented the electric telegraph, you describe both the ideas and the best way you know of to implement them—to build a telegraph.

Applying for a patent is the job of the inventer and his patent attorney. Denying it is the job of the patent examiner. It is up to him to determine whether the application meets the requirements for patentability, whether it is novel, nonobvious, and useful.

Novel means that your idea has not been thought up before, at least by anyone who published it, or publicly practiced the invention, or did other things from which it might have been learned. Nonobvious means that if someone else had wanted to do what you have done, it would not be sufficient for him to simply hire a competent engineer, someone "skilled in the relevant art," and tell him to do it. Something more, vaguely and traditionally seen as inspiration, a flash of genius, a light bulb going off over a cartoon head, is required.

Part of the fun of studying law is the stories, and one of my favorites has to do with the nineteenth-century definition of useful. The case of *Rickard v. Du Bon* arose when Rickard got a patent, Du Bon infringed, and Rickard sued. Du Bon, in his defense, argued that the patented process was useless, so the patent was invalid.

It seems a little odd for a company to go to the trouble of violating a patent on doing something not worth doing. It is even odder given the definition of "useful" in nineteenth-century patent law. Courts held that if an invention was merely of no use to anyone, granting a patent on it did no harm. If the inventor thought it was useful and the patent examiner did not, the inventor was free to waste his own money getting a patent. To be unpatentable, an invention had to be not merely without use but positively pernicious. In the words of Judge Story in *Lowell v. Lewis*:

> All that the law requires is, that the invention should not be frivolous or injurious to the well-being, good policy, or sound morals of society. The word "useful," therefore, is incorporated in the act in contradistinction to mischievous or immoral. For instance, a new invention to poison people, or to promote debauchery, or to facilitate private assassination, is not a patentable invention.

So we have a case in which Du Bon is arguing, first, that Rickard's patented process is wicked, hence should not be patentable, and second that since it is not patentable, he should be free to do it too.

The process was for artificially flecking tobacco leaves. Flecking had no effect on the quality of the tobacco, but flecked tobacco came from places that produced high-quality tobacco, so cigar buyers interpreted a flecked appearance as a signal of high quality. Rickard patented the process. Du Bon argued that the invention was pernicious, since its purpose was to deceive the customer, hence useless, hence unpatentable—so he should be allowed to do it too. He won the case.

Modern courts have strengthened the utility requirement, holding, for instance, that a process for producing a chemical that has no known uses is not useful, and thus not patentable.

In drawing up your patent application you are defining your invention—stating just what ideas you claim to have invented. What makes the project difficult is that ideas do not come with clearly defined boundaries. The same invention can be described narrowly as the exact way in which a particular machine is designed or more broadly, in some cases very much more broadly, as the ideas whose implementation distinguishes that machine from all previous machines. It is up to you to draw the boundary around your invention, to stake out your claim in idea space. It is rather as if a homesteader, instead of being limited to 160 acres, was allowed to decide for himself just how much land he had settled.

In idea space as in geographical space, more is better if you can get it. The problem is that if your claim is broadly defined, it is quite likely that something someone else has already done fits its description or that some way of doing something that fits the description is obvious. If, after inventing the world's first nuclear reactor, you describe it in your patent application as a way of getting power out of matter and claim all ways of doing so, the patent examiner can point out that the steam engine did that quite some time ago.

The narrower the claim, the less likely that problem is to occur. Continuing our geographical analogy, the smaller the territory you claim to have discovered, the less likely it is that someone else can show he got to some part of it first. The problem with making only a narrow claim is that it may not be worth much; next year someone else may invent around your patent, creating a reactor not covered by a narrow description of your invention.

When Samuel Morse drew up the patent application for his telegraph, he had a solution to that problem. His application contained six different claims. The sixth was for all ways of using the electromagnetic force to transmit letters or symbols to a distance. Not only did that include all telegraphs, it covered fax machines, television, and the Internet as well, despite the fact that none of them had been invented yet. The Supreme Court, in *O'Reilly v. Morse*, rejected that particular claim on grounds of overbreadth, while granting the five narrower claims that Morse (prudently) also included. They should have rejected it on the grounds that it was not novel. Signal flags, semaphores, and beacon fires had all been using the electromagnetic spectrum, in the form of visible light, to transmit messages since long before Morse invented the telegraph.

As this description of the patent process suggests, one of its functions is to convert a commons in idea space, a commons consisting of all of the ideas that might be invented, into private property, with each inventor drawing up the lines of his particular claim. One scholar, Edmund Kitch, has argued that this is its principle function. His prospect theory of patents analogizes them to mineral claims. One reason for a mineral claim is to give prospectors an incentive to go out into the desert looking for gold, just as the possibility of getting a patent gives inventors an incentive to make inventions. But a second reason is that in order for the successful prospector to exploit his find he needs mineral rights to the land around it, enough land so that someone else cannot come in, dig a hole next to his, and free ride off his discovery. Similarly, in Kitch's view, ownership of a substantial chunk of idea space permits the patent holder to control and coordinate the further developments of his invention.

As we have seen, patent differs from copyright in a number of dimensions. Copyright applies to expression, patent to ideas. Copyright is obtained automatically, patent only after a laborious application process that many applications cannot survive. Finally, a copyright is good for the author's life plus seventy years; a patent, in U.S. law, has generally lasted for between fourteen and twenty-one years; current patents (with some exceptions) are for twenty years from date of filing.

In the previous chapter I sketched out a framework for determining what sorts of property rights should exist for what sorts of things. We have spent the first half of this chapter examining, in the context of intellectual property, what sorts of property rights do exist for what sort of things. It is time to put the two sketches together.

An Economic Theory of Intellectual Property

In considering the cost of a system of property rights I started with the problem of drawing boundaries. That problem is minor in the case of copyright protection against literal copying. My chapter is or is not a copy of yours. Your copyright over your book is a sharply defined property right.

The same is not true of patent protection. Patent attorneys and patent examiners spend enormous amounts of time and effort haggling over just what should or should not be included in a particular claim. After they are finished and a patent has issued, attorneys for the patent holder and the putative infringer spend more time and energy, both their own and that of judges and juries, determining whether a particular machine or industrial process embodies ideas that are on the protected side of the line. Even after marking out his claim in voluminous detail, the inventor has a less clear idea of what he owns than the author, who has not bothered to mark out his claim at all.

A second and closely related problem is enforcement. Major violations of copyright take the form of publications, publicly observable. Because the right is well defined, both the litigation cost to copyright owners of proving that a violation has occurred and the cost to potential trespassers of avoiding an unintentional violation are usually low. Violations of patent take the form of machines or industrial processes, the details of which are sometimes secret. And even if everything is known, the fuzzy nature of the boundary around the property makes litigation costly and uncertain and accidental trespass, or mistaken charges of trespass that did not happen, almost inevitable.

A third problem is the transaction cost of using the market to move property to its highest valued use. Here again, propertizing expression makes more sense than propertizing ideas. The only way I am likely to copy your copyrighted writing is deliberately, in which case I know whom to apply to for a license. But an inventor risks reinventing bits and pieces of a dozen patented inventions. Avoiding a patent violation may require an extensive patent search, followed by license negotiations for permissions that may or may not be really necessary.

Finally, and perhaps most interestingly, is the issue of incentives to create rights. Providing an incentive to write books or make inventions is one obvious purpose of intellectual property law. What we want, however, is not merely an incentive but the right incentive. The gain to the producer of intellectual property should be at least a rough measure of the value to other people of what he produces in order that he will bear the costs of producing it if and only if it is, on net, worth producing.

When I write a book and enforce my copyright on it, I make it difficult for another author to write the same book; although independent creation is a defense against the charge of infringement, it is, in practice, difficult to prove. I have taken a tiny bit of property out of the commons: the opportunity to write that book. But the number of books that can be written is so enormously larger than the number that will be written as to make what I have taken worthless to anyone but me—nobody else was going to write that book.

It follows that if I write a book, copyright it, and collect royalties, the royalties I collect provide a conservative measure of the value I have produced. It is a conservative measure because, despite the best efforts of my publisher, some readers end up getting the book for less than they would be willing to pay for it. I can ignore the effect of my copyright on the opportunities available to other writers. They lose nothing through not being permitted to write my book, since they wouldn't have written it anyway.

The same is not true when I make an invention. The opportunity to invent something is often quite valuable, as demonstrated by patent races in which two or more teams are competing to make and patent the same invention. The first team to make the invention gets the patent and collects seventeen years of royalties. But if the second team would have made the invention six months later, the social value of the first team's work is six months of the invention, not seventeen years. The commons that the inventor depletes is very much more depletable than the commons depleted by the writer. It follows that the gain to the inventor may in part consist of a transfer from others who might have invented the same idea a little later. So patent royalties may over-reward the inventor, providing too much incentive to make and patent new inventions. If so, invention becomes in part rent seeking, an expenditure of resources by one actor in order to obtain benefits at the expense of another.

Putting all these arguments together, we get a simple explanation for the observed laws. Copyright protection against literal copying creates a form of property that is easy to define, cheap to enforce, relatively easy to transact over, and subject to no rent-seeking problem. Hence we give copyright easily and for a long term. Patent protection creates a form of property that is hard to define, hard to enforce, costly to transact over, and contains a potential inefficiency due to patent races leading to duplication and inefficiently early inventions. Hence we give patents grudgingly and for a short term.

The same analysis explains at least some of the details of intellectual property law. The *scènes à faire* exception to the general rule that expression is copyrightable covers the special case where depletion of the commons is a problem—an expression that is the only way (or one of the few ways) of expressing a particular idea. The patent requirements of novelty and nonobviousness are designed to control the problem of rent seeking by limiting patents to those inventions major enough so that there is a reasonable chance they would not have been made independently anytime early in the patent period. They do so very imperfectly, in part because patent is, with a few narrow exceptions, a one-size-fits-all system; ideas come in a continuous range of size and durability.

Another detail that makes sense is the fair use exception. The smaller the amount you are copying, the greater the transaction cost of arranging permission relative to the value of the permission, hence the stronger the argument for treating the property as a commons. The smaller the effect of your copying on the revenue of the copyright holder, the smaller the reduction in his incentive to produce the work due to his inability to prohibit your use. Even the preference for nonprofit and educational use may make sense, if we believe that those activities produce, on average, positive externalities, and it is thus efficient to subsidize them—in this case at the expense of the copyright holder, in other contexts through tax exemptions and direct government spending.

Consider, finally, the decision by modern courts to put content into the requirement that an invention must be useful in order to be patentable. Given the nature and speed of modern research, this requirement may serve a useful function. Without it, it would be in the interest of companies to search for ways of synthesizing chemicals for which no use was known in the hope that someone would eventually come up with a use and have to go to them for the right to use their synthesis. Since information on how to synthesize a chemical is useful only after some use for the chemical has been found, it is arguably more efficient to put off research on synthesis until you know whether or not the chemical is worth synthesizing.

While this is a plausible argument, it may not be a correct one. One possible response is that whether it is worth looking for a use for a chemical depends in part on how easy it is to make it, so there is some advantage to finding the synthesis first. Another response, based on Kitch's prospect theory of patents, is that by patenting the synthesis the inventor gets de facto ownership of the chemical, at least until his patent expires or someone discovers a different synthesis, giving him both the incentive and the ability to promote and coordinate the search for uses.

Computer Law

Another application of the economic analysis of property is to the question of whether computer programs are writings, and so protectable by copyright. In the early cases judges expressed considerable uncertainty and reached differing conclusions. Some programs, after all, such as machine language programs burned into the ROM chips of a computer, are never intended for human eyes. Such a program is, as John Hersey, a prominent author and the head of the Patent and Trademark Office, argued, more analogous to an elaborate cam, a part of a machine used to control other parts, than to a novel. As some early courts noted, the closest previous case involved the paper tape used to control a player piano, which had been found not to be covered by copyright—because it was not intended to be read and so was not a writing.

Arguing by analogy, Hersey and the judges who rejected copyright for (at least) machine language programs were right. Arguing by function, they were wrong.

The first step of the functional argument is to ask, not whether programs are writings, but why writings are covered by the particular sort of legal rules we call copyright. The previous section of this chapter offered a brief answer. The next step is to ask whether computer programs share the characteristics that make copyright appropriate for writings. The answer, for protection against literal copying, is yes. One program either does or does not contain a substantial amount of code copied from another, and it is usually easy to tell which is the case. Independent creation is unlikely, save in the special case of reverse engineering, where clean room techniques make it possible to prove independent creation. And a bar against literal copying of a particular program imposes an insignificant cost on later programmers, since they could not have copied the program if it had not first been written by someone else and are unlikely to have independently written exactly the same code by accident.

In discussing copyright I have repeatedly limited myself to the case of protection against literal copying. When we go beyond that, when we try to use copyright to protect the Lotus menu tree or the look and feel of Apple's Macintosh interface, the arguments for copyright protection become much weaker. Such extensions make the protected property more like the ideas traditionally protected by patent law. That suggests that we might be better off limiting copyright law to literal copying and using something more like patent law to protect less clearly defined rights.

Copyrightability of programs is one example of a defensible extension of the legal rights designed to protect writing to other sorts of intellectual property. Another example is a state plug mold statute. Such laws prohibited a firm making, say, a boat hull from getting its design by buying a competitor's hull, forming a mold around it, and then using that mold to produce its own hulls. Here again the argument in favor is not that boat hulls are writings but that this particular form of copying has the same features that make copyright law appropriate for controlling the copying of writings.

I referred to state plug mold statutes in the past tense because they have been held unconstitutional by the Supreme Court, presumably on the theory that intellectual property protection is the business of Congress, not the states. Somewhat similar protection is provided at the federal level for computer chips under the Mask Works Act and for boat hull designs under the Vessel Hull Protection Act (Title V of the recent Digital Millennium Copyright Act).

The Case against Intellectual Property

Property rights serve two related functions: They provide both a way of deciding who gets to use what when and an incentive for creating things.

In the case of intellectual property the first function is not merely unnecessary but perverse. We cannot both drive the same car to different places, which is an argument for property rights in cars. But we can both use the same idea to build different machines, or simultaneously read different copies of the same book, which is an argument against property rights in ideas or writings.

Having one more person choose to read a book does not increase the cost of writing it; that must be paid in full in order for there to be any readers at all. Hence when we include in the price of a book a royalty payment to the author, we are, from the standpoint of efficiency, overcharging. If the price of an eleven dollar book represents a ten dollar production cost plus a dollar in royalties to the author, an additional copy produces a net benefit as long as the purchaser values it at more than ten dollars. But if he values it at more than ten and less than eleven, he will not buy it, which is an inefficient outcome. The same is true for the potential user of an idea who values it at more than zero but less than the license fee set by the patent holder. On the dimension of how many people use an idea or a writing, private property gives an inefficiently low result, commons an efficiently high one.

There remains the second function of property. It is hard to read a book if nobody has written it, and authors may choose not to write books if they cannot collect royalties on them. Similarly for inventions. So the protection of intellectual property does provide some benefit. But the case for treating ideas as property is, economically speaking, weaker than the case for propertizing many other things, which may help explain why intellectual property is a relatively recent institution.

Trade Secret: Neither Flesh Nor Fowl

"Trade secret" means information, including a formula, pattern, compilation, program, device, method, technique or process, that: (i) derives independent economic value, actual or potential from not being generally known to, and not being readily ascertainable by proper means by, other persons who can obtain economic value from its disclosure or use, and (ii) is the subject of efforts that are reasonable under the circumstances to maintain its secrecy.
(*Uniform Trade Secrets Act*)

A trade secret is information whose value to its possessor depends on its not becoming generally known. Trade secret law defines the rights that the rightful possessor of a trade secret has against those who have obtained the secret wrongfully, through breach of contract, say, or an employee's violation of his duty of loyalty, or a trespass. It permits him to collect damages based on his loss or the misappropriator's gain. Sometimes, but not always, it permits him to enjoin use of the secret by someone who received it from the guilty party. An injunction will ordinarily not be available against a third party who could not be expected to have known that the trade secret was stolen and has taken actions, such as building a factory using the secret, that would leave him worse off if enjoined than if he had never received the secret.

Unlike patent or copyright, trade secret law does not provide protection against someone who has obtained the secret without the consent of the owner but without violating his legal rights, for example, by reverse engineering a product that embodies the secret. It thus gives protection well short of full-scale property rights.

This brief description suggests two puzzles. The first is why trade secrets are not, like patentable inventions, treated as property. The second is why, if trade secrets are not patentable, they are protected at all, why state trade secret law is not, like state plug mold statutes, preempted by federal patent law.

A legal regime in which trade secrets were entitled to property protection, in which, for example, a competitor who deduced a trade secret, or discovered it by reverse engineering, or invented it independently, could be enjoined from using it, would be a regime of self-claimed patents without examination. Such a regime would be inefficient for the same reasons as a regime in which the patent office granted a patent to the first inventor of every idea. There would be an incentive to waste resources discovering and claiming ideas long before they were of any use to anyone. The incentive to appropriate is in this respect too high, since some of the gains represent transfers to the first inventor from people who could have invented the idea themselves and used it for free but must now pay him a license fee. Thus the ability to freely appropriate property rights in ideas is a potential source of inefficient rent seeking.

Rent seeking appears a second time in the protection of property—as expenditure on prosecuting and defending infringement suits. Such expenditures would be eliminated if the ideas in question were entirely unprotectable. Whether this is an argument against intellectual property protection depends on whether the costs of legal protection, as under a patent system, are higher or lower than the cost of protecting legally unprotected ideas in other ways, most notably secrecy.

One argument for the sort of limited protection that trade secret law provides is that, by making it easier to protect trade secrets, it makes them more productive. Without trade secret law the possessor of a trade secret might be limited to using it in his own factory under his own eye, where he can make sure nobody is stealing it; with legal protection he has the option of licensing it to other people, suing them for misappropriation if they steal it, and enjoining third parties to whom they sell it.

Whether rent seeking provides, on net, an argument for or against legal protection, it is at least an argument in favor of defining protectable rights by criteria that are easy for courts to measure. That may help to explain why trade secrets are not protected against reverse engineering: In most cases there is only a fuzzy line distinguishing reverse engineering, designed to discover a competitor's secrets, from research designed to produce better products. More generally, the requirement that the appropriation of a trade secret must involve some independently wrongful act in order to count as misappropriation provides a convenient bright line rule, one that takes advantage of the existing law that defines the relevant sorts of wrongful acts. Here as elsewhere, bright line rules have the advantage of reducing litigation costs.

This brings us to our second question: Why trade secret law is not entirely preempted by patent law. To answer it, consider an invention that is unpatentable because the patent office considers it too obvious. Such an invention may not deserve seventeen years of protection, but that does not mean that it deserves no protection at all. Trade secret protection provides some reward for the inventor, and thus some incentive to make the invention, without imposing any cost on others who might independently invent it. It thus helps fill one gap in the patent law, the lack of protection for inventions that are only moderately nonobvious.

Trade secret law also helps fill a second gap, the failure of patent law to provide more than seventeen years of protection for very nonobvious inventions. An inventor whose invention can be used without revealing it and who believes that it will take much more than seventeen years for someone else to independently discover it has the option of choosing secrecy instead of a patent. He is, in effect, claiming that the lifetime, and thus the social value, of the invention is greater than the patent law assumes—and offering to prove it. The law of trade secrets assists him in this demonstration by increasing the chance that if someone does duplicate the invention, he will do so by inventing it rather than by stealing it.

Trade secret law also provides assistance for the inventor unable to persuade the patent examiner that his invention deserves protection. The inventor offers to demonstrate that his invention is nonobvious by keeping it secret. If someone else invents the same thing next year, that proves the examiner right, and no harm has been done. But if there is no duplication, he gets at least part of the reward he would have gotten if the invention were patentable—as he should, since he has shown that he was right and the patent examiner wrong.

Finally, trade secret law provides protection for an inventor whose invention, while patentable, is not worth the cost of patenting. An invention of only modest value may qualify for a patent but not be worth the substantial cost of getting one. Trade secret protection is cheaper the less valuable the secret, since the less valuable the secret, the less the effort that will be made to steal it.

In one respect trade secret law actually provides a more efficient structure of incentives than patent law. Making a patentable invention this year instead of next provides only one extra year's use of the invention—but, under a rule that gives the patent to the first inventor, is rewarded with a seventeen-year monopoly. If the cost of making the invention is falling rapidly over time, perhaps due to progress in related technologies, the result will be inefficiently early invention. Under a regime of trade secret protection, on the other hand, the reward to an invention is lower the faster the cost of duplicating it is falling, since an invention that will soon be inexpensive to duplicate will not remain a secret for long. Hence in a regime of trade secret law, unlike one of patent law, an invention whose cost is falling more rapidly will (other things being equal) be made later than one whose cost is falling less rapidly, which is the economically efficient pattern.

Protection without Copyright: First Mover Advantages

> And they asked me how I did it,
>   and I gave 'em the Scripture text,
> "You keep your light so shining
>   a little in front o' the next!"
> They copied all they could follow,
>   but they couldn't copy my mind,
> And I left 'em sweating and stealing
>   a year and a half behind.
>   (R. *Kipling*, *"The Mary Gloster"*)

At the beginning of this century the United States had no copyright treaty with Britain; American publishers were free to pirate books by British authors. Despite the lack of legal protection British authors routinely collected royalties on American sales. How could that happen?

A British author would provide his American publisher with the manuscript of his book before it was published in England, with the result that the English and American editions came out at about the same time. The pirate publisher could not start setting type until the book was available to be copied. With the printing technology of the time, setting type was a slow and expensive operation, so the legitimate publisher got all of the early sales—which, for most books, meant a large fraction of all sales.

If a pirate edition came out, the legitimate publisher could cut his price, issuing a "fighting edition" cheap enough to keep the pirate from making enough money to recover his initial investment. The result of such tactics was that, although piracy occurred, it was not serious enough to keep British authors from making money on their American sales. The publishing technology of the time gave the legitimate publisher enough of a first mover advantage to provide a reasonably good substitute for copyright protection.

And Copyright without Protection

A century later we have almost precisely the opposite situation with regard to computer programs. Having bought a CDR with Microsoft Office 98 on it, I discovered that the license does not permit me to use the program on both my home and office machines. As a matter of law, and, in my view, ethics, I am required to buy a second copy of Word in order to be able to work on this book in both places. But if I chose to violate that legal requirement and use the same CD to install the program on both machines, there is nothing Microsoft could do about it.

Computer programs are covered by copyright law, whether the copying is by a seller, a university, or an individual purchaser. But they are, as a practical matter, protected by copyright law only in the first two cases. If someone buys a copy of Office and a CDR drive and proceeds to make hundreds of copies and sell them over the Internet, he is quite likely to be caught and prosecuted. If my university decides to cut its expenses by buying one copy of Office and installing it on several hundred machines, a single disgruntled employee who knows how to locate Bill Gates's e-mail address could get us in a lot of trouble. But if I install Office on two machines when I am only licensed for one, or if my six-year-old provides all his friends with copies of his computer games, the chance that either of us will be caught and prosecuted is very near zero.

Coming Soon to a World near You

Software companies have responded to the effective unenforceability of their copyrights in several ways. One early solution was to distribute software on disks designed to be uncopyable by the computers that used them. That turned out to provide enough protection to be inconvenient to legitimate customers but not enough to prevent copying by even moderately sophisticated pirates. Programs appeared designed to copy the protected disks. My favorite episode involved a program for TRS80 computers called "Super Utility Plus" that would (among other things) copy most protected disks but was copy protected against itself. So someone else brought out a program, "SuperDuper," whose sole purpose in life was to make copies of Super Utility Plus.

Eventually, after some unsuccessful litigation between a company that provided software for protecting disks and a company that made software for copying protected disks, most of the software producers gave up and abandoned copy protection. But that was only the first round of the battle; another is being waged even as I write, this time with CD-ROMs instead of floppy disks. Currently many programs, especially games, are written to require the presence of the program CD when the program is running. This worked as long as drives for recording CDs were expensive and rare and hard drive space too expensive to be devoted to CD disk images. With hard drives getting steadily cheaper and the price of CDR drives currently near two hundred dollars and falling it seems clear, again, that the end is in sight.

If a software firm finds that it cannot protect its intellectual property directly, one solution is to find other ways of making money from it. Those might include selling support, getting revenue from tie-in sales of products that cannot be easily copied, relying on the honesty of its customers, or getting most of its revenue from firms too large to risk being caught with pirated software.

It also might look for new forms of protection. Technologies continue to change, and it is at least possible that changes currently occurring are moving us toward a world where technology will provide a level of protection far beyond what copyright law is supposed to provide.

One important technology for this purpose is encryption, mathematical procedures for scrambling and unscrambling information. Current developments may make it possible for producers of intellectual property to distribute it in a form that is cryptographically protected, provided with the digital equivalent of a barbed wire fence. The program comes in a digital container; IBM calls their proposed version a crytolope. In order to use the contents, to play a multimedia entertainment package, say, or access a database, you must make a payment, perhaps in digital currency to an online agent of the contents' owner. In exchange for your payment you get controlled access to the contents. Perhaps a dollar buys you an hour viewing of the multimedia or a hundred queries of the database. You can, of course, copy the whole thing, container and contents, and give it to someone else. But if he wants to use it, he too will have to pay.

A variety of projects along these general lines are currently under development; it is still too early to judge whether any will be sufficiently robust to withstand attacks by programmers trying to access the contents without paying for them. One legal issue raised by such technologies is whether programs designed to crack technological protection, digital lockpicks, twenty-first century equivalents of SuperDuper, should themselves be legal. If—as has recently become the case—they are not, and, a much more dubious proposition, if it proves possible to enforce the ban, a container will only have to be strong enough to withstand an attack by an ordinary user, although there is still the risk that an expert might crack the protection and distribute the contents. If programs designed to crack protection are legal, or illegal but widely available, then the protection must be strong enough to withstand a cracking program written by an expert.

At this point the jury is still out. If digital containers turn out to be a viable technology, we will be back in the world of 1900; producers of intellectual property will be able to protect themselves without the assistance of copyright law. And their new protection will be vastly better than the protection they now get from copyright law. Digital containers not only enforce their own restrictions with no need for litigation, they also make possible much more detailed control over the terms on which intellectual property is sold than does copyright.

12

The Economics of Contract

I GIVE YOU money, you give me an apple. No contract, no need for contract law.

I hire you to build a house on property I own. We agree on a price of a hundred thousand dollars. I give you a hundred thousand dollars and, in a world without enforceable contracts, never see you again.

The obvious solution is to make the payment due when the house is finished. You finish building my house and ask to be paid. I suggest that we renegotiate the terms. Until you are paid the house belongs to you, but it is on my land. If you do not want to accept my new and lower price, you are free to tear it down again.

A better solution is to pay you continuously as you build the house, but that too has problems. When the house is three-quarters built, you suggest renegotiating the price—upward. You have been paid for your work so far, and three-quarters of a house is not of much use to me. I could pay someone else to finish it, but without the original contractor's detailed knowledge of just what has been done so far and what remains to be done, that may be a costly proposition.

Another solution, and a very common one, is reputation. You could cheat me but don't, because word will get around and nobody else will hire you to build houses. Reputation may be the most important method for enforcing agreements in our society, although not the one of most interest to lawyers.

You buy a sports jacket from a store that guarantees satisfaction—money back, no questions asked. When you unwrap it, your wife points out that you are a 42 short, not a 40 long, and in any case purple is not really your color. You bring it back to the store, and they give you your money back.

The store knows perfectly well that you are not going to sue them; the time and effort would cost you more than the jacket is worth. They give you your money back any way because they don't want a reputation for cheating their customers.

Department store refunds are an easy case, since the amounts at stake are small, the issues simple, and the parties are engaged in repeat dealings. Quite aside from what you may tell your friends, the store wants to keep you as a customer. Reputational enforcement is harder with larger amounts at stake and more complicated transactions. If your contractor agrees to be paid after the house is finished and you then insist on re-negotiating the price down, you also take the precaution of thinking up some plausible excuse, perhaps a list of complaints about exactly how the house was built. That way, third parties will be unsure who was try-ing to cheat whom. Even if they conclude that you are at fault, it may not matter much, since you are not planning to have another house built any time soon.

Even with large stakes, reputation sometimes provides an adequate mechanism for enforcing agreements. One such situation was explored in a classic article by Lisa Bernstein on the New York diamond industry. Buying and selling diamonds is a business in which people routinely ex-change large sums of money for envelopes containing lots of little stones without first inspecting, weighing, and testing each one.

The New York diamond industry was at one time dominated by ortho-dox Jews, forbidden by their religious beliefs from suing each other—making it a trust-intensive industry conducted almost entirely by people who could not use the legal system to enforce their agreements. While the industry had become more diverse by the time Bernstein studied it, dealers continue to rely almost entirely on private mechanisms to enforce con-tracts—in part for religious reasons, in part to maintain privacy, in part, perhaps, because those mechanisms functioned better than the courts.

At the center of the system is the New York Diamond Dealers' Club, which arranges private arbitration of disputes among diamond mer-chants. Parties to a contract agree in advance to arbitration; if, when a dispute arises, one of them refuses to accept the arbitrator's verdict, he is no longer a diamond merchant—because everyone in the industry now knows he cannot be trusted. Similar arrangements exist elsewhere in the world and exchange information with each other. Presumably the amount diamond merchants are willing to risk on a single deal depends in part on how long the other party has been involved in the industry and thus how much he would lose if he had to leave it.

As this account suggests, trusted private arbitrators provide an alterna-tive to a court system, not by directly enforcing contracts but by gener-ating the public information necessary to allow reputational mechanisms to enforce them. Third parties did not have to investigate a dispute in detail in order to learn who was at fault. They only had to find out which party the arbitrator had ruled against. It also suggests a possible explana-tion for why particular trades are sometimes dominated by a single close-knit ethnic group. If private enforcement of contracts via reputation and social pressure is less expensive and more reliable than enforcement via the court system, people whose social institutions make such private en-forcement practical have a competitive advantage over those who must rely on the courts.

Reputation can do quite a lot to enforce contracts, but it cannot do everything. When I contract to have a house built, the odds are high that the contractor is not a member of the same close-knit ethnic group that I am. If one of us violates our agreement, the other may not be in a position to prove the fact to interested third parties and thus impose reputational costs—either because the third parties do not know the victim exists or because the case is complicated enough so that it is hard for third parties to know who is at fault. And the violator, not being engaged in a trust-intensive industry or repeat dealings, may regard the gain from breaking his agreement as worth any reputational cost it creates.

Even in this situation, private mechanisms may solve the problem, provided that we can agree on a third party we both trust. Each of us posts a bond with the third party. My bond forfeits if, in his judgment, I have broken the agreement, and similarly with yours. But while bonding makes possible private enforcement of some agreements that straight reputational enforcement does not reach, it still does not cover all situations.

My conclusion is that, although enforcement of contracts via courts and contract law is not the only way of solving these problems, and often not the best way, it may still have an important role to play. And whether or not it should play an important role, it in fact does, and is therefore worth studying. In any case, while the rest of this chapter is written in the context of contract law, most of the issues it discusses are issues of contract, not of law. They would arise, in only slightly different forms, for a New York rabbi or a commercial arbitrator.

Why Do We Need Contract Law?

Given a system in which contracts are enforced by courts, why do we need contract law? Why not simply have the court read the contract and enforce the terms as read? That seems the obvious and just solution—and would save law students several semester hours.

There are at least three answers. The first is that courts may not wish to enforce contracts as written because they may believe that they know better than the parties what the terms should have been. A second is that even if you are willing to enforce the contract as written, you still have to decide whether a contract exists and what its terms are, questions about which the parties may sometimes disagree.

A third reason is that even if everybody agrees that a contract exists and should be enforced, and everyone agrees what it says, contracts never say enough. There is not enough fine print in the world to cover every possible contingency. Real-world contracts cover some contingencies, typically ones the drafters think likely to occur, but leave gaps to be filled in by the court.

The Case for Freedom of Contract

You and I are drawing up a contract for a joint business project. It occurs to me that a particular term is inefficient. Giving you an additional month to perform the first stage of the project would save you a hundred thousand dollars, cost me fifty thousand, and thus increase our net gain by fifty thousand dollars.

My first thought is that I should keep my mouth shut, since the change will leave me fifty thousand dollars worse off. But there is a better alternative. I propose to write the change into the contract along with a seventy-five thousand dollar increase in the amount you will pay me for my participation.

This simple example demonstrates a very general point, one that underlies the Coase Theorem. As long as there exists a change in the terms of our deal that would produce net benefits, there is a way of making that change that benefits both of us. Hence we would expect rational bargainers to come up with contract terms that maximize the net gain. If our objective is economic efficiency, that is both an attractive outcome and an argument for enforcing contracts as written.

Courts frequently do enforce contracts as written, but not always. One reason they offer is "unequal bargaining power." The implicit metaphor is a world of conflict rather than cooperation, a war rather than a deal, in which only if each side is sufficiently powerful can it expect its concerns to be included in the final treaty.

That is a widespread and persuasive view of bargaining. To see what is wrong with it, consider a real-world case of unequal bargaining power. Suppose I am the only seller of this book—as, thanks to copyright law, I am. Further suppose that no alternative book is a close substitute for this one. That proposition too is true, as I hope to persuade you by the time you finish the last chapter. I am a monopolist. If you want a book like this, you must buy it on my terms or not at all.

Should I sell the book to you bound and with a cover, as books are usually sold, or simply put the unbound pages in a large envelope and sell that? Binding the book costs me money and provides benefits only for you. If a monopoly can impose its own terms without considering the desires of its customers, why should I bother?

The answer is that even a monopoly cannot force people to buy its products. As a rational monopolist, I am already charging you the highest price you are willing to pay—more precisely, I am already charging the price at which the cost of lost sales from any further increase would at least balance the gain from the higher price. Lowering the quality of the book will have the same effect as increasing the price. Some people (actually, lots of people) willing to pay my price for a bound book will be unwilling to pay the same price for an unbound one. As you may have noticed, this book came bound.

Suppose I think of some way of improving the book, such as a more detailed index or a better binding. The cost to me will be an extra two dollars per book, the increase in value to the customer will be three. It is in my interest to make the improvement and raise the price. The same would be true if instead of selling you a book I was renting you a car, and the improvement I was considering was not in the car but in the contract. If a change in terms is worth more to my customers than it costs me, I should make it and adjust the price accordingly. We are back with our argument for efficient contract. Nothing in that argument depended on assuming that the seller was not a monopoly.

So far I have assumed that the change, in book or contract, has the same value to all customers. Suppose, however, that by improving the index and using higher quality paper I can increase the value of the book by five dollars to readers who really like it but only by one dollar to the more marginal customers. Again assume that the improvements cost me two dollars per book.

Even if the improvement is efficient—produces a net benefit—it is not in my interest to make it. What limits the price I can sell the book for is the value of the book to the marginal customers. The enthusiasts are already getting more than they are paying for.

Following out the logic of that example, we can see that improvements that selectively benefit marginal customers may be made even if not worth making, while improvements that selectively benefit nonmarginal customers may not be made even if worth making. The result might be a level of quality higher or lower than would be efficient. That is a possible source of inefficiency and a legitimate argument against automatically accepting freedom of contract when one party is a monopoly. But it has very little to do with the conventional account of unequal bargaining power.

A second qualification to the conclusion that contracts will be drawn up with terms that maximize the net gain to the parties follows from my implicit assumption that the parties drawing up a contract are free to write into it any price that they can agree to. Suppose I am a landlord renting out an apartment whose market rent would be fifteen hundred dollars a month. Unfortunately for me the apartment is located in New York City and covered by the city's rent control ordinance, which limits the rent to a maximum of a thousand dollars a month.

If the city controls the price but not the other terms of the contract, I respond by lowering the quality of the apartment in whatever ways save me the most money. As long as the value of the apartment is more than a thousand dollars, I will still be able to find tenants. By failing to keep the hot water system in good repair, or keep the building as warm as the tenants' would like it, or fix broken plumbing with reasonable speed, I am imposing a cost on the tenants that is greater than the savings to me; that is why, if I were free to set my own price, I would not be doing those things. But since I am not free to set my own price, lowering the quality of my product is, from my standpoint, the next best alternative.

It follows that one consequence of rent control, more generally of price control, is to subvert the mechanisms that normally keep the quality of products and the terms of contracts efficient, providing an argument for legal restrictions on both.

The Case against Freedom of Contract

The argument I have just given implies that, with a few exceptions, contracts will be designed to maximize the net benefits of those who sign them. But efficiency is supposed to take account of costs and benefits to everybody. In many cases we can ignore effects on other people, for reasons sketched out in chapter 2; in a market society contracting parties, like individual actors, are not ordinarily in a position to impose net costs on third parties without their permission. There are, however, some important exceptions.

When I take out a contract on you with a hit man, I am attempting to impose quite substantial costs on a third party. If my hit man misses, the court will not help me get my money back. Nor will it enforce a contract by which I agree not to testify against someone else's illegal acts. Nor will American courts enforce contracts in restraint of trade, such as an agreement by members of a cartel to maintain a common price. In all of these cases the fact that a contract is signed is evidence that it benefits the parties signing it, but not that it produces net benefits.

Implicit in the argument for freedom of contract, as in most of the economic analysis of law, is the assumption that people who sign contracts are rational, that they know their own interest and act to get it. The argument breaks down where that assumption is implausible, which is why courts will not enforce contracts made by children or lunatics.

A less convincing version of the same justification appears when a court refuses to enforce a contract on the grounds that one of the parties must have been incompetent, since otherwise he would not have agreed to those terms. Implicit in that claim is the court's belief that it knows the interest of the party better than he does and thus is competent to judge his incompetence.

Consider an example, in current legal doctrine, where that belief may well be false:

I agree to deliver ten thousand customized widgets to you by January 10th, for which you will pay me. I further agree that if I fail to meet the deadline, I owe you damages of a hundred thousand dollars. I fail to deliver, you sue. Do you collect?

The answer depends on whether the court believes that a hundred thousand dollars is a reasonable estimate of the cost to you of my failure. If it does, the *liquidated damages* term in our contract is enforceable. But if the court believes that a hundred thousand dollars greatly overestimates the real cost, it may decide that the term is a *penalty clause* and as such unenforceable.

Two assumptions go into this policy: that the court can estimate the real cost of my failure well enough to identify a penalty clause and that penalty clauses are never efficient. The first may be wrong; the second surely is.

To see why, consider the analysis in chapter 5 of the choice between property rules and liability rules. Under a liability rule, if I use your property without your permission, I must pay damages reflecting the injury to you. Under a property rule, if I want to use your property, I must first get your permission; if I don't, I suffer a punishment designed, not to measure the injury to you, but to make sure I won't use your property without your permission.

A penalty clause is a private version of a property rule. I have given you a property interest in my delivering by January 10th. If I want to deliver after that, I must buy your permission. If I neither fulfill my contract nor obtain your permission to void it, I suffer a penalty.

Just as in chapter 5, so here, there are good reasons why parties might sometimes prefer a property rule to a liability rule. They may believe that the cost of moving resources to their highest value use through the market is cheaper than doing it through the court system—because the cost of the relevant market transactions is low, because the cost of using the court is high, or perhaps both.

Perhaps you and I expect to be engaged in many such transactions and so have an interest in maintaining our reputation as reasonable people to do business with. I am confident that if I have problems meeting the January 10th deadline, you will renegotiate on reasonable terms. Further suppose that neither of us has a high opinion of the competence of the court and both prefer spending our money on things other than lawyers. It may be perfectly reasonable for us to choose a penalty clause, in the expectation that it will rarely be invoked, over the alternative of giving the court a free hand to decide damages. Yet the same legal system that routinely enforces property rules created by judges and legislatures refuses to enforce property rules privately created by the people they will bind.

Making Sense of Duress

A mugger catches you alone in a dark alley and offers you a choice: Give him a hundred dollars or he kills you. You reply that your life is well worth the price, but unfortunately you are not carrying that much cash. He offers to take a check. When you get home, should you be free to stop payment? Should a contract made under duress be enforceable?

The argument in favor of enforceability is that if the contract is not enforceable, the mugger will refuse your check—or accept it and then make sure you can't stop payment by killing you and cashing the check before news of your death reaches the bank. Seen from that perspective, it looks as though even a contract made under duress produces benefits for both parties and so should be enforceable. You prefer paying a hundred dollars to being killed, he prefers receiving a hundred dollars to killing you. Where's the problem?

The problem is that making the contract enforceable makes offering people the choice between their money and their life a much more profitable business—most of us have more in our checking accounts than in our wallets. The gain from enforceability is a better chance, if you are mugged, to buy yourself free. It must be balanced against the higher probability of being mugged. It seems likely that the current legal rule, holding contracts made under duress unenforceable, is the efficient one.

But that may not be true under all circumstances. A peace treaty is a contract made under duress—yet most of us think that a world where nations can sign peace treaties and be bound by them is better than a world where the victor must annihilate the vanquished before he can be sure the war is over. Similarly, on a smaller scale, for the transaction by which a prisoner of war gives his parole not to attempt to escape. Indeed, it used to be quite common for a prisoner to be released on parole and permitted to go home—having promised not to rejoin his army until he had been exchanged for a prisoner of equal rank from the other side. The parole system made war somewhat less costly for both sides and so presumably increased the amount of war somewhat, but it seems unlikely that the effect was very great—and it substantially decreased the cost born by captive and captor.

For a example of the same sort of tradeoff in a somewhat different context, consider a case that has recently been in the newspapers—the attempt by a Spanish judge to extradite Augusto Pinochet from England in order to try him in Spain for crimes he is accused of committing while dictator of Chile. Legal rules that immunize ex-dictators make it less expensive for them to commit crimes while in power. But legal rules that hold ex-dictators liable for such crimes make it more expensive for dictators to give up power. Pinochet is one of the rare examples of a dictator who voluntarily relinquished power to an elected government. If he ends up in a Spanish jail as a result, the next dictator may not make that mistake.

So far I have been discussing real duress: Your money or your life. There are other sorts of contracts that courts sometimes refuse to enforce on grounds of duress, but the duress is of a very different kind, and the courts' decisions must be justified, if at all, with other arguments. We will consider two quite different examples, one that I like to think of as semi-real duress, the other as bogus duress.

Bargaining on a Sinking Ship

Your ten million dollar ship has been caught in a storm, disabled, and is gradually going down. Fortunately, a tug comes by and offers to rescue it. Unfortunately, the tug captain, knowing the value of the ship, proposes to charge nine million dollars for his services. If you turn that offer down, he will be happy to take you and your crew to safety, leaving the ship to sink. You agree to his price, he tows the ship safe into harbor, and you refuse to pay, claiming that your agreement was obtained under duress. The admiralty court concludes that a reasonable price for the tow is one million dollars and rewrites your agreement accordingly.

Bargaining with the captain of the tug while the water is rising past your ankles certainly feels like duress to you. But this situation differs from real duress—your money or your life—in one important way. The mugger got you into trouble; the tugboat gets you out. It was not his fault that your ship was sinking.

The argument offered earlier against enforcing contracts under duress here cuts in just the opposite direction. Making it easier for muggers to get your money increases the chance that someone will mug you, which is a bad thing. Increasing the amount tug boats can get for saving your ship increases the chance that, if you are sinking, a tug boat will be somewhere close, which is a good thing. If we are to justify the refusal to enforce such contracts, we need a different argument.

The first step to getting one is to ask what the efficient price is for the tugboat to charge—the price that maximizes the net gain to all concerned. Since the payment itself is merely a transfer, that means asking how the incentives created by the price will affect the actions of people who own tugboats and people whose ships might need a tug.

Consider the question first from the standpoint of the owner of the tugboat, deciding whether to spend an extra hundred thousand dollars to increase by one percentage point his chance of being at the right place in the right time to save a sinking ship. Perhaps he is deciding whether to cruise around in bad weather looking for ships in trouble, or whether to keep his radio receiver manned around the clock in the hope of picking up a distress call. When will he decide to spend the extra money, and when, from the standpoint of efficiency, should he?

He will spend it if the price he can collect is at least ten million dollars, since in that case (assuming away any complications due to risk aversion) his hundred thousand dollar expenditure will produce an average return of at least a hundred thousand dollars. He should spend it if the value of the ship is at least ten million dollars, since in that case the social gain from his acts—an extra one percentage point chance of saving the ship—will be at least equal to the cost. If we want it to be in his interest to take those precautions that are worth taking and only those, we should allow him to collect the full value of the ship as the price for saving it. Any lower price means that, when he takes precautions, some of the benefit goes to the owner of the ship. That is a positive externality, and the result is a lower than optimal level of precautions.

Next consider the situation from the standpoint of the incentives of the ship owner. Suppose that, given whatever tug owners are doing, a sinking ship has a 50 percent chance of being rescued. The ship owner must decide what risks to take in running his ship—whether, for example, he should keep the ship in port during a storm or head out to sea, accepting a small risk that the ship may get into trouble. How will he make the decision, and how, from the standpoint of efficiency, should he?

Sending the ship out in a storm has, we will suppose, a 2 percent chance of getting the ship into trouble. We further suppose, in the light of our analysis so far, that if the ship is rescued, the charge for the rescue will be the full value of the ship. It follows that the cost of to the owner of sending the ship out is a 1 percent chance of the ship sinking plus another 1 percent chance of having to pay the tug ten million dollars to save it. The owner will send the ship to sea only if his benefit from doing so is at least two hundred thousand dollars.

This is the right calculation for him but the wrong calculation for an efficient outcome. Sending the ship to sea results in only one chance in a hundred of its sinking, since half the time it will be rescued. The rescue results in a ten million dollar loss to the ship owner but a matching gain to the tug owner. So it is efficient to send the ship to sea as long as the benefit is at least a hundred thousand dollars. To make it in the owner's interest to act that way, the price charged by the tug should be zero. As long as it is more than zero, the ship owner confers a positive externality on the tug owner every time he risks his ship, so he risks the ship less often than he should.

So far I have assumed away the actual cost to the tug in time, risk, and fuel of bringing the crippled ship back to port. If we redid the analysis including that, the conclusion would be that the price that gave the ship's owner the right incentive to keep his ship out of trouble was just equal to the actual cost of the rescue. Readers interested in a more precise statement of the argument and willing to put up with the necessary mathematics will find it on the web page.

We have just shown that there are two efficient prices. One, the full value of the ship, gives the tug owner the right incentive to be in a position to rescue sinking ships. The other, the cost of the rescue, gives the ship owner the right incentive to avoid getting his ship into a situation in which it needs rescuing. Just where between those two the price should be set depends on how sensitive each party is to the relevant incentives. If there are very few acts the tug owner can take that would be worth taking at a price of ten million but not at a price of five, lowering the price to five million will cause only a small amount of inefficiency on the tow owner's side. Similarly, if there are very few cases where it would be worth putting out to sea if rescuers charged only their costs but not if they charged half the value of the ship, then a price of five million would cause only a small amount of inefficiency on the ship owner's side. By trading off such considerations one could, in principle, find the least bad price, the price that minimized the inefficiencies due to inadequate incentives on both sides.

The logic of the problem should be familiar from earlier chapters. The problem of two efficient prices, which I have gone into in some detail here, is simply Coase's problem of joint causation applied to sinking ships instead of air pollution or airport noise. It will reappear in the next chapter in the context of auto accidents, which are also jointly caused. The reason it looks different here is that those examples involve dual causation of bad things, such as pollution or auto accidents, which we want to deter. This time we are concerned with dual causation of rescues, which we want to encourage. The solution is one we found in chapter 7: Put the incentive where it will do the most good.

Our conclusion so far is that the efficient price is somewhere between the value of the ship and the cost of the rescue. A second conclusion is that there is no reason to expect bargaining to produce it. The bargaining occurs when the ship is sinking and the tug has already shown up, after all the relevant decisions, by ship owner and by tug owner, have already been taken. The only remaining decision is whether to rescue the ship or let it sink, and everyone already knows the right answer to that.

Everyone knows it, but we may not get it. When the bargaining occurs, it is in a setting of bilateral monopoly. Each side is trying to get as much as possible; while they argue, the ship is sinking. That suggests one good argument for the present legal rule, which permits an admiralty court to rewrite a contract that is too favorable to one side. It reduces the risk that the ship will sink while the two sides are haggling.

Alert readers may wonder how this analysis, in which the best possible result involves inefficiency on both sides, can be consistent with the Coase Theorem. The answer is that in a fully Coasian world, a world where all transaction costs were zero, ship owners and tug owners would contract in advance to specify when tugs would be in places where ships might need rescuing, how willing ships would be to put to sea in storms, and the like. A sufficiently elaborate contract, in a world of zero transaction costs, would produce a result that was efficient on every margin. I have implicitly built transaction costs into my analysis by assuming that the contract is negotiated only after the ship gets into trouble. It would be interesting to investigate the actual market for salvage services in order to see where, between that simple picture and the fully efficient version, real arrangements end up.

Bogus Duress: Contracts of Adhesion

A final category of duress accepted by some courts is of a sort familiar to all of us—form contracts, offered on a take it or leave it basis. When you rent a car from Avis you do not get to negotiate either the price or other terms of the contract. You are presented with a series of options to take or refuse and, having done so, have the choice of either signing the contract or going to Hertz or Budget. Current legal jargon, borrowed from the French some decades back, refers to such contracts as contracts of adhesion.

This feels a little like duress. Certainly there is something one-sided about a transaction in which all of the terms are drawn up by one party. If your underlying view of contract formation is a conflict in which each party gets only the terms he bargains for, it is natural to suppose that the contract will end up as one-sided as the bargaining.

The reasons why this is wrong have already been discussed. Avis draws up the contract knowing that they still have to persuade you to sign it. They will, of course, write the most favorable contract to them that they think you will sign. But the way to do so is to draw up an efficient contract, thus maximizing the total gain, and then charge the highest price they think you will pay, transferring as much as possible of that gain to them.

We are left with the question of why Avis, Hertz, and many other firms choose to make use of form contracts. There are two obvious reasons. One is that they want to reduce the costs of drawing up contracts. If you are making similar agreements with millions of customers a year, it is a lot cheaper to draft a single contract with options to cover likely variations among what your customers want than to redraft the contract for each transaction.

The second reason is that a form contract reduces the risk that their employees will cheat them. Suppose Avis left it up to each desk clerk to negotiate the rate of each rental. Five dollars to the desk clerk plus twenty dollars to Avis is a better deal for me than the thirty dollar price the clerk will hold out for if I don't bribe him. But it is a worse deal for Avis.

These arguments are relevant to the question of whether form contracts in general should be legally suspect; my conclusion is that they should not. There remains the possibility that in some cases form contracts may be suspect for special reasons—for instance, when the contract is so complicated that the customer does not know what he is signing.

That situation raises legitimate issues for a court trying to determine what the customer has agreed to; obviously terms printed in six-point gray type and concealed in the contract's ornamental border do not qual- ify. On the other hand, one reason contracts written under our legal system are so elaborate may be the fear that courts will interpret any possible ambiguity as what the court thinks the contract should have said instead of what the parties think it should have said; one way of protecting against that is to specify your contract in great detail. We will return to that problem, and what can be done about it, shortly. Similarly, one reason contracts may contain very one-sided terms is that the parties are trying to limit the ability of courts to interpret the contract, while relying on nonlegal constraints, such as reputation, to prevent those terms from actually being enforced.

Contract, Contract, Who Has a Contract

> Otho would have been Bilbo's heir, but for the
> adoption of Frodo. He read the will carefully and
> snorted. It was, unfortunately, very clear and
> correct (according to the legal customs of hobbits,
> which demand among other things seven
> signatures of witnesses in red ink).
>   (J. R. R. Tolkien, *The Fellowship of the Ring*)

So far I have assumed the existence of a contract while considering various reasons why it might not be enforceable, including the possibility that agreement was not voluntary. A further set of issues arises in deciding whether or not there is a contract there to be enforced.

We agree to meet at a restaurant for dinner tomorrow. If you don't show up, am I entitled to sue you? Probably not. Agreements vary widely in how binding they are intended to be, and not all are properly the business of the legal system. We need ways of drawing lines, distinguishing between an unenforceable statement of intent and an enforceable contract, to enable people to communicate intentions without risking expensive entanglements with the legal system.

One solution is formality. For an agreement to count as a contract it must be signed in red ink, or sealed with purple sealing wax, or notarized, or deposited with the proper official, or all of the above. Such rules define a language, of actions rather than sounds, and so tell us what actions translate as "we intend this agreement to be enforceable."

A variety of other approaches are, in various legal systems, used to determine what is or is not a binding contract. One of the most important ones in our legal system is to count as a contract only an agreement from which each party gains something—known as the *doctrine of consideration*. This raises an interesting problem:

My rich uncle, in an expansive mood at the family Christmas party, announces that a bright boy like me ought to go to college—and he is prepared to pay for it. Six months later, after being accepted by Harvard, I send him the bill: twenty-five thousand dollars for tuition and room and board. He sends it back, with a brief note explaining that he wasn't really serious. When I protest, he refers me to his lawyer, who patiently explains that since I didn't give him anything in exchange for his promise there was no consideration, hence there is no contract to enforce.

Fortunately for me, the situation is not that simple. I sue, invoking the doctrine of detrimental reliance. I did not give him anything in exchange for his promise, but I did spend quite a lot of time and effort, and some of my own money, getting into Harvard, as well as turning down several attractive job offers. These costs, all due to my relying on his promise, establish grounds for my claim that the promise was a contract and should be enforceable.

His promise imposed costs on me, so it makes some sense to hold him liable. It is less clear that contract law is the appropriate way of doing so, given the absence of most of the markers we usually use to tell what is or is not a contract. An alternative might be to count such rash promises as tortious. Another alternative is to impose no penalty at all, on the theory that before relying on his promise I should have gotten it in writing—notarized, sealed, and with the signatures of seven witnesses in red ink.

Interestingly enough, the requirement of consideration does not exist in property law. If I give you a piece of land as a gift, for no consideration, it is still yours; I don't get to change my mind next month and take it back. One possible explanation is that property law has other ways of determining whether a transfer has occurred; under the statute of frauds, all transfers of property must be in writing.

Contracts between Fewer Than Two Parties: Herein of Cats and Crash Victims

Can there be a contract when one party does not know it exists? My cat gets out the door while my back is turned, and I post a fifty dollar reward for her return. The next day a neighbor brings the cat back. The day after that, he happens to see one of my lost cat signs and calls up to demand the reward. Should he have a legal right to get it?

People who see a lost cat and do not know whether there is a reward will be more likely to try to find the owner if they know that, if a reward has been posted, they will be entitled to collect it. Their increased effort increases the chance that my cat will be found. This might in turn reduce efforts by finders who know about the reward, since the more likely someone else is to find the cat, the less the chance that your search will win the reward. But the combined effect must be an increased probability of finding my cat, since it is only if, on average, she is going to be found sooner that there is any reason for informed finders to reduce their effort.

So far we have considered the effect of the legal rule only on the incentives of people who look for cats. What about its effect on the incentives of people who lose them? By making such contracts enforceable we make it more expensive to offer a reward; you may have to pay off even if the finder didn't know the reward has been offered until after he brought back the animal. On average, the result will be fewer offers of rewards. Whether the net effect is to increase or decrease the number of pets found and returned depends on the details of the situation: demand functions for lost cats, supply functions for potential searchers.

> "Contract" is not a preexisting entity of fixed dimensions; it is not a Platonic Form; it is the name given to a promise that courts will enforce. . . . The answer to the question whether the return of the lost article is the acceptance of a contract offer should depend on whether, if so, more lost articles will be returned—a difficult question, as it happens, and one unrelated to logic. (Posner [1973] 1992: 251)

Posner's philosophical point is right, but his economic conclusion is wrong. The return of lost articles, especially ones that purr, is a good. But time spent beating the bushes for a lost cat in hope of reward is a cost. The relevant question is not whether more lost articles will be returned if such promises are enforced, but whether the gain from the return of lost articles, net of the cost of searching for them, will be higher.

For a final puzzle consider the zero-sided contract, one that nobody has signed:

A physician comes upon an auto accident, stops, and treats an unconscious and badly bleeding victim. A week later the victim receives a bill for services rendered. Must he pay it?

Under current U.S. law the answer is yes. To see why, consider again the analysis of the choice between property rules and liability rules. Under almost all other circumstances the purchase of services is handled by a property rule: If I expect to provide you with services and be paid for doing so, I must first get your assent. I am not free to provide the services unasked and then bill you.

Why shouldn't billing for unasked benefits be treated as the flip side of suing for unasked injuries, a Pigouvian subsidy to compensate for a positive externality? The answer is that a property rule usually moves services to their highest-valued use more cheaply and reliably than a liability rule. If the service is worth its price to me, you should be able to persuade me to buy it. That approach provides a cheaper and more reliable measure of the value of the services to me than providing services unasked and then suing for payment.

The accident victim, however, cannot contract for the service, because he is unconscious, even though the service is sufficiently valuable to make it almost certain that it is worth its cost to him. So in this case, unlike almost all others, courts enforce a negative liability rule, a Pigouvian bounty for the conferring of an unasked benefit.

Filling in the Blanks

An opera star's employment contract covers many possible reasons why she might be unable to perform—but probably not the risk that she will be kidnapped by Martians or that a new religion will sweep the land and ban singing as a device of the devil. However carefully parties draw up contracts, there are always contingencies left out, either because nobody thought of them or because they were too unlikely to be worth including.

When the unlikely becomes the certain, or when parties discover that they disagree about what the contract they agreed to means, the dispute may go to court. It is then up to the court to fill in the missing terms or resolve the ambiguity. How should it do so?

One plausible answer is that the court should try to figure out what the parties would have agreed to if they had covered the contingency or resolved the ambiguity. For reasons discussed earlier in this chapter, that means that the court should try to find the efficient terms, the ones that maximize summed gains to the parties.

There are two arguments for doing this. The first is that efficiency is a good thing. The second is that such a policy reduces the cost of drawing up contracts. The parties can leave out unlikely contingencies, knowing that, if they arise, the court will try to fill in the terms they would have agreed to. One cost of the alternative policy of using omissions or ambiguities as an opportunity to implement the court's own agenda is that it gives the parties an incentive to write very long contracts.

If we accept this answer, the problem of interpreting contracts becomes the same as the problem of drafting them—figuring out what terms maximize the parties' summed benefit.

Risk Bearing

I have agreed to deliver ten thousand customized widgets to you by January 10th. Early on the morning of January 1st a drunk driver smashes his car through the wall of my warehouse, crushing half the widgets. One result is that I will have to replace them, at a cost of a hundred thousand dollars. A second is that I will deliver them a month late, costing you another hundred thousand dollars in lost sales. The drunk driver is dead, and his estate bankrupt. Who pays for the losses? In chapter 6 we worked through in some detail the problem of efficiently allocating risk. It is now time to apply our results.

One basis for risk allocation is spreading losses. Suppose I am having a house built by a large firm that builds many houses each year. There is some risk that the house might burn down while it is being built. We could allocate that risk either to me, by specifying that I will have to pay for the additional construction costs in such a case, or to the builder. Since the builder is building many houses in different places, he can spread the risk; I cannot. From that standpoint at least, our contract should specify a fixed price, whether or not something goes wrong. If the contract does not specify who bears the risk, risk spreading provides an argument for assigning it to the builder.

A professional photographer spends six months taking photographs in the Himalayas for *National Geographic*, at a cost of a hundred thousand dollars. When he gets home, he gives his film to the local Walgreen's—which loses it. Do they owe him a hundred thousand dollars?

From the standpoint of risk spreading the answer would be "yes." Walgreen's handles a large number of rolls of films each year, so it can easily pool the risk. From the standpoint of moral hazard, incentives to keep the loss from happening, the answer is "no."

Walgreen's has no way of knowing that there is anything special about these rolls of film. The only way they can prevent the loss is by increased precautions on all rolls. They have the choice of an inefficiently low level of care for ten rolls of film or an inefficiently high level for ten million. The photographer does know that these films are especially valuable and can avoid the problem by taking them to a specialist film lab and making sure the proprietor realizes what they are. The efficient rule from the standpoint of moral hazard is to make the photographer liable, because he is the one in the best position to prevent the loss. That, called the rule of *Hadley v. Baxendale* after an early case, is in fact the law.

In the case of the photographer moral hazard and risk spreading cut in opposite directions; a firm drawing up a contract, or a court interpreting it, has to decide which effect is more important. In the case of a firm that builds houses the two arguments go in the same direction. The builder is not only in a better position than I am to spread the risk, he is also in a better position than I am to keep the house from burning down while he is building it.

A third factor relevant to allocating risk is adverse selection. Consider again the New Year's widget catastrophe. I did not know that that particular drunk driver was going to crash through that particular wall. But I probably do know a good deal more than you do about the chance that something—accident, strike, or bad planning—will prevent me from delivering the widgets to you on schedule. If our contract makes me liable for the resulting loss, you don't have to worry about that risk in deciding whom to buy your widgets from. You know what price I am charging, and you know that I am insuring you against the risk of nondelivery. If the contract specified that you had to bear the risk, you would need to know the reliability of alternative sellers as well as their price in order to decide which one is offering the best deal.

As this example suggests, moral hazard and adverse selection tend to cut in the same direction. As a general rule the party with control over some part of the production process is in a better position both to prevent losses and to predict them. It follows that an efficient contract will usually assign the loss associated with something going wrong to the party with control over that particular something.

Getting Out of Contracts: Efficient Breach

The year is 1929. I contract with you to clear land that I plan to develop in a few years; we agree on a price and a schedule. In drawing up the contract we cover a number of problems that may arise—the land might flood, you might face a strike, I might get into a legal dispute over my title to the land. One of the contingencies we do not write into our contract is the Great Depression. Two years later, when you are about to start clearing, the real estate market has collapsed; the value of the cleared land will be less than the cost of clearing it. I tell you I don't want the land cleared; you respond that you have a contract to clear it and expect to be paid for doing so.

As this example demonstrates, breaching a contract is not always a bad thing; there is little point to spending lots of money clearing land that nobody wants to build on. This raises an important question for contract law: Should breach be permitted, and if so, what damages should the breaching party owe the victim of the breach?

The simplest legal rule is to impose no penalties at all. Some problems with that were discussed earlier in this chapter, in the context of *opportunistic breach*—the builder who takes his money and leaves or the buyer who renegotiates the price after the house is built. Others arise even if both parties honestly intended to fulfill the contract at the time they signed it.

We agree to a business deal that we expect will make each of us a hundred thousand dollars better off. After signing, something happens that raises my cost by a hundred and fifty thousand, converting a hundred thousand dollar gain into a fifty thousand dollar loss. Fulfilling the contract is still efficient, since your gain more than balances my loss. But it is a net loss for me, so, in a world without enforceable contracts, I breach.

Or perhaps not. I inform you that I plan to breach the contract, and why. You respond by offering to pay me an additional sixty thousand dollars to fulfill the contract. Fulfilling now makes me ten thousand dollars better off and you forty thousand dollars better off, so there is no longer any reason to breach.

As this example suggests, the Coase Theorem applies even in a world without enforceable contracts. As long as transaction costs are sufficiently low, contracts worth fulfilling will be fulfilled. The problem with unenforceable contracts is that they may lead to continuous costly renegotiation, with parties misrepresenting costs and benefits in an attempt to shift the terms in their favor.

Next consider the opposite extreme, a legal regime in which breach is forbidden. A party to a contract is entitled to demand *specific performance* of the contract. Failure to perform results in severe penalties.

The situation is the same as before, except that this time my costs have risen by three hundred thousand dollars, converting a hundred thousand dollar gain into a two hundred thousand dollar loss. My loss is larger than your gain, so the efficient solution is to cancel the contract. But you are still better off if I fulfill the contract—and this time you have the legal right to make me do it. Fulfilling the contract is inefficient but profitable—for you—so you make me fulfill it.

Or perhaps not. I offer to pay you a hundred and fifty thousand dollars for permission to breach the contract (strictly speaking, it isn't breach once I have your permission, but if I pay attention to that distinction I will have to use "terminate," "rescind," and "breach" in different places to mean essentially the same thing, so I will continue to refer to all of them as "breach"). You accept. Breaching now makes each of us fifty thousand dollars better off than performing, so we breach. Generalizing the argument, we see that as long as transaction costs are low a rule of specific performance produces the efficient outcome. Contracts are breached if and only if performance produces a net loss.

Here again problems arise because of transaction costs. When some unexpected problem makes it extremely costly for one party to perform its part of the contract, a rule of specific performance creates a bilateral monopoly bargaining problem. I am willing, if necessary, to pay you anything up to two hundred thousand dollars for permission to breach. You are willing, if necessary, to accept anything over a hundred thousand. The result may be a lot of costly bargaining, especially if costs and benefits are not as clear in the real world as in my example. Each side has an incentive to lie about its costs in order to get better terms—and to distrust the other side's claims. One result may be a breakdown of bargaining, resulting in the performance of a contract that it would be more efficient to breach.

Both unenforceability and specific performance are property rules in the sense discussed in chapter 5. With unenforceable contracts each party has the right to breach, so performance happens only if both agree. Under specific performance each party has the right to have the other perform, so breach happens only if both agree. In both cases the mechanism for producing an efficient outcome, moving the rights to their highest-valued use, is bargaining. And in both such bargaining has the potential to produce large costs.

Unenforceable agreements are common—although we do not call them contracts. Specific performance is an uncommon rule except in contracts for the sale of real property. Performance of such a contract is unlikely to be very inefficient; if the property I agreed to sell you is now worth more to me and I cannot persuade you to cancel the contract, I can always sell the property to you and then buy it back.

The alternative to a property rule is a liability rule: Permit breach, but make the breaching party liable for damages. That makes sense if we believe that the costs of controlling breach by renegotiation are unacceptably high. But it also raises a new problem: How to set the damages so as to produce the efficient result.

The answer seems obvious. If I want to breach the contract, I must pay you enough to make you as well off as if I had fulfilled it—the Pigouvian solution to the problem of externalities. By making me liable, the law forces me to take account of all the costs due to my action. If my gain from breaching is more than your loss, I should breach and will. If not, I shouldn't and won't. The legal term for this rule is *expectation damages*. If I breach, I must pay you enough to give you the result you expected from my performance.

The argument can be made clearer by going back to our earlier example. You expect to make a hundred thousand dollars from our contract. Under expectation damages, if I breach the contract, I owe you a hundred thousand dollars. If fulfilling the contract costs me more than a hundred thousand, I will breach and should. If it costs me less than a hundred thousand, I won't breach and shouldn't.

This is the correct rule if our only concern is efficient breach, but (as usual) things are more complicated than that. A single legal rule affects incentives on a variety of different margins; we must take all of them into account in deciding on the right rule. One way of avoiding the costs associated with breaching a contract is to fulfill the contract. Another is not to sign it in the first place. How does the expectation rule affect the incentives relevant to that decision?

Getting into Contracts You Might Want to Get Out of: Efficient Signing

Suppose that, if all goes well, signing the contract and fulfilling it makes each of us a hundred thousand dollars. If something goes wrong, signing the contract followed by my breaching it makes you a hundred thousand dollars better off and me a million dollars worse off. In deciding whether to sign the contract, I will take those facts into account.

The chance that something will go wrong, making breach efficient, is one in ten. Nine times out of ten I make a hundred thousand dollars, one time out of ten I lose a million. On average I am losing money, so I don't sign the contract.

But, seen from our standpoint instead of my standpoint, I should sign it. Taking account of gains and losses to both parties, nine times out of ten we make two hundred thousand, one time out of ten we lose nine hundred. On average we are making money. We need to revise the terms of the contract in a way that makes it in my interest as well as yours to sign it.

Doing so would be easy enough if both of us knew how likely each was to breach. Typically, I am poorly informed about events that could lead to your breaching, and you are poorly informed about events that could lead to my breaching, which creates a problem. So what we want is a rule under which each party has to know only the risk of his breaching in order to decide whether or not a contract is worth signing.

We get it by replacing expectation damages with *reliance damages*: If I breach, I must make you as well off as if we had never signed the contract. I owe you compensation for any expenditures you made in reliance on my fulfilling the contract—hence the name of the damage rule—but I do not owe you for the profits you would have made if the contract had been fulfilled. Similarly, you owe me reliance damages if you breach the contract.

If I breach and then pay you reliance damages, you end up exactly as well off as if you had never signed the contract in the first place. So if I am going to breach, it doesn't matter whether or not you sign. In order to decide whether to sign the contract, all you have to figure out is whether signing benefits you if I don't breach. In order to decide that, you have to know how likely it is that you will breach, since that affects the risk that you will owe me damages, but not how likely it is that I will breach. Similarly, in order for me to decide whether to sign, I have to know how likely I am to breach, but not how likely you are.

Reliance is the correct rule if our concern is whether to sign contracts that might be breached, since it means that you do not have to know the risk that I will breach in order to know whether a contract is worth signing. It produces an efficient outcome on the sign/don't sign margin, assuming each of us knows the probability of events that will lead him to want to breach the contract, but an inefficient outcome on the breach/perform margin, since I will ignore your lost profits in deciding whether to breach. The expectation rule for calculating damages, on the other hand, produces efficient breach but inefficient signing. To put it differently, reliance damages force me to internalize the external cost produced by my signing a contract that I am, with some probability known to me but not to you, going to breach. Expectation damages force me to internalize the external cost produced by my breaching a contract, given that it has already been signed.

Inefficent Reliance

There is a third margin on which both rules produce an inefficient outcome. Imagine that you are deciding how to perform your part of the contract. One alternative is to spend nine hundred thousand dollars customizing your factory to produce the new product. Another is to use the factory as is, making production cost a million dollars higher than it would be in the customized factory.

If nothing is going to go wrong with the contract, you are better off customizing. Suppose, however, that there is one chance in five of some problem that will lead me to breach the contract and cancel my order— after you have customized but before you have produced. Four times out of five, customization saves a hundred thousand dollars. One time out of five it costs nine hundred thousand, since customizing a factory for a product and then not producing it is money wasted. On average it is more efficient to use your existing factory.

But it is more profitable for you to customize. If I breach the contract, I have to make you as well off as if I had not breached. Five times out of five, your decision to customize your factory gains you a hundred thousand dollars. One time out of five, it loses me nine hundred thousand.

Putting the argument more generally, under either rule potential victims of breach decide how much to rely as if the probability of being the victim of breach was zero—because if the other party breaches, the victim will be compensated for the money he wasted by relying on the other's performance. But the efficient policy is to rely only if it is worth doing after allowing for the risk that something will go wrong. Both expectation damages and reliance damages result in an inefficiently high level of reliance.

There is a third alternative that solves that problem: liquidated damages. Instead of having the court set liability on the basis of how much damage it thinks was done, the parties agree in advance on how much each will owe the other if he breaches the contract. Since the victim of breach gets the same amount whatever his reliance expenditures, liquidated damages result in an efficient level of reliance. If they are set equal to what expectation damages would be, they also result in efficient breach; if they are set equal to what reliance damages would be, in efficient signing. It looks as though liquidated damages are unambiguously superior to both the other alternatives.

But liquidated damages must be set in advance, when the contract is signed. A court setting a damage payment after breach has happened has additional information about how much the real damage was. Thus whether liquidated damages are better or worse than the other alternatives depends in part on how serious a problem inefficient reliance is, in part on how well damages can be predicted in advance, and in part on how competent courts are at measuring damages after the fact.

Repeating Ourselves

There is one story and one story only
That will prove worth your telling
  (*Robert Graves, "To Juan at the Winter Solstice"*)

If you think you see something familiar in the analysis of penalties for breach of contract, you are right. The basic arguments are the same as in the analysis of optimal insurance. Expectation damages are a solution to a problem of moral hazard, alias inefficient breach. Reliance damages are a solution to a problem of adverse selection, alias inefficient signing.

One of the problems with eliminating moral hazard by assigning risk to one party is that it increases moral hazard by the other, with the result that, in most cases, efficient risk allocation minimizes the inefficiency due to moral hazard but does not eliminate it. Making Coca-Cola liable for exploding bottles results in efficient precautions on the assembly line but inefficient explosions when someone is shaking a bottle of Coke to make a point at the Fourth of July picnic. Similarly here. The loss due to my breach can be controlled by me by not breaching. It can be controlled by you by not relying too much on my performance. A legal rule that makes me liable for your losses due to my breach gives me the right incentive not to breach but gives you the wrong incentive to rely.

The Boundaries of Fraud

> We fired our guns and the British kept a-coming
> But there weren't near as many as there were a
>   while ago;
> We fired once more and the British started
>   running
> A-down the Mississippi to the Gulf of Mexico.
>   (*The Battle of New Orleans*)

The War of 1812 was fought in America, but the peace treaty was signed in Europe, with the result that the most famous battle of the war was fought after the war was over. The same time delay that made Andrew Jackson a wholly unnecessary hero and, eventually, president also produced a famous case concerning the legal boundaries of fraud: *Laidlaw v. Organ.*

Organ, a New Orleans merchant, got early word of the Treaty of Ghent, which ended the war and, with it, the British blockade of New Orleans. He took advantage of the information by ordering a large quantity of tobacco from the Laidlaw firm. When the news of the treaty became public tobacco prices shot up. Laidlaw tried to renege on the contract. Organ sued—and won.

The economic argument against the verdict should be obvious: If the only reason Organ wants to buy the tobacco today is because it will be worth more tomorrow, the transaction produces no net benefit. Organ's profit comes entirely at Laidlaw's expense. He is engaged in rent seeking, and any resources he spends on that activity, such as money spent making sure he gets the information a day early, are a net waste from the perspective of economic efficiency.

This example suggests the obvious counterargument. The particular use that Organ made of the information may have produced no net gain. But the production of information is itself a very valuable activity, and the opportunity to profit by generating information thus provides a useful incentive. The sooner people in New Orleans know the war is over, the sooner they can get back to the business of exporting tobacco.

Consider a commodity speculator who buys wheat today in the belief that it will be worth more next month. If he is correct, one result is that he makes money at the expense of whoever would otherwise have owned the wheat when its price went up. But another result is to drive up the price of wheat now, when he knows, and the rest of us don't know, that it is going to be scarce in the future. That gives other people an incentive to economize on their use of wheat, arrange for additional imports, and in a variety of other ways adjust in advance to future conditions of which they are as yet unaware.

The popular argument against speculation, that speculators, by keeping goods off the market, create shortages and price instability, is not merely wrong but backwards. A speculator who buys wheat today in order to sell it next month wants the price to be low this month and high next month, but the effect of his actions is precisely the opposite. He is driving the price of wheat up when it is plentiful, by buying it, and driving the price down when it is scarce, by selling it, thus smoothing out price fluctuations. The net effect is not to create shortages and famines but to prevent them, by providing ordinary people an incentive to adjust their present behavior to future conditions that can be foreseen by a sufficiently well-qualified expert.

In order for this to work the speculator must be able to profit by his superior knowledge. If the people who sold wheat to the speculator today were allowed to cancel the transaction after the price went up, there would be little point to being a speculator. If the Louisiana Supreme Court had ruled in favor of Laidlaw rather than Organ, and consistently followed the same rule in other cases, the result would have been less speculation and more unstable prices for agricultural commodities.

But while successful speculation is both productive and profitable, its productivity is not measured by how profitable it is. If Organ buys one day and sells the next, taking advantage of his early knowledge of the treaty, and if it happens that no decisions relevant to producing or using tobacco are made in that interval, he still makes money from the transaction. Thus speculation is an odd case of an economic activity that produces a private benefit that is matched by an external cost—the loss to the party that would have been holding the commodity when its price went up if the speculator had not bought it—along with an external benefit. The net effect is to provide speculators an incentive to produce valuable information and make that information public through the effect of their market transactions on prices, but that incentive is unrelated to just how valuable the information really is.

This analysis suggests a possible defense both for the decision in *Laidlaw v. Organ* and for the willingness of courts in some other contexts to invalidate contracts on grounds of fraudulent concealment of information. We want a legal system in which people who acquire information can sometimes profit by doing so. But we do not want a system in which people who happen to have information highly relevant to the value of what they are selling—for example, the fact that the cow they are selling is afflicted with a serious and not easily observed disease, or the house they are selling has the reputation of being haunted—have an incentive to withhold it, thus producing transactions that may well result in a net loss rather than a net gain.

The haunted house is a real case. The plaintiff was attempting to cancel his purchase after discovering that the house he was buying was widely reputed to be infested by poltergeists. The judge ruled in his favor, at least in part because it was clear that the house's reputation was due to energetic publicity work by the seller. Having told everyone she could reach, including the subscribers of *Reader's Digest*, that her house was haunted, she was not entitled to withhold that information from a prospective purchaser.

> Whether the source of the spectral apparitions seen by defendant seller are parapsychic or psychogenic, having reported their presence in both a national publication (Reader's Digest) and the local press . . . defendant is estopped to deny their existence and, as a matter of law, the house is haunted. . . .
>
> Finally, if the language of the contract is to be construed as broadly as defendant urges to encompass the presence of poltergeists in the house, it cannot be said that she has delivered the premises "vacant" in accordance with her obligation under the provision of the contract rider. (Rubin, J., in *Stambovsky v. Ackely*)

Further Reading

Lisa Bernstein, "Opting Out of the Legal System: Extralegal Contractual Relations in the Diamond Industry," *Journal of Legal Studies* 21 (1992): 115–57.

13

Marriage, Sex, and Babies

In most past societies that we know of, most people got married, most marriages lasted until the death of one of the partners, and most babies were born, although not necessarily conceived, in wedlock. None of these statements is true of the United States at present.

This raises a set of interesting questions. One is whether there is a plausible economic explanation for these changes. Another is what part legal rules have played, either as cause or effect, in the process.

The first step to the answer is another question: Why, in most societies, are childbearing and household production undertaken primarily by couples who have committed themselves to the long-term, often lifetime, partnership called marriage?

Why People Get Married

Many years ago I accepted a position in the UCLA economics department. Doing so required me to move across the country, find a place to live, develop relationships with a new set of friends and colleagues—costly activities that produced a return only if I remained at or near UCLA.

Suppose that when I came I received a salary of forty thousand dollars. A year or two later the department chairman, who is of course an economist, makes the following calculation: "If Friedman was willing to come for forty thousand dollars, despite all of the transitional costs he had to pay, he would be willing to stay for thirty. After all, if he leaves he has no way of getting back his moving costs, or taking his new friends with him, or . . ." The chairman calls me into his office to discuss the tight state of the department's budget.

I am happy to talk to the chairman. I too am an economist and have made my own analysis of sunk costs. I knew, and the chairman presumably knew, that for my first year or two I would not be a very productive member of the faculty, since I would be distracted by the costs of learning a new environment, finding out what colleagues I could usefully interact with, and the like. Now that I have finished that process I am more useful as teacher, researcher, and colleague. If he was willing to pay me forty thousand dollars to come, he should be willing to pay me fifty to stay. After all, there is no way he can get back the money he lost during my first year.

This stylized fiction demonstrates a real and important point: A fundamental reason for long-term contracts, in marriage or business, is the existence of relation-specific sunk costs. Before I came to UCLA both they and I were bargaining on a competitive market; there are other universities and other economists. Once I had been hired and both they and I had adapted to our relationship, we were stuck in a bilateral monopoly with potential bargaining costs. One way of reducing those costs is through long-term contracts—explicit, as in the tenure system, or implicit, as in the general custom of not cutting an employee's salary save under special circumstances.

Marriage is an extreme example. While many of us like to believe that our husbands or wives are uniquely suited to that role, it is not true; if it were, the chance of finding them would be remote. At one time I did some rough calculations on the subject and concluded that my present wife is about a one in two hundred thousand catch. That seems reasonably consistent with the fact that I found her, given the mechanisms our society provides for the early stages of the search process, such as sorting people socially by interests and educational status. I was lucky, but not unreasonably lucky. It is also consistent with the fact that in the years since finding her I have met one or two other women who might have been as well suited to me.

They might have been as well suited to me, but it would have been foolish to investigate the matter. Once a couple has been married for a while, they have made a lot of relationship-specific investments, borne costs that will produce a return only if they remain together. Each has become, at considerable cost, an expert on how to get along with the other. Both have invested, materially and emotionally, in their joint children. Although they started out on a competitive market, they are now locked into a bilateral monopoly with associated bargaining costs.

One way of reducing those costs is a long-term contract, till death do us part. There remains room for bargaining within the marriage, but the threat of walking out is removed. And bargaining within the marriage can be reduced by well-defined social roles, laws and customs prescribing each party's obligations, as well as by the knowledge that when the bargaining is over the two parties will still have to live with each other.

There are costs to that solution. The most obvious is that people who make the wrong choice are stuck with it. That problem that can be reduced by more careful search, but not eliminated. Clearly defined sexual roles may result in an inefficient division of labor, a husband who is good with children working while a wife who is good at earning money stays home. And even within the prescribed pattern, each partner still has available the threat of adhering to the letter but not the spirit of the contract. So far as I know, nobody has ever been divorced for cooking, or making love, badly.

My favorite evidence of the limits to contract enforcement in a traditional system of marriage is provided by al-Tanukhi, a ninth-century Arab judge who produced a volume of anecdotes for the entertainment of his contemporaries:

> A woman stood waiting on the road for the Vizier Hāmīd ibn 'Abbas and complained to him of poverty, asking alms. When he had taken his seat, he gave her an order for two hundred dinars. The paymaster, unwilling to pay such a sum to a woman of her class, consulted the vizier, who said that he had only meant to give her two hundred dirhems. But as God had caused him to write dinar for dirhem, gold for silver, so the sum should be paid out as it was written.
>
> Some days later, a man put a petition into his hand, wherein he said that the vizier had given his wife two hundred dinars, in consequence whereof she was giving herself airs and trying to force him to divorce her. Would the vizier be so good as to give orders to someone to restrain her? Hāmīd laughed and ordered the man to be given two hundred dinars.

In traditional Islamic society men could divorce their wives, but women could not divorce their husbands. Yet the vizier, and presumably al-Tanukhi, took it for granted that as a practical matter the wife could force a divorce, and not even the vizier could prevent it.

If traditional marriage provides a solution to the problems of relationship-specific sunk costs, why have we abandoned it? One answer is that in traditional societies child rearing was something close to a full-time job, and child rearing plus household management at least a full-time job. One profession, housewife, absorbed almost half the labor force. Most individual women were specialized to the job of being the wife of a particular man.

Two things changed that. One was the enormous drop in infant mortality over the past two centuries. It used to be the case that in order to be reasonably sure of ending up with two or three children, a woman had to produce children practically nonstop during her fertile years. Today a family that wants two children has two children.

The second change was the shift of production out of the home. Clothes are now made in factories by machines, bacon is cured by professionals. Clothes may be washed in the home, but most of the work is done by the washing machine. The job of housewife has, for most families, gone from a full-time to a part-time job. The result is that women are less specialized to a particular job and a particular man. There are still substantial costs to breaking up a marriage, but they are considerably lower than two hundred years ago, and, as a result, more marriages break up. Our legal institutions have changed accordingly, shifting away from indissoluble marriage to something close to divorce on demand.

I Gave Him the Best Years of My Life: The Problem of Opportunistic Breach

Two firms agree on a long-term joint project. One will research and design a new product; the other will produce and market it. The first, having done its part of the job, hands over the designs—and, in a world without enforceable contracts, the second firm dissolves the agreement, produces and markets the product, and keeps the money. This is the problem of opportunistic breach, discussed in the previous chapter in the context of building houses.

A couple marries. For the next fifteen years the wife is bearing and rearing children—a more than full-time job, as those who have tried it can attest. The husband supports the couple, but not very well, since he is still in the early stages of his career.

Finally the children are old enough to be only a part-time job, and the wife can start living the life of leisure that she has earned. The husband gets promoted to vice president. He divorces his wife and marries a younger woman.

It makes a better soap opera than my first story, but the economics are the same. In a traditional marriage the wife performs her part of the joint project early, the husband late. That timing, combined with easy divorce, creates the potential for opportunistic breach—encouraged by the fact that most men find women more attractive at twenty-five than at forty.

Once women recognize that problem, as by now they have, they adjust their behavior accordingly. One way is to become less specialized to the job of housewife, to have a career and hire someone else to clean the house and watch the kids. Another is to postpone or spread out child-bearing, so as to make the pattern of performance by the two partners more nearly the same. Both adjustments fit, and may help explain, changes in recent decades, including the increase in both age at first marriage and age at first child.

Another solution is to make the contract more nearly enforceable by imposing substantial damage payments on the breaching spouse. While that happens to some extent, there are a number of practical problems. One is the difficulty of enforcing such rules. Human capital is mobile, and a man ordered to pay alimony or child support may move to another jurisdiction, making collection hard. A second is the problem of monitoring quality, discussed earlier. If a husband who asks for a divorce must pay large damages, he has the alternative of trying to make his wife's life so miserable that she is willing to give him a divorce without being asked. And if we try to prevent that with a legal rule that automatically gives the wife a large compensation whenever a marriage breaks up, we create a risk of opportunistic breach in the opposite direction. The net result at present appears to be that, although husbands are sometimes required to pay money to their wives when there is a divorce, the ex-wife ends up, on average, worse off, and the ex-husband better off, after the divorce.

So far I have mostly been concerned with one oddity of modern society: the historically extreme ease and high frequency of divorce. The same arguments help explain a less striking oddity: the substantial number of people who never get married. We are left with a third puzzle: the large and perhaps historically unprecedented number of people who don't get married but do have children.

Out-of-Wedlock Births

One popular explanation for the sharp increase in the illegitimacy rate over the past few decades is that it is a consequence of welfare laws. Poor women are, in effect, paid to have children—perhaps not enough to make having children profitable in an accounting sense, but enough to make it profitable for some in the more relevant economic sense, which includes nonpecuniary benefits as well as pecuniary ones. A woman who is not quite willing to have a child if she knows she must support it herself may be just barely willing if she knows that the state will pay part of the cost.

The problem with this explanation is that although the highest illegitimacy rates occur in low-income populations, illegitimacy rates in parts of the population to which welfare is almost irrelevant have also risen. So although welfare might be one cause of the changes, it cannot be the only cause. A second piece of evidence in the same direction is that, despite recent decreases in the real subsidy to childbirth, the illegitimacy rate continues to rise.

A second explanation, proposed by my friend James Woodhill, is that the illegitimacy rate, like the divorce rate, has increased as an indirect consequence of reduced mortality—this time not infant mortality but mortality in childbirth. Until recent times the single most dangerous thing that an ordinary person could do was to have a baby. He argues that the result was a world where, in the age groups relevant to marriage, men outnumbered women. Women were thus in a sufficiently strong market position to be able to demand support for their offspring as a condition for sleeping with a man and bearing his children. As medicine improved and the numbers shifted, women's market position became weaker, with the result that some who wanted children were unable to find a man willing to support them.

To make the story more vivid, add in one more factor. Women typically marry men a few years older than they are. In the mid-sixties, as the children of the baby boom reached marriageable age, women born in 1947 were looking for men born in 1945—and there weren't very many of them. Some, unable to find a husband, accepted a lover instead. And so the sexual revolution was born.

A different and more elaborate explanation has been offered by two economists, George Akerlof and Janet Yellin, who argue that the increase in illegitimacy was an indirect consequence of the widespread availability of abortion and contraception. On the face of it, that seems backwards: Abortion and contraception prevent unwanted children, and we would expect that, on average, people who are not married are less likely to want children than people who are. Their argument, in my words, not theirs, goes as follows:

In a world without contraception or abortion, sex and childbearing are linked; they are, in the jargon of economics, *joint products*. Each act of intercourse produces both sexual pleasure and, with some probability, a baby. Both women and men enjoy children, but not equally; women have a higher demand for children than men do.

Here as elsewhere in economics, "demand is higher" means that the quantity demanded is higher at any given price. In a world where men father children but women raise them at their own expense, men may well want more children than women since, in that world, having children is expensive for women and inexpensive for men. But in a world where the costs were evenly divided, women would choose more children. That, at least, is the underlying conjecture.

As long as sex and childbearing are linked, someone who wants sex can only get it combined with a possibility of children. That is a good reason for women to refuse to consent to sex unless the man guarantees support for any children that result, either by marrying her or by committing himself to do so if she gets pregnant. She can expect to get those terms because other women face the same risk and thus make the same demand.

We now add in legal abortion and widely available contraception, breaking the link between sex and childbearing. Women who don't want children are willing to provide sex on much less demanding terms, since they enjoy it too. Women who want both sex and children must compete for men with women who want only the former. They end up getting them, on average, on less favorable terms. Some women who want children must have them without husbands.

There is an empirical problem with this explanation. Both reliable contraception and safe illegal abortions were available to middle- and upper-class women before they were available to poorer women. If the Akerlof-Yellin explanation is correct, high illegitimacy rates should have appeared first near the top of the income scale and then worked their way down. What actually happened was the reverse. To explain that one must combine their explanation with something else, perhaps the role of welfare payments in encouraging illegitimacy at the bottom of the ladder.

Before closing, I should add one more possible explanation: rising incomes. The richer people are, the easier it is for a woman to support children by herself. Some women may regard a husband as a net cost and so prefer, if possible, to do without one.

Explaining Sex Law

Many societies, including ours, forbid prostitution. Many societies, until recently including ours, forbid fornication and adultery. The arguments in favor of permitting people to engage in transactions in their mutual benefit seem to apply to sex as to anything else, so why do these laws exist?

The easiest to explain is the law against adultery—especially, although not exclusively, female adultery, which in most societies is more severely sanctioned than male adultery. The terms of a traditional marriage include sexual exclusivity. From the standpoint of the husband, one reason is that he wants to be sure the children he is supporting are his own. The wife does not have that problem, but she would like to be sure that her husband is not spending money that should go to her and her children on another woman and other children instead. For both there is also a link between sexual fidelity and emotional commitment—and emotional commitment, or if you prefer mutual altruism, helps reduce the problems of a bilateral monopoly bargaining game, which is one of the things a marriage is.

The Akerlof-Yellin argument provides a possible explanation for laws against fornication and prostitution. Even in a world without reliable birth control, it was still sometimes possible to get sex without marriage, and that fact weakened the bargaining position of women who wanted sex, babies, and husbands. Laws making sex outside of marriage illegal improve the bargaining position of women who want to get married, or stay married, or to maintain a strong bargaining position within marriage. Hence it is rational for such women to support such laws.

It may also be rational for at least some men to support them. If the argument is right, a longer-term result of access to sex without marriage may be a partial breakdown of the institution of marriage. If, as seems to be the case, children brought up by two parents end up on average as better people, more valuable trading partners and fellow citizens, than children brought up by one, preserving the institution of marriage may be desirable for men as well as for women.

Glittering Bonds

Premarital sex is not, popular opinion to the contrary, a new discovery. In most societies we know of, however, men prefer to marry women who have never slept with anyone else. This creates a problem. Unmarried women are reluctant to have sex for fear that it will lower their ability to find a suitable husband, and as a result unmarried men have difficulty finding women to sleep with.

One traditional solution to this problem is for unmarried couples to sleep together on the understanding that if the woman gets pregnant the man will marry her. This practice was sufficiently common in a number of societies for which we have data that between a quarter and half of all brides went to the altar pregnant.

One problem with this practice is that it creates an opportunity for opportunistic breach by the man, the strategy of seduce and abandon familiar in folk songs, romantic literature, and real life. That problem can be reduced by converting the understanding into an enforceable contract. Under traditional common law a jilted bride could sue for breach of promise to marry. The damages she could collect reflected the reduction in her future marital prospects. They were in fact, although not in form, damages for loss of virginity.

Starting in the 1930s U.S. courts became increasingly reluctant to recognize the action for breach of promise to marry, with the result that between 1935 and 1945 it was abolished in states containing about half the population. This created a problem for women who wanted to engage in premarital sex but did not want to end up as single mothers in a society in which that status was both economically difficult and heavily stigmatized.

The solution they found was described in "Rings and Promises," an ingenious article by Margaret Brinig. The practice of a man giving his intended a valuable diamond engagement ring is not, De Beers' ads to the contrary, an ancient custom. Data for diamond imports in the early part of the century are not very good, but Brinig's conclusion from such information as she was able to find was that the practice became common only in the 1930s, peaked in the 1950s, and has since declined.

Her explanation was that the engagement ring served as a performance bond for the promise to marry. Instead of suing, the jilted bride could simply keep the ring, confiscating the posted bond. The practice eventually declined not because of further legal changes—at present no states recognize the action for breach of promise to marry—but as a result of social changes. As premarital sex became more common, contraception more reliable, and virginity of less importance on the marriage market, the risk of opportunistic breach, and thus the need for a bonding mechanism, declined.

Byways of Seduction Law

A few years back, while investigating the history of punitive damages, I stumbled across an odd and interesting bit of nineteenth-century law. In both England and America, when a man discovered that his daughter had been seduced he could sue the seducer—even if the daughter was an adult. The grounds on which he sued were that he, the father, had been deprived of the daughter's services. Suits for seduction were thus treated as a special case of the doctrine under which a master could sue for injuries to his servant.

In one case a judge held that it was sufficient basis for the action if the daughter occasionally acted as hostess at her father's tea parties. Once the father had standing to sue as a master deprived of his servant's services, he could then base his claim, not on the actual value of the services, but on the reputational injuries suffered by the family as a result of the seduction.

The obvious question is why, given that seduction was considered a wrongful act, the law took such a roundabout approach to dealing with it. The explanation I found in the legal literature was that one party to an illegal act cannot sue another for damages associated with the act. If you and I rob a bank and you drop the loot on the way out, I am not entitled to collect damages for your negligence. Fornication was illegal, hence a seduced woman was party to an illegal act, hence she could not sue for damages. So the law substituted the legal fiction of the father suing as a master deprived of his daughter's services.

It occurred to me at the time that there was another, and perhaps more plausible, explanation of what was going on. In traditional societies, including eighteenth- and nineteenth-century England, fathers attempt to control whom their daughters marry. One tactic available to a daughter who disagrees with her father's choice is to allow herself to be "seduced" by the man she wants to marry, in the expectation that her father, faced with a fait accompli and possibly a pregnancy, will give his consent. That tactic appears explicitly in Casanova's *Memoires*, which provide a vivid and detailed firsthand account of life in eighteenth-century Europe.

A legal doctrine that gave the daughter the right to sue would lower the risk of the daughter's tactic for evading parental control by making it possible for her to punish a seducer who refused to marry her, and would thus weaken paternal authority. A legal doctrine that gave the father control over the action gave him a threat that could be used to discourage enterprising, and unacceptable, suitors.

In chapter 1 I described the economic analysis of law as involving three different projects: predicting the effect of legal rules, explaining legal rules, and choosing legal rules. In discussing the second project I offered as an example the Posner conjecture that common law rules tend to be economically efficient.

I have just provided a different example. My explanation for why common law treated seduction in the peculiar way it did depends on the assumption that the people shaping the law wanted fathers to be able to control whom their daughters married. I do not assume that such control was efficient.

Buying Babies

Some years ago I came across an article in the *Wall Street Journal* that astonished me for the degree of economic ignorance displayed by a publication whose writers I expected better of. Its subject was the adoption market. The writers discussed how that market has swung between shortage and surplus, between periods when infants were unable to find adoptive parents and periods when potential parents were unable to find suitable infants to adopt. They concluded that it demonstrated a failure of the free market.

There was one small point that the article omitted. Under U.S. law it is illegal for prospective adoptive parents to pay a mother for permission to adopt her infant. The adoption market is thus a "free market" on which the price is set, by law, at zero. The observation that price control leads to shortages when the controlled price is below the market price and surpluses when it is above is neither surprising nor a failure of the free market.

There are at least three ways in which shortages produced by price control can be dealt with. The simplest is queuing. When the United States experimented with gasoline price control under President Nixon, one result was long lines at gas stations. Waiting in lines is a cost, so when the lines get long enough the sum of the money cost of gasoline plus the time cost becomes large enough to drive quantity demanded down to quantity supplied. In the adoption market at present prospective parents must often wait years to adopt an infant.

A second way of dealing with the problem is rationing. Some authority decides which prospective buyers are given how much of the limited supply. In the case of the adoption market, the rationing is done by adoption agencies that are authorized to arrange legal adoptions. They impose their own criteria in order to eliminate enough prospective parents so that they can provide adoptions for the remainder. Some of the criteria they have used may be defensible as attempts to select the applicants best suited to be parents. Others, such as the requirement that the adoptive parents be of the same religion as the infant's natural mother, seem to make sense mainly as a way of reducing the number of applicants.

The third possibility under price control is a black market. It is legal for adoptive parents to make payments to lawyers to arrange adoptions and to the infant's biological mother to cover her medical costs. Currently, the cost of arranging a private adoption of a healthy white infant is in the tens of thousands of dollars, which is quite a lot more than the pecuniary costs usually associated with childbirth. Presumably some of that ends up as an illegal payment to the mother for her consent, disguised as something else, and some goes to the lawyers who arrange the transaction.

On this market as on others, the problem could be eliminated by eliminating price control, permitting adoptive parents to negotiate mutually acceptable terms with the natural mother. That solution has been proposed by, among others, Judge Posner. It is widely believed among his fellow legal academics that that fact alone makes it almost certain he will never be on the Supreme Court, despite being one of the most distinguished jurists and legal scholars of his generation. What senator would vote for the confirmation of a candidate who had openly advocated selling babies?

Why does the proposal produce such a strong negative reaction? The obvious answer is that it involves selling human beings, and human beings should not be owned. But what an adoptive parent gets is not ownership of a baby but parental rights (and obligations) with regard to a baby. If "owning" a child in that sense is objectionable, why is it not equally objectionable when the owner is a natural or adoptive parent under current law?

A better argument against a free market in adoptions is that, while it will maximize the joint benefit to the parties to the transaction—adoptive parents and natural mother—it may ignore costs and benefits to the child. But it is hard to see why that should be more true than under current institutions; in neither case do the infants get a vote. People willing to pay money to adopt a child are typically people who very much want to be parents—which is, after all, one of the chief qualifications for the job. Why is the willingness to wait three years and fill out lots of forms, or the ability to find and willingness to pay a lawyer with the right connections, better evidence? Adoption agencies claim to impose their restrictions with the welfare of the child as their chief objective—but why should we expect them to be more concerned with the welfare of a particular infant than either its natural mother or the couple that wants to adopt it? Infants have considerable influence over their parents, natural or adoptive, and very little over the running of adoption agencies.

A more interesting argument, and one with a much broader range of applications, goes under the name of "commodification." The idea is that a transaction between two parties affects others, not in the direct ways economists normally include in their analysis of externalities but in a more subtle fashion—by changing how people think. If we permit payments of money in exchange for babies—even for parental rights with regard to babies—we will start thinking of babies as things like automobiles and jewelry, commodities, not people. If we permit cash payments between a prostitute and her customer, we will start thinking of sex as a service that women sell rather than part of a loving relationship. Thus, argued Margaret Radin in a widely cited law review article, even if permitting prostitution makes both prostitutes and their customers better off, it might still be proper to prohibit it on the grounds that permitting it commodifies sex and so makes men and women in general worse off. On similar grounds it might be proper to prohibit a free market in adoptions.

I find the argument ingenious but unconvincing. Even where prostitution is common, very few people—prostitutes, customers, or others—regard it as a model for what sex is supposed to be. Men sleep with prostitutes not because they would not prefer to sleep with women who love them but because there are no suitable women who love them and are willing to sleep with them.

Also implicit in the argument is the assumption that what matters is what the law says rather than what people do. Prostitution, as Radin recognizes, exists at present throughout the United States, even though it is legal only in two rural counties in Nevada. Adoptive parents pay money at present to get an infant, probably more than they would pay if direct payments were legal, since the real cost of price-controlled goods, including waiting time, covert payments, and the like, is usually higher than the cost of the same goods on legal markets without price control.

To argue that legalizing such transactions will also make people see them as legitimate requires two assumptions, both implausible. The first is that if anything is not illegal it must be good, which suggests a view of society along the general lines of T. H. White's ant nest, where everything was either forbidden or compulsory. In a nation where private gambling is illegal but many states conduct lotteries, it is hard to believe that many of us make a close identification between good/bad and legal/illegal.

The second necessary assumption is that people view government as a source of moral authority. Current polling results put government fairly far down on the scale of public approval. As William Godwin put it almost two hundred years ago, in his response to the argument that we need government-run schooling in order to teach people morality, one should hope "that mankind will never have to learn so important a lesson through so corrupt a channel."

Commodification is an ingenious argument, but less novel than it appears. It is simply a new version of the traditional social conservative argument against both immoral behavior and free speech: that ideas matter, that preaching, or demonstrating, bad principles leads to bad behavior.

Seen from this standpoint, Radin's argument for why laws against prostitution might be justified fits oddly with the jurisprudence of the First Amendment. Courts routinely hold that acts that might properly be banned as acts, such as burning the American flag, are also speech, and because they are speech are legally protected. The commodification argument holds that some acts that ought not to be banned as acts, such as the transaction between a prostitute and her client, are also speech, and because they are bad speech ought to be banned. There is nothing logically indefensible in the claim, but once it has been accepted it becomes hard to see why one should not accept broader arguments in favor of government censorship of bad ideas.

I have devoted so much time to this set of arguments not only because they are interesting but also because they relate to an important set of legal issues raised by new reproductive technology. One such technology, in vitro fertilization, has now become both common and widely accepted. A second and technologically simpler practice, the use of surrogate mothers, is still controversial, with courts generally reluctant to enforce a contract by which a woman agrees to be artificially inseminated with sperm from a man whose wife is infertile and to turn over the resulting infant to the couple for adoption. A third, producing an infant by cloning a cell from an adult human, has not, so far as we know, happened yet but is almost certainly possible now. Coming up in the near future is the possibility of giving parents some control over which of the children they could produce they do produce, and perhaps, in the somewhat further future, giving their children characteristics that no child naturally produced by those parents would have. Other technologies, some of which have already been implemented in mice and could be in humans, could permit a lesbian couple to produce a child genetically related to both of them.

All of these practices have been or will be criticized in ways similar to current criticisms of legalizing the adoption market. Arguments will include claims that even though the transactions are voluntary, some participants are being taken advantage of. They will include arguments based on the presumed interest of children, with the implicit assumption that parents who employ new technologies will be less committed to their children than parents who produced them the old-fashioned way. They will get much of their force from a deep-seated belief that these things are contrary to nature, that they treat human life in ways it ought not to be treated. New things are frightening:

> What this new technique, and so many others like it, tell us is that there is nothing special about human reproduction, nor any other aspect of human biology, save one. The specialness of humanity is found only between our ears; if you go looking for it anywhere else, you'll be disappointed. (Mouse geneticist Lee Silver, responding to a bioethicist concerned that a technique that might make it possible to produce human sperm by implanting human cells in the testes of an animal challenged "the specialness of humanity")

While arguments against the transactions associated with new reproductive technologies will probably prevail in many courts, that may have very little effect on how widely such technologies are used. Consider the case of host mother contracts. Such contracts are criminal in at least one state and to varying degrees unenforceable in most. But that has very little effect on what actually happens, because people who want to make such contracts can choose where to do so—and, of course, choose states with favorable legal rules. Even where the contract is not entirely enforceable, that fact has become relatively unimportant as firms in the business of arranging host mother transactions have learned to identify and avoid potential host mothers who are likely to try to renege on their agreement after the fact.

Rationing Surplus Kittens: A Feline Digression

Some time back my children decided that they wanted kittens, so we took a trip to the local humane society. It was an interesting experience. We ended up spending several hours waiting in line to receive one of a small number of permissions to "adopt" a pet, filling out forms, and then being interviewed by a humane society employee to make sure we were suitable adopters.

What was puzzling about the experience is that kittens are a good in excess supply. The humane society has more of them (and of cats, puppies, and dogs) than it can find homes for and, although it does not like to say so, routinely kills surplus animals. Rationing goods in excess supply is not usually a problem. Yet the humane society was deliberately making it costly, in time and effort, to adopt a kitten and trying to select which lucky people got to do so, despite their knowledge that the alternative to being adopted was not another adoption but death. Why?

Part of the answer was that they gave out only seven adoption permits in each two-hour interval because that was as many as they could process, given a limited staff and the requirement that each adopter be suitably checked and instructed. But that raises a second question. Since they did not have enough staff to process everyone who came, why insist on extensive interviews? Better owners are no doubt superior, from the standpoint of a kitten, to worse owners, but almost any owner is better than being killed, which was the alternative.

So far as I could tell, the only real function of the process was to make the employees feel important and powerful, handing out instructions and boons to humble petitioners. That suspicion was reinforced when the woman interviewing us insisted very strongly that cats should never be permitted outdoors, stopping just short of implying that if we would not promise to keep our new pets indoors, she would not let us have them. On further questioning it turned out that she did not apply that policy to her own cat.

We left the center petless, obtained two kittens from a friend (and very fine cats they have become), and I wrote an unhappy letter to the local newspaper with a copy to the humane society. The result was a long phone conversation with one of the women running the shelter. She explained that there were two models for such shelters: one in which animals were given out on a more or less no-questions-asked basis and one involving the sort of "adoption procedures" I had observed. When pressed on the fact that the real effect of her shelter's policy was to discourage adoptions and thus kill animals that might otherwise have lived, she responded that if they followed the alternative policy, nobody would be willing to work for the shelter, since employees would feel they were treating the animals irresponsibly. That struck me as a kinder version of the explanation I had already come up with.

When the decision of what baby goes to what parent is made by an adoption agency, there is no good reason to expect the people making it to prefer the baby's welfare to their own. When the equivalent decisions are made for pets, there is no good reason to expect the people making them to put the animal's welfare—or life—above their own feelings.

Are Babies a Good Thing?

In recent decades it has been widely argued that babies are a bad thing, that when I decide to have one more child the predictable result is that other people are worse off and the world a less pleasant place. This belief, which has led to a variety of proposals for laws and policies designed to reduce the birth rate, is based in part on bad economics and in part on possible, but contestable, empirical claims.

The argument starts with the idea that more people mean less resources for each—less land, water, minerals, petroleum, and the like. The statement may be true, but the conclusion that by having a child I make yours worse off does not follow. Children are not born clutching deeds to a per capita share of the world's land and oil. In order for my child to acquire land he must buy it, which means that he must produce, or I must provide him, enough valuable resources to compensate the previous owner for giving up his land. The same is true for any other owned resource.

By buying land my child may (very slightly) bid up its price. But while that is a bad thing for those who are buying, it is a good thing for those who are selling. The externality, as I pointed out in chapter 3, is only pecuniary.

A better argument looks to real externalities associated with childbearing. My child may use the public schools. He may pollute. He may become a criminal. He may go on welfare. In these and other ways he may impose net costs on other people.

The list of externalities is too selective. My child may find the cure for cancer, and so save your child from an agonizing death. He will pay taxes, some of which will go to help pay fixed expenses such as the national debt or veterans' pensions that your child would otherwise have to pay. More people means a bigger market, more competition, more customers to share in the fixed costs of designing goods or writing books. An additional child generates positive as well as negative externalities. In order to argue for policies designed to reduce the birth rate, one must show not merely that there are some negative effects but that the net effect is negative.

As it happens, my first piece of economic research dealt with just this question. In it I attempted to estimate the size of the relevant externalities in order to calculate whether the net effect was positive or negative, whether someone having one more child makes the rest of us, on average, better or worse off. I concluded that the numbers were too uncertain to permit me to calculate with any confidence the sign of the result.

The point is not limited to this particular issue. Any time you are involved in a political controversy and somebody argues for taxing or banning something because it produces negative externalities, or for subsidizing something because it produces positive externalities, it is worth trying to draw up your own list of externalities—of both signs. It is only too easy to generate an apparently objective argument for either conclusion by suitable selection.

Two Routes to Efficiency

Perceptive readers may have noticed that in this chapter I have invoked two different sorts of arguments for the efficiency of law and custom. One derives efficiency from standard economic arguments, expansions of the simple case for laissez-faire presented in chapter 2. The use of engagement rings as bonds, for example, is a rational response by individuals to the problem of making possible sex before marriage while controlling the risk of opportunistic breach by the male partner. The increased instability of marriage over the past century would have happened in a world where marriage contracts were explicitly negotiated as couples rationally adapted the terms of their agreement in response to a decrease in the sunk costs associated with it. The same individualistic approach can sometimes also be used to derive from rational behavior the existence of inefficient outcomes, such as opportunistic breach due to women performing early in marriage and men late.

The same cannot be said of arguments that interpret laws against adultery or prostitution, or legal rules designed to protect children, as efficient adjustments to the corresponding problems. It cannot even be said of changes in marriage law as they actually happened, since in our society terms of marriage are not individually negotiated; contractual agreements on terms such as easy divorce would almost certainly be held unenforceable as contrary to public policy. Such arguments require some more general mechanism to push legal rules toward efficiency. It is not obvious, *pace* Posner, that such a mechanism exists. It is particularly puzzling if we wish to explain legal rules designed to protect children. Children, after all, neither vote, lobby, nor litigate, which ought to eliminate their welfare from influencing the mechanisms that most obviously determine law.

Altruistic parents care about the welfare of their own children—but not, or not very much, about the welfare of other people's children. If I care about the welfare of my children, I have no need to lobby for laws against abuse, or to make divorce more difficult; I know I am not going to abuse my children and that I will take due account of their welfare when deciding whether to get a divorce.

The distinction between arguments for efficiency based directly on individual rationality and those that require some more elaborate mechanism runs through the analysis of the law. The efficiency of the terms of a negotiated contract follows directly from the rationality of the parties. The efficiency of the law of contracts—supposing that it is efficient—is harder to explain. We will return to that topic in chapter 19.

Further Reading

The anecdote of the poor woman and the two hundred dinar is slightly condensed from *The Table-Talk of a Mesopotamian Judge*, by al-Muhassin ibn Ali al-Tanukhi, trans. D. S. Margoliouth.

Both the idea and the title of one section of this chapter are borrowed from Lloyd Cohen, "Marriage, Divorce, and Quasi Rents; or, 'I Gave Him the Best Years of My Life,'" *Journal of Legal Studies* 16 (1987).

The classic presentation of the commodification argument is Margaret Radin, "Market-Inalienability," 100 *Harvard Law Review* 1849 (1987); you may find it more convincing than I did.

Lee Silver, *Remaking Eden*, provides an entertaining and informative account of reproductive technology, current and forthcoming.

14

Tort Law

IF SOMEONE shoots you, you call a cop. If he runs his car into yours, you call a lawyer. Crimes are prosecuted publicly, torts privately. This chapter is devoted to torts, the next to crimes. A later chapter examines both, asking whether there are good reasons to have two different systems, whether there are good reasons why each is associated with a particular set of legal rules, and whether there is a good reason why our legal rules sort offenses into the categories of crime and tort in the way in which they do—whether, for example, it might be better to treat burglary as a tort and auto accidents as crimes.

The Logic of Tort

A tort is a wrong that is privately prosecuted, typically for damages, although some tort suits seek injunctions. Unlike contract law, which enforces obligations voluntarily agreed to, tort law deals with obligations imposed by law. To do so it must answer four questions:

1. *What makes an act wrongful?* When I go into competition with you I make you worse off, yet competition is not a tort. Implicit in tort law is some set of rights defining what acts are or are not wrongful.

2. *What does it mean to say that my act* caused *your loss?* Events in the real world have multiple causes. I would not have run you over had you not been walking down the road to have dinner with a friend—did he cause the accident?

3. *Under what circumstances is someone liable for a loss he causes?* What if I caused an accident, but there was no reasonable precaution by which I could have avoided it? What if both parties were negligent: I was driving too fast, but you were standing in the middle of the road paying no attention to traffic?

4. *If I am liable, how much am I liable for?*

As we will see, all of these questions can be analyzed in terms of economic efficiency. Whether doing so explains current law is less clear.

When Is an Act Wrongful?

Think of tort damages as a way of forcing potential tortfeasors to take account of the costs their acts impose on other people, a legal mechanism to internalize externalities and thus produce efficient choices. As I argued in chapter 3, your loss when I go into competition with you is only a pecuniary externality, not a net externality—you are worse off, but our customers are better off. On net, I impose no external cost, so I should not be charged for your loss. Competition should not be a tort and, at least since the fifteenth century, has not been.

To make the point clearer, imagine that I become my city's 101st physician. Before I hung out my shingle, the other 100 physicians were each seeing 100 patients a month at $10 a visit. My competition drives the price down to $9.90. At the lower price patients are a little more willing to see a doctor—total visits increase by 100 a month, just enough to keep me busy.

Each of the other physicians is now worse off by $10 a month as a result of my entering the business, ten cents less a month for each of 100 patients, which may explain why none of them invite me to join their golf game. That loss, however, is precisely matched by their patients' gain, since the patients of each doctor are now paying a total of $10 a month less in medical bills. The additional 100 visits that are being made as a result of the lower price must be worth less than $10 apiece to the patients, since they did not make those visits at the old price, but more than $9.90 apiece, since they do make them at the new. So my services must be worth between $990 a month and $1,000 a month. I am getting $990 a month for them. My reward almost precisely measures the value of what I produce, so I have almost precisely the correct incentive to become a physician. Competition is not a tort.

Neither is dressing badly. When I wear an orange shirt with purple pants or forget to mow my lawn for a month, I impose a real externality on my neighbors. Yet the former is never tortious and the latter rarely. The externality is hard to measure, and its size too small to be worth the cost of dealing with it through the legal system, so we use less formal mechanisms instead. Acquaintances ask, in a pointed way, if perhaps I am color blind. My neighbors mow my grass for me—along with my newly planted fruit tree (true story).

Ordinary tort damages are a liability rule, so another reason not to treat something as a tort is that we prefer a property rule. If I steal your car, you don't sue me for the resulting inconvenience, you call the cops. Since I do not want to be arrested, I buy your car instead.

So we now have three different reasons why acts that impose costs might not be tortious: that they result in a transfer, not a net cost, that they impose a net cost but are not worth controlling through the tort system, or that they are best controlled by a property rule rather than a liability rule. Acts that impose costs on others but do not fit any of those categories are quite likely to meet the requirements for a wrongful, hence tortious, act.

The next question is, given that a cost was imposed, what does it mean to say that I imposed it—that I caused the loss.

Causation Part I: Falling Safes and Very Dead Hunters

I stop my friend in the street to chat. He continues on down the street. As he passes by an office building, a safe falls out the window and crushes him. Have I caused his death? Should I be liable?

One sense of "I caused his death" is "had I not acted as I did, he would not have died"—the "but for" definition of causality. In that sense I killed my friend—if I had not delayed him, he would not have been under the safe when it fell. Yet it would seem odd to blame me and odder still to hold me liable. Why?

This puzzle is based on a real case. A tree fell on a moving trolly, injuring passengers. One of them sued. He succeeded in demonstrating that in order for the trolly to be where it was when the tree fell on it the driver had to have driven faster than the speed limit at some point during the trip. Breaking the law is per se negligence, so the driver was legally negligent whether or not his driving was actually unsafe. If he had not driven over the speed limit, the trolly would not have been under the tree when it fell, so, the plaintiff argued, the driver's negligence caused the injury.

The plaintiff lost; the court held that the driver's negligence had not caused the accident in the legally relevant sense. Logically, the court was wrong; economically, it was right. Why?

The driver decided how fast to drive before he knew when and whether the tree would fall. Driving faster did not increase the *ex ante* probability that the tree would fall on the trolly; if it had fallen a few seconds later, the extra speed would have prevented the accident instead of causing it. We could, in principle, give the driver the right incentives by penalizing him when his decision causes an accident and rewarding him when his decision prevents one, but it is a great deal easier to do neither. Since his decision imposes no *ex ante* cost, imposing no liability gives him the right incentives.

The same argument applies to the falling safe. *Ex post*, judged by what actually happened, my decision killed my friend. *Ex ante*, judged by the information available to me at the time, my decision had no effect on the probability my friend would die. There was a very tiny chance that delaying him would put him under a falling safe, just balanced by the very tiny chance that not delaying him would put him under a falling safe. I caused my friend's death. But for the law to take notice of that sort of causation produces less efficient outcomes than for the law to ignore it.

Coincidental causation is an extreme case of the general problem of foreseeability. The main reason to award tort damages, from the economic standpoint, is to give people an incentive not to do things that impose costs on others. But that does no good if the actor does not and cannot know that his action will impose costs and so lead to his paying damages. Hence unforeseeability is a defense to tort liability. That conclusion does not apply where the actor did not know the consequence of his actions but readily could have found out. In such situations the fact that he will be liable if damage is done gives him a desirable incentive—to find out what the consequences of his actions are likely to be and, having found out, to modify his behavior accordingly. Many real cases fall somewhere between "was, or easily could have been, foreseeable" and "entirely unforeseeable," leaving a difficult line-drawing exercise for the courts. We will leave them with it and go on to a second complication in the logic of causation.

Two hunters simultaneously, independently, and accidentally mistake a third hunter for a deer and shoot him, one through the head and one through the heart. The widow sues. Each hunter responds that he will be happy to pay for the damage he has caused, but that the difference between the effect of one bullet and of two is small—perhaps a slight increase in the undertaker's bill. Put in the language of economics, each points out that while the average cost per bullet was half a life, the cost imposed by the marginal bullet was close to zero and, if we conceive of tort law as a system of incentives, it is the marginal cost that matters. The conclusion seems paradoxical, yet the argument is logically sound.

If you find that implausible, try working the problem through with numbers. Suppose that if either Al or Bill hunts, his chance of shooting Carl is 10 percent. If both of them hunt, each has a .1 probability of shooting Carl, but Carl has only a .19 probability of being shot—a .09 probability that Al will shoot him, a .09 probability that Bill will, and a .01 probability that both will.

Suppose we (somehow—see chapter 9) value Carl's life at a million dollars. Further suppose that the law accepts the argument offered above. If either Al or Bill shoots Carl, he pays a million dollar fine. If both of them shoot Carl, neither pays anything. Does this give them the right incentives—make it in their interest to properly allow for the probabilistic cost they impose on Carl by deciding to go hunting?

If Al is not hunting, Bill's decision to hunt imposes a .1 probability of a million dollar loss, giving an expected cost of $100,000. It also costs Bill $100,000 in expected damages, in the form of a .1 probability of having to pay a million dollars to Carl's widow. Bill has the right incentive. He will go hunting only if doing so is worth $100,000 (perhaps he is a very enthusiastic hunter).

Next suppose that Al is hunting. Bill's decision to hunt now increases the probability of Carl dying from .10 to .19, imposing an expected cost of only $90,000. Bill's expected damages are also $90,000, since he has a .09 chance of killing Carl all by himself and owing a million dollars in damages and a .01 chance of firing one of the two bullets that kills Carl and owing nothing. Again the rule gives Bill the right incentive.

Repeat the argument for Al to get the same result. Substitute a different rule, say one in which a two-bullet accident results in each hunter owing half a million, run through the calculations, and you will find that each has an inefficiently high incentive to stay home.

The argument clashes sharply with most people's intuition of what the law should be. One reason is that, in the two-bullet case, it provides no money for Carl's widow. If the purpose of the tort system were providing insurance, making neither Al nor Bill liable wouldn't do it.

Tort law also provides Carl's widow nothing if Carl trips over a root while he is hunting and shoots himself. For reasons that will be covered at greater length later in the chapter, tort law is a poor way of providing insurance. It makes more sense to use insurance companies to provide insurance and tort law to deter actions that impose costs on others.

A second reason it seems wrong is that the numbers don't add up. Al and Bill, between them, have done a million dollars worth of damage, yet I am claiming that the sum of the damage done by Al and the damage done by Bill is zero. The confusion here is between marginal damage and average damage. The marginal damage done by Bill, given what Al did, is zero; Carl is no more dead than if Bill hadn't been hunting. Ditto for Al. The average damage is half a life each.

If this seems puzzling, consider one of the most famous puzzles in the history of economics—the diamond/water paradox. Diamonds are much less useful than water—compare a world with no diamonds to a world with no water. Yet they cost much more. Why?

The answer is that although the total value of all the water I use is very large, the marginal value of the last gallon, used to water the lawn, is low. In market equilibrium (for details, see a good price theory book) price equals marginal value, because people keep increasing the amount they use of something as long as a little more costs less than it is worth. They stop when the value to them of one more gallon of water is just equal to its price. They pay the same price per gallon for all of the gallons they get, including the (very valuable) gallon that makes the difference between life and death. They are buying water at its marginal value, which is much lower than its average value. Similarly, Al and Bill each pays the marginal cost he imposes, which is much less than the average cost.

Why do I spend so much time on such a counterintuitive argument? Precisely because it is counterintuitive. As long as economics tells us things we already believe, it is easy to ignore the logic and focus only on the conclusion. An economic argument that logically derives a conclusion that feels wrong forces us to think more carefully about both the argument and the intuition it contradicts.

In this particular case the logic of the argument is correct, but the legal conclusion, at least for the case of two hunters, is wrong. To see why we must expand the argument beyond the issue of causality.

One problem with the conclusion is that it depends on my assuming that Al and Bill are acting independently, that the double killing was a freak accident. If we accept the legal principle of no liability for double shootings, the next one may not be an accident. My proposed legal rule presents an obvious opportunity for getting away with murder.

A second problem arises from my implausible assumption that Al and Bill could actually pay fines that properly compensated Carl for the cost of being killed, at least in the sense explained in chapter 9. This brings us back to the issue of *ex ante* versus *ex post* punishment discussed in chapter 7. One argument for *ex ante* punishment is that *ex post* requires large punishments (imposed with low probability), which the offender may not be able to pay. We then have the choice of either a fine that is lower than the damage done and so underdeters the offense or a more severe but more costly punishment such as execution or imprisonment.

One solution to the problem posed by judgment-proof hunters is to supplement the inadequate *ex post* damage payment for killing Carl with an *ex ante* punishment for careless hunting. One way of doing so is to fine the hunters in the double-bullet case. Neither hunter did any serious damage, since Carl would have been just as dead from only one bullet. But the fact that they shot him is evidence that they were hunting carelessly. Hunting carelessly is an activity we would like to punish. On exactly the same grounds, we would also punish them for a near miss, assuming we could prove it, although that, too, does no harm.

While this argument implies that Al and Bill ought to be liable even in the two-bullet case, it would be a mistake to generalize that conclusion. One can imagine other cases of redundant causation where independence was clear, the parties were not potentially judgment proof, and the argument I have offered would go through, implying that neither party should be liable.

One can also imagine cases where the same line of argument leads to a counterintuitive result in the opposite direction. Suppose two people independently commit tortious acts such that either act alone does no damage, but the two together do a great deal of damage. This time marginal damage is greater than average damage; the same argument that implied that neither Al nor Bill owed anything now implies that each party should be separately liable for the full amount of the damage. Ingenious readers are invited to invent their own examples.

There is a delightfully logical illogic to causation in law, examined through an economic lens. In the case of coincidental causation, you did in fact cause your friend's death—but for your act he would be alive—yet the law pretends you did not and, economically speaking, is correct to do so. In the case of redundant causation neither Al nor Bill caused Carl's death, yet the law pretends they did and, economically speaking, is correct to do so.

Causation Part II: 9 Percent Guilty

Someone running a nuclear reactor makes a mistake, and radioactive gas leaks out. Careful calculations predict that the result will be to increase the local cancer rate for the next twenty years from ten cases a year to eleven. Is the owner of the reactor liable, and if so for how much to whom?

Under traditional common law the answer was "no." If a cancer victim sues, the defendant points out that since only one cancer case in eleven is due to his negligence, the odds are ten to one that this particular case would have happened anyway. A tort plaintiff must prove his case by a preponderance of the evidence, which is usually interpreted as requiring him to show that it is more likely than not that the defendant is guilty. Since the probability that the defendant is responsible for the injury is only about 9 percent, the plaintiff loses.

How might the legal system handle such cases? Not, surely, by holding the reactor liable for all the cancer cases. If we do that, the reactor is charged eleven times the damage done by its negligence, which is both excessive and inefficient. Generalizing that principle, any time a hunter is injured by a stray bullet and the guilty party is unknown, every hunter in the woods would be found guilty and required to pay the full cost of the injury.

One possibility might be to permit tort actions for probabilistic wrongs. A cancer patient could demand 1/11th of the damages he would have received if the reactor had been solely responsible. Alternatively, everybody in the area could sue, asking damages based on the *ex ante* cost, the increased risk of getting cancer.

There are problems with this approach. To begin with, if we are going to apply it consistently, all civil verdicts should take a probabilistic form. If someone who is 9 percent likely to have caused a loss owes 9 percent damages, then someone who is 60 percent likely should owe only 60 percent damages and not, as at present, 100 percent. An additional problem, if we permit suit for the risk of cancer cases that have not yet happened, is that before the cases have occurred we have very little evidence on what effect the radiation release actually had. And pooling claims by, say, a hundred thousand people requires a class action or something similar, raising serious incentive problems—how to make sure the attorney serves the benefit of the class instead of his own. Given the limitations of a trial as a way of solving a complicated problem, there seems much to be said for the all or nothing nature of verdicts under present law.

A less radical and more elegant solution would be suits by groups of victims. Suppose 110 cancer victims pool their cases and sue together. They have no way of showing which of them got cancer because of the release. But they can use statistics to show that the best estimate of the consequence of the release is that among them they suffered ten more cases than they otherwise would have, and that the defendant therefore owes the group a corresponding amount of damages. Alternatively, if our legal system treated tort claims as transferable property (as the legal system of Iceland, which we will encounter in chapter 17, did a thousand years ago), a law firm could buy up the claims of a large number of victims and then sue the reactor owner. That is a possibility we will return to in chapter 18.

So far as I know, the joint-suit approach was never actually applied to such cases. But there is at least one famous case that was handled in an analogous way, with the roles of plaintiffs and defendants reversed. It involved Diethylstilbestrol (DES), a fertility drug that turned out to produce medical complications in the daughters of some of the women who had taken it. The complications took a minimum of ten to twelve years to appear, and the most serious, a form of cancer, appeared, according to varying estimates, in between one in 250 and one in 10,000 of the daughters.

The case raised two issues. The first was whether there was any basis for holding the producers of the drug liable. In order to avoid releasing a drug with a side effect that takes a generation to manifest itself, a drug company would have to test each new drug for a full generation before releasing it, carefully monitoring the medical condition of not only everyone who took it but all of their children as well. And they would have to do it on a very large scale in order to detect so small an effect. That seems an excessive level of precaution, likely to result in much more expensive drugs and a lot of unnecessary death and misery to those denied new drugs during such an extensive testing period. So one could plausibly argue that the effect was not foreseeable at any reasonable cost, and the drug companies therefore ought not be held liable. By reaching the opposite result, the court provided no benefit in greater precautions, since even if the companies were liable the precautions necessary to prevent such a problem were not worth the cost of taking, and it generated a considerable cost in expensive litigation.

The other issue was, if the producers were liable, which producer was liable to which victim. DES was an unpatented drug produced by a number of different companies, no one of which had a majority of the market. By the time the side effect finally manifested itself, there were few surviving records to show which company had made the dose used by any particular woman. If a woman sued a drug company for damages, the company could (truthfully) reply that the odds were much less than even that it had produced the dose she took. The court settled the problem by allocating damages to the drug companies in proportion to market share, thus involuntarily pooling the defendants in a way roughly analogous to the voluntary pooling I have suggested for plaintiffs.

Liability: How to Get Only Efficient Accidents

> It is just and reasonable that if a person uses a
> dangerous machine, he should pay for the damage
> which it occasions; if the reward which he gains
> for the use of the machine will not pay for
> the damage, it is mischievous to the public
> and ought to be suppressed.
> (*Bramwell, L.J., in* Powell v. Fall, 5 Q.B. 597
> [*1880*])

After a long detour through the jungles of causation, it is time to return to a very simple question. I take actions that may impose costs on others—drive a car, shoot a rifle, blow up rocks with dynamite. The size and likelihood of those costs depend on what precautions I take. How can we use tort law to give me an incentive to take those precautions that are worth taking, and only those?

Our objective is not to eliminate the risks entirely—we could do that by banning cars, rifles, and dynamite. Our objective is to get the efficient level of precautions, and thus the efficient level of risk. We want a world where I get my brakes checked one more time if, and only if, doing so reduces expected accident costs by at least as much as it costs. We want a world where I break up rock with dynamite instead of a sledge hammer if and only if the savings in cost to me at least makes up for the increased risk to my neighbors. What we want is not a world of no accidents—that costs more than it is worth—but a world with only efficient accidents, only those accidents that cost more to prevent than preventing them is worth. We want the world we would have if everyone took all and only cost-justified precautions.

To simplify things, I start with the simplest case—unicausal accidents. I am engaged in an activity, flying a small airplane, which has some chance of injuring other people's persons and property. The probability of such injury depends on what precautions I take but not on what precautions they take. There is nothing other people can do, short of armoring their roofs with several feet of reinforced concrete, a precaution we are confident is not worth the cost, to protect themselves against the risk that I might crash my plane into their houses.

We also start with a simple legal rule—strict liability. If I cause damage, I am liable. In deciding whether and how often to fly, how safe (and expensive) a plane to use, and how often to get it checked, I will now take account of both costs to me and costs to others, since I bear the former and am liable for the latter (we will assume that if my plane goes down I will have time to get out with a parachute and will thus survive to pay damages). So it is in my private interest to take all precautions that are worth taking. Strict liability leads, in this case at least, to the efficient level of precautions.

Next consider a different legal rule—negligence. Under a negligence rule, at least as economists define it, I am liable for an accident if and only if I did not take all cost-justified precautions to prevent it. This view of negligence appears in the law as the Hand formula: A party is negligent if there is a precaution he could have taken to reduce the probability of the accident such that the cost of the precaution was less than the reduction in probability times the cost of the accident. A more intuitive way of putting it is that a party who imposes costs on others does so negligently if he has failed to take precautions that a reasonable person would have taken if he himself were the one bearing the cost of the accident.

Suppose airplane crashes are governed by a negligence rule. I have two alternatives: I can take all cost-justified precautions (taking account of costs to others as well as to myself) or not. If I do not take all cost-justified precautions and there is an accident, I will be liable, just as if the rule were strict liability. But as we have just seen, if I am going to be liable, it is in my interest to take all cost-justified precautions. So under a negligence rule, just as under a rule of strict liability, it is in my interest to take all and only cost-justified precautions.

How does which rule we use affect how much litigation we can expect? Under strict liability I am liable even if I took all cost-justified precautions, so we would expect strict liability to lead to more lawsuits than negligence. On the other hand, under strict liability lawsuits ought to be simpler, since the plaintiff does not have to prove that the defendant was negligent. So the overall effect on litigation cost is unclear.

So far I have assumed that courts are fully informed, that they know not only what the damage was and who caused it but also what precautions the tortfeasor took and what precautions he should have taken. Let us now weaken that very unrealistic assumption. Precautions are of two sorts: observable and unobservable. In the case of observable precautions the court knows both what you did and what you should have done. In the case of unobservable precautions the court either does not know what you did (whether, for example, I was paying attention to traffic while driving down the road or thinking about how to revise this chapter) or it does not know what you should have done. Since, in the case of unobservable precautions, the court cannot tell whether you were negligent, negligence now means failure to take all cost-justified observable precautions.

Under the new assumptions strict liability and negligence produce different results. Under strict liability the court does not have to know what precautions you took or should have taken, so the result is unchanged; it is in your interest to take all and only cost-justified precautions. But under negligence you have a more attractive option available. You take all precautions that are both observable and cost justified. Having done so you are non-negligent, so if an accident happens you will not be liable. You now choose the optimal level of unobservable precautions based on the cost of an accident to you but ignoring the cost to the victim.

Suppose I am involved in a minor auto accident. At trial I succeed in showing that I was driving at a reasonable speed, swerved when a deer ran in front of my car, and as a result dented a parked car. No cost-justified improvement in how I drove would have prevented that accident.

I could, however, have prevented the accident by not driving. A perfectly informed judge might calculate that the net value to me of that particular trip was only ten cents, the expected damage to people and property I might run into in the course of the trip was twenty cents, so not taking the trip would have been a cost-justified precaution. If so, then I was negligent from the moment I started the car and should be held liable for any damage I did thereafter.

In the real world judges do not have that sort of information; they know whether I took the trip but not whether I should have. How much I drive, my *activity level*, is thus an unobservable precaution. In the law and economics literature the distinction between observable and unobservable precautions is often given as the distinction between precautions and activity level. That is a convenient shorthand, since activity level is an important unobservable precaution, but a misleading one, since it is not the only such.

Strict liability does, and negligence does not, give me an incentive to take account of external costs in deciding on unobservable precautions such as activity level. So the more important unobservable precautions are, the stronger the case for strict liability over negligence. Judge Posner has proposed this as an explanation for the legal rule that holds ultra-hazardous activities, such as removing tree stumps with dynamite or keeping a pet lion in a cage in your back yard, to be subject to strict liability. His (plausible) argument is that "ultra-hazardous" is simply the legal term for the sort of activities for which the efficient precaution is often not to do them.

To see the same argument applied in the opposite direction, consider the Texas Supreme Court's decision in *Turner v. Big Lake Oil Company*, mentioned several chapters ago in my description of how courts make law. The question was whether or not to follow the precedent of *Fletcher v. Rylands*, the English case that established strict liability for bursting reservoirs. The court declined to do so, in part on the grounds that storing large quantities of water might have been an unusual use of land in England but was essential if one wished to grow anything on the parched lands of West Texas. Putting their argument in our terms, there was no point in using strict liability to give farmers an incentive to prevent accidents by not having reservoirs, since they were going to have reservoirs on their property whatever the legal rule was.

One common feature of the two cases, one in England and one in Texas, is that in each the court was clearly conscious of the wider implications of its verdict. The English judges discussed the potential loss of life from bursting reservoirs, despite the fact that the actual accident being litigated killed nobody. Presumably they had in mind catastrophes earlier in the century in which bursting dams had killed hundreds—in one American case thousands—of people and wanted to establish legal rules that would make such accidents less likely in the future. The Texas court based its result in part on the importance of reservoirs for agriculture, although the particular reservoir whose failure was being litigated contained, not water for irrigation, but salt water produced as a by-product of pumping oil. Both sets of judges were looking at the case from what I earlier described as a forward-looking perspective. They were determining not merely how to deal with a particular accident that had already happened but how future accidents would be dealt with, and thus affecting the incentives of the people whose future actions would determine how likely future accidents were to occur.

Dealing with Problems of Dual Causality

So far, by assuming that only one party can take precautions, I have avoided the complications that Coase introduced to the theory of externalities. We now shift the example from flying a plane, which might crash into a house, to driving a car, which might run into someone else's car. How likely I am to run into you depends both on how I drive and on how you drive. Auto accidents are subject to dual causation; how likely they are to happen depends on decisions by both parties.

Auto accidents are also dual events in another sense: When two cars run into each other, both are damaged. That feature of the problem makes the analysis somewhat more complicated without adding anything interesting to its essential logic. I will therefore simplify the discussion by assuming that all collisions occur between automobiles and tanks. Both drivers affect the chance of the collision, but only the car is injured. If we wanted to drop that assumption, we could do it by treating each collision as two torts, one each way, and applying our analysis to each in turn.

Start with a legal rule of no liability; if a car gets crushed, that is the driver's problem. Drivers have the proper incentive to take precautions, since they will have to pay the cost of any accident. Tanks bear no costs and so take no precautions. The rule leads to efficient behavior by drivers of cars but not by drivers of tanks.

To solve that problem, we switch to a rule of strict liability: tanks are strictly liable when they damage cars. Now the tank driver takes full account of accident costs in deciding how to drive (and how often to have his treads checked and whether to engage in random target practice while rolling down the highway). But the driver of the car, knowing that if a tank crushes his car the driver will have to pay to replace it (all cars in my hypothetical are equipped with ejection seats, so only the car is injured), takes no precautions at all. We have solved the incentive problem for the tank but created one for the car.

Next consider a negligence rule. When an accident occurs the tank driver is liable if and only if he was negligent. If we assume a fully informed court, the result is efficient. Tank drivers take all cost-justified precautions, for the same reason as in our earlier discussion: If they don't, they will be liable, and if they are going to be liable, it is in their interest to take all cost-justified precautions. Since tank drivers take all cost-justified precautions, tanks are never negligent, hence never liable. Since tanks are never liable, car drivers know they will have to pay the cost of accidents. So it is in their interest to take all cost-justified precautions as well. A negligence rule solves the problem of getting efficient incentives in a world of double-sided causation.

So does a rule of strict liability with a defense of contributory negligence. Under that rule the tank is strictly liable unless the car was negligent. Car drivers know that if they fail to take all cost-justified precautions they will have to bear the full costs of accidents, and if they are going to bear the full cost it is in their interest to take all cost-justified precautions. Since car drivers are never contributorily negligent, tank drivers know they will be held strictly liable, so it is in their interest to take all cost-justified precautions as well. We now have not one solution to the problem but two.

To make these solutions work we had to assume that the court was fully informed, that it knew what everybody did and what everybody ought to do. But under that assumption there is an even simpler solution to the problem of dual causation. The court announces that, any time there is an accident, any driver who has not taken the cost-justified level of precautions will be shot. Nobody wants to be shot, so everybody takes the cost-justified level of precautions.

We have just worked our way back to the simplest solution to the problem of externalities—a central authority who figures out what everyone should do and tells him to do it. Both evidence and theory suggest that, save in very simple situations, that solution does not work very well. It requires the central planner to have information he is unlikely to have, and it depends on the interest of the planner being the same as the interest of the planned, which is rarely the case.

In order to include some of these problems in our analysis, we again drop the assumption of fully informed courts and divide precautions into observable and unobservable. The result, applying the earlier arguments to the more complicated case of dual causation, is summarized in table 14.1.

The table has an interesting symmetry: Columns 1 and 2 are identical, save that the roles of tank and car are reversed, and similarly for columns 3 and 4. That is not an accident. No liability and strict liability are the same rule, with the parties reversed: Under no liability the car always pays for the damage; under strict liability the tank does. Negligence and strict liability with a defense of contributory negligence are the same rule as well: One party pays the cost unless the other party is negli-

TABLE 14.1
Results of Alternative Legal Rules

Optimal Level of	No Libability (1)	Strict Liability (2)	Negligence (3)	Strict + Contributory (4)
Care by tank	No	Yes	Yes	Yes
Activity by tank	No	Yes	No	Yes
Care by car	Yes	No	Yes	Yes
Activity by car	Yes	No	Yes	No

gent, in which case the negligent party pays. The rules seem different because it is the car and not the tank that gets smashed, so if the law does nothing, it is the car owner who must pay the cost. But if we think of the cost as jointly produced by the decisions of both and the liability rule as a way of deciding who will bear it, the symmetry becomes clear.

Table 14.1 might be useful if we were actually designing a legal system. Suppose there is some category of accident that produces a cost initially born by one party (car) as a result of decisions by both (tank and car). If the party in the best position to take precautions is car, if there are lots of things worth doing by the driver of the car to prevent the accident and few or no cost-effective precautions that the tank can take, then no liability is a sensible rule. If we reverse the assumption, strict liability is a sensible rule.

Suppose neither works. Some of the precautions worth taking should be taken by the car, some by the tank. The next step is to separate precautions into observable and unobservable ones. Suppose the important precautions cars can take are observable—not driving drunk, not veering in front of tanks, and the like—but the main thing tanks can do to reduce the number of accidents is to stay off the road. Staying off the road counts as an unobservable precaution, since although the court knows whether the tank was on the road—if it had not been on the road, it would not have run over my car—the court does not know whether it should have been. Under these assumptions, the efficient rule is strict liability with a defense of contributory negligence. Reverse the pattern, and the efficient rule would be negligence.

There is one more rule we ought to consider. Suppose we make tank drivers strictly liable, but instead of paying damages to car drivers they pay a fine to the state. Now both tanks and cars have an incentive to take the efficient level of precautions, observable and unobservable alike. Tanks bear the full cost of accidents in the form of a fine; cars bear the full cost because the driver receives no damage payment if a tank crushes his car. And under this rule the court no longer needs to either observe or evaluate precautions, so it requires less information than under a rule of either negligence or contributory negligence.

This elegant solution to the problem of dual causation has one unfortunate consequence: Accidents never get reported. After a tank crushes a car, the tank driver pays the car driver not to report the accident. That becomes even clearer if we shift to a more realistic picture: Everyone is driving a car, and a collision injures both vehicles. The rule now takes the form of double liability. Each driver is responsible for his own costs and pays a fine to the state equal to the other driver's costs. That gives both drivers an efficient incentive to avoid accidents, provided that accidents are reported and fines collected, but it provides no reason for either driver to report, since by not reporting he avoids the fine.

What I have been discussing is a normal part of our legal system—but not of tort law. When we convert the damage payment into a fine we also convert the offense from a tort to a crime and must shift the enforcement mechanism from private law suits to enforcement by the state. For more on that subject, stay tuned.

We have made our assumptions significantly more realistic and have shown why some legal rules are better suited to some sorts of accidents. But we have still not explained why, under a negligence rule, anyone is ever found liable. The argument so far implies that actors will always choose the efficient level of observable precautions—and it is observable precautions that determine the court's judgment of negligence.

The next step is to recognize that both the court and the parties may make mistakes. The court might be wrong about what the efficient level of precautions is and so find someone negligent when he was not or not negligent when he was. Tortfeasors might underestimate the efficient level of precautions or gamble that the court would underestimate it. Once we introduce court error some actors will find it in their interest to take more than the efficient level of precaution, in order to make it less likely that a court will (mistakenly) find them negligent when they are not. Others will find it in their interest to take less than the efficient level, in the hope that if there is an accident the court may mistakenly find them non-negligent. All parties will find it in their interest, if an accident occurs and someone is sued, to spend resources trying to generate court errors in their favor. Including such possibilities substantially complicates the analysis. It also explains why people are sometimes found negligent and why there are so many jobs for lawyers—and law professors.

One reason courts may make mistakes is that they do not know enough about the characteristics of the actors whose precautions they are judging. The optimal speed for you to drive depends, among other things, on how fast your reflexes are and how well you deal with emergency situations in real time. Since courts do not have that sort of information, they generally define negligence not in terms of what precautions are cost effective for you but in terms of what precautions would be cost effective for an imaginary "reasonable man."

Suppose you are a professional race driver and believe, correctly, that the speed at which it is safe for you to drive is substantially faster than the speed which is safe for the average driver. Further assume there is no speed limit, but that if you have an accident how fast you were going at the time will be one of the things determining whether a court will hold you negligent. Finally assume that the court, following a reasonable man standard, considers any speed above sixty miles an hour to be negligent. How fast should you drive?

You have two options. You can stay down to sixty, thus guaranteeing that if you are in an accident you will not be found negligent. Or you can drive faster than that, at the cost of being found liable if there is an accident. The second option puts you, in effect, in a strict liability world, where you will, for the usual reasons, choose the efficient speed.

In deciding between those alternatives you must trade off the benefit of being able to drive at what is, for you, the optimal speed against the cost of being liable for whatever accidents occur at that speed. If the cost happens to be larger than the benefit, it will be in your interest to drive inefficiently slowly. The same argument, applied to someone who is an unusually bad driver, implies that it may sometimes be in his interest to drive at sixty even though that is inefficiently fast for him, since at sixty he will still not be liable for any accidents he causes, and if he is not liable, it is in his interest to drive inefficiently fast.

Strict liability eliminates the problem. The court does not have to decide what the optimal level of precaution is; the driver, knowing he will bear all of the costs, makes that decision for himself, incorporating all of his private information about his own abilities.

It follows that if Posner's conjecture that the common law is efficient is correct, courts should tend to impose strict liability for torts where potential tortfeasors vary a great deal in characteristics relevant to the optimal level of precaution, since in such cases a negligence rule based on the characteristics of a reasonable man will overdeter some and underdeter others. More generally, we should see strict liability rules not merely where activity level is important (Posner's point) but where unobservable precautions are important—including precautions that are "unobservable" not because the court cannot see them but because the court cannot judge if they are worth taking. I do not know whether such a pattern actually exists or not.

Amount of Damages

You negligently injure me; I sue and win. How much do you owe me? The traditional answer is "enough to make the victim whole," to make me as well off as if the injury had not occurred. Chapter 9 dealt with one problem raised by that rule, the problem of adequately compensating someone for being killed or injured. Here we will consider others.

Enough to make whole the injury appears, at first glance, to be exactly what is implied by the Pigouvian approach to externalities, putting aside complications of double causation and the like. I impose a cost on you, so I pay a sum equal to the damage done, giving me an incentive to properly include the external cost in my decisions.

That works if every tortfeasor is detected, sued, and loses. But in the real world information is imperfect, litigation is costly, and courts less than omniscient. We can expect real-world tortfeasors to be found liable with a probability less, perhaps substantially less, than one. If so, tortfeasors will, on average, pay out as damages less than the full damage they do, giving them an inefficiently low incentive to avoid doing it.

One solution might be to scale up the amount awarded to compensate for the less than unit probability of a successful suit. Criminal law sometimes works that way. When you pay a hundred dollar fine for littering, the reason is not that your one Coke bottle did a hundred dollars worth of damage but that a high fine is required to make up for the low chance that any single act of littering will be detected. Tort law, however, only requires that the victim who prevails in his suit be made whole. It calculates damages as if they were imposed with certainty. One reason why that may be a sensible rule will be discussed in chapter 18.

There is an exception to this rule that has become increasingly important in recent decades: punitive damages. Ordinary damages are supposed to be based on damage done. Punitive damages may be more, sometimes much more.

Making Sense of Punitive Damages

Until very recently almost all damage awards in civil suits were based on the rule "enough to make the victim whole." Punitive damages, also called exemplary damages, were rare, so rare that in the nineteenth century a respectable minority opinion (supported by, among others, the Supreme Court of New Hampshire and one of the chief legal commentators) held that no such thing existed.

Before trying to make sense of punitive damages, it is worth looking at some of the early cases. One of the earliest, *Huckle v. Money*, involved a conflict between the British Crown and its critics. An anonymous article appeared in an antigovernment publication. Some King's Messengers—roughly speaking, the eighteenth-century equivalent of Secret Service agents—illegally forced their way into the house of the suspected author, holding him prisoner while they searched his papers. He sued. They argued that they owed him only for the actual cost inflicted by their efforts, a few hours of his time plus the inconvenience of cleaning up the mess. They lost; the court awarded him punitive damages.

A slightly later example involved a case of deliberate insult. One landowner swore that he would shoot birds on another's property without the owner's permission—and did. The owner sued and was awarded damages for substantially more than the damage actually done.

In the eighteenth and nineteenth centuries such cases were rare; more recently awards of punitive damages have become much more common. The legal requirement is that the tort be deliberate or reckless. The law puts no limit on the damages that may be awarded.

I have so far collected six different explanations for this doctrine, four that are explicitly economic, two that are not. I start with the latter:

1. *Punitive damages do not exist. What are misinterpreted as punitive damages are simply damages for hard-to-measure injuries. Having someone hold you prisoner in your house or shoot on your land without your permission humiliates you and lowers your reputation, and the court includes those costs in calculating damages.* This explanation is consistent with the early cases I mentioned and was a respectable minority opinion in the nineteenth century. If it is correct, then modern punitive damage law is a mistake.

2. *Ordinary damages imply no moral judgment of the tortfeasor—he is merely required to make up for the injury he has done. Punitive damages serve to express public condemnation.* But why express outrage by giving a windfall gain to the victim? Indeed, why use tort law at all, why not use criminal law instead to deal with outrageous behavior?

The next two are economic explanations, offered by Judge Posner and his frequent coauthor, William Landes:

3. *Punitive damages are a probability multiplier to compensate for the chance that a tortfeasor may never be sued or the victim may be unable to win his case.* If so, why is the criterion "deliberate or reckless?" One might argue that someone who commits a deliberate tort will also try to hide it, making detection less likely, but that hardly applies to a reckless tort such as riding down the street in the back of a pickup firing your rifle into the air. If punitive damages are a probability multiplier, they ought

to be based on how likely the offense is to lead to a successful tort suit, not on whether it was reckless or deliberate.

4. *Punitive damages are a way of playing safe if damage is hard to measure but efficient offenses are unlikely.* To understand this argument we start by asking what is wrong with imposing too large a penalty. One answer is that it gives people an incentive to be too careful, deterring efficient offenses. So if we are confident that all offenses of a particular sort, all deliberate torts, for example, are inefficient, we don't have to worry about the risk that we are imposing too high a punishment. If we are not sure exactly how much damage the tort did, we might as well guess high.

This explanation works a little better than the previous one. Part of what makes us describe a tort as reckless is the failure of the tortfeasor to take even the simplest and most obvious precautions. That suggests that his behavior was clearly inefficient, so we need not worry about over deterring it. In the case of a deliberate tort, the tortfeasor is paying some cost to commit it, unlike an accident, where you must pay a cost to avoid it. So the optimal level might well be zero.

Then again, it might not; perhaps the benefit to the tortfeasor is sufficiently large to more than cover the cost to both tortfeasor and victim. Even then, permitting the tort is inefficient if the same benefit could be obtained at lower cost via a market transaction. In the case of an accidental tort I do not know whom I am going to injure, which makes it hard to buy his permission in advance. In the case of a deliberate tort that is less of a problem. I could have paid you for permission to shoot birds on your property if my doing so was worth more to me than my not doing it was to you. So one way of viewing punitive damages is as a tool for enforcing a property rule.

But what about a tort that is both deliberate and efficient: polluting when you know it is tortious, are willing to pay for the damage, but cannot arrange the transaction because there are too many victims? What about throwing sparks in the cases where doing so, and paying damages, is efficient? In any case where damages can be measured accurately, setting the damage payment equal to damage done will be sufficient to deter all inefficient torts, so additional offenses deterred by a higher damage payment must be efficient ones—which we don't want to deter.

The final two explanations for punitive damages are my own. I am not entirely satisfied with either, but I think I prefer them to the alternatives.

5. *When we correctly take account of the cost of litigation in calculating efficient damages, it turns out that more deterrable torts should be punished more severely than less deterrable torts relative to the damage they do. Punitive damages are for a class of particularly deterrable torts.*

In order to explain this I must introduce a factor so far ignored: litigation cost. We would like to deter all inefficient torts, but not at any cost. If a particular offense does net damage, damage to victim minus gain to tortfeasor, of a hundred dollars, but deterring it costs a thousand dollars in litigation costs, we are better off not bothering.

The next chapter works through the logic of optimal punishment in some detail in the context of criminal law. Its conclusion is that the Pigouvian rule of imposing a punishment equal to the damage done in order to deter all and only inefficient acts is efficient only if doing so is costless. If detecting, litigating, and punishing offenses is costly, the rule for calculating the efficient level of damages becomes more complicated; the result depends both on the damage done and on how the number of offenses and the associated costs vary with the punishment.

If the supply of offenses is very inelastic, if it requires a large (and costly) increase in punishment to produce a modest decrease in the number of offenses, it is then only worth deterring offenses that are not merely inefficient but very inefficient. We do so by making the punishment less than the damage done. We thus deter only very inefficient torts, torts for which the benefit to the tortfeasor of committing them (or, equivalently, what it would cost the tortfeasor to take the precautions necessary to avoid committing them) is much less than the damage done.

Higher damage awards lead to more litigation cost per case. But if the supply of offenses is very elastic, higher damage awards also result in many fewer cases. In such a situation increasing the punishment, for example by imposing punitive damages, lowers litigation costs. It becomes efficient to set the damage payment higher than the actual damage done, deterring some efficient offenses in order to avoid the cost of litigating them.

The details of the analysis can be found in chapter 15 and, in a more mathematical form, on the web page. What is important here is the relation between this argument and punitive damages. Arguably, deliberate torts are particularly deterrable. In the case of an accident liability simply adds one more cost to whatever costs the actor already bears from the accident. The actor cannot simply choose to avoid liability by not having the accident, he can only, at some cost in precautions, decrease its likelihood. Deliberate torts are deliberate, so the actor can deliberately not commit them. Reckless torts are a harder case, but presumably part of what makes them reckless is that the tortfeasor easily could have, and should have, avoided them.

If this argument is right, punitive damages are awarded for torts in relatively elastic supply, ordinary damages for torts in relatively inelastic supply, and doing so is at least roughly efficient. Ordinary damages undercompensate, because they contain no probability multiplier—and they should undercompensate, since the optimal punishment, allowing for the cost of imposing it, is less than damage done if the supply of offenses is sufficiently inelastic. Punitive damages overcompensate, and should, since the optimal punishment is more than the damage done if the supply of offenses is sufficiently elastic.

6. *Punitive damages are designed to deter strategic torts.*

Consider a simple example of a deliberate tort: beating up the guy who is trying to date the same girl you are. The reason you do it is not that you enjoy beating people up but that you want to deter people from going out with "your" girl.

If ordinary damage payments fully compensate the victim of a tort, this won't work. You beat me up, I sue you, the court awards me enough money to fully compensate me for being beaten up. I have suffered no net injury, so neither I nor anyone else has a good reason to avoid offending you in the future. In the words of a popular bumper sticker, "Hit me, I need the money."

But ordinary damage payments do not fully compensate the victim of a tort, for at least three reasons. One is that damages are not imposed with certainty, so *ex ante* the victim is only partly compensated. Another is that (under U.S., but not British, law) the victim normally must pay his own attorney's fees. Finally, ordinary damages often ignore costs such as pain and suffering that are hard to quantify. The result is that if I expect to get beaten up for trying to date your girl I may date someone else instead, even though I know I can sue you and may collect. You have successfully employed the same strategy as the railroad company, in chapter 5, when it successfully deterred the farmers into switching to clover and saving it the cost of a spark arrester.

When you beat me up, was that an efficient tort? Probably not. Your gain may well have been greater than my loss, as suggested by the fact that you chose to do it even though you knew you might end up having to pay for both my damages and your lawyer. But I am not the only one who lost. By demonstrating your willingness to beat people up, you also imposed a cost on everyone else who might have wanted to do something you disapproved of, including all of the other men who might have wanted to date "your" girl—and on her. Hence in the case of a strategic tort the damages observed by the court and used to calculate what it takes to make the victim whole may greatly underestimate the real damage done.

Beating someone up, in our legal system, is usually treated as a crime rather than a tort, making my example an artificial one designed to link with the analysis of the economics of bar room brawls in chapter 8. For more realistic examples consider the early British cases, with a few added details.

I am a wealthy landholder in eighteenth-century England. One cause and consequence of my wealth is that I control several seats in Parliament. The reason I control them is that my tenants vote the way I tell them to, my neighbors' tenants vote the way they tell them to, and, in matters political, my neighbors follow my lead.

Recently one of my neighbors has been acting uppity, threatening to run his own candidate for a seat where his tenants make up a sizable fraction of the voters. Something must be done; it is time to teach him a lesson.

I publicly announce, toward the end of a local ball, that my neighbor is a rascal and a coward, that nobody with any sense would have anything to do with him, and that I think so little of him that I plan to shoot birds on his property next weekend, whether he likes it or not. I do it. He sues for trespass. I hire a good lawyer. Five years, many hours of time, much frustration, and many thousands of pounds later, he wins his suit. I pay him the cost of a day's rent of a grouse shooting field—and nobody else challenges my control over local politics. I have successfully committed a strategic tort. In order to stop me the court must award my victim punitive damages. Doing so not only raises the cost of my tactic, it also reduces its effectiveness, since what I am losing my neighbor is getting.

A similar analysis can be used to make sense of the earlier case. One objective of the King's Messengers was to find out who wrote the anonymous article. Another was to make it unpleasant to be known as a critic of the Crown. If the court had awarded only ordinary damages, they would have succeeded.

Punitive damages are not, as it happens, available against our equivalent of the King's Messengers. Our government, under the doctrine of sovereign immunity, can be sued only with its permission. The Torts Claims Act, which waives sovereign immunity for the federal government in a variety of contexts, does not permit punitive damages. When a Texas court found that the Secret Service, in the course of its search and seizure of Steve Jackson Games, not only acted in direct violation of federal law but continued to do so for several months after the relevant facts had been pointed out by the victim's attorney, it awarded the victim only a very conservative estimate of ordinary damages.

Why Pay the Victim?

One difference between tort law and criminal law is that under tort law the offender pays a damage payment to the victim instead of a fine to the state. Why do it that way?

One answer was mentioned earlier—to give the victim an incentive to prosecute. This is a good reason, but not quite as good as it might seem. If the punishment is a fine going to the state, the victim still has an incentive to prosecute—and then offer to drop the charges in exchange for suitable compensation. Arguably this is what happened in English criminal law in the eighteenth century, under a system in which criminal prosecution was not by police—there were no police—but by a private prosecutor, usually the victim.

If the fine goes to the state, any settlement greater than zero makes the victim better off than if he continues to press charges, and any settlement less than the fine makes the tortfeasor better off. Having the fine go to the victim instead of the state reduces the bargaining range, since he will only accept a settlement that gives him at least what the court would have awarded, net of any legal costs avoided by settlement. Reducing the bargaining range is likely to reduce bargaining costs.

That argument would apply to any private prosecutor, not just the victim—and under eighteenth-century English law any Englishman could prosecute any crime. There are, however, three good reasons for giving the right to prosecute to the victim, as is done in modern tort law. One is that the victim is the person most likely to know that the tort occurred, hence the one in the best position to report it if given a suitable incentive to do so. A second is that the victim is likely to be an important witness, so giving him the right to the fine eliminates transactions that would otherwise be required between him and the prosecutor. A third reason is that the victim has an additional incentive to prosecute: Prosecuting this offense may deter future offenses against him. A rule that gives the victim the fine combines the incentives in one person, eliminating costly transactions. These argument will appear again in chapter 18.

A more common, but less persuasive, justification for awarding tort damages to the victim is that doing so compensates him for his loss. As I have already suggested, and will discuss at greater length shortly, tort law makes a poor form of insurance. And, as we saw in the case of the car and the tank, compensating the "victim" can have perverse incentive effects, since the compensation reduces his incentive to take precautions to prevent the accident.

One exception is the case of the strategic tort where, as we saw in chapter 5, compensation reduces the effectiveness of the tortfeasor's threat. When the fine for starting fires was converted into a damage payment, in a world without complications such as litigation costs, the railroad's strategic position collapsed, and it installed the (efficient) spark arrester.

This suggests the importance of distinguishing between an anonymous tort, such as an auto accident, and a tort such as deliberate trespass where the tortfeasor knows the identity of the victim. With an anonymous tort, strategic behavior is not an option. I could drive dangerously in the hope that others would respond by being very careful, but, since I am only one driver out of many, the effect on their behavior would be negligible. The closest I can think of to a real-world example of that tactic is a friend who never took dents out of her car, on the theory that other drivers would conclude that since she wasn't careful they should be.

Nonanonymous torts create not only the risk of strategic behavior but also an opportunity for bargaining. In interactions between neighbors we may not need tort law to move us to the right outcome. As we move toward less anonymous torts we also move toward a world where property rules may make more sense than liability rules.

Dual Causation and Product Liability or Who Pays for Coke Grenades?

Product liability, a legal issue located on the border between tort and contract, has been responsible for a great deal of litigation in recent decades. The fundamental question is who is to be held responsible when something unexpected goes wrong in the use of a product, when a Coke bottle explodes or a lawn mower injures the person pushing it. Do we follow a rule of *caveat emptor* (let the buyer beware), under which the buyer takes the good as he finds it, complete with any defects, or a rule of *caveat venditor*, under which, if anything goes wrong, the seller is liable? Or are there, perhaps, better alternatives?

This way of putting it makes the distinction too sharp. If your wife takes out your gun and shoots you, something has gone wrong; that isn't what you bought the gun for. But even under *caveat venditor* the manufacturer of the gun is unlikely to be held liable. Product liability law deals with the subset of "things going wrong" associated with defective products. Even then the category is large and vague. Lawn mowers are supposed to cut things; when they cut the wrong things it is not always clear whether the defect is in the machine or the man pushing it.

The obvious basis for choosing a liability rule is its effect on the incentives of people to do things that prevent accidents, to make Coke bottles that don't blow up, or to design safer mowers. If Coca-Cola is liable, that gives them an incentive to maintain high levels of quality control in order to make sure bottles rarely blow up, which is an argument for *caveat venditor*.

The problem is more complicated than that for two reasons. The first is that users can also prevent accidents—by not shaking Coke bottles in hot weather, by wearing shoes while mowing the lawn, and by having a couple of beers after mowing the lawn, not before. When I looked through some real cases involving exploding Coke bottles—all of them, of course, dating from before Coca-Cola switched from glass to plastic—I came across one where the bottle had been out of refrigeration for thirty-six hours, in Fresno, California, before it exploded. To the extent that liability law insures the user against accidents, it reduces his incentive to prevent them, which is an argument for *caveat emptor.* We are back with the problem of moral hazard discussed in chapter 6, and the same answer: Put the incentive wherever it will do the most good.

A second complication is that even if Coca-Cola is not liable it may still have a good reason to make sure its bottles don't explode: reputation. If consumers have a reasonably accurate idea of how risky their bottles are, poor quality control will be punished by lost sales. In a world of fully informed consumers *caveat emptor* results in efficient precautions by both sides, by Coca-Cola to maintain its reputation and by users because they will bear the cost of any accidents. The same would be true of *caveat venditor* if Coca-Cola were fully informed about what each customer was going to do with each bottle and could adjust its price accordingly, but it is hard to be fully informed about things that have not yet happened.

In order for reputation to provide Coca-Cola with the proper incentives, consumers must be well informed not merely about the risk of bottles blowing up, but about the risk of Coke bottles blowing up, so that it is Coca-Cola, not the whole industry, that gets reputational benefits from Coca-Cola's quality control. How plausible this assumption is will vary from one product to another. If consumers are entirely uninformed about product quality, if, for instance, they are buying medical drugs whose side effects may not show up for many years, reputation might give little or no incentive to the seller. If so, that is an argument for making the seller liable.

One way of not being blinded by an exploding Coke bottle is to take precautions—keep it cold, and, if for some reason you must handle warm bottles, wear leather gloves and glasses. Another way is not to buy it. If consumers are fully informed about risks, one result is that producers have the right incentive. Another is that consumers can make the correct decisions about what to buy. If they are ignorant of an important dimension of quality, such as the risk of defects, that no longer works. A consumer who seriously underestimates the risk of defects may buy something worth less to him than the price, while a consumer who overestimates the risk may make the opposite mistake. We are again back in chapter 6, this time with the problem of adverse selection.

If the seller knows the risk and the buyer does not, the solution is for the seller to insure the product, which is what *caveat venditor* makes him do. Coca-Cola is selling a bottle of Coke with an insurance policy attached and, knowing the risk, knows what both cost. The buyer is buying a bottle and an insurance policy, and, because the policy will cover his losses if the bottle proves defective, he does not have to know how great that risk is in order to decide if the package is worth its price. The same argument implies that if it is the buyer who best knows the risk—knows, for example, that he plans to use his new car for drag racing, not commuting—the seller should not be liable.

These arguments give us a fairly straightforward result, although one not always easy to apply in practice. If buyers have accurate information about how risky each firm's products are, the right rule is *caveat emptor.* If buyers do not have such information but sellers do and sellers are in the best position to prevent accidents, the best rule is *caveat venditor.* In more complicated situations, such as ones in which sellers know the risk but buyers can best control it, we must either figure out which consideration is more important or go with some intermediate solution, such as making the seller liable for only part of the risk.

That compromise, the liability law equivalent of coinsurance, may be the one implicit in much of tort law. Traditionally damage awards were based on a narrow definition of costs; although that has changed somewhat, they are still low enough on average so that (bumper stickers to the contrary) very few people really want someone to run into them so that they can sue him. Hence even with tort rules that make someone else liable, most of us still have at least some incentive to avoid being victims.

So far I have neglected one argument often used to justify making producers liable—the fact that they are usually in a better position than consumers to spread the risk. I may, if I am very unlucky, have one Coke bottle blow up on me in the course of my life. Coca-Cola sells many millions of bottles a year. Their loss, if they are liable for such accidents, like the loss borne by an insurance company insuring many houses, is reasonably predictable.

The reason I have neglected the issue of risk spreading is that although consumers want protection against risk and tort law can provide it, there is a better alternative. Insurance policies have two important advantages over liability law as a mechanism for protecting people from risk. The first is that liability law is too selective. If I hurt my hand because a Coke bottle explodes, liability law may reimburse me for the loss, but if I slip on my own icy front stairs and hurt my hand, there is nobody to sue but myself. What I want protection against is not risk due to defective products, or risk due to other people's negligence, but risk in general. That is an argument for using insurance policies to provide protection against accidents and tort law to give people the proper incentive to prevent them.

A second advantage of insurance over tort law is that an insurance company wants a reputation for being generous in paying out benefits— not so generous as to encourage fraudulent claims, but generous enough

so that people want to buy insurance from it. A litigator wants the opposite reputation. The harder he makes things for the plaintiff in this suit,
the less likely it is that the next plaintiff will try his luck. The adversarial
relation between plaintiff and defendant is likely to result in much higher
costs than the (relatively) cooperative relation between an insurance company and a customer filing a claim. On average, of every dollar paid out
by tort defendants in damages and attorney fees, tort plaintiffs, after paying their attorneys, receive about fifty cents.

This suggests a further consideration relevant to the choice of a liability
rule: litigation costs. Under *caveat emptor* nobody is liable, nobody is
sued, and nobody has to pay any lawyers. Under *caveat venditor* the injured consumer must sue, or at least threaten to sue, in order to collect
damages. That is a general argument, here and elsewhere in the law, for
letting losses remain where they fall, to be weighed against the gains we
sometimes get by shifting them somewhere else.

We have been talking in terms of two simple alternatives: *caveat emptor* and *caveat venditor*. Courts might distinguish more finely, imposing
caveat emptor for some sorts of risks and *caveat venditor* for others,
along the lines we have just been sketching out. Or they might apply
negligence principles, holding Coca-Cola liable only if it could be shown
that it had failed to take appropriate precautions (negligence liability) or
holding it liable unless it could show the user had failed to take appropriate precautions (strict liability with contributory negligence).

So far I have assumed that the liability rule, whatever it is, is to be set
by courts or perhaps legislatures. There is another alternative: contract.
Every time an auto company provides a thirty thousand mile guarantee,
it is imposing a rule of *caveat venditor* on itself for the particular sorts of
defects covered by the guarantee.

Under a legal regime of freedom of contract courts set default rules but
leave parties free to change them. If the court imposes *caveat emptor* and
sellers believe that the shift to *caveat venditor* would be worth more to
buyers than it costs them, then sellers offer guarantees and raise their
price accordingly. If the court imposes *caveat venditor* and buyers value
the resulting legal protection at less than it costs sellers to provide it, then
buyers agree to sign waivers of liability, converting the rule to *caveat
emptor* in exchange for an appropriate reduction in price. The economic
analysis of what liability rule is most appropriate to any given situation
is still useful under freedom of contract, both to courts choosing default
rules and to parties deciding whether or not it is worth contracting
around them. But the final decision is made by the parties, not the court.

The argument for permitting freedom of contract depends on consumers and sellers being rational and having some information, but it does
not require the sort of full information that is needed to make *caveat*

emptor automatically the right rule. Consumers do not have to know what the risk of Coke bottles blowing up is. They only have to know enough to decide whether, on average, they are better off with or without a guarantee, whether, for one part or another of their economic dealings, they prefer *caveat emptor* or *caveat venditor*, given the price of each.

The discussion of freedom of contract points out an important distinction that can easily be missed: between deciding what the right legal rules are and deciding what mechanism will be most likely to produce them. The analysis of the choice between *caveat emptor* and *caveat venditor* focused on the first question: When is one rule or the other superior? The analysis of the choice between freedom of contract and mandatory liability rules set by courts or legislatures focused on the second question— which mechanism is most likely to generate the superior rule.

Poker, the Value of Information, and Judicial Negligence

> Now, even if you do get information that you did
> not expect, it means nothing if this new, surprising
> information does not change your strategy.
> (*David Sklansky*, Fighting Fuzzy Thinking in
> Poker, Gaming & Life)

Sklansky is discussing poker—specifically the question of when it is worth paying for information about another player's strategy by making bets that reveal information but, on average, lose money—but his analysis applies more widely, as the title of his book suggests. Providing and evaluating information is costly for both producer and consumer; whether it is worth doing depends on how much the information is worth. If a bottle of Coke is worth a dollar to me and sells for fifty cents, learning that it carries with it a risk of explosion that I would evaluate as a two cent cost has no effect on my behavior. The bottle is still worth more than it costs, so I still buy it. If the bottle was worth 51 cents to me, the information does affect my behavior (value $51 - 2 = 49$ cents, cost 50 cents, so I don't buy it), but since the bottle is actually worth only a penny less than it costs, buying it would be only a very minor mistake.

Generalizing the argument, information that has only a small effect on how much a good is worth to a consumer is unlikely to affect whether he buys it; if it does push him over the edge into not buying, the result is only a small savings. So adverse selection is important only if the missing information has a large effect on the value of the good—for example, whether a car is a lemon or a cream puff. It follows that failure to provide information should not be actionable unless the information has a substantial effect on the value of the good to the consumer. Failure to recognize that principle gives us a world where the instruction manual for every product starts with fifteen pages of warnings aimed at the jury in some future damage suit, all of which the rational consumer ignores.

To see how this requirement plays out in real-world law, consider the polio vaccination cases. About one person in a million who was inoculated with the Sabin live virus vaccine got polio as a result. Since there was no known way of immunizing against polio without that risk, courts held that the vaccine was "inherently dangerous," hence not a defective product.

While there is no way of making an inherently dangerous product safe, one can still avoid the danger by not using the product. Hence the question arose of whether the producers of the vaccine were negligent, not for producing the vaccine but for failing adequately to warn those who used it. The producers provided warning information to physicians and others who dispensed the vaccine but did not take precautions to make sure that everyone who got the vaccine also got an individualized warning.

Whether that was negligent, at least in the economist's sense, depends on whether the warning would have made a difference, whether there was a significant chance that someone who was informed of the risk would conclude as a result that it was not in his interest to be vaccinated. In *Davis v. Wyeth Laboratories, Inc.* the court accepted that argument and attempted to calculate the relevant costs and benefits:

> The Surgeon General's report . . . predicted that for the 1962 season only .9 persons over 20 years of age out of a million would contract polio from natural sources. . . . Thus appellant's risk of contracting the disease without immunization was about as great (or small) as his risk of contracting it from the vaccine. Under these circumstances we cannot agree . . . that the choice to take the vaccine was clear.

If the mistake is not obvious, read it again. The court is comparing the risk to Davis from being immunized—about one chance in a million of contracting polio—with the risk of not being immunized. To estimate the latter it uses the fraction of the adult population that could be expected to contract polio from natural sources *in one year.* But immunization lasts for life, so the relevant comparison is to his lifetime chance of ever contracting polio, perhaps with a weighting factor to take account of the fact that the later he contracts it the smaller the fraction of his life affected.

If we assume that the risk was constant over time and measure the cost of getting polio by number of years of normal life lost, the court's calculation was off by about a factor of twenty-five, making the benefit of the vaccine more than twenty times the cost. The mistake is one that a bright high school student should have caught. If judges, like pharmaceutical companies, were legally liable for the consequences of their negligence, the judge who wrote that opinion and those who joined in it would have owed Wyeth a very large amount of money.

Eggshell Skulls and Inconsistent Legal Rules

> The plaintiff was about 14 years of age, and the
> defendant about 11 years of age. On the 20th day
> of February, 1889, they were sitting opposite
> to each other across an aisle in the high school of
> the village of Waukesha. The defendant reached
> across the aisle with his foot, and hit with his toe
> the shin of the right leg of the plaintiff. The
> touch was slight. . . . In a few moments he felt
> a violent pain in that place, which caused him
> to cry out loudly. . . . He will never recover the
> use of his limb.
> (Vosburg v. Putney, *80 Wis. 523, 50 N.W. 403
> [1891]*)

So begins one of the odder cases of the common law. For reasons nobody seems to have understood, something serious went wrong with Vosburg's leg after it was lightly kicked by Putney. The court concluded that although there was no way Putney could have foreseen the result, nonetheless his kick was tortious and he, which is to say his parents, legally responsible for the consequences. The result is a legal rule that still survives: A tortfeasor takes his victim as he finds him. Even if the victim happens to be unusually vulnerable, even if he turns out to have an "eggshell skull" that can be broken by a light blow, the tortfeasor is still liable for the actual costs due to his tort.

On the face of it, making me pay more when I do more damage makes sense only as long as the loss is foreseeable. If I have no way of telling who does or does not have an eggshell skull, I cannot adjust my precautions to respond to the incentive of greater liability. Yet there is an efficiency argument for the rule, based not on the (unforeseeable) damage in a single case but on the average damage across many cases.

Potential tort victims vary in how vulnerable they are. If the legal rule limited damages to what could reasonably be foreseen, then tortfeasors with the bad luck to injure particularly fragile victims would pay average damages, tortfeasors with the good luck to injure particularly sturdy victims would pay below average damages, and the average tortfeasor would pay less than the average damage done by his tort. By instead requiring tortfeasors to take their victims as they find them we give potential tortfeasors the right average incentive to take precautions.

If you find this argument for the efficiency of the rule persuasive, think back to the Himalayan photographer's lost film in chapter 12. The logic of that problem and the logic of this are strikingly similar. In each case the party at fault has less information about the amount at risk than the victim. While Vosburg could not have known just how fragile his leg was, he knew more about the subject than Putney since he knew, and Putney did not, that he had a previous injury to that leg that was still healing. In the more general case the fragile victim is quite likely to know he is fragile, certainly more likely to know than is the tortfeasor.

Precisely the same argument I have just made to defend the rule implied by *Vosburg v. Putney* could have been used to attack the rule of *Hadley v. Baxendale* under which Walgreen's escapes most of the liability for losing the photographer's film. That rule implies that negligent parties, film developers in the example, will pay below average damages for losing especially worthless films, average damages for losing especially valuable films, and hence on average will pay less than the damage they do. Precisely the same argument I used to defend the rule of *Hadley v. Baxendale*, that it gave the party with more knowledge an incentive to take the appropriate precautions, could be used to attack the rule of *Vosburg v. Putney*. If you have an eggshell skull, it is easier to deal with the problem by having you wear a protective helmet than by having everyone in the world treat everyone else like an egg.

This matched pair of legal rules, along with the accompanying justifications (in both cases borrowed from Judge Posner), nicely illustrate the risks of evaluating the efficiency of the legal system after the fact. Once we know what the rule is, we can usually find an argument, even a plausible argument, for why it is efficient. Often enough there is a matching argument that we could have used with equal effect if the rule had come out the other way. For a second example of the same point, consider the following.

A Convenient Miracle

You tortiously injure someone, and the court awards him damages. What form should the compensation take? Should you owe your victim each year for that year's medical costs and lost earnings, or should the court award a lump sum based on its estimate of the present value of the total stream of costs resulting from the injury?

One argument against annual payments is that they require continued involvement by the court. Another is that they distort the victim's incentives. If he succeeds in getting a job, thus demonstrating that his injury is not, after all, totally incapacitating, his damage payment will be reduced accordingly. If the court awards a lump sum instead, the victim is left free to do whatever he can to reduce the cost due to his injury without being penalized for it. This is the policy usually followed by modern courts.

There are two problems with this policy. The first is that it requires the court to estimate costs in advance. Victims who recover faster than the court expected are overcompensated, victims who recover more slowly are undercompensated, and both kinds have an incentive to spend time and effort persuading the court to make a high estimate of the unknown future costs.

The second problem may be illustrated by a simple story:

> A tort plaintiff succeeded in collecting a large damage judgment. The defendant's attorney, confident that the claimed injury was bogus, went over to the plaintiff after the trial and warned him that if he was ever seen out of his wheelchair he would be back in court on a charge of fraud.
>
> The plaintiff replied that to save the lawyer the cost of having him followed, he would be happy to describe his travel plans. He reached into his pocket and drew out an airline ticket—to Lourdes, the site of a Catholic shrine famous for miracles.

Lump-sum payments do indeed reduce the cost of being injured. They also reduce the cost of pretending to be injured, since you can end the pretence as soon as you cash the check.

To Think about

> Traffic on the highways . . . cannot be conducted
> without exposing those whose persons or
> property are near it to some inevitable risk;
> and that being so, those who go on the highway,
> or have their property adjacent to it, may well be
> held to do so subject to their taking upon
> themselves the risk of injury . . . and persons
> who . . . pass near the warehouses where goods
> are being raised or lowered, certainly do so
> subject to the inevitable risk of accident. In neither
> case, therefore, can they recover without proof of
> want of care or skill occasioning the accident.
> (*Blackburn, J.,* Fletcher v. Rylands
> *L.R. 1 Ex. 265 [1866]*)

The quotation is from the most famous of the early cases on the choice between negligence and strict liability. Is Judge Blackburn correct in arguing that negligence is more appropriate than strict liability for the particular cases he mentions?

Hint: Whose activity level will be (efficiently) reduced if we shift from strict liability, in which victims are always compensated, to negligence, in which they are compensated only if the tortfeasor was negligent?

15

Criminal Law

SOMEONE COMMITS a crime. He is arrested and punished. That is a cost to him, hence a reason not to commit the crime. Seen from this perspective, the explanation of criminal law is simple: It is a way of enforcing property rules. If your car is worth more to me than to you, I can buy it from you. If the law prevents me from stealing it from you, that changes the outcome only when it is worth less to me than to you, in which case the efficient outcome is for you to keep the car.

This argument assumes that crimes always have a cheaper market substitute, purchase instead of theft. What about assault? I get enormous pleasure from responding to your unkind remarks about my beloved Macintosh by slugging you. The consensual equivalent, a boxing match, say, would be no substitute. It is at least possible that my pleasure from slugging you is greater than your displeasure from being slugged, in which case that particular assault may be an efficient crime. Perhaps what we should aim for, in criminal law as in tort law, is not enough punishment to always deter but a punishment—more precisely, since not all criminals are caught, a combination of punishment and probability of being punished—that imposes the damage done on the one doing it. I will then assault you only when doing so is efficient.

Judge Posner has offered an example of an efficient crime that may seem more plausible than mine, especially to readers running Windows. A hunter, lost in the woods and starving, stumbles across a locked cabin containing food and a telephone, breaks in, feeds himself, and calls for help. His gain is more than the owner's loss, so his crime is efficient. It cannot be replaced by a market transaction because the owner of the cabin is not there to transact.

One way the legal system might permit such an offense is by setting the expected punishment roughly equal to damage done. The hunter then demonstrates that the crime is efficient by his decision to commit it. The value to him of breaking into the cabin must be more than the cost, which he pays in his punishment, or he wouldn't do it. Arguably, that is how we enforce parking laws. Illegal parking imposes costs on others. If it is sufficiently important to me, I demonstrate that by being willing to pay the price of occasional parking tickets.

Another way in which we might permit efficient crimes is by modifying the law so that they are no longer criminal. That is how we actually handle the lost hunter problem; he is excused from criminal liability under the doctrine of necessity. Similarly, if the reason you are driving seventy-five is that your wife is in the back seat going into labor, the traffic cop may escort you to the hospital instead of writing you a ticket. This method works only when the special circumstances that make your act efficient are ones the court, or cop, can observe.

To test just how strong your support for efficiency is, consider a case of efficient murder. A wealthy sportsman concludes that the only game dangerous enough to be really worth hunting is man. He offers ten adventurers one hundred thousand dollars each in exchange for their agreeing that he may choose one of the ten at random and attempt to kill him. They agree. Should the law recognize the agreement and, if his hunt is successful, hold him innocent of murder on grounds of consent, or is that pushing freedom of contract a little too far?

The killing is efficient. It produces a net gain *ex ante*, as demonstrated by the assent of all concerned. Yet most of us would find it objectionable. Some might defend that conclusion along the lines of the commodification argument of chapter 13. Others might argue that the hunt is too likely to impose costs on innocent third parties caught in the line of fire. But one can always modify the scenario to eliminate such problems; perhaps the sportsman owns his own private hunting preserve. Such modifications are not likely to eliminate our reservations. Perhaps we have finally found a limit to efficiency as a source of law.

Coming to Terms with the Poverty of Our Circumstances

I have offered two models for criminal law: enough punishment always to deter and enough punishment to eliminate all and only inefficient offenses. Neither describes what we have. Crimes occur, so we do not have enough punishment always to deter. And almost all of the crimes that occur are inefficient ones, crimes in which the damage to the victim is more than the gain to the criminal.

If the punishment lottery for murder, the probability of being caught and convicted along with the resulting punishment, is at its optimal level, we ought to have only efficient murders, murders where the killer's gain is more than the victim's loss. If that is how our system works, the reason we don't try to catch more murderers or punish them more severely is that if we did there would not be enough murders. That does not sound like any world I have lived in recently. Nor does our present law fit the Pigouvian prescription: Expected punishment equals damage done. To make that work for murder, where the damage done is a life, we would have to combine the less than unit probability of conviction with some punishment worse than death, perhaps lengthy torture.

The reason we do not catch all, or even almost all, murderers is that doing so would cost more than it is worth. Part of the cost would be in extra police and courts. Part of it would be in the punishment of innocent defendants. A standard of proof low enough to convict everyone who is guilty will also convict some who are not.

Taking Enforcement Costs Seriously

Making sense of criminal enforcement requires us to think seriously about its costs. To deter crime we must catch offenders and punish them. Both activities are costly, so we should take those costs into account in deciding what punishment to impose. The cost per offense usually increases with both probability of apprehension and severity of punishment, so a higher expected punishment costs more per offense to impose. It may sometimes, however, cost less in total, since a higher punishment will deter some offenses and offenses that are deterred do not have to be punished.

It is obvious why the cost per offense increases with probability of apprehension: It takes more police to catch fifty murderers out of a hundred than to catch twenty-five, and it takes more prosecutors and court time to convict them. To see why it also increases with the severity of the punishment, it is worth thinking a little more about punishment cost.

When a convicted criminal pays a thousand dollar fine to the state, the cost to him, which is what gives the punishment its deterrent effect, is a thousand dollars, but the net cost is zero. Every dollar the criminal loses the state collects. Punishment cost, defined as the difference between the cost the punishment imposes on the criminal and the benefit it provides to others, is zero.

Suppose the criminal cannot pay enough to provide the amount of deterrence we want to impose. Instead of (or in addition to) fining him, we imprison him for a year, which is equivalent, from his standpoint, to, say, a ten thousand dollar fine. The punishment costs him ten thousand dollars, but the enforcement system receives nothing. Instead the rest of us must spend money, say another ten thousand dollars, to run the prison. The net cost of the punishment, the criminal's loss plus the enforcement system's loss, is twenty thousand dollars. It is as if he had paid a fine of ten thousand dollars but we had collected a fine of minus ten thousand.

As we increase the size of the punishment we wish to impose, the number of offenders who can pay it as a fine decreases, so we tend to shift to

more costly punishments such as imprisonment. Hence increasing the severity of the punishment typically increases the punishment cost per offense punished.

This observation solves a puzzle first raised by Gary Becker in the article that started the modern economic literature on crime. Suppose we
currently deal with some offense by imposing a 20 percent probability of
a ten thousand dollar punishment. Why not switch to a 10 percent probability of a twenty thousand dollar punishment? The effect on the criminal
will be the same, assuming he is risk neutral, so the deterrence will be the
same. We will only have to catch and try half as many criminals, so we
can save money by firing some police, judges, and prosecutors.

It works, so we repeat the process: 5 percent and forty thousand. And
repeat it again. The conclusion seems to be that the efficient punishment
lottery is a corner solution, an infinitely severe punishment imposed with
an infinitesimal probability.

The reason this does not work is that we cannot simply double the fine
forever; the criminal who can pay ten thousand dollars may be unable to
pay twenty. As the punishment increases we are forced to shift to less and
less efficient punishments, raising the punishment cost. An efficient system will accordingly choose, among combinations of punishment and
probability that are equivalent from the standpoint of the offender and so
have the same deterrent effect, the one that minimizes the sum of punishment cost and apprehension cost. Whatever level of deterrence we provide will then be provided with the least-cost combination of punishment
and probability.

The next question is how much deterrence that should be. How many
offenses should we deter, and how many should we fail to deter? It is
inefficient for me to steal a television set that is worth five hundred dollars
to you and only four hundred dollars to me. But it is still more inefficient
to prevent me from stealing the set if the cost of doing so is two hundred dollars spent on police, courts, and prisons. The rule "prevent all
inefficient offenses and only inefficient offenses" is correct only if doing
so is costless. The correct rule in the more general case is to prevent an
offense if and only if the net cost from the offense occurring is greater
than the cost of preventing it. The reason we do not increase the punishment for murder may be, and probably is, that although we would
like to prevent more murders than we do prevent (indeed, we might like
to prevent all murders), the cost of doing so is more than we are willing
to pay.

While the cost per offense increases with increases in expected punishment, the number of offenses decreases, since a higher expected punishment deters some offenses. The fewer offenses occur, the less must be
spent to apprehend and punish offenders. If the decrease in offenses out-

weighs the increase in cost per offense, increasing the expected punishment reduces total enforcement and punishment cost. A system with higher punishments and thus fewer offenses then costs less than a system with lower punishments and more offenses. The additional cost of deterring one more offense is negative, making it efficient to prevent not only all inefficient offenses but some efficient ones as well—in order to save the cost of punishing them. In the extreme one could imagine a society where the penalty for shoplifting was death, with the result that there were no shoplifters and nobody ever had to be executed.

The Theory of Optimal Punishment

The next step is to make the argument more precise in order to see how, in principle, we would calculate the efficient punishment for any crime.

Consider a crime that does a thousand dollars worth of damage each time it is committed. We start by setting the expected punishment for the crime at $900; each time the crime is committed, the offender is subject to a punishment lottery, a combination of probability and punishment, that is equivalent, from his standpoint, to a $900 fine collected with certainty.

By raising the expected punishment to, say, $901 we can deter one more offense. Unfortunately, imposing a slightly higher punishment on a slightly smaller number of offenders will increase our total cost of catching and punishing criminals by $50. Should we do it? The answer depends on how large the net benefit is from deterring the crime.

Deterring the crime saves the victim a thousand dollars, but we must also take account of the effect on the criminal. If he got nothing from committing the crime, he wouldn't commit it. To calculate the net benefit from deterrence, we must subtract the gain the criminal would have gotten from the crime from the loss the crime would have imposed on the victim. How do we measure the criminal's gain? Not by asking him but by watching him. He will commit an offense if and only if its value to him is more than the punishment he expects for committing it.

We are interested, not in criminals in general or offenses in general, but in the gain that the criminal committing the particular offense we are deterring would have received by committing it. If that gain had been less than $900, he would have been deterred even before we increased the punishment. If it was more than $901, he would not have been deterred even by the higher punishment. It follows that the offense we deterred was worth between $900 and $901 to the offender. It did $1,000 in damage. So the net damage done by the offense was about $100. By deterring the offense we eliminated $100 of net damage at a cost of only $50, so it was worth doing.

Following out this argument, we keep raising the expected punishment as long as the gain is more than the cost. The process stops when the last offense deterred costs just as much to deter as the net damage it does. Putting it a little more formally:

Net damage = damage to victim – gain to criminal.

For the marginal offense, the one that will be deterred if we raise the punishment just a little more,

Gain to criminal = expected punishment,

hence

Net damage = damage to victim – expected punishment.

For the optimal punishment,

Cost of deterring one more offense = Net damage = damage to
victim – expected punishment.

Rearranging gives us

Expected punishment = damage to victim – cost of deterring
one more offense,

or, in the more compact notation of mathematics,

$\langle P \rangle = D - MC.$

If the cost of deterring one more defense is positive, as it will be if the supply of offenses is very inelastic so that it takes a lot of increased punishment to deter an offense, we should set expected punishment below damage done. We want to deter only very inefficient offenses, ones that will be deterred even by a low punishment, because only they do enough net damage to be worth the cost of deterring. If the cost of deterring one more offense is negative, as it will be if the supply of offenses is very elastic so that a small increase in expected punishment deters a lot of offenses, we should set expected punishment above damage done. We are deterring not only all inefficient offenses but some mildly efficient ones as well, a few hungry hunters and outraged Macintosh users, in order to save the cost of punishing them. We are still not deterring the very efficient offense, the lost hunter who is not just cold and wet but literally starving. He is willing to buy the use of someone else's cabin even at our inflated price.

This solution to the problem of setting the level of punishment combines elements of two different intuitions: punishment equal to damage done ("an eye for an eye," "make the punishment fit the crime") and enough punishment to deter. If catching and punishing criminals is easy and inexpensive, the optimum is about equal to damage done; enforcement and punishment costs are unimportant, so we simply design our system to deter all inefficient and only inefficient crimes. If the supply of offenses is highly elastic at some particular level of punishment, so that below that level there are many offenses and above it very few, and if we expect few offenses to be efficient, then we set the punishment at the point where any further increase would have very little deterrent effect to balance its cost—just enough punishment to deter most offenses.

So far I have been describing offenses as efficient if the gain to the criminal is more than the cost to the victim, with the lost hunter as my standard example. We can now see that there is a different sense in which some offenses can be described as efficient. There are some offenses that we would like to deter if we could do so costlessly, but not given the actual cost of doing so. These are offenses that it is inefficient for the criminal to commit but also inefficient for the rest of us to deter, given the cost of deterring them.

The analysis of optimal punishment brings us back, in a somewhat more sophisticated form, to our earlier discussion of property rules versus liability rules. Where the marginal cost of deterring offenses is low—where, as we put it in chapter 5, allocating resources via the court is inexpensive—we want a liability rule, setting damages roughly equal to damage done. Where the low cost of voluntary transactions makes efficient involuntary transactions rare and the cost of using the court is high, we want a property rule, setting damages high enough to deter almost all involuntary transactions and thus eliminate the cost of litigating them.

Why Count Benefits to Criminals?

You may have found something very odd about the last few pages. In considering the net benefit from deterring a murder I subtracted out the gain to the murderer. In analyzing punishment costs I treated the fine collected by the state as a benefit but the fine paid, or life or liberty lost, by the criminal as a cost. Throughout this discussion I have taken it for granted that costs and benefits to criminals go into the calculations that generate efficient law in the same way as costs and benefits to anyone else.

The obvious response is that costs and benefits ought to have a moral as well as an economic dimension. I have a right to my life and property, so my loss as the victim of murder or theft counts. You do not have a right to my life and property, so the loss to you when we prevent you from killing or robbing me does not count.

This is a persuasive argument, but, for the purposes of this book, it is a mistake. It is a mistake because it assumes its conclusions instead of proving them.

One of the attractions of the economic analysis of law is that it provides a way of answering questions about what the law ought to be, what rights we ought to have. It starts with what looks like a very weak premise—that one should design legal rules to maximize the size of the pie. It assumes nothing at all about the sorts of things we expect legal and ethical rules to be based on: desert, rights, justice, fairness.

Starting with this premise, economic theory, and very little else, one produces—by the end of this book we will have produced—a long list of prescriptions. They include:

> Theft and murder should be punished. Contracts should be enforced. The imposition of criminal penalties should require higher standards of proof than the imposition of civil penalties.

We start with economic efficiency and end with conclusions that fit reasonably well both existing legal rules and our ethical intuitions. Somehow we get out quite a lot more than we put in. That is one of the reasons the project is interesting. If instead of treating all benefits to everyone equally we first sort people into the deserving and the undeserving, the just and the unjust, the criminals and the victims, we are simply assuming our conclusions. Benefits to bad people don't count, so rules against bad people are automatically efficient. We cannot deduce moral conclusions from economics if we start the economics by assuming the moral conclusions.

What acts are or are not crimes is one of the things our theory is supposed to tell us. Murder may be a simple case, but what about speeding? What about breaking into an empty house when you are lost and starving? What about slugging someone who has the presumption to suggest that Windows is a better operating system than the Mac OS? Economic analysis provides tools for answering these questions. If we treat it, instead, as an elaborate machinery for justifying the answers we already have, we will learn little that we do not already know.

A second reason to include costs and benefits to criminals in our calculations, and one that links back to our moral intuitions, is that even if we agree that it is good to prevent crimes, we must still decide how good it is and hence how hard it is worth trying to do it. Compare a poor man who shoplifts with an arsonist who burns down buildings for the fun of it. Over the course of a year each happens to impose the same costs. Both are committing crimes we would like to prevent. But we are willing to go to a lot more trouble to stop the arsonist than to stop the shoplifter—because his crime is such a waste. Similarly, most of us are far more willing to excuse a murderer when his murder was committed "out of necessity"—when, as in a lifeboat situation, the only alternative was his own death. Not only does economic theory imply that gains to criminals count, but a more careful examination of our own moral intuitions, motivated by economic theory, suggests that gains to offenders are not entirely irrelevant to our moral judgments.

I conclude that I have been doing it right. Economic analysis should give equal weight to the costs and benefits of murderer and victim. If doing so produces the conclusion we want—that murder is a bad thing— that is interesting. If it does not, that too is interesting.

The Most Efficient Punishment of All

You are convicted of embezzling money from your employer. One consequence is that you spend the next year in jail. A second consequence is that, when you get out and go on the job market, your superb qualifications for the job of corporate treasurer get you no job offers. Your punishment consisted of both a jail sentence and stigma, the cost to you of other people's knowledge of your crime.

Stigma is a very real punishment. Economist John Lott has done two empirical studies of its size, one dealing with white-collar criminals and one with corporations charged with cheating their customers. The first found that the loss of income after conviction made up a substantial part of the total punishment. The second found that the loss in corporate value, measured by stock value, due to stigma was many times larger than the nominal punishment.

How do you measure the loss due to stigma? Lott looked at the stock price of companies accused of offenses against their customers. Using a multiple regression, he calculated how in the past the stock price of each company had been related to other variables, such as the stock price of other companies in the same industry. He then predicted from the regression what the company should have been worth just after the charges, compared that with what its stock actually was worth, and interpreted the difference as the loss in company value due to the charges. The loss he found was, on average, many times higher than the highest fine that would be imposed if the charges turned out to be true. He concluded that most of the loss was due not to the prospect of paying a fine but to the loss of reputation. The real function of the court process was not to provide punishment directly but to generate information.

Stigma differs from other punishments in at least two interesting ways. The first is that, unlike all other punishments, it can, and usually does, have a negative net cost. To prove that, try a simple experiment. First get convicted of embezzlement and serve out your term. Then go to a prospective employer and tell him that you realize he is reluctant to hire a convicted embezzler as company treasurer, but you will make it worth his while by agreeing to work for a lower salary than other candidates for the job. If you can agree on a salary, you have demonstrated that the value to you of getting the job was more than the cost to him of giving it to you. If, as I think more likely, there is no salary he will offer and you accept, you have demonstrated that the cost to him of having an embezzler as treasurer is more than the value to you of getting the job.

Stigma is information, and information is, with rare exceptions, valuable, since it allows people to make more nearly correct choices. The knowledge that you are a crook is valuable to potential employers. If you can still persuade them to hire you by offering to work for less, the stigma has simply transferred money from you to them since, without that information, they would have hired you at the normal wage. If you cannot persuade them to do so, the information must have been worth more to them than it cost you. So stigma can be, and often is, a form of punishment with net negative cost, one that benefits other people by more than it hurts the person being punished.

Stigma has another special characteristic: How efficient a punishment it is depends on whether the person who was convicted was guilty. If we convict someone who is innocent, stigma becomes a very inefficient punishment, since the information we are creating is false. So the fact that criminal conviction usually does, and civil conviction usually does not, impose stigma is another reason why it makes sense to require a higher standard of proof for the former.

Should the Rich Pay Higher Fines?

A very long time ago, when I first started teaching economic analysis of law, one question routinely came up: If we punish offenses with fines, should the fine be the same for rich and poor? I thought it should; my students thought it should not.

My argument followed directly from the Pigouvian approach to law. A particular offense imposes some number of dollars worth of damage. If the benefit to the offender is more than that, his offense produces a net benefit; if less, a net loss. By setting punishment equal to damage done we get the efficient result, for both rich and poor. Rich people may end up committing more assaults, just as they buy more Cadillacs, but that is a feature, not a bug.

John Lott carried the argument one step further, in one of his more politically incorrect (which for John means very politically incorrect indeed) articles. He observed that rich people who commit crimes are, on average, less likely to get convicted than poor people, because they have better lawyers, and offered that fact as evidence of the efficiency of our legal system. Most crimes, after all, are punished by imprisonment, not fines. Two weeks in jail represents a larger dollar cost to a rich man than a poor man, so if we want both to face the same expected cost in dollars we must balance the higher cost with a lower probability of conviction.

The argument, mine and John's, is straightforward. It is also wrong, as I eventually realized when I stopped explaining to my students why they were wrong for long enough to start thinking about the problem and, in particular, the implication of enforcement costs. Equal dollar expected punishment is the right rule in a world where both catching and punishing criminals is costless, so all we have to worry about is deterring all and only inefficient offenses, but that is not the world we live in. The reason we do not raise the punishment for murder is not the fear that if we did we would have too few murders.

Once you take account of enforcement cost, the optimal punishment depends not only on damage done but also on how hard it is to deter offenses. In many cases the answer to that question is different for different people. As my students kept pointing out—to my deaf ears, since I already knew they were wrong—it takes a higher punishment to deter a rich criminal than to deter a poor one. If deterrence is expensive, it may make sense to impose on each sort of criminal just enough punishment to deter most offenses, which requires different punishments for different people.

Consider two sorts of offense—those that have a roughly equal payoff in utility for rich and poor and those that have a roughly equal payoff in money. Stealing a hundred dollars provides the same amount of money to a rich man as to a poor man, so the same fine should deter it. Indeed, since the time of the rich man is worth more dollars per hour than that of the poor man, if it takes each of them the same amount of time to steal a hundred dollars, the rich man should be deterred by a lower fine than the poor one.

Contrast that with an offense such as slugging someone you are mad at or saving ten minutes by speeding. The money value of the offence is higher to the richer offender, so it takes a higher (money) punishment to deter him. That may be an argument for imposing higher fines on richer defendants or equal jail sentences with equal probability.

As I discovered, my students' intuition was in part consistent with a more sophisticated application of economic analysis than I was offering them, but only in part. If you work through the analysis, the efficient rule sometimes involves charging the rich higher fines. But sometimes, with some assumptions about supply curves and cost of enforcement, the efficient rule is to punish the poor and ignore the rich—because a punishment high enough to deter rich offenders costs more than it is worth.

There is a second difference between rich and poor with slightly less ambiguous implications. Fines are more efficient punishments than imprisonment, and richer offenders can pay higher fines. Even if neither offender can pay a sufficiently high fine, imposing a given dollar punishment via imprisonment requires fewer days in jail for a higher-income offender and is therefore cheaper. So punishment costs (per dollar of punishment) should decrease as income rises, which implies a higher efficient dollar level of punishment for richer offenders.

Or perhaps not. Punishing rich criminals is cheaper than punishing poor criminals. But convicting rich criminals is more expensive because, as John Lott pointed out, they have better lawyers. In designing an efficient legal system, we must take account of both sorts of costs. That might, depending on the numbers, bring us back to letting the rich get away with murder or, more plausibly, drunk and disorderly. If so, you will have to decide for yourself whether justice is worth the cost.

What I Have Left Out

Throughout this chapter I have taken it for granted that the purpose of the criminal law is deterrence, making it in the interest of potential criminals not to commit crimes. While that assumption greatly simplifies the analysis, it may also ignore some relevant considerations.

One is that some sorts of criminal punishment achieve a different objective—incapacitation. Someone in jail may still be able to commit crimes, but his opportunities, and his potential victims, are much more limited than if he were free, so jailing a criminal should reduce the damage he does. Hanging him reduces it even more.

In a simple Pigouvian world where convicting criminals is costless and all punishments are fines, criminals do no net damage; only efficient crimes occur, and we do not want to prevent those. In that world incapacitation is worthless. But in the more difficult world of positive enforcement and punishment costs, preventing a crime by incapacitating the potential criminal saves the cost of catching him, the cost of punishing him, and the net damage done by the crime, which is almost always positive. Hence incapacitation is a net benefit.

A more elaborate version of my analysis would include that benefit as a subtraction from punishment cost. Locking someone up costs his freedom and some of our taxes, but it also provides a benefit by reducing his opportunity to commit crimes, so imprisonment is a more efficient punishment than a simple calculation would suggest. Similarly for execution.

The logic of the argument remains the same, but the relative efficiency of different punishments might change.

A second argument offered for locking up criminals is that it gives us an opportunity to change them into good citizens, to rehabilitate them. This belief has been in and out of fashion several times over the past two centuries; the original penitentiaries, built in the early nineteenth century, were called that because they were places where people were supposed to learn to repent their crimes. Methods for teaching penitence included shaved heads, prison uniforms, hard work, solitary confinement, and Bible study. My own suspicion is that if we cannot teach people to be virtuous with twelve years of public schooling, a few more years of imprisonment are unlikely to do the job. I will therefore continue, for the most part, to ignore rehabilitation, while noting that insofar as it does exist it too can, in principle, be folded into the calculation of punishment cost as a subtraction, a negative cost.

Another way in which I have implicitly simplified the analysis is in considering only one crime at a time. As I pointed out back in in chapter 1, that is sometimes a mistake. If two crimes are substitutes for each other—armed robbery and armed robbery plus murder, in my earlier example—raising the punishment for one may deter the criminal into committing the other instead. An efficient legal system must take account of that possibility, a problem known in the literature as "marginal deterrence." Doing so makes the analysis, and its explanation, considerably more complicated. Interested readers can check that claim by looking at an article that I co-authored with William Sjostrom, in which we show how the problem of marginal deterrence could be incorporated into the analysis of efficient punishment.

A final objection that may be offered by some is that my central assumption, that punishment deters, is false. One answer is that it is not an assumption but a conclusion; the assumption is rationality. A second answer is that, popular myth to the contrary, the evidence is overwhelmingly in favor of deterrence in the economist's sense. There have been many statistical studies measuring the effect on crime rates of changes in either the probability of apprehension, the punishment, or both; with few exceptions, they show that increasing expected punishment reduces crime rates.

Such studies also consistently show that crime rates are more sensitive to probability than to punishment. Increasing the chance of being caught and convicted from 10 to 20 percent reduces crime more than increasing the penalty from one year to two. This is sometimes interpreted as showing that criminals are risk preferrers, that they prefer the riskier 10 percent chance of a two-year sentence to the less risky 20 percent chance of one year, even though the expected cost in years is the same.

There is a simpler explanation. The cost of being tried for an offense is not limited to the punishment imposed by the court after conviction; it also includes time spent awaiting trial or money spent raising bond by offenders who have the good luck eventually to be acquitted, litigation costs in time and money, and stigma. Suppose the combined effect of all of those costs is equivalent to an extra year in jail. We then have

10 percent chance of 2 years in jail = .1(2 years in jail + 1 year in other costs) = .3 years,

20 percent chance of 1 year in jail = .2(1 years in jail + 1 year in other costs) = .4 years.

The example generalizes. If the number of years in jail represents only part of the punishment and the other part is fixed, a given percentage increase in the jail term raises the expected cost to the criminal by less than the same increase in the probability of conviction and therefore has less deterrent effect even if criminals are risk neutral with regard to punishment.

Why Not Hang Them All?

Suppose armed robbery is currently punished by a ten-year prison term imposed on offenders with a probability of .6. Research on the tastes of potential criminals demonstrates that they are indifferent between a 60 percent chance of ten years in jail and a 10 percent chance of death. Obviously a reform is in order. We shut down the prison. Every time we convict a criminal, we roll a die. 1–5 we let him go, 6 we hang him.

On the face of it this is an unambiguous improvement. The criminal is as well off *ex ante*, we are getting the same deterrence so victims are no worse off, and we no longer have to spend money on prisons. There is, however, room for still more improvement. Why waste time and energy catching and convicting criminals only to turn them lose? We reduce our expenditure on courts and police until we are convicting only one criminal in ten, thus saving money on apprehension as well as on imprisonment.

The argument applies to any crime currently punished by imprisonment. If the sentence is only a month, we use a 720-sided die instead of a six-sided one. It follows that an efficient legal system will make no use of imprisonment. Defendants who can pay fines will be fined, since fines are more efficient than execution. Defendants who cannot pay fines will be executed, with probability scaled to the seriousness of the offense. No penalty will ever be used if there exists another penalty that is both more severe and more efficient, since we can always make the system more efficient by substituting the higher penalty at a lower probability.

If we are going to be serious about constructing an efficient set of punishments, we should consider a wider set of options. In many historical societies, prisoners were required to work off their sentence. One could imagine a modern society where a criminal had the option of X years or Y dollars. The X years could be served out in a conventional prison. Alternatively, a private prison factory could obtain possession of the prisoner, with his consent, by posting a bond for Y dollars. The agreement between prison and prisoner would specify the terms of employment under which he would work off this fine. A sufficiently trusted prisoner could take an ordinary job, live an ordinary life, and pay his fine from his income. A more dangerous prisoner would require more guarding, would work inside the prison, and would pay off his fine more slowly. Prisoners too dangerous or unproductive to be employed at a profit could simply serve out their terms.

Whether a convicted criminal is judgment proof depends in part on whether it is in his interest to be; the same person might be "unable" to pay a fine but willing and able to pay a gambling debt of the same amount—given the alternatives. A legal system that routinely allowed convicted criminals to choose between fines and less attractive punishments, whether imprisonment or probabilistic execution, would make it in the interest of criminals to make sure that if they were caught they could pay.

Another alternative is to make execution more efficient. In eighteenth-century England corpses were routinely sold to surgeons for dissection. In twentieth-century America their value would be much higher. Execution presents the ideal environment for harvesting organs for transplant, giving the body of a criminal in good health a market value in the tens of thousands of dollars.

We can now see what an efficient system of criminal punishment might look like. It would be designed to squeeze the largest possible fines out of convicted criminals, using the threat of more unpleasant alternatives for those who failed to pay. If the fines that victims can pay, even under such threats, are inadequate, they are supplemented by penal slavery for criminals who can produce more than it costs to guard and feed them, execution with the organs forfeiting to the state for those who cannot. Any prisons that do exist and do not pay for themselves are as unpleasant as possible, so as to produce as much punishment as possible per dollar of imprisonment cost. It is a consistent picture, and considerable parts of it can be found in the not very distant past, but not a pretty one. Nor does it much resemble the system of punishment actually existing in modern societies. It looks as though someone is making a mistake. Either there is something wrong with my analysis of what an efficient system would look like or our system is far from efficient.

Some Inadequate Responses

One argument offered against execution is that it is irreversible and courts sometimes make mistakes. But imprisonment is also irreversible. We cannot get back the years spent in prison any more than we can get back a life. The loss from one mistake is less, of course, but since imprisonment must be applied with higher probability than execution to get the same deterrent effect, there will be proportionally more mistakes. Imprisonment does have the advantage that we can partly correct errors if we discover them before the sentence has been served out, and we can to some extent compensate a prisoner after the fact for his false imprisonment. But both happen so rarely as to be an implausible explanation for the choice of imprisonment over execution.

Incapacitation provides a reason why imprisonment might sometimes be a more efficient punishment than execution or a fine. So does rehabilitation, assuming that we actually know how to change the tastes or skills of criminals in a fashion that makes them unlikely to commit further crimes. While these complications might modify the implications of a straight deterrence model, it is hard to believe that they could justify the modern system of punishments, in which imprisonment is heavily used, execution and penal slavery rare, forfeiture of organs unknown.

Execution in America at present is very expensive, due to the protracted litigation it requires; that could be seen as an economic argument against it. But it seems more natural to interpret this as a consequence of our reluctance to employ execution than as a cause. The argument for the superiority of execution does not require any increase in how careful we are about whom we convict. Historical societies that made extensive use of execution, such as eighteenth-century England or nineteenth- and early-twentieth-century America, did so without extensive and expensive litigation.

A final defense of our present legal rules is that they are a consequence of the tastes of the populace. Modern people would find execution, penal slavery, penal torture, or the dismemberment of executed criminals to provide organs for transplant distasteful. Such punishments thus generate large negative externalities. Given the existence of those tastes, our present legal rules are efficient.

I reject that explanation for the same reason that I earlier rejected the idea that benefits to criminals should not count in defining efficiency. An economic theory that is free to eliminate anomalies by explaining them away as due to someone's unexplained and peculiar tastes has very little in the way of testability or predictive power. Our objective is explanation, not description. It is possible that people do have those tastes, but if unexplained tastes are the sole reason for the institutions we wish to explain, we have failed to explain them. And our project is much more interesting if we can show that the institutions our tastes favor are in fact efficient, implying that our peculiar tastes are actually an efficient set of norms.

The Virtue of Inefficient Punishment

Consider the world of efficient punishment from a more symmetrical viewpoint than we have so far employed, one that takes account of the incentives of all relevant actors. It is a world where, by persuading a court that someone is guilty of a crime, I can expropriate large amounts of the defendant's financial, human, and perhaps biological capital. In a world of efficient punishments, somebody gets most of what the convicted defendant loses. It is in that somebody's interest to convict defendants, whether or not they are guilty.

The conventional analysis of optimal punishment on which my analysis up to this point has been built is based on a mistake that has been extensively criticized in other contexts: the philosopher-king view of government. The old textbook literature on regulation and related topics treated market participants as rational, self-interested actors, but the state as a proxy for the author—a wise, benevolent, wholly altruistic organization, doing whatever would best correct the failures of the market. It was by abandoning that model that we got public choice theory and the modern analysis of regulation.

The orthodox theory of optimal punishment makes the same mistake. It treats criminals as rational, self-interested actors. But it treats the enforcement apparatus of police, courts, prosecutors, and legislature as a philosopher-king, with imperfect knowledge but only the best of motives.

One cost of that approach is that it makes it harder to include tort law and criminal law in the same theory, despite their obvious similarity of means and end. Tort law is enforced by the actions of private parties, criminal law by the actions of the state. It seems obvious that private plaintiffs ought to be treated as rational self-interested actors, and that is how they generally have been treated in the law and economics literature. By treating state actors differently, we not only obscure the similarities, we also make it harder to think clearly about the choice between privately and publicly enforced law—the project of chapter 18.

Once we start treating all actors symmetrically it becomes obvious that a system of efficient punishments has a substantial cost as well as substantial benefits. The cost is rent seeking. The legal system becomes a mechanism to be used by some people to expropriate other people—who respond by taking expensive precautions to avoid being expropriated. The population as a whole might well be better off with less efficient punishments.

This is not a purely theoretical problem. Consider some real-world examples:

Modern tort law offers opportunities for plaintiffs, or at least plaintiffs' attorneys, to engage in extensive rent seeking via class actions and claims for punitive damages. It is widely alleged that the result has been a host of unjustified legal actions, with attorneys enriching themselves at the expense of defendant corporations and their insurers. One example, discussed in chapter 3, was the popularity of Fraud on the Market claims. Even a small probability of a very large damage judgment may give an innocent defendant good reason to accept an out-of-court settlement. The elimination of American production of small airplanes can be, and has been, plausibly explained as a defensive reaction to that sort of rent seeking: Firms found that they were better off exiting the industry than risking future litigation.

Civil forfeiture law creates a similar incentive for public law enforcement officials. Under current law property used in the commission of certain crimes can be seized by the state. Seizure does not require evidence that the owner of the property violated any law—the case is against the property, not the owner—nor does it require the criminal conviction of anyone, owner or user. It is up to the owner who wishes to get his property back to demonstrate, in a civil action, that it was not used to commit a crime.

Since forfeiture under federal law is to the federal government, one might expect it to provide an incentive only to federal law enforcement agencies, but that ignores the relevant market transactions. The Coase Theorem is alive and well in the law enforcement industry. Federal agencies divide the gains, and thus the incentives, with local law enforcement agencies. After federal law was altered to authorize such sharing there was a striking shift of local law enforcement effort toward the enforcement of drug laws, which provide lots of opportunities for forfeiture. Many states have their own forfeiture statutes as well, some of which provide for directing forfeited assets to the law enforcement agency responsible for obtaining them. The incentives implied by such institutions pose an obvious risk—that law enforcement will be directed toward seizing property rather than preventing crime.

For the same problem in the context of criminal law, consider the Ruby Ridge killings. One point on which all parties seem to agree is that the origin of the conflict was an attempt by the Bureau of Alcohol, Tobacco, and Firearms (BATF) to entrap Randy Weaver by persuading him to sell a BATF informer two shotguns whose barrels had been shortened to slightly below the legal length. The reason to do so was to force Weaver to spy for the BATF on other people who shared his (white separatist) political views. The intended gain to the enforcers was in services not cash, but the logic of the situation was the same. Since law enforcement agencies make extensive use of informers, it seems likely that similar actions have occurred in many less publicized cases.

Consider next a fictional example, now slightly dated:

> In 1993 Vermont passed the first of the organ bank laws. Vermont had always had the death penalty. Now a condemned man could know that his death would save lives. It was no longer true that an execution served no good purpose. Not in Vermont.
>
> Nor, later, in California. Or Washington, Georgia, Pakistan, England, Switzerland, Rhodesia.

Despite the new legislation transplant organs are still in short supply. The legal system responds to the resulting political pressures. At the end of the story the prosecution reads the capital charge for which the defendant is being tried:

> The state will prove that the said Warren Lewis Knowles did, in the space of two years, willfully drive through a total of six red traffic lights. During that same period the same Warren Knowles exceeded local speed limits no less than ten times, once by as much as fifteen miles an hour. (From Larry Niven, "The Jigsaw Man," in *All the Myriad Ways*)

All of these examples demonstrate a common problem—the effect of efficient punishment on the incentives of enforcers, public (civil forfeiture and BATF entrapment) or private. The same institutions that, seen from the perspective of a philosopher-king model of law enforcement, produce an unambiguous improvement by lowering the cost of enforcing the criminal law have the potential, seen from a perspective of rational self-interest, to set off a costly rent-seeking struggle, a war of each against all, with each side trying to use legal institutions to expropriate others and avoid being expropriated.

Cannibalism, Rent Seeking, and Rape

For a more distant example of the same issue, consider the universal human prejudice against cannibalism. On the face of it the prohibition is irrational and inefficient. Once I am dead I have no more use for my body, so why not let someone else get some useful protein out of it?

The answer should now be obvious. In a society in which cannibalism is an accepted practice, everyone is at risk of becoming someone else's dinner. Each of us must go to a good deal of trouble to make sure that nobody has a safe opportunity to kill him. The ban on cannibalism means that most people, most of the time, have no good reason to kill each other, making life a good deal easier for all of us.

One of the Greek historians commented that the Persian empire was so well ruled that a virgin with a sack of gold could travel from one end of the Great Road to the other unharmed. The two values at risk in that case differ in an important respect relevant to this discussion. People who own sacks of gold rarely send them wandering about the countryside unprotected; they can, and usually do, keep them locked up safe. For a woman to lock up her virginity is, modern fantasies about medieval chastity belts to the contrary, a lot harder.

Rape may be the most common really serious crime. One reason is that most women have something—the use of their bodies—that many men want and that there is no inexpensive way of protecting. Some societies have solved that problem by literally locking up women's bodies, sequestering women, at least upper-class women, somewhere where only trusted men would have access to them. In a modern society that would be a very costly solution. Our society solves, or attempts to solve, the same problem by treating rape as a serious crime.

For another example of the same issue consider the question of whether there should be an entirely free market in organs for transplant. Organs are currently in short supply, and legalizing the market seems an obvious way of dealing with the problem. It would give individuals an incentive to sell the rights to their organs in advance, with the organs harvested only when the individual died, or to agree that organs could be sold at the time of death, with the money going to their heirs. More controversially, if the price were high enough, it would give people with two kidneys an incentive to sell one of them.

The best argument I know of against a completely free market in organs is the rent-seeking problem. Few of us carry more than a few hundred dollars in cash, but every healthy individual carries with him at all times tens of thousands of dollars worth of internal organs. With a completely free market, there would be a substantial incentive to kidnap people in order to dismember them, raising the risk of murder and the costs of defending against it. It has been alleged that this already is happening in some parts of the world, and organnapping features in a widely circulated urban legend, involving someone who wakes up, after a wild night, minus his kidneys.

One solution would be a market, but one with adequate precautions to establish chain of title to any organs sold. Another would be a legal regime in which organs could be sold by their owner, in advance or at time of death, but not resold.

> Among nations of hunters, as there is scarce any property, or at least none that exceeds the value of two or three days' labour, so there is seldom any established magistrate or any regular administration of justice. Men who have no property can injure one another only in their persons or reputations. But when one man kills, wounds, beats, or defames another, though he to whom the injury is done suffers, he who does it receives no benefit. It is otherwise with the injuries to property. The benefit of the person who does the injury is often equal to the loss of him who suffers it. . . . The acquisition of valuable and extensive property, therefore, necessarily requires the establishment of civil government. Where there is no property, or at least none that exceeds the value of two or three days' labour, civil government is not so necessary. (Adam Smith, *The Wealth of Nations*, book 5, chapter 1, part 2)

Further Reading

David Friedman and William Sjostrom, "Hanged for a Sheep: The Economics of Marginal Deterrence," *Journal of Legal Studies* (June 1993).

The title is lifted from an old English proverb: "As well hang for a sheep as for a lamb." At one time stealing either a sheep or a lamb was a capital offense, so you might as well steal the more valuable animal. The proverb nicely illustrates both the application of rationality to criminals and the fact that you do not have to be an economist to think like one.

16

Antitrust

Part I: Economics

IN CHAPTER 2 I offered a simple argument for laissez-faire. If you leave people free to exchange goods on mutually acceptable terms, the result is to move all goods to their highest-valued uses, producing the efficient allocation of existing goods. If a good is worth more to a potential consumer than it costs a potential producer to produce it, the latter will find it in his interest to produce the good and sell it to the former, with the result that goods get produced if and only if they are worth producing.

This argument assumes that the only cost to me of selling one more unit of a good is the cost of producing it. But what if one effect of trying to sell more units is to drive down the price? Suppose, for example, that I own the only grocery store in a small town. The cost to me of selling an extra ten gallons a week of milk is not only what it costs me to get and sell the additional milk but also the lost revenue on milk I could have sold at a higher price if I had been content with selling less.

A numerical example may make the argument clearer. I am choosing whether to sell a hundred gallons a week at $2 a gallon or a hundred and ten at $1.90. The cost to me of the extra ten gallons is $1.50 a gallon. Expanding output gives me $19 of revenue, ten gallons of milk at $1.90 a gallon, at a cost of only $15. That sounds like a good deal until it occurs to me that it also costs me $10 of lost revenue on the hundred gallons that I could have sold at the higher price and must now sell at the lower.

If I considered only the cost and revenue directly associated with the additional gallons, I would keep selling more milk as long as the price was above my cost, since as long as price is above cost I am making money on each additional gallon. That describes the behavior of a seller in a perfectly competitive market—one with so many firms that his sales have no significant effect on price. But a monopoly, more generally a firm with some market power, knows that it can only sell more by selling at a lower price—which costs it revenue on the units that it could have sold at the higher price if it had been content with a lower volume. For me that lost revenue is a cost. For everyone put together it is only a transfer; what I lose on milk that my customers were willing to buy at the higher price, they gain.

To see why selling at a price above cost is inefficient, consider a customer to whom an additional gallon of milk is worth $1.80—less than the price I am selling milk for but more than the cost to me of providing it. If I produced the extra gallon and gave it to him, I would lose $1.50, he would gain $1.80, for a net gain of thirty cents. The net gain would be the same if I produced the milk and sold it to him for $1.50, although the division of the gain between us would be different. As long as I am selling milk for more than its cost to me, customers who value the milk at more than its cost but less than its price will not get it, which is inefficient. This simple point, usually illustrated with a diagram showing the monopoly's cost curves, demand curve, and profit-maximizing price, is the standard economic argument for the inefficiency of a monopoly seller.

The failure to sell to everyone who values milk at more than it costs me is a problem for me as well as for economic efficiency; I am missing out on potential profits. One solution is to find some way of selling milk at different prices to different customers, charging a high price to those willing to pay it and a lower price to those who will only buy at a low price. In some cases such price discrimination is a practical option, but in many others it is not, either because I cannot tell who will or will not pay a high price or because I cannot prevent people to whom I charge a low price from reselling to people to whom I am trying to charge a high price.

If I somehow solve these problems, and do it well enough so that I can sell to every customer at the highest price he is willing to pay, the standard argument against monopoly vanishes. As long as there is a customer who values milk at more than it costs me, it is in my interest to sell it to him. The result is that with perfect price discrimination it is in my private interest to sell the efficient quantity of milk, the quantity such that everyone who values it at more than its cost of production gets it.

Perfect price discrimination is perfectly efficient, at least so far as quantity is concerned, although that is not true for the imperfect price discrimination that is usually the best a seller can do. Perfect price discrimination also results in all of the gain from the transaction going to the seller and none to the buyer, like a bilateral monopoly bargain in which one side is a much better bargainer than the other. But since economic efficiency is concerned with the size of the net gain, not who gets it, that should be irrelevant to efficiency. Or perhaps not. Stay tuned for late-breaking updates.

In a competitive industry above-normal profits, profits that more than pay the normal rate of return on capital, make it in the interest of someone to start a new firm, driving output up and prices and profits down. So in a competitive industry in long-run equilibrium, firms sell at a price that just covers all of their costs, including a market return on the stockholders' capital. Economic profit, defined net of the normal cost of capital, including the capital of the stockholders, is zero. In a monopoly industry, however, there is room for only one firm. The result is at least the possibility of monopoly profit.

The Inefficiency of Monopoly: Part II

The year is 1870. Somewhere west of civilization is a valley of fertile farmland, into which it will some day be worth building a rail line. Whoever builds the first line will have a monopoly; it will never pay to build a second. If the line is built in 1900, the total profit it will eventually produce after paying all costs, including a normal market return on the capital used to build it, will be $20 million. If the railroad is built before 1900, it will lose a million dollars a year until 1900 because there will not be enough people in the valley to support the cost of maintaining the rails.

I, knowing these facts, propose to build the railroad in 1900. I am forestalled by someone who plans to build in 1899; $19 million is better than nothing, which is what he will get if he waits for me to build first. He is forestalled by someone willing to build still earlier. The railroad is built in 1880. The builder receives only the normal return on his capital for building it. The logic of the situation is identical to the logic of inefficiently early homesteading in chapter 10 and inefficient theft in chapter 3.

In such a situation monopoly profit ends up not as a transfer to the firm from its customers but a net loss. The higher the monopoly profit, the more resources firms burn up competing to be the one that gets it. If so, perfect discriminatory pricing is not the best solution to the problem of monopoly but the worst. Since each customer is buying at the highest price he is willing to pay, all of the gain from the firm's production is transferred to the firm as monopoly profit—and all of the monopoly profit is burned up in the cost of acquiring the monopoly. So the distribution of the gains from trade does matter after all, not as part of the definition of efficiency but, in this situation at least, as an incentive to inefficient behavior.

We now have two arguments for the inefficiency of monopoly—each presented in a simplified scenario but with more general application. One is that a monopoly, in the process of maximizing its profit, sells too low a quantity at too high a price; if it expanded output, its customers would gain more than it would lose. The second is that the opportunity to acquire monopoly profits creates an incentive for inefficient rent seeking, for spending resources making sure that your firm, rather than someone else's, ends up with the monopoly.

If monopoly is inefficient, what can we do about it? Before attempting that question, there is another we must answer first.

Why Is Monopoly?

The only grocery store in a small town is a *natural monopoly*. If someone tried to start a second store, one of the two would eventually go out of business because one store selling to everyone has lower average costs, and so can afford to sell at a lower price, than two stores each selling to only some of the customers. The same thing could happen on a larger scale in an industry in which a large part of production cost was independent of how much was produced—the cost of designing a product, writing a computer program, tooling up a factory. The more units the fixed cost is divided among, the lower the average cost, so big firms can undersell small ones.

Almost all firms have some fixed costs, so why isn't every industry a natural monopoly? One reason is that economies of scale in production are balanced by administrative diseconomies of scale. The bigger a firm is, the more layers there are between the president and the factory floor, and the harder it is for the former to control what is happening on the latter. Once a firm has gotten big enough to take advantage of most of the potential economies in production cost, further growth may cost it more in higher administrative costs and less carefully managed factories than it gains in lower production costs. That is one reason that most industries consist of many firms.

One reason there may be only one firm in an industry is natural monopoly. Another is that if someone tries to compete with him, the monopolist will call the police. The original meaning of "monopoly" was an exclusive right to sell something. Typically such monopolies were either sold by the government as a way of raising money or given to people the government liked, such as relatives of the king's mistresses. Monopolies of this sort are still common. An example is the Post Office: The private express statutes make direct competition illegal.

For a third source of monopoly, and one that brings us closer to legal issues associated with antitrust, consider an industry made up of only five large firms. It occurs to the president of one of them that if they all reduce production, prices will rise; they will gain more from higher prices than they lose from lower sales. The result is a cartel: a group of firms coordinating their behavior to hold output down and prices up as if they were a single monopoly.

One problem for the cartel members is that while each of them is in favor of the others keeping output down and price up, each would like to expand its own output to take advantage of the high price. It can do so by chiseling on the cartel price, selling additional output for a little less to favored customers, defined as customers who can be lured away from a competitor and trusted not to tell anyone about the deal they are getting.

Each cartel member gains by chiseling—at the expense of the others. If they do enough of it, they drive the price back down to what it was before the cartel was formed.

One solution is for the members of the cartel to sign a contract agreeing to keep their output down and to prevent chiseling by doing all of their selling through a common agent. In much of the world such contracts are both legal and enforceable. In the United States they are neither. They have long been unenforceable as contracts in restraint of trade; under current antitrust law they are also illegal.

That is not true of a cartel agreement enforced by the government, such as the airline industry prior to deregulation. The enforcement agency enforcing the domestic airline cartel was the Civil Aeronautics Board, which had veto power over fare changes, including fare cuts. A similar function was served in the international market by the International Air Transport Association (IATA), most of whose members were government airlines whose owners could enforce the agreement by denying nonmembers landing rights in their countries.

Another solution is for the firms to merge into a monopoly. This may raise costs somewhat, since the reason there were originally five firms instead of one was that the firms were already up to the size at which average cost was minimized. But it may also raise profits if the merged firm has enough of the market to be able to restrict output and drive up price. In the United States such mergers are subject to disapproval by the antitrust division of the Justice Department.

A friend of mine has suggested an ingenious way in which the antitrust division could distinguish "procompetitive" mergers, mergers designed to join firms that can produce more cheaply by combining their assets, from "anticompetitive" mergers designed to create a monopoly. A procompetitive merger makes things worse for other firms in the industry, since it produces a more efficient competitor. An anticompetitive merger makes things better for other firms in the industry, since they will benefit when it restricts output in order to drive up the price at which it—and they—can sell. All the antitrust division has to do, when a new merger is proposed, is see who objects. If the other firms in the industry object, it approves the merger; if they don't object, it rejects it. Unfortunately, this only works until the other firms catch on and revise their tactics accordingly.

Cartels and anticompetitive mergers both result in both of the sorts of inefficiency described earlier. In either case one consequence of the monopoly is to push prices above marginal cost, reducing output below its efficient level. In the case of a cartel, rent seeking takes the form of expenditures by the cartel members to enforce, and evade, the cartel restrictions, as well as bargaining costs over creating and maintaining the cartel.

In the case of merger the inefficiency of having a firm too big to minimize average cost is a rent-seeking expenditure, paid by the merging firms in the process of getting a monopoly in order to transfer money from their customers to themselves.

Artificial Monopoly

Suppose that in some industry economies and diseconomies of scale roughly balance; over a wide range of output big firms and small firms can produce at about the same cost. It is widely believed that such a situation is likely to lead to an *artificial monopoly*; the usual example is the Standard Oil Trust under John D. Rockefeller.

I am Rockefeller and have somehow gotten control of 90 percent of the petroleum industry. My firm, Standard Oil, has immense revenues, from which it accumulates great wealth; its resources are far larger than the resources of any smaller oil company or even all of them put together. As long as other firms exist and compete with me, I can earn only the normal market return on my capital.

I decide to engage in predatory pricing, driving out my competitors by cutting my prices below my (and their) average cost. Both I and my competitors lose money; since I have more money to lose, they go under first. I now raise prices to a monopoly level. If any new firm considers entering the market to take advantage of the high prices, I point out what happened to my previous competitors and threaten to repeat the performance if necessary.

This argument is an example of the careless use of verbal analysis. "Both I and my competitors are losing money . . ." sounds as though we are losing the same amount of money. We are not. If I am selling 90 percent of all petroleum, a particular competitor is selling 1 percent, and we both sell at the same price and have the same average cost, I lose $90 for every $1 he loses.

My situation is worse than that. By cutting prices, I have caused the quantity demanded to increase; if I want to keep the price down, I must increase my production—and losses—accordingly. I lose, say, $95 for every $1 my competitor loses. My competitor, who is not trying to hold down the price, may be able to reduce his losses and increase mine by cutting his production, forcing me to sell still more oil at a loss. He can cut his losses by mothballing older refineries, running some plants half time, and failing to replace employees who move or retire. For every $95 I lose, he loses, say, fifty cents.

But although I am bigger and richer than he is, I am not infinitely bigger and richer; I am ninety times as big and about ninety times as rich. I am losing money more than ninety times as fast as he is; if I keep trying to drive him out by selling below cost, it is I, not he, who will go bankrupt first. Despite the widespread belief that Rockefeller maintained his position by selling oil below cost in order to drive competitors out of business, a careful study of the record of the antitrust case that led to the breaking up of Standard Oil found no evidence that he had ever done so. The story appears to be the historian's equivalent of an urban myth.

In one incident a Standard Oil official threatened to cut prices if a smaller firm, Cornplanter Oil, did not stop expanding and cutting into Standard's business. Here is the reply Cornplanter's manager gave, according to his own testimony:

> Well, I says, "Mr. Moffett, I am very glad you put it that way, because if it is up to you the only way you can get it is to cut the market, and if you cut the market I will cut you for 200 miles around, and I will make you sell the stuff," and I says, "I don't want a bigger picnic than that; sell it if you want to" and I bid him good day and left. That was the end of that. (Quoted in John S. McGee, "Predatory Price Cutting: The Standard Oil [NJ] Case," p. 137)

Predatory pricing is not logically impossible. If Rockefeller can convince potential competitors that he is willing to lose an almost unlimited amount of money keeping them out, it is possible that no one will ever call his bluff, in which case it will cost him nothing. But the advantage in such a game seems to lie with the small firm, not the large one, and the evidence suggests that the artificial monopoly is primarily a work of fiction. It exists in history books and antitrust law but is and always has been rare in the real world, possibly because most of the tactics it is supposed to use to maintain its monopoly do not work.

Solutions and Problems Therewith

Since competition is efficient, one might think that the solution to the inefficiency of monopoly is to break up the monopoly firm. But if a natural monopoly is broken up into smaller firms, average cost will go up—that is why it is a natural monopoly. Since average cost falls as output increases, one of the firms will expand, driving (or buying) out the others. We end up where we started, with a single monopoly firm.

The inefficiency of monopoly is an argument for breaking up artificial monopolies or preventing their formation by laws against predatory pricing, but I have just argued that artificial monopolies created by predatory pricing are for the most part mythical. It is also an argument for breaking up monopolies created by government regulation of naturally competitive industries. But in the case of natural monopoly, perfect competition is simply not an option. We don't want every small town to have ten grocery stores.

The cure that economics textbooks traditionally offered for the efficiency problems of natural monopoly was government regulation or ownership. One problem with this approach is that a regulator, or an official running a government monopoly, has objectives of his own— some combination of private benefit to himself and political gains for the administration that appointed him. A sensible policy for the regulator might be (on the historical evidence often is) to help the monopoly maximize profits in exchange for campaign contributions to the incumbent administration and a well-paid future job for the regulator.

Suppose we somehow solve that problem and put a natural monopoly under regulators who have only the best of intentions. After reading the first half of this chapter, they conclude that the solution is to force firms to charge marginal cost, to sell a gallon of milk, or, more realistically, a kilowatt hour of electricity, at exactly what it costs to produce.

This leads to several problems. The first is finding out what the firm's costs are—real monopolies, outside of textbooks, do not come equipped with a diagram showing their cost curves. One approach is to simply watch, see what it costs to produce each unit of output, and set prices accordingly. But relating costs to output is not a simple matter of observation. To determine marginal cost we have to know not only the cost of the quantity the firm is producing but also what it would cost to produce other quantities.

A second problem is that the regulator observes what the firm does, not what it could do—and the firm knows the regulator is watching. It may occur to the firm's managers that if they arrange to produce the last few units in as expensive a fashion as possible, the regulators will observe a high marginal cost and permit them to charge a high price.

Suppose the regulators see through any such deceits, correctly measure marginal cost, and set price equal to it. A natural monopoly exists because the cost of producing additional units decreases as output increases, giving a larger firm a cost advantage over a smaller firm. But if marginal cost is falling, then average cost, which includes the cost of the earlier and more expensive units, is higher than marginal cost. So if a natural monopoly is forced to sell at marginal cost, it will eventually go broke or, if the regulation is anticipated, never come into existence. To prevent that the regulator must find some way of making up the difference between price and average cost.

One solution might be a subsidy paid for by the taxpayers. While this arguably makes economic sense it is in many cases not a practical option, since regulatory agencies are rarely provided, by Congress or state legislatures, with a blank check on the treasury. The usual alternative is to get the money from the monopoly's customers. Instead of requiring it to charge marginal cost, the regulators require it to charge average cost, a less efficient outcome but still better than the price the monopoly would set for itself.

How does the regulator find out what average cost is? If he simply asks the firm's accountants to calculate how much it spent this year and sets next year's prices accordingly, the management of the firm has no incentive to hold down costs, especially the cost of things that make the life of management easier. Here again management knows that the regulator is watching and modifies what it does accordingly.

The real-world version of this approach to controlling natural monopolies is called "rate of return" regulation. The idea is to set a price that gives the stockholders of the regulated utility—the most common example of a regulated natural monopoly in the United States at present—a "fair rate of return" on their investment. The cost of inputs other than the stockholder's capital is set at what the regulatory commission thinks it ought to be, based on the experience of past years.

How much do investors have to get to make it worth investing in utilities? The obvious answer is "the market rate of return"—but on how much capital? If regulators measure the size of the investment by how much investors initially put in, investors in new utilities face an unattractive gamble: If they guess wrong, the company goes bankrupt and they lose everything; if they guess right, they get only the market return on their investment. So a regulator who bases rate of return on historical costs must somehow add in a guesstimate of the risk premium that investors would have required to compensate them for the chance of losing their money.

What about measuring the current value of the investment by the market value of the utility's stock and allowing the utility to set a price that gives a market return on that value? Unfortunately, this ends up as a circular argument. The value of the stock depends on how much money investors think the company will make, which depends on what price they think the regulators will permit it to charge. Whatever amount the regulators allow the utility to make will be the market return on the value of the stock, once the value of the stock has adjusted to the amount the utility is making.

Regulatory commissions exist in the real world, hold hearings, and publish press releases describing what a fine job they are doing in protecting customers from greedy monopolies. What they really do, however, and what effect they really have are far from clear. In a famous early article on the economics of regulation, George Stigler and Claire Friedland tried to determine the effect of utility regulation empirically, by looking at the returns to utilities in states where regulation came in at different times. So far as they could tell, there was no effect.

Extending the Monopoly

One issue that antitrust law has paid a good deal of attention to is the possibility of a firm that has a monopoly in one market using it to somehow get a monopoly in another. A prominent recent example is the controversy over charges that Microsoft is trying to use its near monopoly in the market for desktop operating systems to get a second monopoly in the market for web browsers. This issue appears in at least three different legal contexts: vertical integration, retail price maintenance, and tie-in sales. In all three contexts, as we will see, the legal analysis that has been widely accepted by the courts is inconsistent with the relevant economic theory. And in all three cases the result of showing that is to leave us with a puzzle. Having shown that the court's explanation of these practices is wrong, we have to explain why they nonetheless exist.

Vertical Integration

Suppose steel production happens to be a natural monopoly and I have it. It occurs to me that making cars requires steel, and I am the only source. I accordingly buy up a car firm, refuse to sell steel to its competitors, and soon have a monopoly in cars as well. I am now collecting monopoly profit on both the steel industry and the auto industry, so I, and my stockholders, are happy.

What is wrong with this strategy is not that it will not work but that it is unnecessary. If I want to drive the price of cars up, I don't need a car company to do it. All I have to do is raise the price at which I sell steel to the existing companies. The car companies will pay the higher price to me, pass the increase on to their customers, and so provide me with my monopoly return without any need for me to get into the car business.

The reason this argument matters to the law is that one of the things antitrust law regulates is vertical mergers, regarded as suspect on the theory that they make it possible for the monopolist to expand his monopoly. The argument so far suggests not only that vertical mergers should not be suspect but also that they should not happen, leaving us with the question of why they do.

One reason, of course, is that it is sometimes cheaper for a firm to make its own inputs or sell its own output, with the result that, even where no question of monopoly is involved, we observe quite a lot of vertical integration. A more interesting reason, where a firm does have a monopoly at one stage of the production process, is that vertical merger is a way of reducing the inefficiency due to its monopoly and, in the process, increasing the firm's profits.

When my steel monopoly pushes up the price of the steel it sells to auto companies, they respond by using less steel and more aluminum and plastic. To the extent that the substitution is driven by my monopoly price, it is inefficient. The car company is using a hundred dollars of aluminum to substitute for steel that costs it a hundred and twenty dollars to buy but costs me only eighty dollars to produce. That represents a net loss of twenty dollars to efficiency and, potentially, to profit.

One solution is for me to buy the car company. I then instruct its managers that in deciding when it is cheaper to use steel they should base their calculations on its real cost of eighty dollars, but that in pricing cars they should do their best to extract as much monopoly profit as possible. I thus eliminate one of the inefficiencies due to my monopoly price on steel, while still selling autos at a monopoly price and collecting the corresponding monopoly profits.

Retail Price Maintenance

Retail price maintenance is the practice of a producer controlling the price at which retailers are permitted to sell his products. For many years federal law permitted states to decide whether or not such contracts were permitted and enforced. Under current law explicit contracts of that sort are illegal everywhere, although in practice that rule is widely evaded—as you can easily check by a few on-line price comparisons of, for example, the latest Macintosh models.

One argument for banning retail price maintenance agreements is that they are a way in which the producer, who has a "monopoly" of selling his own products to retailers, extends that monopoly to the retail market, presumably in exchange for a share of the monopoly profits that doing so produces for the retailers. Here again the problem with the argument is not that the strategy would not work but that it is unnecessary. A producer is free to charge retailers whatever price they are willing to pay. If he wants to raise the retail price, all he has to do is raise the wholesale price. Without any price maintenance agreement the retailers will compete down their margin until it just covers their costs. Instead of getting a share of the increased revenue from the higher retail price, the producer gets all of it.

Having explained why retail price maintenance does not exist, we are left with the puzzle of explaining why it does, why some producers attempt to make and enforce agreements controlling the price at which their goods may be sold.

I am a retailer of expensive hi-fidelity audio equipment. In order to sell it I spend a considerable sum maintaining a showroom where potential customers can listen to different producers' equipment, consult with my expert salesmen, and so decide which products to buy.

Judging by the state of my showroom, all is going well; my salesmen hardly have a free moment. Judging by my books, however, something is wrong; lots of people are looking, but almost nobody is buying. While trying to solve this puzzle, I decide I am in need of some fresh air, so I go out for a stroll. Just around the corner I find the explanation—a new catalog discount store, with a small office and no showroom, selling the same products I sell at 80 percent of my price. Taped to the door is a map showing the location of my showroom.

This is a problem both for me and for the producers of the audio equipment I sell. Since customers can get my expensive presale services for free and then buy from my lower-cost competitor, I stop offering the presale services. I close down the showroom, fire most of my salesmen, and cut prices to match the competition. Customers no longer have the option of trying my goods before they buy. They respond by going to competing retailers selling different brands of equipment, brands whose manufacturers insist on a minimum price for their equipment sufficient to cover the cost of salesmen and showroom. Those retailers provide the presale services, secure in the knowledge that nobody can undercut their prices.

Tie-in Sales

Long ago, when computers required rooms instead of desktops and belonged only to large firms and governments, there was a company called IBM. Earlier still, IBM produced card sorting machines—dumb predecessors of the digital computer that processed information by sorting paper cards with holes punched in them. IBM had something close to a monopoly on selling and leasing such machines. One term in their agreement, one eventually declared illegal, was that customers had to use IBM punch cards. Why?

Here again, the obvious answer is in order to extend the monopoly from card sorters to cards. Here again, that answer does not work.

Punch cards are not exactly high tech items; lots of firms could produce them and did. IBM could require its customers to use its punch cards but had no control over what cards were used by people using other machines. If IBM took advantage of its monopoly on punch cards used with IBM sorters by raising their price, the result would be to make using IBM machines more expensive. But they could have done that much more easily by simply raising their prices. Insisting that their customers use expensive punch cards instead of cheap ones is an indirect way of raising the price of the card sorting machine.

It is tempting to reply that IBM can get away with expensive punch cards because their customers have nowhere else to go. But that is wrong. To begin with, their customers have the option of not using a sorter at all, an option many firms took. They also have the option of using machines made by other firms—and will take it if IBM gets too expensive.

The more fundamental response is that if IBM can insist on expensive punch cards without losing any customers, that is evidence that they could also have raised the price of their machines without losing any customers, in which case they should have done so. Once they have gotten to the profit maximizing price, the price at which further increases lose them more in sales than they gain in revenue per sale, any further increase, whether per machine or per card, makes profits lower, not higher.

Again, I have explained too much. Having shown that IBM had no reason to insist on a tie-in between cards and sorters, I must now explain why they did.

One mundane explanation is that IBM cared about the quality of the punch cards. If something went wrong, they might have to service the machine, and if too many things went wrong, their reputation might suffer. One way of controlling quality was by making the cards. A similar explantion has been offered for an earlier round of antitrust cases involving a giant company, the IBM of its day, making shoe-manufacturing machinery.

A more interesting explanation is that IBM was engaged in a clever form of discriminatory pricing. The value of the same machine is different to different customers; ideally, IBM would like to charge a high price to a firm that gets a lot of use out of the sorter, and is therefore willing to pay a high price, while charging a lower price—but enough to more than cover production cost—to more marginal users.

Customers willing to pay a high price are unlikely to mention that fact to IBM. But, on average, high-value customers are also high-use customers. High-use customers use a lot of punch cards. By requiring all customers to use IBM cards and charging a high price for them, IBM is, in effect, making the same machine more expensive to customers who use it more. Combining expensive cards with somewhat less expensive machines lets it keep the low-use users, who are compensated for the high price of one with the low price of the other, while milking the high-use users, who are the ones least likely to abandon their machines.

I do not know when this explanation for tie-in sales was first offered by an economist, but I suspect that a lawyer beat us to it. The earliest tie-in case I have come across involved not a computer but a printing press. The tie-in was with the paper the press used. The attorney defending the company's right to require a tie-in offered a simple explanation. If the company covered all of its costs, fixed and variable, in the price of the press, small printers would be unable to afford it. By charging a lower price for the press and a higher price for the paper, the company made the combination affordable for small printers, who didn't use all that much paper, while covering its fixed cost with the extra money it made from big printers, who did. It was precisely the economist's explanation of tie-in sales as a form of discriminatory pricing—presented, as favorably as possible, from the monopolist's point of view. And it correctly pointed out the efficiency advantage produced by price discrimination—a larger quantity of output, due to the ability to cut prices for some customers, in this case indirectly, without cutting them for others.

While these arguments imply that tie-in sales are sometimes efficient, it does not follow that they always are. One cost of requiring customers to buy expensive punch cards is that they will take expensive precautions to avoid using any more of them than necessary. That is inefficient if the cost of the precautions to the user is higher than the cost of the cards saved to IBM. The inefficiency due to overpricing the cards must be balanced against the efficiency gain due to making computers available to the lower-use customers who would otherwise be priced out of the market. There are no theoretical grounds on which we can predict what the net effect will be; it might go either way.

Conclusions?

This chapter has been devoted mostly to explaining issues rather than analyzing legal alternatives. One reason is that both antitrust theory and antitrust law are complicated areas, and I have done little work in either. But at this point it is worth at least trying to summarize the subject from a legal rather than a purely economic point of view.

Antitrust law ultimately involves three different approaches to reducing the costs associated with monopoly: controlling the formation of monopolies, regulating monopolies, and controlling efforts to misuse a legal monopoly.

The formation of monopolies is controlled in three different ways. One is by restrictions on the mergers of large firms, where the antitrust division believes that the merger will have an "anticompetitive" effect. If two firms wish to merge, one of which controls 40 percent of the pickle market and one 50 percent, the antitrust division may decide that 90 percent of pickles is too near a monopoly for comfort. In principle their decision is based not only on the percentage of the market but also on how easy it is, if the merged firm tries to exploit the consumers of pickles with high prices, for other pickle producers to expand or for new firms to enter the market, and on how willing consumers are to substitute other things for pickles if pickles become too expensive. If the conclusion goes against the merger, the firms have the choice of either remaining separate or having one of them spin off its pickle business before merging.

A second way in which formation of monopolies is controlled is by restrictions on behavior believed to create them, in particular on predatory pricing, selling below cost in order to drive competitors out and establish a monopoly. I argued earlier that such restrictions are a cure for an imaginary disease, but the antitrust division may not always agree. Similar arguments apply to controls over tie-in sales and retail price maintenance agreements.

A final, and perhaps most important, way of controlling the formation of monopolies is by making it harder for firms in concentrated industries to cooperate, to form a virtual monopoly, a de facto cartel, by jointly holding quantity down and price up. One way of preventing that is by refusing to enforce cartel agreements, as is done in the United States and—more recently—the United Kingdom. Another is by making such agreements, including secret price-fixing agreements, illegal.

Regulated monopolies in the United States are mostly public utilities—electricity, natural gas, water, telephones—and regulation is mostly at the state level. For reasons I have already discussed, it is unclear whether utility commissions can be trusted to try to produce efficient outcomes, whether they can do so if they try, and even whether they have any significant effect on the industries they regulate. The theoretical rule—set price equal to marginal cost, and find the money somewhere to cover the difference between that and average cost—is straightforward. The practical application is not.

Controlling attempts to misuse a legal monopoly gets us into the topics I discussed under the general subject of extending monopolies. My arguments suggest that, while the behaviors in question may be a result of monopoly and may increase the monopoly's profits, it is not clear that they make the rest of us worse off. It is therefore also unclear whether there is any good reason to restrict them.

Antitrust, the Next Generation

For about a decade, roughly the eighties, federal antitrust activity was at a relatively low level, in part due to the influence of the sort of arguments I have just offered, arguments that suggest that antitrust activity often does more harm than good. More recently it has revived again, largely targeted at the computer industry. The current showpiece is the Microsoft antitrust trial.

One reason may be that software provides a particularly striking example of a natural monopoly. Once a computer program is written, the cost of producing additional copies is close to zero, so the more copies you sell the lower the average cost. The result is that, at any given time, there is likely to be a single dominant product in each niche—one dominant word processor, one dominant photo-editing program. Current champions are Microsoft Word and Adobe PhotoShop.

Stanley Liebowitz, an economist studying these markets, tried an interesting experiment. He graphed market share in each of a variety of niches against average rating in computer magazine reviews. The pattern was striking. At any one time there was usually a dominant product. It stayed dominant until one of its competitors started getting consistently better reviews, at which point the competitor rapidly took over the market. In an industry where, once a program is written, it costs relatively little to crank out another million copies, market share can change with startling speed.

Just as the American form of marriage has been described as serial polygamy, so the software industry provides a striking example of serial competition. At any given instant there is a dominant product, but which one it is changes over time. During the relatively short history of the personal computer, the dominant spreadsheet on Intel machines has gone from VisiCalc, the original spreadsheet, to Lotus 123 to Microsoft Excel. The dominant word processor has gone from WordStar to WordPerfect to Microsoft Word.

You may think you see a pattern there. So did the antitrust division. Microsoft has not always been the winner; Adobe, for example, continues to dominate a group of related niches involving graphics and desktop publishing. But Microsoft's share of successful software applications is high and increasing. One explanation offered by its competitors is that ownership over the operating system, first MS DOS and later Windows, gave Microsoft an unfair advantage in writing software, since they knew more than anybody else about the underlying code with which that software interacts.

While that explanation sounds plausible, it does not do a very good job of explaining what actually happened. Insofar as Microsoft has such an advantage, it is limited to machines running their operating systems, so Microsoft applications ought to succeed only, or at least mostly, on Intel platforms. But Word and Excel are not only the dominant word processor and spreadsheet under Windows, they are the dominant ones on Macintosh computers as well.

An obvious explanation is that Microsoft used its operating system advantage to obtain a dominant position in the Intel world and then spread from there to the Macintosh, taking advantage of the desire of Macintosh owners to use products compatible with what other people were using. While that sounds plausible, it does not fit the historical facts. In the early years of the Macintosh the dominant word processor on Intel machines was WordStar. The dominant word processor on Macs was Word. In both the word processor market and the spreadsheet market, Microsoft first obtained a dominant position in the Macintosh market, where it had no more access to the operating system than anyone else and less than Apple (which produced a competing word processor) and then extended that to the DOS/Windows world.

Something Old, Something New: Network Externalities and the Qwerty/Dvorak Myth

The latest version of an economic theory to explain monopoly and justify antitrust action goes by the name of "network externalities." The underlying idea is that there can be economies of scale associated with consumption as well as production. It is convenient for me to use the same word processor as people with whom I want to exchange documents, so the more people are using Word the greater the incentive for me to abandon my trusty WriteNow and go with the crowd. It is convenient for my telephone to be able to reach as many other people as possible, so the larger the size of the telephone network the greater the value it provides to each customer. As with economies of scale in production, the likely result is a natural monopoly.

The classic example offered for the real-world importance of this effect is the Qwerty keyboard, the arrangement of keys on a conventional typewriter. According to the widely accepted story, the Qwerty layout was originally designed to slow typists down, in order to reduce the problem of keys jamming in early typewriters. It achieved success as a result of being used by the world's only touch typist in a crucial early typing contest. Once established, it maintained its position through the power of network externalities despite the existence of a greatly superior alternative, the Dvorak keyboard. In a world dominated by Qwerty machines, practically nobody wanted to learn Dvorak.

Some years ago Stanley Liebowitz and Stephen Margolis published an article, "The Fable of the Keys," demonstrating that every single fact in the above story was false. Qwerty was designed to prevent key jamming not by slowing typists but by putting pairs of letters that frequently followed each other on opposite sides of the keyboard, thus alternating between the two banks of keys in the early machines; that pattern is still a desirable one, since it means that typists tend to type with alternate hands, which is faster and less tiring. There were many early typing contests, different machines won different contests, and the recorded scores make it clear that there was no single typist with a large speed advantage over everyone else.

Perhaps their most damning result concerned not Qwerty but its competitor. So far as they were able to determine, the great superiority of Dvorak was demonstrated only in tests run or supervised by August Dvorak, its inventor. The advocates of network externalities, in taking the Dvorak/Qwerty case as evidence for their theory, were treating advertising puffery as scientific data. Tests by independent third parties interested in the possibility of adopting the new layout showed it to be at most a few percent faster than the existing standard.

Liebowitz and Margolis did not claim that the network externality argument was impossible, although they have argued that it is mostly a relabeling of phenomena already familiar in the context of economies of scale and natural monopoly. What they claimed was that, at least in the typewriter case, its effects were unimportant. After all, while some typists need to be able to move from one typewriter to another, many others do not. Many writers preferred to do all their work on a single typewriter, especially back in the days of mechanical typewriters, which varied a good deal more than computer keyboards today. The costs of modifying a typewriter to change the keyboard layout were never terribly high and became much lower when IBM introduced the Selectric, a model that permitted multiple interchangeable type balls. They became lower still when the world switched from typewriters to word processors, since a computer's keyboard layout can be remapped in software. Every Apple IIc made came with a built-in switch that toggled the keyboard between Qwerty and Dvorak.

If Dvorak had been as much better as its advocates claimed, it should have rapidly established a dominant position among typists who did not have to be able to use other people's machines. Having demonstrated its superiority there, it should have spread. By now Qwerty should have been relegated to the dustbin of history. It didn't happen that way.

A similar issue arises in the context of computer software, where compatibility is again of significant value. Here again Liebowitz and Margolis offer evidence that while the fact that other people are using a word processor may increase its value to me, the effect does not seem to be very large. If the main question deciding what word processor I use is what word processor everyone else uses, and similarly with other products, then the first dominant product should also be the last, since no competitor will ever have a chance to compete. It follows that I must be currently running WordStar or MacWrite, and that VisiCalc still owns the world of spreadsheets. It didn't happen that way.

They also offer some less direct evidence. Suppose there are two equally good word processing programs, one with 95 percent of the market, one with 5 percent. If network externalities are important, the dominant program should be worth substantially more than its competitor to users, say a hundred dollars more. The rational monopolist should raise his price accordingly, to take advantage of his customers' willingness to pay. He won't raise it by the full hundred dollars, since at that price his competitor might start to expand, but raising it by somewhat less, say, fifty dollars, permits him to both maintain his monopoly and exploit it.

It follows that if externalities are important, the dominant product in each niche should cost more than its competitors. Empirically, that does not seem to be the case. Here again, the conclusion is not that network externalities do not exist but that they do not seem to matter very much, at least in this market.

I have said a good deal about the background to recent antitrust actions but very little about the case that is the current high-profile example. One reason is that by the time this book is published the Microsoft case will probably be over and something else occupying the headlines. Another reason is that I do not know enough of the detailed allegations in that case, or the evidence for and against them, to want to offer an opinion as to whether Microsoft has or has not been doing the various wicked things that its competitors accuse it of doing.

17

Other Paths

THE SUBJECT of the economic analysis of law is law—all law in all times and places. So far, however, we have applied it almost exclusively to modern Anglo-American law. In this chapter I expand the discussion to cover three very different systems of legal rules. Two are historical legal systems: saga period Iceland and eighteenth-century England. The third is a system not of law but of norms, privately enforced rules that exist a few hours from where I live and, for some categories of disputes, override the public law of the state of California.

One reason to look at such systems is to see how well our theory fits them. Another is to stretch our thinking, to bring to our attention other possible solutions to the problems our legal system deals with. A third is to provide real-world evidence of how such alternative solutions might work and what problems they might encounter, evidence that will be useful in the next chapter, where I consider possibilities for a radical redesign of our legal system.

Private Law—with a Vengeance

Standing at the beginning of the mythic history of every country is the good, strong ruler who brought it into existence: George Washington, Alfred the Great, Charlemagne. The history of Iceland starts with a strong ruler too. His name was Harald Haarfagr. He lived in the ninth century; his accomplishment was to convert a group of small kingdoms with weak kings into one large kingdom with a strong king.

The large kingdom was called Norway. The chief occupations of its inhabitants were farming, fishing, and piracy; they were what we now call Vikings. Quite a lot of them were unhappy with Harald's revision of their traditional political system, so they loaded their longships with families, friends, and as many farm animals as would fit and left for a newly discovered island out in the wastes of the North Atlantic. That is the origin of Iceland as the Icelanders told it.

When, early in the tenth century, the Icelanders got around to setting up their own legal system, they based it on traditional Norwegian law—with one major omission. They decided they could do very well without a king. The result was a polity that included a legislature and courts but no central executive and only one government employee: the law-speaker (*logsogumaðr*), whose job was presiding at the legislature, providing legal advice, and reciting the entire law code publicly once over the course of his three-year term. Putting the matter in modern American terms, they had left out an entire branch of government. Without an executive branch of government to prosecute crimes, it is hard to have a system of criminal law. They left that out too.

The Icelandic system was centered around the office of *Goði*, usually and misleadingly translated "chieftain." An ordinary landowning Icelander plugged into the legal system by being the thingman of a particular goði. The relationship was a voluntary one; the thingman was free to switch from his current goði to any other who would have him. There were thirty-nine *Goðar* (plural of *Goði*) in Iceland when the system was established, later expanded to forty. The right to be a goði, called a *goðorð*, was a piece of transferable private property, like a McDonald's franchise. You could become a goði by inheritance or by purchasing a goðorð from someone willing to give it up.

We are tenth-century Icelanders; I suspect you of cutting wood in my forest and decide to take legal action. The first step is to ask you publicly who your goði is, since the relation between our goðar will determine in what court I can sue you, just as the question of what states two modern-day American litigants are citizens of may determine what court has jurisdiction over their case.

Once the court is determined, I sue for damages as in a modern tort suit. You do or do not show up to defend your case, as you prefer; there are no police available to arrest you and hold you for trial as there would be in a modern criminal case. The court gives a verdict: You owe me a damage payment of twenty ounces of silver. The court goes home. You do or do not pay.

If you do not pay, I institute a second legal procedure to have you declared outlaw. Once you are outlawed I, or anyone else, can kill you with impunity. Anyone who helps defend you is himself in violation of the law and can in turn be sued.

Modern tort and contract law are sometimes described as private law in contrast to public (criminal) law, since the former are enforced by private prosecution by the victim, the latter by public prosecution by the state. But the Icelandic civil system was private law in a stronger sense. Not only was the prosecution of the case private, enforcement of the verdict was private too. And under the Icelandic system all law was civil. The legal procedure I have just described for your violation of my property rights to my forest could equally well have been describing the legal consequence of your killing my brother.

This description of the Icelandic legal system suggests some obvious problems. One is stability: What is to keep a good fighter with lots of tough friends from violating the law and ignoring any verdicts against him, secure in the knowledge that nobody will dare attack him? A similar problem occurs when the victim is relatively poor and friendless, with inadequate resources to prosecute a case and enforce the verdict. Further problems include offenses that are hard to detect—nine times out of ten, the thief gets away clean, one time out of ten he is sued and must give back the money—and judgment-proof defendants. Why bother to sue someone if he has no money to pay a fine?

The Icelandic legal system provided solutions, although not perfect solutions, to all of these problems. Consider first the most serious threat, the risk that powerful men would routinely ignore court verdicts, bringing down the entire system.

Powerful men in the Icelandic sagas do occasionally try to ignore court verdicts, or forcibly block the working of the legal system, but in the long run they rarely succeed. Part of the reason is that any clash between the two sides will generate injuries and a new set of cases, which the side defending the outlaw will lose, since defending an outlaw is illegal. The losing side then has the choice of either paying the resulting damage payments or ignoring them and, by doing so, pulling more and more people into the coalition against the outlaw and his supporters.

My favorite example of the inherent stability of the system is a scene in *Njalsaga*. A lawsuit is being tried, and things have gotten so badly out of hand that it looks as though violence may break out between the two sides in the middle of the (open air) courtroom. Someone on one side of the case asks a friendly neutral what he will do to help. He replies that he will draw up his supporters, armed. If his friend's side is losing, they can retreat behind his people. If his friend's side is winning, he and his people will break up the fight before the winners have killed more men than they can afford to pay for. The clear implication is that, even when things are going very badly, everyone knows that in the long run killings are going to have to be paid for—which, given how high the damage payment for a killing was, made killing your opponents an expensive proposition.

So far I have assumed that even if the defendant in a tort suit was more powerful than the plaintiff, had more friends willing to fight for him, the plaintiff at least had enough resources to prosecute the case. But what if the defendant was relatively poor and powerless—an elderly man, say, with no sons?

The solution was to make tort claims transferable. The weak tort victim sells his claim to a neighbor with sufficient force to prosecute it. How much he gets depends on how much the neighbor expects to collect and how difficult he expects the prosecution to be. If the defendant is a

sufficiently tough case, the victim may have to give the case to his neighbor for free, or even offer to help pay the costs. What he gets in exchange
is deterrence—a demonstration that people who injure him will be forced
to pay damages, even if he doesn't end up collecting them. His situation
is the same as that of a modern tort victim whose damage judgment just
covers his legal cost—or a modern crime victim. Convicted criminals pay
fines, if any, to the state, not the victim.

Our legal system does not permit unresolved tort claims to be transferred. In that respect we are at least a thousand years behind the cutting
edge of legal technology. But we achieve a similar effect in a clumsier and
less direct way. When an attorney agrees to prosecute a case on a contingency basis, he is accepting a share in the claim as the payment for his
services. If he loses, he gets nothing; if he wins, he gets a percentage of the
damage judgment.

What about offenses with a low probability of being detected? The
Icelandic system dealt with that problem by treating the concealment of
a crime as a further offense. A law-abiding Icelander who happened to
kill someone—such things can happen in a society in which going off on
a Viking expedition played the same role that a college education, or a
few years abroad, play in ours—was expected to promptly announce the
fact of the killing and the names of both himself and the victim to someone living nearby. If he failed to do so—worse still, if he concealed the
body—he was guilty not merely of killing but of the more serious offense
of murder. Not only was his legal position worse if he got caught, but the
action of concealing his crime was regarded as shameful.

The problem of judgment-proof defendants was solved in a variety of
ways. One was through informal credit arrangements; a convicted offender might get help with his fine from friends and kin in an implicit
exchange for future services. Another was through a form of temporary
slavery—debt thralldom—under which the offender worked off his punishment. Finally, the fact that an offender who failed to pay would be
outlawed and face the choice of leaving Iceland or being killed made it in
the interest of offenders to do their best not to be judgment-proof.

The Icelandic system was set up in 930 A.D. The first serious difficulties
arose just before the year 1000, in the form of violence between the majority pagan and minority Christian factions, the latter supported by the
King of Norway. The two sides agreed to arbitration by the (pagan)
lawspeaker. His verdict was that Christianity would become the official
religion of Iceland, with pagan worship still permitted in private.

About 150 years later another serious problem arose, a feud between
two powerful factions, one of which used force to prevent the other from
going through the legal procedures necessary to sue them. Cooler heads
prevailed, and that case too was settled by arbitration.

Finally, starting about the year 1200, there came a period of increasingly violent conflict, leading to the final breakdown of the Icelandic system. In 1262 three of the four quarters of Iceland voted to turn the country over to the king of Norway. In 1263 the north quarter agreed, and the Icelandic experiment was over. It had lasted for three hundred and thirty-three years.

The Icelandic system of fully private law appears obviously unworkable to modern American eyes. Yet it worked well enough to function for more than three hundred years and generate one of the world's great literatures. Our word "saga" comes originally from a body of histories and historical novels composed in Iceland during and just after the period I have been describing, many of which are currently in print in English paperback translations. For a population of seventy thousand people living in a far corner of the world a very long time ago, that is a considerable achievement.

Without Police or Prosecutor: Criminal Law in Eighteenth-Century England

Our next episode is closer to home in both time and law. England in the eighteenth century had, on paper, a legal system much like ours, including our distinction between criminal and tort law. But while it had criminal law, there were no police to enforce it; the first English police force was not established until the 1830s. Nor were there public prosecutors. This raises an obvious puzzle. With neither police nor prosecutors, who would catch criminals and prosecute them?

The answer is that, under English law, any Englishman could prosecute any crime. In practice the private prosecutor was usually the victim.

That raises a second puzzle. A tort plaintiff has an obvious incentive to sue; if he wins, he gets to collect damages. A private plaintiff in a criminal suit stands to collect nothing; if he wins the case, the defendant is hanged, or transported, or perhaps pardoned. So why prosecute?

One possible answer is that the reason to prosecute was the hope of settling out of court before the trial. The plaintiff might gain nothing from a conviction, but the defendant stood to lose quite a lot, possibly his life, and might therefore be willing to pay the plaintiff to drop charges. Such agreements were legal and approved of in misdemeanor prosecutions; they were illegal in felony prosecutions but seem to have happened nevertheless.

A second reason to prosecute was, just as in saga period Iceland, to buy deterrence. Suppose I am running a business particularly vulnerable to theft, say a cloth-dying establishment with lots of valuable pieces of cloth drying in the open air. By prosecuting one thief I buy a reputation that will deter others. Precisely the same incentive, deterrence as a private good, still operates today, as witness "we prosecute shoplifters" signs in department stores. And, as that example suggests, even in our legal system criminal prosecution is in practice at least partly private, since the victim often has to go to a substantial amount of trouble in the process of helping to get the criminal convicted.

Most people do not expect to be victims of multiple offenses and so cannot reasonably expect to establish a reputation by prosecuting them. For them, Englishmen in the eighteenth century came up with an ingenious alternative: societies for the prosecution of felons.

Such societies, of which thousands were formed, typically operated in a single town. Each member contributed a small annual sum. The money was available to be spent on prosecuting anyone who committed a felony against any member. The list of members was published in the local newspaper—to be read by the local felons. Thus a prosecution society served as a commitment mechanism, a way in which a potential victim could assure potential felons that felonies against him would be prosecuted, converting deterrence from a public good into a private good. Instead of my prosecution slightly raising the general rate of conviction and so producing an infinitesimal increase in deterrence for everyone, it substantially raises the rate of conviction for people who commit felonies against members of my association, producing a substantial increase in deterrence for us.

In order for deterrence to be a private good the criminal must know who the victim is—in the eighteenth-century context, that he is a member of a particular association for the prosecution of felons. This raises a problem with anonymous-victim offenses such as highway robbery, offenses where the criminal does not know who the victim is and thus does not know whether he is precommitted to prosecute. In the middle of the century, in response to a perceived problem of inadequate incentives for prosecution, English authorities at both the national and local levels instituted a system of rewards, sometimes quite generous, for successful prosecutions. This led to some new problems, which we will return to in the next chapter.

In addition to private prosecution the English system of criminal law in the eighteenth century had another odd feature: the pattern of punishments. But first a historical digression:

In medieval England (and elsewhere) the Catholic Church claimed ultimate authority over clerics, such as priests and monks. A clergyman accused in the royal courts of a capital offense could "plead benefit of clergy" and so have his case transferred to the church courts, which did not impose capital punishment. In a society without extensive bureaucratic record keeping, this raised a further problem: Who counted as clergy, and how could the court know whether a particular defendant qualified? The problem was solved with a simple rule: A clergyman was defined as anyone who could read. Traditionally, the ability to read was tested by asking a defendant to read a particular verse from the Bible, which came to be known as the neck verse, since knowing it saved your neck. Criminals who were both illiterate and prudent memorized it.

Over time two developments made this system increasingly unsuited to its intended purpose. One was the spread of literacy, which meant that more and more laymen could claim benefit of clergy. The other was the Protestant Reformation. By the sixteenth century there no longer were church courts in England handling the sorts of offenses for which defendants were likely to plead benefit of clergy. The result was to convert benefit of clergy from a legal rule giving the church jurisdiction over its own officials into a get out of jail free card for felons.

The legal system responded in a variety of ways. One was to declare the more serious offenses "nonclergyable": Defendants charged with them no longer had the option of pleading benefit of clergy. By the eighteenth century virtually all serious offenses, including theft of forty shillings or more and any burglary that put the inhabitants of the burgled home in fear, had become nonclergyable felonies. According to the law the penalty for a nonclergyable felony was hanging. Eighteenth-century England thus presents, at first glance, the spectacle of a legal system in which all serious crimes were capital ones.

The appearance is misleading in several ways. A jury that thought the defendant guilty but the legally mandated punishment too severe might convict the defendant of a lesser included offense instead, a process referred to as "pious perjury." If a defendant was convicted of a capital offense, the court might offer to pardon him on condition of transportation, his agreement to be shipped off to the New World and sold into fourteen years of indentured servitude. If a war was going on, defendants might be pardoned on condition that they agreed to enlist in the army or navy. A pregnant woman could plead her belly—get off with a noncapital punishment on the grounds that even if she had committed a capital offense her unborn child had not. And a substantial number of defendants, after being convicted and sentenced to hang, were simply pardoned and sent home.

How did this system, known to later historians as the "bloody code" for its reliance on execution, work in practice? One study of records from a particular set of courts concluded that, of defendants charged with nonclergyable felonies, only about 40 percent were convicted of those charges, with some others being convicted of lesser, noncapital offenses. Of those convicted, only about 40 percent were executed. So, at least for that sample, someone charged with a capital offense had about one chance in six of being executed—a lot higher than in our legal system, but considerably short of what the formal legal rules suggest.

Something is missing from this picture: imprisonment, which we consider the normal punishment for serious crime. In eighteenth-century England imprisonment was sometimes used as a punishment for minor offenses such as vagrancy. Other than that, jails were used to hold accused felons until trial and convicted felons until they were hanged or transported. Imprisonment as a punishment for serious crime did not exist until late in the century.

Can we make sense out of this pattern of punishments from an economic standpoint? I think the answer is yes.

Imprisoning a dangerous criminal is expensive, and England in the eighteenth century was, by our standards, a poor society. Both execution and transportation were much less expensive punishments. When a convicted felon enlisted in the army in order to save his neck, the cost of the punishment to the government imposing it was negative, since the Crown got a soldier for less than it would have had to pay to hire him on the open market.

One obvious alternative to our usual form of imprisonment—if we drop, for a moment, our late-twentieth-century sensibilities—is penal slavery, prisons whose occupants are forced to work. My conclusion, from such evidence as is available, is that penal slavery was not normally an attractive option from the standpoint of the government; the cost of housing, feeding, and guarding dangerous criminals was substantially more than the amount that could be made from their labor. That, at least, seemed to be the implication of a brief experience with penal slavery in the 1770s, when the American Revolution cut off the option of transporting convicted felons to the New World.

Further evidence comes from the history of galley slavery. Contrary to *Ben Hur* and other works of fiction, galley slavery is a Renaissance invention; the warships of the Greeks and Romans were normally rowed by free men. Sometime around the end of the fifteenth century the Mediterranean powers started using condemned criminals as rowers. The practice spread rapidly, resulting in a mass shift from execution to galley slavery as the preferred sentence for healthy male criminals.

To understand why that happened, it is worth thinking a little about the economics of slavery. In order to use slaves profitably their owner must make more money from their labor than the cost of feeding, guarding, and supervising them. How easy that is depends, to a considerable degree, on what the slaves are doing.

Supervising galley slaves is easy; since they are all rowing in unison, it is obvious if one is not doing his part. Keeping them from escaping is easy too, since it is hard to swim with chains on. Rowing a galley was the ideal form of slave labor from the standpoint of the slaveowners. The history of criminal punishment suggests that it provided the Mediterranean powers something they had previously not had, a form of penal slavery that produced more than it cost and so was preferable, from the standpoint of the state, to execution. Galleys don't work well in the rougher waters of the Atlantic, so England used transportation instead.

This account raises another puzzle: Why did galley slavery arise when it did? I have a simple, although speculative, answer. In classical antiquity and through most of the Middle Ages, sea warfare consisted in large part of hand-to-hand combat, land battles on ships. The last thing you wanted on your warships was a crew that was unarmed, chained, and hated you. It was only when cannon became sufficiently effective to convert warships from floating armies to floating gun platforms that galley slavery became a practical military technology.

So one explanation for the observed pattern, in England and elsewhere, is that legal systems were looking for inexpensive, better yet profitable, forms of punishments. This provides an explanation not only for the existence of execution and transportation and the absence of imprisonment, but for pardoning as well. If the judge concluded that this particular defendant was merely a good boy who had yielded to temptation, not a hardened criminal, he might also conclude that telling the defendant he was going to be hanged by the neck until dead and then pardoning him would provide a sufficient fright to deter any future offenses. Much the same principle explains discretionary sentencing in modern law. It also explains the legal rule that allows (sufficiently) insane criminal defendants to get off. If someone is too crazy to be deterred, it may be worth institutionalizing him in order to prevent future problems, but there is little point to punishing him. In the one case you let the defendant off because punishing is unnecessary, in the other because it is useless.

A second explanation of selective pardoning is that it provided a way of reducing the negative externalities imposed by execution. Hanging almost always imposes a large cost on the person most directly affected; that is one of the reasons for hanging people. It may also impose substantial costs on others: friends, relatives, employers, and taxpayers potentially responsible for supporting the convicted criminal's dependents. Those costs serve little deterrent function. If many such people are willing to go to some trouble to testify in favor of the criminal at trial or sign a petition asking the Crown to pardon him, that is evidence that such costs are substantial and so a reason to avoid them by pardoning the convict.

So far I have assumed that pardons are based on information the court system receives about the prisoner. An alternative way of looking at them is as a good sold on a market. A petition from the convict's employer might provide information about the character or productivity of the convict. A petition from a politically influential nobleman, who might never have met the convict and was unlikely to know much about him, provided no such information, at least not directly. Yet such a petition would probably have more effect on the outcome of the case than one from the convict's closest friends.

Imagine that you are an ordinary Englishman who wishes to save the life of a friend convicted of a capital felony, say sheep stealing. One way of doing so is to go to some high-status person you know, perhaps the local squire, and ask him to intervene on your friend's behalf. You are engaged in an implicit exchange of favors. Low-status people sometimes have opportunities to benefit high-status people, and you have implicitly committed yourself to do so, whether by being suitably deferential to the squire in public or by supporting the parliamentary candidate he recommends.

The local squire has more influence with the authorities than you do but not enough to save a convict from the gallows. He accordingly writes to a politically influential local peer, requesting him to intervene in behalf of one of the squire's people, a worthy young man led astray by bad companions. Here again the exchange is not primarily of information but of services. One of the things that makes local peers politically influential is the support of local squires.

The court, by considering and acting on such petitions, is implicitly offering the convicted felon a choice between a fine and execution. The fine is paid not by the felon but by his friends and takes the form not of money but of favors. It goes, possibly through intermediaries, to people who can influence the granting of pardons. To the extent that those who will end up paying such fines are in a position to prevent their friends from committing felonies, such a system gives them an incentive to do so. It thus functions as a collective punishment similar to those observed in some primitive legal systems, in which fines are paid not by the offender alone but by other members of his kinship group as well—not too far from what we observed happening in saga period Iceland.

Pardons procured in this way substitute an efficient punishment, a fine, for a less efficient punishment, execution. In doing so they provide resources to the state and those who control it. Thus the legal system, in addition to providing a mechanism to reduce crime, also increases the ability of the state to maintain its authority. Considered from the standpoint of public relations, it is an elegant way of doing so. Nobody is threatened save the guilty convict. The squire is not oppressing his tenants but doing them a favor, at their request. The knowledge that such favors may occasionally be needed gives everyone in the village an incentive to be polite to the squire. In the Middle Ages English kings openly sold pardons as a way of raising money. One way to interpret pardoning in the eighteenth century is as a subtler version of the same thing.

To the modern mind eighteenth-century English law enforcement, with no police or public prosecution and no imprisonment for serious crime, seems clumsy and unworkable. What is the evidence on how well it worked compared to other systems that existed at the time or compared to a modern system?

Unfortunately, there is not much good data on crime rates prior to this century. Such information as we have suggests that the very long term trend for the English murder rate over a period of many centuries is downward. For a specific comparison between the situation in the late eighteenth century, with private prosecution, and in the early twentieth, with public police and prosecutors, we have a little more than that: The figure for indictments for homicide in the former period is similar, on a per capita basis, to the figure for murders known to the police in the latter, which suggests that the eighteenth-century system and the modern system may have worked about equally well. But it is not clear how comparable the two statistics are. And even if we knew that crime rates were about the same under the two systems, we do not know how other changes over the course of the century might have affected them.

A more interesting comparison may be between England and France. France in the eighteenth century had a modern system of criminal law enforcement: paid professional police, public prosecutors, imprisonment (as well, until midcentury, as galley slavery). At the end of the century it was the French state with its modern system that collapsed, while England went on to rule much of the world. Of course, there may have been other reasons.

Finally, there is the question of why the English did not adopt a modern system earlier, as some contemporary writers argued that they should. Perhaps it was because the French did have such a system and French institutions, as every good Englishman knew, were wicked and tyrannical. A more sympathetic explanation is that England spent the seventeenth and early eighteenth centuries in a civil war followed by a military dictatorship followed by a series of successful coups: the reestablishment of the Stuart monarchy, its replacement by William and Mary in the Glorious Revolution of 1688, and finally the installation of the Hanoverian dynasty. One thing that may have become clear during those conflicts was that, if criminal prosecution was controlled by the Crown, the king's friends could get away with murder.

That problem is still with us. Consider the final outcome of three putative violations of the law committed in my lifetime by law enforcement agencies: The shooting deaths of two (sleeping) Black Panthers by Chicago police in 1969, the illegal search and seizure of Steve Jackson Games (entertainingly recounted by Bruce Sterling in *The Hacker Crackdown*) by the Secret Service in 1990, and the killings by federal marshals and the FBI in the Ruby Ridge case in 1992. In each case perpetrators either were never prosecuted for any criminal offense, were charged with a much less serious offense than they appeared to be guilty of (obstruction of justice rather than murder), or, in one case, charged by a different level of government than the one that employed him. None of the government agents in question suffered any criminal penalty. But in each case the government or agency involved ended up paying either civil damages or a large civil settlement to the victims or their heirs. Criminal prosecution is controlled by the state, civil prosecution by the victim.

These examples suggest an important point too often forgotten in the economic analysis of law: The rationality assumption applies to enforcers as well as enforcees. In constructing legal institutions we cannot simply assume that legislators, judges, and police will go out and do good—in the economist's version, promote efficiency. We have to think about their incentives too.

Order without Law: Private Norms in a Modern Society

Our third story brings us even closer to home, to a rural California county in the late twentieth century. It starts with Ronald Coase and cattle.

Consider two neighbors. One is a farmer, the other a rancher whose cattle occasionally stray onto the farmer's land and eat his crops. Under the legal rule of *closed range*, the rancher is responsible for the resulting damage; he has a legal duty to fence in his cattle. Under the alternative rule of *open range*, it is the farmer's duty to fence the cattle out; if they get in, the rancher is not liable.

One implication of Coase's analysis of the problem of externalities, discussed in chapter 4, is that as long as transaction costs are low, which rule we have has no effect on how ranchers and farmers behave. If the efficient solution is for the farmer to fence the cattle out (typically the case if there is lots of grazing land with free-ranging cattle and a few scattered farms), that will happen, whether because the farmer is liable (open range rule) and wishes to avoid the uncompensated damage or because the rancher is liable (closed range) and pays the farmer to fence the cattle out to avoid the greater cost of fencing them in himself. Similarly, if the efficient solution is to fence the cattle in, that will happen. All the legal rule determines is who pays for it.

Shasta County California, by historical accident, is a patchwork of open and closed range; in some parts of the county owners of straying cattle are liable for the damage their cattle do, in some parts they are not. It occurred to Robert Ellickson, a legal scholar, that this provided a perfect opportunity to test Coase's argument against the real world.

What he discovered was very odd indeed, as sometimes happens when scholars temporarily abandon theory in favor of observation. Coase's prediction was correct. Farmers, ranchers, and people who combined both functions behaved in the same way with regard to straying cattle whether in open or closed range. But Coase's explanation was wrong: There were no side payments. Farmers in open range were not paying ranchers to fence their cattle into their own fields; ranchers in closed range were not paying farmers to fence cattle out of their crops.

Further study yielded a simple and surprising explanation. When it comes to matters of trespassing cattle—and some other things—the law of the state of California does not run in Shasta County. The resolution of such disputes is determined instead by a system of informal norms of neighborly behavior, a private system of rules privately enforced.

Suppose some of my cattle get into your fields and start eating your tomato plants. You call me up to complain. If I am a good neighbor, I come over promptly, remove my cattle, apologize, and, if there has been substantial damage, offer to help you repair it.

Suppose I am a bad neighbor: I show up three hours later, don't apologize, don't offer to help. Your first response is true negative gossip, telling other people in the community about my unneighborly behavior. People start showing me the cold shoulder, my wife doesn't get invited to neighborhood bridge games, my children don't get invited over to play at other children's houses.

Suppose it doesn't work; perhaps I don't have a wife and children and am an unsociable type, just as happy not to have to exchange friendly chit-chat with neighbors. After the second or third time my cattle stray into your field, you escalate the conflict. Instead of calling me up to remove my cattle, you drive them out of your field yourself and keep driving them for several miles in the direction away from my farm. Eventually I notice that my cattle are missing and have to spend considerable time and effort finding and retrieving them.

It may occur to some readers, especially after the discussion of alternative punishments in the previous part of this chapter, that there is a more efficient punishment I could impose. Eight of your cattle wander into my field. I convert one of them into hamburger in my freezer—this is, after all, a rural county—and call you up to tell you that seven of your cattle are trampling my tomatoes. After a few such incidents you count your herd and get the point.

That punishment may be more efficient, but it is forbidden by this particular system of norms. The reason, I believe, is that it is too efficient—

with the result that it is in my interest to impose it even when you are not really guilty. Not only is the system of private norms we are discussing privately enforced, it is also (unlike the Icelandic system) privately judged. When I decide what punishment to impose on you for the misdeeds of your cattle, I am acting as judge and jury in my own case, limited only by the willingness of our neighbors to accept my side of any subsequent dispute about what happened.

As long as all the punishments I can impose hurt me as well as you, my judging my own case is not too serious a problem. I don't really want to spend the next two hours driving your cattle away from your ranch. But if I have the option of imposing a punishment that makes me better off at your expense, that changes the situation. Now, when you tell our neighbors that I am really a cattle thief rather than a wronged farmer, they may believe you. By restricting the range of permitted punishments in the way it does, the system of private norms of neighborly behavior avoids that problem.

So far I have discussed the application of the norms to only one issue, trespassing cattle. They apply to some other issues as well, such as the mutual obligation of neighbors to build and maintain fences. There too the norms, in practice, trump California law.

The reason norms trump law in Shasta County is simple: One of the strongest norms is that neighbors don't sue neighbors. Anyone who goes to court to enforce his rights automatically loses his case in the court that matters most, the court of local public opinion.

Of course, the system of norms does not cover everything. California law still applies to murder, marriage, and many other things. It even applies to cattle when they are run down by cars. People driving through Shasta County are not neighbors, hence not a part of the system of self-enforced norms, so suing them is a perfectly legitimate activity and being sued by them a real risk.

Having stumbled over the norms of Shasta County, Ellickson went on to investigate a variety of other systems of private norms, including those of whalers in the nineteenth century and modern American academics. The last example was the cruelest, at least so far as his fellow law professors were concerned, since he offered evidence that professors, when photocopying each other's articles, blithely ignore the relevant copyright laws while adhering to professional norms designed to serve the interests of the academic community, in some cases at the expense of their publishers. His central thesis was a simple one: Close-knit groups tend to develop efficient norms. He concluded that while formal law is important, it is less important than generally believed. In a wide variety of situations people not only succeed in resolving their conflicts without recourse to law, they do it by mechanisms that work considerably better than the legal system.

Two important questions these stories suggest are how norms arise and why they tend to be efficient. If rules are well designed, the obvious explanation is that someone designed them. While this may explain some systems of religious norms, it tells us little about norms that apply to straying cattle and fence building in Shasta County, or, in the nineteenth century, to who owned a whale when two different ships had been involved in killing it.

An alternative to deliberate planning is evolution. Perhaps, over time, societies with better norms conquer, absorb, or are imitated by societies with worse norms, producing a world of well-designed societies. The problem with that explanation is that such a process should take centuries, if not millennia, which does not fit the facts as Ellickson reported them. Whaling norms, for example, seem to have adjusted rapidly to changes in the species being hunted.

Perhaps what is happening is a form of evolution involving smaller and more fluid groups than entire societies. Consider a norm such as honesty that can be profitably followed by small groups within a society, applicable only within the group. Groups with efficient norms prosper and grow by recruitment. Others imitate them. Groups with similar norms will tend to fuse, in order to obtain the same benefits on a larger scale. If one system of norms works better than its competitors, it will eventually spread through the entire society. When circumstances change and new problems arise the process can repeat itself, generating modified norms to deal with the new problems.

This conjecture about how norms arise and change suggests a prediction: Even if a norm is efficient, it will not arise if its benefits depend on everyone following it. It is in the interest of any pair of captains to agree in advance to an efficient rule for dealing with whales that one ship harpoons and another one brings in, just as it is in the interest of a pair of individuals to agree to be honest with each other. But a rule for holding down the total number of whales killed so as to preserve the population of whales is useful only if everyone follows it. The former type of norm existed, the latter did not, with the result that nineteenth-century whalers did an efficient job of hunting one species after another to near extinction—which was probably not the efficient outcome.

Where Are They Now?

Iceland today is a conventional Scandinavian democracy, with public prosecution, public law enforcement, and other familiar institutions. England today has a legal system very much like America today. What happened?

A possible explanation for the final collapse of the Icelandic system is external pressure. In the thirteenth century Norway emerged from a long period of civil war with a strong and wealthy monarchy. During the Sturlung period, the final fifty years of increasing violence leading to the collapse of the Icelandic system, the Norwegian Crown repeatedly meddled in Icelandic politics, supporting one faction or another in the hope of setting up a native ruler subservient to Norway. They never succeeded—their clients tended to abandon their Norwegian allegiance once it looked as though their side could win without it—but the continuing civil war eventually convinced most of the Icelanders to give up on independence.

An alternative explanation is that the Icelandic system depended on political power, in particular the ownership of goðorðs, being widely dispersed. The Sturlung period saw an increasing concentration of power, with a few factions controlling many goðorðs. That may have subverted the competitive balance of power on which the system depended.

Yet another possible explanation is that what destroyed the system was a foreign ideology: monarchy. As long as the function of feud was to resolve claims by people who thought they had been wronged, the system worked reasonably well. But when the feuds changed into a civil war over who was going to end up ruling the country when its traditional system collapsed, it was a different game with a different logic. Imagine, for a rough modern equivalent, what our legal system would look like if judges routinely got elected for the chief purpose of jailing all opponents of their political patrons, or if juries routinely acquitted murderers on the grounds that they approved of the murder. The form of the system would be the same as it now is, the substance very different.

What about the changes in the English system in the late eighteenth and early nineteenth century that converted it into something more like a modern system of public prosecution of crime? One possible explanation is that private prosecution depended on reputational incentives, on potential victims, individually or in prosecution associations, committing themselves to prosecute in order to buy a reputation that would deter crimes against them. Such incentives work better in a small town, where everyone knows everyone else, than in a big city, and the cities were getting bigger. It was in London in the 1830s that Robert Peel established England's first system of paid, professional police.

That may explain the shift from private to public prosecution, but what about the shift from execution, transportation, and pardoning to imprisonment? That may, in part, have reflected rising incomes. Imprisonment was more expensive than execution but permitted a more continuous range of punishment (and was less offensive to the views of much of the population) than a legal system that, at least sometimes, hanged people for minor crimes. So once England was rich enough to afford to lock up violent criminals, it started doing so. In addition transportation was becoming less effective as transport became less expensive, making it easier for transportees to escape and return to England illegally.

A second factor seems to have been ideological. Eighteenth-century penal theorists had a view of criminal behavior very much like that of twentieth-century economists: Criminals were criminals because it paid. To stop them from being criminals, you imposed punishments severe enough to make some other option more attractive. The early nineteenth century saw a shift toward the idea that rehabilitation rather than punishment was the proper goal. Criminals were criminals because they didn't know any better; if properly reeducated via religion and hard work, they would become law-abiding and productive members of the community. Hence the rise of the penitentiary, where criminals would learn to repent of their moral failings and from whence they would go forth and sin no more.

Lessons We Can Learn

I have described three different societies, each of which had or has a system of rules to deal with the same problems, or at least some of the same problems, as our legal system, and each in a different way. What can we learn from them?

The first and most general lesson is that the solutions we are used to are not the only possibilities. Crimes do not have to be prosecuted by police and public prosecutors, as we can see by both historical examples. Punishments do not even have to be enforced by the government, as we can see in both Iceland and Shasta County.

These societies not only tell us that alternatives are possible, they also tell us something about what problems they encounter and how they might be dealt with. Systems of private prosecution, including modern tort law, depend on someone having an adequate incentive to prosecute and the resources to do it. The Icelanders came up with some interesting solutions to that problem, as did the English in the eighteenth century.

Ellickson's work on norms also suggests an interesting possibility for making sense of crime rates in the United States at present. Our murder rate is not only unusually high by the standards of other developed countries, it is also very uneven—low in most places, very high in poor parts of the inner city. Perhaps the reason is that the system of legal control over crime that legal scholars, including economists, spend their time studying doesn't really matter very much on the south side of Chicago, just as it doesn't matter very much in Shasta County. The main reason not to commit crimes in most of the United States, indeed most of the world, might be that if your neighbors suspect you are a criminal they will be reluctant to give you a job, or rent you an apartment, or let you date their daughters.

If that system of private enforcement breaks down in subgroups of our society where major sources of income are welfare and crime, where both sex and childbearing are largely divorced from marriage and parents have little control over the sex lives of their children, the criminal law may prove a weak substitute.

Further Reading

Readers interested in more information on these three societies may want to look at two articles and a book review by me, all of which can be found on my web page, and a book by Robert Ellickson:

"Making Sense of English Law Enforcement in the Eighteenth Century," *University of Chicago Law School Roundtable* (spring/summer 1995): 475–505.

"Private Creation and Enforcement of Law: A Historical Case," *Journal of Legal Studies* (March 1979): 399–415.

"Less Law Than Meets the Eye," a review of Robert Ellickson, *Order without Law*, *Michigan Law Review* 90, no. 6 (May 1992): 1444–52.

Robert Ellickson, *Order without Law* (Cambridge, Mass.: Harvard University Press, 1994).

18

The Crime/Tort Puzzle

OUR LEGAL SYSTEM has two quite different sets of rules designed to do the same thing: Deter people from injuring others by making it costly to do so. This apparent redundancy was demonstrated in two recent high-profile cases. In one, O. J. Simpson was first acquitted of the crime of killing his wife and then convicted of the tort of killing his wife. In another, Michael Jackson was accused of child molestation. The civil case settled out of court, at which point the criminal case was dropped, presumably because the witnesses were no longer willing to testify.

The existence of two sets of legal rules for the same purpose raises at least three interesting questions:

1. Is one approach clearly superior for some sorts of offenses and the other for other sorts, providing a good functional reason for the existence of both, or could we have a functioning legal system in which all offenses were treated as torts or all offenses as crimes, perhaps with some modifications to existing tort or criminal law?

2. Is there a reason to sort offenses between the two systems as we do, a reason, for example, why a burglary is normally treated as a crime rather than a tort and an auto accident as a tort rather than a crime?

3. Tort law and criminal law are each a bundle of legal rules. Is there a reason why the rules are bundled in that particular way, why, for example, the system in which offenses are prosecuted by the victim requires a lower standard of proof for conviction and relies more heavily on monetary punishments than the one in which offenses are prosecuted by the state?

Part I: Should We Abolish the Criminal Law?

We know it is possible to have a functioning legal system in which all offenses are torts because the Icelanders had such a system, and it functioned for more than three centuries. But that does not tell us whether such a system would work for us, nor does it tell us whether it would be for us (or was for them) superior to a system in which some offenses are torts and others crimes. So it is worth examining the theoretical question of whether there are good reasons why some offenses should be publicly prosecuted, as in current criminal law. A variety of such reasons have been proposed. They include:

1. *The victim of an offense may not have sufficient resources to prosecute it.* This problem can be dealt with by making tort claims transferable, as was done in saga period Iceland. A victim with inadequate resources gives or sells his claim to someone better able to prosecute it. He might, as a result, end up with no compensation for his loss—but then, under criminal law at present, victims receive no compensation either.

2. *Some offenses cause diffuse injury, so nobody has an adequate incentive to prosecute them.* This is dealt with under current law by class actions. It could be better dealt with by making claims for torts that had not yet been litigated, including ones that had not yet occurred, transferable. Middlemen would buy bundles of small claims from potential plaintiffs, then rebundle them for sale to prosecution firms, with each firm buying claims associated with the particular offenses it is litigating.

3. *Some offenses result in a diffuse injury difficult to observe, along with an observable injury to a single victim.* The standard example is a crime that both injures the victim and imposes fear on potential victims. This problem is less severe under tort law, where the victim/prosecutor, if successful, gets reimbursed for his injury, than under a criminal system, where the victim gets nothing. But even under tort law victims are not fully reimbursed *ex ante*, since there is some chance they will fail to collect

damages, and, in most circumstances, they must pay their own legal costs, so there is still good reason to fear being a victim. One possible solution, discussed in chapter 14 in the context of punitive damages, is to increase the amount of damages to allow for such problems.

4. *If an offender is judgment-proof, there is no incentive for the victim to prosecute him, so prosecution must be by the state.* There are at least three possible responses to this problem:

Whether defendants are judgment-proof is in part a function of the legal rules on collecting judgments. If convicted defendants who were unable to pay money damages could be sold into slavery or dismembered for organ transplants, fewer defendants would be judgment-proof, not only because some would have sufficient value as slaves or spare parts but because the existence of such unattractive outcomes would provide offenders an incentive to make sure they were able to pay damages in money instead. Some of the risks of such a system were discussed in chapter 15.

The state could pay the fines of judgment-proof offenders to the victim/prosecutors, thus providing them an incentive to prosecute, and impose criminal punishments, thus deterring offenders. Such a bounty system, analogous to a voucher system for schooling (or the GI Bill, which was a voucher system for higher education), combines private prosecution with public funding.

The victim of a tort may commit himself to prosecute even judgment-proof defendants in order to deter offenses against him, provided that the legal system provides nonpecuniary punishments for convicted defendants unable to pay damages. We saw an example of this pattern in the prosecution associations of eighteenth-century England.

5. *It is impossible to construct legal rules that give victims the optimal incentive to prosecute.* Hence the best possible system of private enforcement is inferior to an ideal system of public enforcement, although not necessarily to an actual system of public enforcement.

This, the most sophisticated and interesting of the arguments against private enforcement, is due to Landes and Posner. As we saw in chapter 15, for any offense there exists some optimal amount and probability of punishment. But once we set the amount of punishment in a system with private prosecution we have no way of controlling the probability. That will be determined by the profit-maximizing behavior of the victims—how much they find it worth spending on identifying and convicting offenders in order to collect damages from them. There is thus no way save luck of getting to the optimal combination of probability and punishment.

To put the argument more mathematically, we are trying to separately get two variables, probability and punishment, to their optimal values. But we have only one control variable to do it with: the level of punishment. An ideal public enforcement system, on the other hand, could set probability and punishment independently, making an ideal public enforcement system superior to even an ideal private one, at least in that respect.

A Solution to the Landes/Posner Impossibility Proof

The solution to this problem is for the legal system to set, not the punishment if convicted, but the expected punishment: fine paid times probability of conviction. To make that possible we must first add a set of middlemen to our privately enforced legal system, prosecution firms that buy claims from victims, prosecute them, and collect the fine, if any. As in chapter 15 we will limit ourselves for simplicity to a single crime, say mugging.

Think of any punishment as consisting of a fine paid and a fine collected. The fine paid measures how much worse off the convicted criminal is as a result of having the punishment imposed on him. The fine collected measures how much better off other people are as a direct result of having the punishment imposed on him. The difference between fine paid and fine collected is the punishment cost. Consider some examples:

1. A cash fine, with no administrative costs of collecting it. Fine paid equals fine collected, punishment cost equals zero.

2. Execution. Fine paid equals the value of one life. Fine collected equals zero—a little less if execution has positive costs.

3. Imprisonment. Fine paid equals the value to the criminal of not being in prison. Fine collected is negative—the cost to the rest of us of running the prison.

Suppose a prosecutor has bought a thousand offenses, for each of which he is permitted (and required) by the court to collect an expected punishment, a fine paid, of a thousand dollars. If he catches and convicts every offender—an expensive proposition—he charges each a thousand dollar fine, collecting a total revenue of a million dollars. If he catches and convicts only a hundred offenders, he is legally entitled to impose a ten thousand dollar fine on each, but, since many cannot pay that much, he ends up having to imprison some instead—and pay for the prisons. In deciding how many to catch and convict he must trade off the lower apprehension cost of catching fewer criminals against the higher punishment cost of punishing those he catches more severely.

Generalizing the argument we can see (the formal demonstration is at the end of the chapter) that it is in the private interest of the prosecutor to choose the optimal punishment/probability combination, the combination that minimizes the sum of apprehension cost and punishment cost. He wants to minimize the sum of the two costs because he is paying both: apprehension cost directly, since it is up to the prosecutor to apprehend and convict offenders, and punishment cost indirectly, because the higher the punishment cost, the less of what offenders lose goes to him and the more he has to pay to punish them.

So all the court has to do is to set the correct expected value for fine paid. Profit maximization by the enforcer will produce that expected value in the optimal way, solving the problem raised by Landes and Posner.

But . . .

There is a problem with this approach to expanding tort law to provide private prosecution of offenses that are now crimes. Consider an offense for which the average return from catching and punishing an offender is negative: It costs more to catch and convict him than the fine collected. In order for prosecutors to stay in business, victims must pay enforcers to take over their claims and prosecute them. The victims are still selling their claims but at a negative price.

A victim who sells an offense for a negative price is paying for the enforcer's agreement to impose a specific expected punishment on the offender. The reason to do so is deterrence. The victim wants potential offenders to know that if they commit an offense against him they risk punishment.

This works for offenses for which it is possible to make deterrence a private good, such as burglary. A potential victim pays an enforcer to agree to prosecute his claim for any offenses committed against him. The victim passes on the relevant information to potential burglars by posting a notice on his door announcing that that particular enforcer has purchased his claims and will enforce them. The victim has sold his claims, in advance, at a negative price, and has gotten deterrence in exchange.

This is not a purely imaginary arrangement. Even in our present system, in which the enforcement of criminal law is nominally entirely public, there are firms that sell similar services. In eighteenth-century England potential crime victims joined prosecution associations, paying a price to buy deterrence.

So private enforcement, generalized tort law, could work for all offenses that sell at a positive price, offenses for which the amount collected from convicted offenders is, on average, more than the cost of catching and convicting them. It also could work for offenses that sell at a negative price but for which deterrence can be made a private good. It does not work for offenses that sell at a negative price for which deterrence cannot be made a private good because the offender does not know enough about the victim to be deterred—*anonymous victim offenses*. These were the sort of offenses—highway robbery, for example—that provided a special problem for the system of private enforcement of criminal law in eighteenth-century England.

How serious the problem is depends in part on the technology of committing offenses and apprehending and punishing offenders and in part on features of the legal system that affect the cost of apprehension and punishment. A legal system that permitted penal slavery, or one that allowed the sale of organs from executed felons, or one set in a society where individual reputation was important and stigma thus provided a powerful and efficient punishment, would have lower punishment costs than one without those features.

Part II: Sorting Offenses

In modern legal systems some offenses are privately prosecuted as torts, others publicly prosecuted as crimes. This raises an obvious question: Does the tort/crime distinction in modern law correspond reasonably closely to the distinction between those offenses that are and are not dealt with adequately by private enforcement?

Landes and Posner argue that it does. They argue that torts are, generally speaking, offenses detected with probability near one, hence for which the problem of getting the proper probability/punishment combination disappears.

But even if detecting many torts is cheap, prosecuting them is not. The more the victim spends, the more likely he is to win his case. The higher the damage payment he will receive if he wins, the greater the incentive to spend money in order to win it. The damage payment set by the law is both the punishment for committing a tort and the reward for successfully prosecuting one. There is no reason to suppose that the same damage payment produces the optimal levels of both punishment and prosecution. The problem Landes and Posner raised in order to show why it is inefficient to apply tort law to crimes also implies that it is inefficient to apply tort law to torts!

An alternative defense of the current crime/tort division is the argument that criminals are more likely to be judgment-proof against the optimal punishment, unable to pay the corresponding fine, than are tortfeasors. Translated into the language I am using here, this suggests that tort offenses are more likely to sell at a positive price, more likely to produce more in fines than it costs to prosecute them, than are criminal offenses.

There are two reasons why we might expect criminals to be more often judgment-proof than tortfeasors. One is that (some) crimes, such as burglary, are hard to detect, so the optimal probability of conviction is low, so the fine must be high in order to give an adequate expected punishment. The other is that, if offenses are hard to detect, producing even a small probability of conviction may be costly. Both of these are related to the fact that crimes are intentional, so criminals are likely to spend resources concealing them.

One problem with this comparison is that it is based on a biased sample of torts: the ones that get litigated. Since tort law is privately enforced, anonymous victim torts with negative price don't get litigated. The offenses we observe being prosecuted in the tort system tend to be the ones with positive value.

A second problem is that while the offenses we now classify as crimes are more likely than torts to be negative price offenses, they are less likely than torts to be anonymous victim offenses. A burglar deciding which house to burgle can choose to avoid houses with notices saying that their owners have paid in advance to have burglars prosecuted. A driver cannot readily adjust his level of care to take account of which other cars have notices on them saying that their owners have paid in advance to have drivers who run into them prosecuted. So intentional offenses, typically crimes rather than torts, are less likely to be anonymous victim offenses, hence more likely to be offenses for which deterrence can be made a private good.

Another important issue, touched on in chapter 15, is the problem of deliberately fraudulent claims. Under any system in which offenses sell at a positive price, there is an incentive to manufacture them, to frame potential defendants. Hence any legal changes that shift the system toward more efficient punishment by, for example, making it easier to collect fines also risk encouraging prosecutorial fraud.

The English criminal system encountered this problem in the mid–eighteenth century. Because of concern that incentives for private prosecution were too low, the Crown established substantial rewards for successful prosecution of certain offenses such as highway robbery. The result was a series of scandals in which it appeared that the convicted offender either had been entrapped into committing the offense in order that he could then be betrayed for the reward or had been framed for an offense that had not occurred. Analogous modern cases arise under both civil forfeiture and punitive damages.

This problem provides a possible explanation for one of the more puzzling features of tort law, the absence of probability multipliers. A successful litigant is entitled to have his injury made good, to receive a damage payment equal to the damage done. But if victims of torts are successful litigants with probability less than one, as is surely the case, the result is an expected punishment predictably less than the damage done. The obvious solution is to add in a probability multiplier, to scale up the punishment of tortfeasors who are successfully sued to compensate for the failure to punish those who are not.

One explanation for the lack of such probability multipliers is that they would be an invitation to fraud. Under current law someone is never better off as a result of being a victim of a tort; even if he successfully litigates it, all he gets is an amount sufficient to make up for the damage he has suffered. With a substantial probability multiplier, someone who could set up bogus torts, with witnesses suitably placed and primed to guarantee successful litigation, might do very well for himself. He faces much the same incentives as the homeowner whose insurance company has carelessly permitted him to insure his house for twice its value.

This suggests a second category of offenses for which private enforcement may work poorly: positive value offenses for which it is relatively easy to manufacture false positive verdicts. It is not clear, however, that public enforcement avoids the problem. Public enforcers must have some incentive to get convictions if they are to do their job, hence some incentive to get false convictions. Furthermore, public enforcers frequently use the threat of conviction to extract services in the form of information or testimony. The threat need not involve a real offense, as a number of examples, including a recent police scandal in Philadelphia, have demonstrated. While a legal system that limits enforcers to inefficient punishments makes prosecutorial rent seeking more difficult, it does not

eliminate it, since an inefficient punishment can be converted into an efficient one by an out-of-court settlement.

This suggests one important way in which the incentives of an enforcer
whose objective is private deterrence are superior to those of an enforcer
whose incentive is the profit from collecting an efficient punishment or the
political or bureaucratic gains from maintaining a high conviction rate. A
policy of arresting the first indigent who passes a crime scene, convicting
him in front of a hanging judge, executing him, and auctioning off his
organs may be an effective way of collecting income through prosecution,
private or public. But since your chance of being punished under such a
policy does not depend on whether or not you are guilty, it is a very
ineffective way of deterring crime. Private deterrence is the one incentive
that makes it in the direct private interest of the prosecutor to convict the
right person.

Part III: Bundling Legal Rules

I have written so far as if the defining difference between criminal law and
tort law was the distinction between public and private prosecution.
While that approach seems natural to an economist, other differences
might seem more central to scholars approaching the question in other
ways. Thus, for example, it is sometimes said that the essential difference
is that a crime is seen as a moral fault, a source of stigma, and a tort is not;
accusing someone of being a criminal is more of an insult than accusing
him of being a tortfeasor. Crimes are sometimes thought of as distinguished by certain sorts of punishment, notably imprisonment and execution. And criminal law is distinguished from tort law, at least in modern
Anglo-American legal systems, in a variety of other respects. Crimes have
a high standard of proof, require intent, are guaranteed a jury trial, have
punishments often much higher than the damage done, pay fines to the
state rather than the victim, and so on.

This suggests an obvious question: Are there good reasons why these
features go together? Are there good reasons why we have one category called "tort" with one set of rules, another called "crime" with another set?

The answer, as I will attempt to show below, is that there are reasons,
although perhaps not always compelling ones. I begin with a list of features in tabular form (see table 18.1).

The tort and crime columns in the table represent stylized versions of
the two systems. Fines are used in criminal law, but they tend to be for
offenses, such as speeding or illegal parking, that have some of the other
characteristics of torts. A parking ticket does not convey stigma and, in

TABLE 18.1
Characteristics of Tort and Criminal Systems

Characteristic	Tort	Crime
Who controls prosecution	Victim	State
Who collects punishments	Victim	State
Form of punishment	Fine	Imprisonment, execution
Standard of proof	Preponderance of the evidence	Beyond a reasonable doubt
Probability multiplier?	No	Yes
Right to jury trial?	Maybe	Yes
Desired level of offenses	> 0	= 0
Requires intent	No	Yes
Stigma to conviction	No	Yes

practice, does not require proof to the criminal standard. Punitive damages can be interpreted as a form of probability multiplier, and have been by some scholars, but they are also connected with stigma. For purposes of simplicity the table ignores such intermediate cases.

The table also ignores features that have dropped out of modern law. Eighteenth-century English criminal law combined private prosecution with criminal punishments. Early medieval English law went even further; the appeal of felony was, like a modern tort action, entirely private—the private prosecutor could drop charges, and the Crown could not pardon a convicted offender—but a successful prosecution resulted in criminal penalties. These systems provide important evidence of alternative ways in which legal rules might be bundled, but I am concerned here with a narrower range of options.

Looking at the table, we observe that under both systems the same actor controls prosecution and collects punishments. There are two obvious reasons for this. One is that collecting a damage payment provides an incentive to prosecute. The other is that the party who controls the prosecution can also drop the prosecution or, if that is forbidden, prosecute badly. Any system in which one party controls prosecution and another collects the punishment raises the possibility that the former will divert the fine to himself via an out-of-court settlement.

There is also a disadvantage to the combination: the opportunity it provides for fraudulent prosecution. If the claim and the right to prosecute are held separately, fraudulent prosecution requires a transaction between the owner of the claim and the prosecutor.

The victim of an offense has an incentive to prosecute in order to deter future offenses against him. He is also, in many cases, the chief witness. By making him the owner of the claim we unite in one person two incentives to prosecute plus an important input to successful prosecution, eliminating the transaction costs of getting separate people playing those roles to work together. Here again there is also a possible disadvantage: The greater the victim's incentive to get a conviction, the less trust can be put in his testimony. One of the reasons for the abandonment of the system of rewards in eighteenth-century England was that juries, knowing that witnesses might share in the rewards, rationally distrusted their testimony. The same problem arises today when juries know that witnesses for the prosecution in criminal trials are paid informants or have agreed to testify in return for a reduced sentence.

Having the claim belong to the victim has both advantages and disadvantages so far as its effect on the victim's incentive to prevent the offense, for reasons that will be discussed later in the chapter.

We next notice that the tort system is associated with relatively efficient punishments, the criminal with relatively inefficient. That makes sense in terms of the previous analysis, since offenses that require inefficient punishments are likely to be negative price offenses and so more difficult to prosecute privately. Of course, the fact that an offense is currently subject to inefficient punishment does not guarantee that it must be.

The inefficiency of criminal punishments provides, as first pointed out in chapter 1, an explanation for the higher standard of proof required to impose them. The lower the cost of punishment, the lower the (net) cost of imposing it incorrectly. So it makes sense to combine less efficient punishments with a higher standard of proof.

Or perhaps not. One problem with efficient punishments is that, by making successful prosecution profitable, they create an incentive for fraudulent prosecutions. One way of controlling that is a high standard of proof. An alternative way is by making fraudulent prosecution—in the limiting case, any unsuccessful prosecution—itself tortious. A weaker version of that is to require the losing party in a tort suit to pay the other side's legal expenses as is currently the rule in England, although not in the United States.

There are three plausible explanations for the absence of probability multipliers in tort law. One I have already mentioned: Probability multipliers make it profitable to be the victim of an offense, provided your probability of successful prosecution is sufficiently high relative to the average probability from which the multiplier is calculated. In a privately prosecuted system that provides an incentive for fraudulent prosecution.

A second explanation is that, because torts are not intentional, they are usually not concealed, and the probability of apprehension and conviction is thus arguably higher than for crimes. If so, the need for a probability multiplier is less. It might be argued in the opposite direction, however, that where the probability is low, it is the privately enforced system that particularly requires the multiplier. In both systems the multiplier is desirable in order to provide adequate deterrence. With private prosecution it may also be desirable in order to give an adequate incentive to the prosecutor. That relation is made explicit in the efficient system for private prosecution that I described in part I, which differs in important ways from tort law as it actually exists.

A third explanation links the lack of a multiplier to the importance of efficient punishments. The higher the punishment, the less likely it is that the offender can pay it as a fine. Hence one problem with probability multipliers is that they may push the punishment too high, increasing the fine paid but decreasing the fine received and thus reducing the incentive to prosecute.

The fact that Anglo-American law guarantees the defendant the opportunity for a jury trial for criminal cases but not always (except in the United States) for civil cases is puzzling. One possible explanation is that it serves the function of making fraudulent prosecution more difficult. Under a criminal system the prosecutor, judge, and claimant are all, in some sense, the same party; despite attempts to guarantee judicial independence, judges are ultimately employees of the state. Hence in a corrupt criminal system, a single party is sufficient to indict and convict. Introducing a jury changes that situation. Of course, there is still the risk that, under a corrupt civil system without juries, judges could conspire with fraudulent claimants. That risk is particularly serious when agents of the state play the role of civil plaintiff, as they do in forfeiture cases.

The category "desired level of offenses" requires some explanation. There is a sense in which the desired number of murders is positive—given the cost of preventing them. And the desired number of auto collisions would be zero—if we could avoid collisions at no cost.

What I mean here by the desired level is the level that would be efficient if the cost to the legal system of achieving that level were zero. If we could costlessly deter all murders, we would, despite the inconvenience to those of us with rich uncles. If we could costlessly deter all traffic accidents, we would not, because the ways in which people avoid having traffic accidents when the expected penalty is high, for example, by not driving, sometimes cost more than the reduction in accidents is worth.

As this example suggests, part of the reason the desired level of crime is typically zero is that crimes are intentional; perpetrators benefit by the occurrence of successful crimes and so spend resources to make them occur. This makes it likely that crimes will be inefficient for two reasons. First, many crimes are transfers, and if we add to a transfer the cost of bringing it about, the result is a net loss. Second, since the auto thief typically chooses whom he will steal a car from, he could choose to buy it instead. Where market transactions are practical they are typically less expensive than coerced transactions, since in the latter case the other party is spending resources trying to prevent the transaction.

This brings us to the issue of intent. Given that intentional offenses are more likely to be inefficient, and thus worth deterring if doing so were costless, why are they also worth prosecuting publicly rather than privately?

Two answers have already been suggested in earlier discussions. One is that intentional offenses are more likely to be concealed, hence harder to detect, hence more likely to be negative price offenses. The other is that intentional acts are more likely to have market substitutes than accidental acts, making it less likely that they are efficient, and may be more deterrable. If so, it makes sense to use a property rule, enforced by criminal law, rather than a liability rule, enforced by tort law, to deal with them. An argument in the opposite direction is that intentional offenses are less likely to be anonymous victim offenses, hence it is easier to deter them by making deterrence a private good.

We come finally to the question of stigma, the one punishment with negative cost. It is an unusual form of punishment in another respect as well: The direct benefit from imposing it is a public, not a private, good. A successful prosecution produces information about the defendant that is valuable to those who will deal with him in the future, but that value is not available to help pay the cost of prosecution. Stigma does, however, help solve the problem of deterring offenses that are costly to punish. Hence it is not surprising to see its use combined with the use of inefficient punishments—that is, with the criminal law.

Suppose we used stigma to punish offenses that we wished to ration but not to eliminate, such as traffic accidents. There would be a risk of overdeterrence, especially since the amount of stigma, unlike the size of a fine or the length of a prison sentence, is not something that the criminal justice system has direct control over. This is not a problem for murder. That suggests a second reason why it makes sense for stigma to be associated with criminal rather than civil offenses. A third reason is that, since stigma imposes costs on the defendant and provides its benefits to people other than the prosecutor, a private prosecutor may be willing, for a suitable consideration, to agree to a secret out-of-court settlement, thus keeping the information that would have been generated by a guilty verdict from those who could have used it to guide their future dealings with the defendant.

Why Burglary Should Be a Tort and Denting Fenders a Crime

Legal rules affect behavior on many margins. They affect incentives to commit offenses, incentives to prosecute them, and incentives to prevent them. For some offenses tort law may provide better incentives than criminal law on one of those margins and worse on another. If so, the question of what ought to be a tort and what ought to be a crime will be ambiguous, at least until we develop a theory good enough to predict not only the sign but also the size of such effects.

In the next few pages I will take one of the margins and argue that, judged by the incentives provided by the alternative legal regimes on that margin, our rules are backwards. Things we treat as crimes, such as burglary, ought to be torts; things we treat as torts, such as auto accidents, ought to be crimes. By doing so I hope to demonstrate one reason why figuring out whether our present allocation of offenses between the two systems is efficient is a hard problem.

The incentive I have chosen to examine is the incentive for potential victims to prevent offenses. From that perspective there is a simple and striking difference between tort law and criminal law. The victim of a tort suffers an injury but also obtains an asset, a claim for damages against the offender. The victim of a crime suffers an injury but obtains no corresponding asset since the fine for the offense, if any, goes to the state. So one effect of treating an offense as a tort instead of a crime is to reduce the net damage suffered by the victim and thus his incentive to prevent the offense.

Reducing the incentive to prevent the offense is not necessarily a bad thing; here as elsewhere, what we want is the right incentive, neither too much nor too little. The ideal legal system, seen from this standpoint, is one in which the potential victim receives exactly the net benefit produced by his defensive precautions and thus has an incentive to take them if and only if they are worth the cost. The question for any particular class of offense is whether the reduction in incentive provided by tort law moves the potential victim toward or away from the efficient level of precaution.

A World of Costless Enforcement

To make the argument easier, we start with a world in which catching and punishing offenders is costless. All offenders are detected, and none are judgment-proof. Within this simplified framework what is the right incentive for the victim to prevent the offense and what system gives it?

Start with automobile accidents. For simplicity consider accidents in which a car runs into a pedestrian and only the pedestrian is injured. We may attempt to deter such accidents either with a tort rule, in which the driver of the automobile is liable to the victim for the damage done, or with a criminal rule, in which the driver pays a fine but the victim does not receive it.

From the standpoint of the driver, the two rules (with the same penalty) generate the same incentive. Any reduction in the probability of an accident due to the driver's precautions reduces his liability by an amount equal to the savings in net social cost. What about the pedestrian?

Under the tort rule the pedestrian suffers no cost from being run into, since his damages are fully compensated by the driver. It follows that the pedestrian has no incentive to take precautions. Under the criminal rule, on the other hand, the pedestrian pays the full cost of the accident. It follows that he has the efficient incentive to take precautions to prevent it. It follows that, from the standpoint of the incentive for victim precautions, such offenses should be crimes, not torts.

Generalizing beyond the simplified example in which only one party suffers a loss, the efficient rule is that each party bears his own loss and pays a fine equal to the loss that the accident imposes on the other party. Thus each bears the full cost of the accident and has an incentive to take any cost-justified precautions to reduce its probability.

Consider next burglary, still in a world of costless enforcement. The legal system sets the penalty for burglary equal to the damage done, the value of what is stolen. Any burglar willing to pay that price commits an offense—and should. The system generates only efficient burglaries, those for which the gain to the offender is greater than the loss to the victim. The textbook example is Posner's hunter, lost and starving, who comes across a locked cabin in the woods, breaks in, feeds himself, and telephones for help.

In this world a homeowner who puts a lock on his door is wasting his own money and the burglar's time. He is better off leaving the door open and (costlessly) collecting the value of whatever goes out. The optimal level of precaution to prevent burglary is the same as the optimal level of precaution for a supermarket to take in preventing its customers from buying its vegetables: zero.

Under a tort rule that is the level of precaution the victim will take. He knows he will be fully reimbursed for whatever he loses, so he has no incentive to spend resources preventing burglary. Under a criminal rule, on the other hand, the criminal takes from the victim but repays the state, so the victim has an incentive to prevent the burglary. Hence, at least in the simplified world of costless enforcement and considering only the incentive of the victim to defend himself, burglary ought to be a tort.

Readers interested in a formal demonstration of the same result in a slightly more realistic world will find it on the web page.

Of course, there is no guarantee that we would reach the same conclusion if we analyzed the question in terms of incentives on other margins—for example, the incentive of the victim (under tort law) or the public prosecutor (under criminal law) to prosecute the offense. If it turns out that tort law gives the right incentives for some decisions by some parties and criminal law gives the right incentives for other decisions by other parties, we are left with no clear answer in theory to the question of which offenses should be under which legal system—and the difficult practical problem of trying to figure out which of the two imperfect solutions we should prefer.

Conclusion

There is a set of offenses that are especially difficult for private enforcement to deal with: negative price offenses with anonymous victims. Such offenses provide a plausible argument against a pure tort system. There is a further set of offenses that are difficult to deal with either privately or publicly: offenses where the probability of apprehension is low, requiring a probability multiplier in order to get an adequate expected punishment, where efficient punishments are possible, making successful prosecution profitable, and where it is difficult to detect fraudulent prosecutions.

The current sorting of offenses between the categories of crime and tort has at most a modest relation to what that analysis suggests would be an efficient division. In examining the bundling of legal rules into the forms we call "tort" and "crime," on the other hand, we can find plausible, but not always compelling, efficiency explanations for most of its features.

Efficient Institutions for the Private Enforcement of Law: A Postcript for the Mathematically Inclined

I am a prosecutor who has purchased from the victims the right to prosecute 1,000 offenses of a particular sort. The court has set an expected punishment of \$1,000. That means that I may catch all offenders and impose on each a fine paid of \$1,000, catch 100 and impose on each a fine paid of \$10,000, or catch 10 and impose on each a fine of \$100,000.

In choosing among these alternatives I wish to maximize the total of fines collected minus enforcement costs. Let F_p be the fine paid by each convicted offender, F_c the fine collected, making $F_p - F_c$ the punishment cost. N is the number of offenders convicted and punished. N/1,000=p, the probability of conviction and punishment. $E(p)$ is the per offender cost of catching an offender with probability p. P_o is the price the enforcer has paid each victim for the right to enforce his claim and collect the resulting fine.

The enforcer receives the fine collected, pays for enforcement, and pays to buy offenses, so he faces a profit function:

$$\pi = NF_c - 1000E(p) - 1000P_o = NF_p - N(F_p - F_c) - 1000E(p) - 1000P_o.$$

The court has set $pF_p = \$1000$, hence $NF_p = \$1,000,000$; hence we have

$$\pi = [\$1,000,000 - 1000P_o] - [N(F_p - F_c) + 1000E(p)].$$

Profit = [total fine paid–price paid to buy 1,000 offenses]–[the sum of total punishment cost (difference between fine paid and fine collected) and total enforcement cost].

The enforcer must decide how hard to try to catch the offenders, as measured by p, the probability with which he catches them. That decision will determine the fine paid, which he will collect in the most efficient form possible. The first bracketed expression in the second equation is independent of p, so he maximizes his profit by choosing the value of p that minimizes:

$$N(F_p - F_c) + 1000E(p).$$

$F_p - F_c$ is the punishment cost for one offense punished, $N(F_p - F_c)$ is therefore the total punishment cost; $NE(p)$ is the total enforcement cost. So the enforcer is choosing the level of p (and the punishment that, combined with that p, yields the set value of expected punishment) that minimizes the sum of punishment and enforcement cost—which is to say, the least cost combination of probability and punishment. So all the court has to do is to set the efficient value of expected punishment, fine paid times probability of punishment, and the enforcement agency, in the process of maximizing its profit, will produce that value with the optimal combination of probability and punishment.

19

Is the Common Law Efficient?

> The common law method is to allocate
> responsibilities between people engaged in
> interacting activities in such a way as to maximize
> the joint value, or, what amounts to the same
> thing, minimize the joint cost of the activities.
> *(Posner 1973: 98)*

ALMOST THIRTY years ago Richard Posner, then a law school professor, now the chief judge of the Seventh Circuit, proposed a simple conjecture: that the common law could best be understood as a set of rules designed to maximize what we have been calling economic efficiency. Over the years since he and others have offered a number of arguments for why we would expect that to be true—none of which I find entirely convincing. But Posner has also offered empirical evidence on a heroic scale. In a research project lasting decades and attracting the efforts of a large part of the law and economics community, he and his coworkers have scanned the common law, attempting to determine in each case what legal rules would be efficient and how they correspond to the legal rules that exist.

In past chapters we have seen some of the results of that project—skewed, of course, toward my interests and contributions. In this chapter I first sketch the arguments for why we might expect common law to be efficient and then offer a brief survey of the evidence.

The A Priori Case for Efficiency

> In searching for a reasonably objective and
> impartial standard, as the traditions of the bench
> require him to do, the judge can hardly fail to
> consider whether the loss was the product of
> wasteful, uneconomical resource use. In a culture
> of scarcity, this is an urgent, an inescapable
> question. And at least an approximation to the
> answer is in most cases reasonably accessible to
> intuition and common sense.
> *(Posner 1973: 99)*

The quoted passage, from the first edition of Posner's *Economic Analysis of Law*, a treatise masquerading as a textbook, provides one-half of his explanation of why judges can be expected to make efficient law: Efficiency is a widely held value, and judges, even without the apparatus of economic theory, can figure out more or less what rules are efficient. The other half is the claim that there is no other widely held value that judges are in a position to achieve.

One obvious alternative, income redistribution, is difficult to achieve through general legal rules, for reasons discussed in chapter 1. If courts consistently interpret contracts in a way favorable to some class of litigants, tenants in disputes with landlords, say, or workers in disputes with employers, other features of the transactions will adjust; rents will rise or wages fall to take account of the changed terms. The end result is unlikely to benefit the favored class and may well injure both sides by forcing on them less efficient terms than they would have agreed to on their own. So it might be prudent for judges, even egalitarian judges, to concentrate on maximizing the size of the social pie, the objective that Posner calls wealth-maximization and I have been calling economic efficiency, and leave to legislatures the dispute over how it is to be divided.

Even if judges are unable to redistribute among groups, they can still redistribute among the parties to the particular case they are deciding, and it is those parties who are most obviously and directly affected by the judge's decision. If in some category of disputes, landlord-tenant litigation for example, one party consistently appears more deserving than the other, the result may be a consistent bias in the resulting legal rules unrelated to economic efficiency. This problem is reduced but not eliminated by a legal system that distances the appeals courts making the rules from the parties whose cases they are deciding.

A more serious problem with Posner's argument is that it assumes that judges understand enough economics to realize that they cannot use general rules to benefit favored groups. As any economics teacher can testify, most of his students and acquaintances do believe that "pro-tenant" legal rules benefit tenants, "pro-labor" legal rules benefit workers, and "pro-business" legal rules benefit capitalists and executives. Why should we expect judges to be any better informed? Quite a lot of twentieth-century law, including such economically unconvincing concepts as contracts of adhesion and unequal bargaining power, seems to bear the stamp of economic ignorance. As Posner himself put it in *Economic Analysis of Law*, criticizing the verdict in the Baby M case (holding the enforcement of surrogate motherhood contracts contrary to the public policy of the state of New Jersey), "The court gave a number of reasons for this conclusion that demonstrate a lack of economic sophistication and a need for a book like this."

A further problem is that judges may care about things other than either efficiency or redistribution, values summed up in vague but emotively powerful terms such as "justice" or "fairness." One possible reply is that those values can themselves be viewed as in large part reflecting social concerns with economic efficiency. In chapter 17 I argued that private norms among close-knit groups, which may be one source of our intuitions of justice and fairness, have some tendency to be economically efficient.

Even if judges know enough economics to realize that they ought to be making efficient rules, it does not follow that they know enough to do it. Determining what legal rules are economically efficient can be a hard problem. Posner himself is one of the most intellectually able and economically sophisticated judges of this century. Yet in his academic work he has quite often proposed economically incorrect arguments for economically mistaken conclusions. We can hardly expect less qualified judges to do better, or even as well.

Economists routinely expect business firms to act efficiently, although there is little reason to expect that executives are any smarter than judges. But there is a crucial difference between the two cases. An executive who makes the wrong decision loses money. The market provides feedback, positive and negative reinforcement, to guide business firms toward efficient behavior. No comparable mechanism exists to push judges toward efficiency. A catastrophically bad decision might mean a reduction in national income of a tenth of a percent a decade later. That is an enormous amount of damage for one human being to do, billions of dollars down the drain, but it is not a signal that the judge making the decision is likely to pick up and respond to.

Another approach to arguing that legal rules should be efficient is to start with the incentives of the parties to litigation rather than the incentives of the judges. An inefficient rule makes the people it affects on net worse off, giving them an incentive to keep trying to contract or litigate around it. Eventually the water wears down the rock; after enough law cases a court finally gets the right answer.

This argument cannot explain the efficiency of legal rules with widely dispersed effects, since no one affected person has the necessary incentive to try to litigate to change them. And even if effects are concentrated, there is no reason to expect benefits and costs of alternative legal rules to be equally concentrated. If a particular legal change produces benefits for a small and well-organized group, well enough organized to fund repeated litigation aimed at establishing the necessary precedents, and spreads its costs widely enough, the argument implies that we can expect to get it even if it is, on net, inefficient. A cynical observer of the past century or so of legal change might argue that that is precisely what has been happening. The concentrated interest group consists of attorneys; the result of their efforts has been a body of law designed to maximize the demand for their services.

Ultimately, Posner and those supporting him have established no more than a possibility—that judges, especially nineteenth-century judges in a culture favorable to the value of economic efficiency, might decide cases in ways that tend to produce efficient rules. The serious defense of his thesis depends not on the a priori argument but on the evidence.

The Case for the Defense: Efficient Legal Rules

In chapter 5 I introduced the distinction between property rules and liability rules: "steal my car, go to jail" versus "dent my car, get sued." Under property rules rights get allocated to their highest-valued use through voluntary exchange; if the right to use your car is worth more to me than to you, I buy it. Under liability rules they get allocated by appropriation followed by a court-determined reimbursement of the victim by the appropriator.

As we saw, property rules are efficient in settings where private transaction costs are low and allocation via litigation costly and inaccurate; liability rules are efficient under the opposite circumstances. Roughly speaking, that corresponds to what we observe in the law. While there are some exceptions—I cannot sell you one of my kidneys, although that would be a straightforward private transaction—goods that should be allocated through property and trade are; goods that cannot be, at any reasonable cost, such as your right not to have me carelessly run my car into yours, are handled by liability rules instead.

This provides some evidence for the Posner thesis, but not much. The problem is that it is too easy a case. Consider the alternative: a system in which I was free to steal your car any time I wanted and your only recourse was to sue me for damage done, but in which driving down the street required me first to purchase permission from every other driver on the road. Such a system would be not merely inefficient but wholly unworkable. Economic analysis helps us understand why such a system would not work, but we do not need to assume that legal rules are efficient in order to predict that we will not get those ones. All we need is some mechanism to eliminate legal rules whose consequences are immediately catastrophic.

The background rules for property—in particular, the fact that if I own a right I can, under most circumstances, transfer my ownership to someone else—are again about what we would expect under an efficient legal system. As we saw in chapter 2, transferability provides a simple mechanism for moving goods to those who value them most. And at least some of the exceptions in our legal system—I cannot, for example, transfer my parental rights with regard to my child to someone else without first getting permission from the legal system, or openly sell my vote—can be defended as ways of dealing with potential third-party effects.

The general pattern of the law of real property, the way in which property rights to land are bundled, also seems at least roughly consistent with economic efficiency. The person who owns the right to plant crops on the land also owns the right to decide who walks on it, which make sense, since the two rights are worth much more combined than separated. He does not own the right to decide whether airplanes fly a mile over his land or radio stations broadcast electromagnetic waves through it, which again makes sense for similar reasons. And, as I argued at some length in chapter 11, the broad pattern of intellectual property law, in particular the difference between the legal rules for patent and copyright, looks like a system of economically efficient rules.

In tort law, too, much of the general pattern seems consistent with economic efficiency. The requirement that the tortfeasor must make the victim whole gives us the Pigouvian solution to the externality problem—charge the person responsible an amount equal to the external cost—at least as long as we ignore both litigation costs and the risk that some tortfeasors may escape unscathed. Negligence rules offer a solution to Coase's problem of double causation: The tortfeasor takes optimal precautions in order not to be found negligent; the victim, knowing that the tortfeasor will not be found negligent, takes optimal precautions because he expects to bear the cost of the tort himself. Strict liability with contributory negligence achieves the same objective in a mirror image form: The potential victim takes precautions in order not to be contributorially negligent, so the tortfeasor knows he will be liable, so it is in his interest to take optimal precautions too. Both rules, along with a few other alternatives, are observed in common law settings.

A negligence rule generates inefficient incentives with regard to precautions that the court cannot readily monitor, such as activity level: Was it efficient to take the trip during which I (non-negligently) ran my car into yours? The common law deals with that problem by imposing strict liability, which gives the correct activity level incentives for the tortfeasor but not the victim, on abnormally hazardous activities, activities for which it is quite likely that reducing the activity level is an efficient way of reducing the problem. And (some) courts substitute negligence for strict liability where the activity is a normal and necessary part of the use of land, hence unlikely to be deterred. If strict liability produces additional litigation costs but little or no additional deterrence, we are better off with negligence, as the Texas Supreme Court concluded in *Turner v. Big Lake Oil.*

Some differences between tort and criminal law also make sense in terms of economic efficiency, as we saw in chapter 18. Torts are usually punished with money damages, crimes with imprisonment or execution. The former is a more efficient punishment, hence false convictions are less costly, which justifies the lower standard of proof in tort law.

Many other detailed rules in the legal system also seem to fit with economic efficiency. One example is the defense of necessity, under which Posner's starving hunter could successfully avoid criminal prosecution for breaking into an empty house and using the telephone to call for help. His crime is an efficient one, so we don't want to deter it, and, since he has made no attempt to conceal his crime, he will be detected with certainty, making tort damages sufficient to deter him from breaking into houses when he is not starving. Another example is the rule of foreseeability. It is the Himalayan photographer, not the film developer, who bears most of the cost when the latter loses the former's film, since it is cheaper for the photographer, who knows the special value of the film, to take precautions than for the developer, who does not. A third example is the refusal of admiralty law to apply unlimited freedom of contract in salvage cases, thus discouraging ship captains from continuing to bargain as the water rises past their ankles.

The Case for the Prosecution: Inefficient Legal Rules

If we look past the general pattern to the details, the Posner thesis becomes considerably less convincing. The fact that organ sales by the owner are illegal is one example. A completely free market in organs for transplant might raise problems, since it makes murder followed by medical dismemberment profitable, creating serious negative externalities for potential victims. But that problem would not apply to a market in which individuals were free to accept payment now in exchange for selling the right to harvest their organs after death. A less exotic example is the failure of current law to support freedom of contract in the context of product liability and related issues—as I argued, in chapter 14, would be efficient.

Posner has defended the efficiency of current product liability law, arguing that in a complicated modern society the costs to consumers of evaluating the mix of waivers and guarantees produced by free contract would be unreasonably high. The obvious response is that if general rules are superior to case-by-case decisions, rational consumers can adopt general rules. Instead of imposing mandatory terms for product liability, as they now do, the courts could require contracts that deviate from the court's default rules to provide clear notice—in bright red fourteen-point type on the first page. Consumers who agreed with Posner that the courts were more competent than they were to set the terms on which they purchased goods could follow a policy of never signing a contract with red print on the first page; consumers who believed the courts frequently got it wrong could follow a different policy. If Posner is right and consumers are rational, the result will be the same as without freedom of contract; if he is wrong, rational consumers can and will contract around inefficient default rules. Posner's argument requires him to assume not merely that consumers are ignorant about the details of optimal contracts but that they do not know that they are ignorant and would therefore choose to waive the superior liability regime offered by the courts.

The refusal of modern courts to enforce agreements to waive claims for product liability or medical malpractice is one example of a more general pattern, the retreat from freedom of contract over the past eighty years or so. Another is the reluctance of courts to recognize the enforceability of mass market form contracts, so-called contracts of adhesion. A third example is their unwillingness to enforce penalty clauses, agreements for liquidated damages that the court considers excessive. As I pointed out in chapter 12, a penalty clause in a contract is simply a privately negotiated property rule. It makes sense in the same contexts as other property rules: where the cost of moving resources to their highest-valued use is lower through private transactions (one party buys permission from the other to void their contract) than through litigation.

There are many other examples of inefficient features in the common law. Perhaps the most striking is the refusal of the common law to include, in calculating damages for wrongful death, the value of the victim's life to himself. Insofar as that pattern is now changing, it is mostly through wrongful death statutes—and legislation is the part of the legal system that Posner does not claim is efficient.

Another example is the refusal of the common law to make tort claims, including inchoate tort claims, marketable. In chapter 9 I showed how doing so would help solve problems associated with tort damages for loss of life, in chapter 17 how it could be, and once was, used to solve the problem of victims too poor to prosecute, and in chapter 18 how it would make possible a superior alternative to the class action.

Earlier I offered intellectual property law as evidence in favor of efficiency. But Posner's thesis is about common law, not legislated law—and both patent and copyright are the product of federal statutes. Of course, statutes must be interpreted, so even statutory law, by the time it get down to the litigants, has a substantial common law element. But if we look at that dimension of intellectual property law, the case for efficiency is not so clear.

Consider the issue of whether or not computer programs in machine code, the form of the program actually used by the computer, are copyrightable. In the early cases some courts concluded that they were not, on the plausible enough grounds that something that was not intended to be read by a human being was not a writing. That argument was ended not by the courts but by Congress, which revised the copyright act to include software in both source code and object code forms. Insofar as that feature of intellectual property law is evidence for efficiency, it is evidence for the efficiency of statutory law.

For evidence in the other direction, consider the question of how long a patent lasts. The optimal term of patent protection depends on the technology of making and marketing inventions. The faster the rate of innovation, the more likely it is that what you invented today I would have invented tomorrow, hence the more likely that a long term of protection will over-reward you for your invention. During the past century the technology of making and marketing inventions has changed enormously. Throughout that time the term of protection provided by U.S. patent law has been somewhere in the range of fourteen to twenty-one years.

Fuzzy Law and Fuzzier Economics: The Case for Ignorance

So far I have been evaluating the thesis that the common law is efficient by listing features of the law that do or do not fit its predictions, that are or are not efficient. As you can see, there are quite a lot of both. A more serious problem with testing the thesis is that often we simply do not know what the efficient rule is. In many cases a clever theorist can come up with plausible economic arguments in favor of either of two alternative legal rules: negligence or strict liability, accepting or rejecting the defense of coming to the nuisance, including or not including probability multipliers in calculating tort damages.

I spent all of chapter 18 on one example of that sort of problem, the division in our legal system between crimes and torts. The existence of criminal law can be defended as a way of dealing with judgment-proof defendants. That defense can be answered by proposing that tort defendants be made less judgment-proof, by proposing a bounty system to combine private prosecution with some public funding, or by pointing out that deterrence can be made into a private good and even judgment-proof criminals are worth deterring.

A more sophisticated defense of current law, due to Landes and Posner, points out that in order to create a fully efficient system of privately enforced criminal law one must optimize two outcomes using a single control, which is, in the general case, mathematically impossible. There is no reason, short of blind luck, why the same fine would generate both the optimal probability of punishment (through the incentive that the opportunity to collect that fine gives the enforcers) and the optimal amount of punishment. I offered a solution to that problem by describing institutions for private enforcement under which profit maximization by the enforcement firm generates the optimal probability/punishment mix for any level of expected punishment, leaving one outcome to be optimized by one control. That solution can in turn be critiqued by pointing out that if the cost of apprehending and convicting an offender is greater than the fine he can be made to pay, offenses will sell at a negative price: Victims must pay prosecution firms to prosecute crimes against them. That critique can be answered by again noting that deterrence can be a private good, with the real-world example of eighteenth-century prosecution associations, a system of institutions in which potential victims did pay to have offenses against them prosecuted. And that reply can be answered by raising the problem of anonymous victim offenses, for which deterrence can not be made a private good.

I have just run one argument—about whether we should abolish criminal law, a central feature of our legal system—through seven rounds, four or five more than you are likely to encounter if you take a law and economics course from anyone but me. At each step the conclusion reversed. I offer that as evidence of how risky it is to go from the existence of an argument for the efficiency of some particular rule to the conclusion that the rule is in fact efficient.

And we are not done; I omitted a second line of criticism of the Landes and Posner argument, itself one of the more sophisticated defenses of the tort/crime distinction in the literature. Their problem of optimizing two variables with one control is not limited to crimes; it applies to torts as well. Just as the fine in a private criminal system is both the disincentive to the criminal and the incentive to the prosecutor, so the damage payment in a civil system is both the punishment for committing a tort and the reward for successfully litigating one. There is no reason to expect the optimal incentives for the two purposes to be the same. Insofar as Landes and Posner have explained why private prosecution of crimes is a mistake, they have shown why private prosecution of torts is a mistake too, thus undercutting their argument for the efficiency of our current legal institutions.

The problem is not merely ambiguity but selection bias as well. Suppose you are a legal scholar who believes in the Posner thesis. You observe that the common law accepts the coming to the nuisance defense; the pig farm, sued by the neighboring development for creating an olfactory externality, can defend itself by pointing out that it was there first. After thinking about the problem for a little, you come up with an explanation. The problem is produced not by having a pig farm but by having a housing development next to a pig farm. It is easier to relocate a housing development, or a pig farm, before it is built than after, so whoever came second was the lower-cost avoider of the problem.

Suppose, however, that you encounter the same issue a few decades later and find that the courts have become increasingly unwilling to accept that defense in nuisance suits. It occurs to you that while the developer can relocate his development, the owner of the land he was planning to build on cannot relocate his land. If urban expansion makes suburban housing the highest-valued use for all of the land surrounding the pig farm, a legal rule of coming to the nuisance allows the pig farmer to impose large external costs on the owners of all the surrounding land. By rejecting that defense, we force him to take account of those costs—and move.

As this example shows, and as many others could show, a scholar looking for evidence that the common law is efficient can almost always find it—by figuring out what is efficient after he finds out what the law is. In most cases the range of plausible arguments is wide enough so that an ingenious searcher can find at least one that justifies existing law. Sometimes, on sufficiently careful examination, it turns out that the argument, although plausible, is wrong. Sometimes it doesn't. And sometimes, when we are looking at a very large number of legal rules, the argument never gets a sufficiently careful examination.

My own conclusion is that the jury is still out on the Posner thesis. Some features of the common law make sense as what we would expect in an efficient legal system, some do not, and in many cases we simply do not know with any confidence what the efficient rule would be.

The case may be a little stronger for a modified version of the thesis, one that holds that common law used to be economically efficient, perhaps because it inherited its doctrines from efficient systems of private norms or from efficient legal rules generated by the competing court systems of medieval England, but has been gradually drifting away from efficiency for most of the past century. That would explain the retreat from freedom of contract, although not the tort law's long-standing refusal to award damages for the value of a victim's life to himself or to make tort claims marketable.

In Defense of Richard Posner

> Hence the economic analyst can move easily not
> only within common law fields but between them.
> Almost any tort problem can be solved as a
> contract problem, by asking what the people
> involved in an accident would have agreed on
> in advance with regard to safety measures if
> transaction costs had not been prohibitive. . . .
>
> Equally, almost any contract problem can be
> solved as a tort problem by asking what sanction
> is necessary to prevent the performing or paying
> party from engaging in socially wasteful conduct,
> such as taking advantage of the vulnerability of a
> party who performs his side of the bargain first.
> And both tort and contract problems can be
> framed as problems in the definition of property
> rights. . . . The definition of property rights can
> itself be viewed as a process of figuring out what
> measures parties would agree to, if transaction
> costs weren't prohibitive.
>
> (*Posner [1973] 1992: 252–53*)

Whether or not Posner has correctly explained the common law as it now exists, he has done something else that may be just as important. In trying to demonstrate that the law is efficient, he (along with many others) has demonstrated the essential unity, not necessarily of the law as it exists, but of the problems the law exists to solve. We do not know whether the law is efficient. We do know that the question "What is the efficient legal rule?" converts the study of law from a body of disparate doctrines into a single unified problem, where the same arguments—moral hazard, holdouts, public good problems, adverse selection, *ex ante* vs *ex post* rules, and many others—help make sense of a wide variety of legal issues. The Posner thesis, whether true or false, has clearly been useful.

Further Reading

The best source for Judge Posner's work in the economic analysis of law is R. Posner, *Economic Analysis of Law* (Boston: Little, Brown, 1973; 2d ed. 1977, 3d ed. 1986, 4th ed. 1992).

His defense of the absence of freedom of contract in product liability law can be found in Posner and W. Landes, *The Economic Structure of Tort Law* (Cambridge, Mass.: Harvard University Press, 1987).

For a general review of his work, inside and outside of economics, see D. Friedman, "Richard Posner," in *The New Palgrave Dictionary of Law and Economics* (New York: Stockton Press, 1998).

What We Have Been Doing for the Past Nineteen Chapters, or a Rough Sketch of an Elephant

THE WORLD HAS limited space and resources and is occupied by people with differing beliefs and objectives. From those simple facts comes the potential for conflict. I want to hunt a deer across the field where you are trying to grow wheat. You want to go swimming in the stream where I am trying to catch fish.

The simple and obvious solution is the direct use of physical force. You plant a thorn hedge around your wheat field to persuade me to hunt deer somewhere else. I hit you over the head with a tree limb to convince you to swim somewhere else.

This is not a very satisfactory solution to the problem; it is expensive in time and effort, scratches and bruises, and frequently fails of its objective. The direct use of force is so poor a solution to the problem of limited resources and diverse ends that it is rarely employed save by small children and great nations.

A more sophisticated version of that solution, substituting threats for violence, works considerably better—well enough to be observed in a considerable number of historical societies. You and I somehow work out a division of our claims to resources. I know that the field is yours—meaning that if I trample it, you will do things I don't like, such as hitting me over the head or swimming in my pool. You know that the pool is mine, meaning that if you swim in it I will do things you don't like, such as hitting you over the head or trampling your wheat field.

With only two people, there is an obvious temptation to solve the problem once and for all by sneaking up on you when you are asleep and hitting you over the head very hard. With a society of more realistic size, that is prevented by my knowledge that if I kill you, your friends and relatives will kill me in revenge. The result is a feud society (not to be confused with a feudal society), in which legal rules are privately enforced by the threat of private retaliation against those who violate them.

Consider Greece at the time of the Homeric epics. When Agamemnon comes home victorious from the Trojan war he is promptly murdered by his wife and her lover. Nobody calls the police and has him arrested, because there are no police to call. Murder, even murder of the king, is a private affair. It is up to his kin to avenge him.

The king's kin, in this case, means his son, Orestes. The problem is that one of the murderers against whom he owes vengeance is his mother. A similar conflict about two thousand years later generates much of the plot of *Gislisaga*. Gisli takes vengeance against Thorgrim, one of the killers of his blood brother (and brother-in-law) Vestein but leaves the other, Thorkell, untouched—because Thorkell is Gisli's brother. Orestes chose the other horn of the dilemma, killing his mother and providing the plot for plays by, among others, Aeschylus and Euripides.

Feud systems have functioned tolerably well in a variety of historical societies. To some extent they still do. The privately enforced norms of Shasta County are, in essence, a feud system, although one in which the range of retaliation is considerably more restricted than in Homeric Greece or saga period Iceland. And many other human interactions can be understood as systems of private rules privately enforced by the threat of one party doing things the other party will not like.

One can imagine a modern society built on a more elaborate and formalized version of such a system of decentralized law and law enforcement. Thirty years ago I devoted about a third of my first book to sketching out how such a society might work, with private firms enforcing the rights of their customers and bargaining among themselves to establish private courts to settle disputes among them. That is not, however, the society we live in. Hence, despite digressions on Iceland and Shasta County, this book is dedicated to making sense of a different solution to the problem of human conflict.

Direct private force is the obvious decentralized solution. The obvious centralized solution is dictatorship. Someone appoints himself ruler and gives orders. I am not allowed to trample the wheat; you are not allowed to scare the fish. If anyone does something he is not allowed to do, the dictator or his helpers beat him up.

This solution also exists in a variety of contexts in the modern world. The patriarchal family is one example, the firm another, government a third. While it can work tolerably well for small groups and simple problems, it works badly, often catastrophically badly, for large groups of people doing complicated things.

It works badly for two reasons. The first is that individuals control themselves in their own interest; the dictatorial solution requires some mechanism to force them to do what the dictator wants instead of what they want. The second is that information is dispersed; each of us has a lot of specific knowledge about his own abilities, circumstances, and desires. In order for the dictatorial method to work well, to produce attractive outcomes for the people it is applied to, that information has to be somehow passed up a hierarchy of command from us to the dictator, then crunched by the dictator in order to figure out what all of us should do, then passed back down to us as orders. In practice, most of it gets lost in the process—which is one reason why large, centrally controlled organizations usually work very badly.

For large societies it turns out that the best solutions are decentralized ones, built on the institutions of private property and trade. Each individual owns himself; land and things are mostly owned by particular individuals. If I want your services or the use of your property, I make you an offer you are willing to accept; if getting what I want is worth more to me than giving it costs you, there should be some such offer that I am willing to make.

This sounds simple, but implementing that solution raises a considerable variety of problems. Legal rules, defining what rights each person has and how disagreements or deliberate violations of rights are to be dealt with, are one approach to dealing with those problems.

Property, Contract, Tort, and Crime in Three Paragraphs

In a system of private property we need some way of defining what the boundaries of my property are, not only in physical space but in rights space as well—what uses of my neighbor's property violate my rights in mine and vice versa. We need some way of determining who owns a particular piece of property and establishing property rights over previously unowned property. We need mechanisms for enforcing these rules and for settling disputes over them. And all of this must be generalized from the special case of real property—property in land—to the more general case that includes property in things and intellectual property. Hence property law, including intellectual property.

One of the things I can do with my property is to sell it to you. Part of the reason the decentralized solution works is that it permits things, and rights in things, to move via trade to whatever person values them most. In order for that mechanism to work beyond the simplest cases (I give you an apple in exchange for your orange), we need contracts, agreements specifying the mutual obligations of the parties to more complicated exchanges. Contracts can lead to disagreements in interpretation, honest or otherwise, and so require some body of rules to determine when a contract exists and how disputes are to be resolved. Even in the simplest case of exchange, we need enough legal rules to determine whether I was trading my apple for your orange, in which case it is now my orange and your apple, or merely letting you hold my apple while I inspected your orange. Hence contract law.

To prevent me from violating a legal rule, there must be some mechanism to make something I don't like happen to me when I do. That mechanism, whatever it is, will also have to deal with cases in which one party believes a rule was violated and another does not. Hence we require tort law and criminal law to specify the relevant rights and the mechanisms by which they are enforced, and we require procedural rules and a court system to settle disputes.

Economics

This book is about a particular approach to understanding legal rules, developed by economists and by legal scholars influenced by economics. The central question around which that approach has been organized is a simple one: What set of rules and institutions maximize the size of the pie—resulting, so far as is possible, in everyone achieving his objectives? What legal rules are economically efficient?

There are at least three reasons why that is the question we ask. The first is that while economic efficiency—roughly speaking, maximizing total human happiness—is not the only thing that matters to human beings, it is something that matters quite a lot to most human beings. That is true both for selfish reasons—all else being equal, the larger the pie the larger I can expect my slice to be—and for unselfish reasons. Since the objective is important to almost everyone, it makes sense to think about what rules best achieve it.

A second reason is that there is evidence that considerable parts of the legal system we live in can be explained as tools to generate efficient outcomes. If so, the economic approach may provide a correct description of why law, or at least much law, has its present form, and thus a way of understanding it. It is a lot easier to make sense out of a tool if you know what it is designed to do.

A final reason is that figuring out what rules lead to more or less efficient outcomes is one of the things economists know how to do—and when you have a hammer, everything looks like a nail.

Efficient Legal Rules and How to Get Them

The first approximation to a system of efficient rules is simple—private property and trade. I belong to me, everything belongs to someone, and if you want the use of me or mine, you make me an offer I am willing to accept. Through trade all goods and services move to their highest-valued use, producing an efficient outcome.

This description implicitly assumes that the real world can be divided up into unrelated pieces, each belonging to one person—or, to put it differently, it assumes that how I use my property does not affect you and how you use your property does not affect me. Sometimes that is true. Often it is not, giving us the problem of externalities; a standard example in both economics and law is air pollution. If I do not bear all of the costs of my action, I may take it even though the net effect, including the cost I am imposing on others, is negative. If so, my action is inefficient—it makes the size of the pie smaller even if it increases the size of my slice.

There are at least four different ways in which such problems may be dealt with. The first and perhaps most obvious is direct regulation—someone decides what people should do and requires them to do it. This works if the regulator is benevolent, omnipotent, and omniscient. In practice none of those conditions is likely to be met. It is the dictatorial solution to social order, applied within the decentralized solution to resolve some of its problems.

A second alternative is a liability rule requiring me to pay someone, the state or my downwind neighbor, the cost of the damage I do. Since I am now bearing the full cost of my action I will take it only if the net effect is positive, in which case the action is efficient. This works if we have some mechanism that accurately measures external costs and forces the responsible party to pay for them.

There is a problem hidden in the idea of a "responsible party"; the cost I am being made to bear is not entirely due to me. My air pollution would do no damage if nobody happened to be living downwind. What we call an external cost is, in almost every case, due to the actions of multiple people. Choosing one of them and making him responsible may result in a costly solution by him instead of a less costly solution by someone else. This suggests a generalization of the approach: Put the incentive where it does the most good. Try to design legal rules so that the party in the best position to reduce a cost is the one who must bear it.

A third solution is to apply the same approach to rights that we are already applying to goods and services: private property and trade. The right to pollute belongs to someone; if that someone is you, the polluter, and the right is worth more to me, your downwind neighbor, then I buy it from you. This works well in contexts in which the costs of such private transactions are very low, not so well when they are high, and not at all when they are very high—air pollution in Southern California, for example.

A final solution, and a very common one, is to do nothing—to permit inefficiencies due to externalities because eliminating them costs more than it is worth.

My example was air pollution, but the analysis applies across a wide range of legal issues. When I breach my contract with you I impose a cost on you—and might choose to breach even though the net effect, taking account of your costs as well as my benefits, is negative. One solution is administrative—a court decides whether my breach is on net efficient, permits it if it is, forbids it if it is not. A second is a rule of expectation damages: I am permitted to breach but must reimburse you for the resulting costs. A third is private negotiation: I am permitted to breach only if I first buy your permission. A fourth is to do nothing at all—in which case what we have is not a legally enforceable contract but an unenforceable agreement: When you fail to show up for my dinner party, despite having accepted my invitation, I can complain but have no grounds to sue. These alternatives apply to the control of externalities in a variety of contexts—risk allocation in insurance or contract design, product liability law and tort law more generally, and elsewhere through the legal system.

The control of externalities is not the only common thread that runs through our analysis, although it may be the most central. In a system of private property there must be some way of defining what rights ownership implies and whom they belong to. If I own a piece of land, can I forbid you from digging a hole on your side of the property line into which my house slides? From digging a coal mine on your property and mining coal under mine? From playing loud music at 3:00 A.M. on your front porch, twenty feet from my bedroom window? If we live on a river bank, what happens to our property rights when the river shifts? What if I build a house on what both my neighbor and I think is my land, only to discover, when one of us actually checks the survey, that part of it is on his?

Another set of issues concern the problem of how to enforce whatever legal rules we have: the choice between *ex post* and *ex ante* punishment, the problem of giving enforcers the right incentives, costs of apprehending, convicting, and punishing offenders, and the implication of those costs for optimal enforcement.

What comes out of nineteen chapters of this is a general approach to designing an efficient legal system:

Choose an appropriate combination of property and liability rules taking account of the costs of both.

Define and bundle property rights in a way that minimizes costs associated with defining and defending them and transacting over them.

Enforce the whole by some mix of public and private action under a suitable set of rules of proof and liability.

Throughout the project consider the incentives of all parties, including the enforcers, transaction costs, and the problem of using dispersed and imperfect information. Where possible, create institutions that make it in someone's interest to use such information to generate the appropriate rules.

I have described one direction in which the analysis can be applied—figuring out what legal rules would be efficient. Running the project in the opposite direction, what comes out is a way of understanding the legal system we have—on the conjecture that it, or at least large parts of it, can be explained as a system of efficient rules.

An important thing to remember in either version of the project is that utopia is not an option. As Coase argued, in the same essay that gave us the Coasian approach to externalities, in the real world all solutions are imperfect. Our project is not to eliminate costs but to minimize them, to find the least bad system of legal rules. Even that we can do only imperfectly; we do not know enough to reduce legal design to mathematical calculation. What we can do is to understand the advantages and disadvantages of alternative rules as a first step toward choosing among them.

For example, strict liability in tort law compensates the victim and so gives him no incentive to take precautions to reduce the cost or probability of accidents. Negligence solves that problem at the cost of eliminating the incentive for the tortfeasor to take those precautions that the court cannot observe or cannot judge. Hence strict liability is most attractive where victim precautions are unimportant and unobservable precautions by the tortfeasor important, negligence under the opposite circumstances.

A rule of *caveat venditor* in product liability eliminates the consumer's incentive to minimize risk and cost and produces litigation and associated costs; a rule of *caveat emptor* eliminates the litigation, restores the consumer's incentive, but eliminates the producer's incentive to control risks that customers are unaware of. Hence the choice between the rules hinges on who can best control the risk (putting the incentive where it does the most good), on how costly and accurate litigation is, and on how well informed consumers are with regard to at least the average level of risk of a particular brand. Freedom of contract provides a private mechanism for choosing among alternative rules, provided that consumers are sufficiently well informed, not about the risks of particular products, but about the value to them of guarantees.

An *ex ante* punishment such as a speeding ticket provides incentives based on the information available to the enforcement apparatus but not the (usually much more detailed and less costly) information available to the actors. An *ex post* punishment such as tort liability for automobile accidents gives the actor an incentive to use his private information but requires large punishments imposed with low probability, hence typically results in high punishment costs. So the choice between the two depends on the relative quality of the information available to enforcers and to actors concerning what the actor is and should be doing and on the size and resulting cost of *ex post* punishment. One conclusion is that where even *ex post* punishments are small enough to raise little problem of risk aversion or judgment-proof defendants, they are unambiguously superior to *ex ante* ones, unless for some reason the enforcement apparatus has better information about what the actor is and should be doing than the actor does. Another is that a pure *ex ante* system is almost never efficient, since it can be improved by adding an *ex post* punishment low enough not to impose significant punishment costs.

A legal system might choose to treat the same act as tort, crime, both or neither. Treating an offense as a tort raises potential problems with judgment-proof defendants, especially in contexts in which deterrence cannot easily be made into a private good. Where the probability of catching and convicting an offender is low, it raises a further problem of inadequate punishment if damages awarded are not scaled up to compensate for the low probability and a risk of fraudulent prosecution if they are. Treating an offense as a crime solves the problem of judgment-proof defendants but raises incentive problems both for victims, who may have an inadequate incentive to report crimes and assist in prosecuting them, and for enforcers. More generally, it has the problems usually associated with centralized forms of production. And where deterrence can be produced as a private good, the privately enforced solution has the advantage of a built-in incentive to convict the right person.

Antitrust law has the potential to reduce both rent-seeking costs associated with the attempt of firms to get monopoly profits via price-fixing agreements or merger and monopoly dead weight costs due to inefficiently high prices when such attempts succeed. But it raises the risk of hindering productive transactions made in the shadow of antitrust law, such as mergers designed to reduce costs, and contractual terms, such as retail price maintanance, that are best explained as means of increasing the value that firms produce, not merely the price of what they sell. In the worst case—the history of the Interstate Commerce Commission provides an instructive example—antitrust may be used to impede competition and promote monopoly.

The Modesty of Our Circumstances

As these examples suggest, we rarely if ever know enough to be able to provide a precise solution to the question of what legal rules are efficient—to calculate that the optimal punishment for robbery is three years two months and a day in jail or that conviction should require at least a .932 probability of guilt. Most of the time the best we can hope for is to understand enough of the logic of the problem to yield an informed guess about what a reasonably good solution would look like. That is the process that I worked through to exhaustion—probably yours as well as mine—in chapter 5, analyzing a simple legal problem involving railroads, farmers, and sparks.

What I am offering in this book are not answers but ways of finding them. That is not because I do not have opinions as to what the law ought to be but because, in most cases, I do not believe that I have arguments for those opinions that are strong enough so that any reasonable person who understands the arguments must agree with me. One reason for that view is the existence of other economists, including some of whose ability I have a high regard, who understand the arguments but, on one point or another, have reached different conclusions.

My own view of antitrust law, for example, is that, with the exception of the refusal of courts to enforce contracts in restraint of trade, we would be better off without it. But what I want you to end up with is not necessarily that conclusion—offered by an economist with no expert knowledge of the field—but the analysis that led me to it and might lead someone else to a somewhat different conclusion. Similarly, my own view is that our legal system would be improved by a substantial shift in the direction of tenth-century Iceland—a redefinition of the boundaries of criminal and tort law moving us toward greater reliance on private enforcement, with appropriate adjustments in the relevant law. But what I want you to end up with is not that conclusion but an understanding of how one can usefully think about the choice between private and public enforcement and the appropriate legal institutions for each. Similarly with such other issues as freedom of contract, the marketability of organs and parental rights, and much else.

Economics is neither a set of questions nor a set of answers; it is an approach to understanding behavior. What comes out of that approach depends not only on the economic theory but also on the facts of the real world to which the theory is applied. I know a great deal about the real world—as do you, and every other sane human past the age of one—but there is a great deal more I do not know. And while I have thought through substantial parts of the logic of law, doing so in one mind and a reasonable length of time has often required me to ignore complications that might turn out to be important.

So I will end with a brief list of some of the more relevant parts of my ignorance. I do not have:

An adequate theory of transaction costs, although fragments of such a theory can be found in chapter 5 and elsewhere.

An adequate theory of the incentives of public employees such as police and judges. Such analysis as I provide depends mostly on the very weak assumption that they must have some incentive to do what they are doing, else they would not be doing it, plus the assumption that they desire the same sorts of things as other human beings.

An adequate theory of the mechanisms that generate legal rules narrowly defined—statute and common law. I do offer at least a brief sketch of the mechanisms that generate private norms in chapter 17, and elsewhere I have offered an analysis of the mechanisms that would generate legal rules in a system where law and law enforcement were produced as private goods.

In addition to these major gaps, the theoretical analysis I offer ignores many of the relevant complications of the real world to which legal rules apply.

For example, I have implicitly assumed that all offenders face the same probability of being apprehended, which is obviously not true. The analysis of efficient punishment could and should be redone with that assumption dropped.

Also, I have made no serious effort to analyze the interaction between public enforcement of law and private enforcement via reputation and private norms—beyond a very brief discussion of the way in which stigma imposes costs on someone convicted of a crime, costs due to private parties taking into account the information generated by his conviction.

While information costs have occasionally played a role in the analysis, I have for the most part used the rationality assumption of economics in its simplest form—individuals take the right action—rather than assuming that individuals make the right choice about gathering costly information and then take action based on the imperfect information they have found it worth obtaining. Thus, for example, I have assumed, explicitly or implicitly, that everyone knows the legal rules that apply to his actions—surely false.

I could go on, but I will leave you to list additional omissions—and, if sufficiently ambitious, attempt to repair some of them.

INDEX

accident, 59

accidents, unicausal, 198

activity level, considered as an unobservable precaution, 200

adhesion, contracts of, 156

adoption, free market in: arguments against, 181

adoption market, economics of, 182

adultery, explaining laws against, 177

adverse selection, 65, 69–71, 73, 162, 217, 307; in the market for used cars, 70; in product liability law, 214; reliance damages as a solution to a problem of, 168

airport noise, as a jointly produced external cost, 37

Akerlof, George, 176

Annie Lee Turner et al. v. Big Lake Oil Company et al., 103

anonymous victim offenses, 212–13, 268, 285–86, 292, 295, 305

antitrust law, 254, 262; advantages and disadvantages of, 316; author's view of, 317; network externalities, 262; predatory pricing, 250; retail price maintenance agreements, 255; tie-in sales, 257

appeals, role in maintaining a consistent legal system, 107

attempts, punishment of, 79, 83; considered as an ex ante punishment, 74; impossible, punishment of, 81–82

auto accidents, argument for treating as a crime, not a tort, 295

bargaining, analysis of, 86

bargaining breakdown, risk of, 94

bargaining costs, related to size of bargaining range, 94

bargaining power, unequal, 148

bargaining range, size of related to bargaining costs, 93

Becker, Gary, 226

bees and externalities, 41

benefit of clergy, 268

bilateral monopoly, 87, 88, 89, 92, 93, 94, 155, 164, 172; in bargaining with small children, 87; with high stakes likely to

produce large costs, 93; in marriage, 177; marriage as an example of, 172

Blackstone, Sir William, 9

bloody code, the, 269

bonding, as a form of private contract enforcement, 147

boundaries of property, problem of defining, 119; problem of enforcing, 119

breach of promise to marry, suits for, 178

bright line rules, 43

Brinig, Margaret, 178

Buchanan, James, 45

bully, considered as a Doomsday Machine, 89, 93

bundle of rights, ownership as a, 39

bundling rights, Coaseian approach to, 44; constructing efficient bundles, 113–14; in the form of ownership of land, 112

burglary, argument for treating as a tort not a crime, 295

cannibalism, taboo against as a way of reducing rent-seeking, 241

cartels, 247; chiselling as a problem for, 247; CAB and IATA as enforcers of, 248

causation in tort, 189, 197; coincidental causation, 192; probabilistic causation, 197; redundant causation, 195

caveat emptor, 213, 214; advantage of lower litigation costs with, 216; advantages and disadvantages of, 315; when the right rule, 215

caveat venditor, 213, 214; as a solution to adverse selection, 214; disadvantage of requiring litigation, 216; disadvantages of, 315; guarantee as a voluntary form of, 216; when the right rule, 215

chicken, game of, 85

Civil Aeronautic Board (CAB), 248

civil forfeiture, as an efficient punishment leading to rent-seeking, 240; effect on incentives of law enforcement, 240

civil law, normally plaintiff a private party, 108; saga period Iceland as an extreme example of, 264